LAG legal aid handbook 2015/16

Legalaidhandbook.com

Legal Aid Handbook 2015/16 is supported by legalaidhandbook.com

Readers of the book have access to a supporting website containing the full text of the Handbook, which we will keep up to date between editions alongside regular news, updates and case reports and a comprehensive resources page.

Register to receive email updates at www.legalaidhandbook.com

Follow us on Twitter 🐦 @legalaidhbk

Available as an ebook at www.lag.org.uk/ebooks

LAG legal aid
handbook 2015/16

Edited by Vicky Ling and Simon Pugh

with Anthony Edwards

 Legal Action Group
2015

This edition published in Great Britain 2015
by LAG Education and Service Trust Limited
3rd floor, Universal House, 88–94 Wentworth Street, London E1 7SA
www.lag.org.uk

This book has been produced using Forest Stewardship Council (FSC) certified paper. The wood used to produce FSC certified products with a 'Mixed Sources' label comes from FSC certified well-managed forests, controlled sources and/or recycled material.

FSC
www.fsc.org
MIX
Paper from
responsible sources
FSC® C020438

Print ISBN   978 1 908407 58 0
ebook ISBN   978 1 908407 59 7

Typeset by Regent Typesetting, London
Printed in Great Britain by Hobbs the Printers, Totton, Hampshire

This book is dedicated to the memory of Andrew Wilson,
a fine lawyer who believed passionately in justice for all, fought
tenaciously for his clients, and inspired all who worked with him.

Preface

Our thanks go again to Esther Pilger, Steve Hynes and Nim Moorthy from Legal Action Group (LAG), whose support for the Handbook is greatly appreciated. Once again, Esther has proved unflappable in the face of delays and uncertainty, particularly following the challenges to the crime tender. We must also acknowledge the contribution made by our long-suffering families who have supported us as ever as we wrote this book.

We should like to thank all those who commented on the last edition of the Handbook and provided ideas for this update, as well as those who commented or emailed us via the website.

We welcome our new contributors, Solange Valdez and Richard Charlton, who bring their expertise in their own fields to bear on the immigration and mental health chapters. We are particularly pleased that Tony Edwards has provided his unrivalled knowledge and experience in the crime chapters, and that Steve Hynes has contributed his usual thoughtful survey of the policy scene. Our thanks to them all.

We have endeavoured to give as complete an account of the civil legal aid scheme as at 1 September 2015 as we can. The crime chapters cover the new criminal legal aid contracts coming into force in January 2016.

Any errors or omissions are, of course, our responsibility.

The Handbook's supporting website, www.legalaidhandbook. com, will continue to be used for updates, news alerts and other material of interest, and readers can register to receive email updates and alerts, and will have access to the full text of the Handbook, which we will keep updated between now and the next edition in 2017. Readers can also follow us on Twitter @legalaidhbk.

We welcome comments on the *LAG legal aid handbook 2015/16* as we want to make it as relevant and useful to legal aid practitioners as we can, and readers can contact us at admin@legalaidhandbook.com or via Legal Action Group at lag@lag.org.uk.

Once again, our final thanks go to the readers of the Handbook, those hard-pressed but dedicated legal aid lawyers determined to do their best for their clients in difficult times. We hope we have made your task a little easier.

Vicky Ling and Simon Pugh
September 2015

Contributors

Vicky Ling is a Chartered Quality Professional and management consultant. Vicky worked for the Legal Aid Board in the early 1990s at the inception of 'franchising', has experience of managing organisations with legal aid contracts and has written and lectured extensively on legal aid practice management.

Vicky is a founder member of the Law Consultancy Network, a team of highly experienced law firm management consultants and is an associate consultant at Infolegal, providing compliance and practice advice. She has advised over 200 firms of solicitors and not-for-profit organisations on all aspects of legal aid contract and quality standards.

Vicky is co-author, with Matthew Moore, of *The Solicitors Office Procedures Manual*, now in its second edition: www.solicitors-opm.co.uk and a commissioner of The Low Commission.

Simon Pugh has extensive experience of legal aid practice management and contract compliance across the private practice and not-for-profit sectors and civil, criminal and family law. He has written and spoken widely on legal aid and related issues. He is a solicitor, currently non-practising, and was previously head of legal practice at Shelter, the housing and homelessness charity.

Richard Charlton is a solicitor and specialist in mental health law at Richard Charlton Solicitors. He was selected as the first mental health legal aid lawyer of the year at the LALY awards and is currently President of the Mental Health Lawyers Association. Richard is a Law Society assessor for the Mental Health Tribunal Panel and a senior peer reviewer in mental health for the Ministry of Justice. He was shortlisted for the Law Society Excellence Awards in the human rights category.

Anthony Edwards is a criminal solicitor at TV Edwards LLP. He is a higher courts advocate and duty solicitor. He is a visiting professor at

Queen Mary, University of London and a member of the Law Commission's advisory panel on criminal law.

Anthony writes and lectures widely on criminal law. He is on the editorial boards of *Criminal Law Review* and *Blackstone's Criminal Practice* and author of *Advising a Suspect in the Police Station* (Sweet & Maxwell), contributing author to *Blackstone's Criminal Practice, Police Station Handbook, Magistrates' Court Handbook* and *Youth Court Handbook* (all OUP), *Criminal defence: a guide to good practice* (with Roger Ede) and *Fixed fees in the criminal courts* (both Law Society).

Steve Hynes is director of the Legal Action Group (LAG). Steve has written extensively and appeared in the broadcast media commenting on legal aid and access to justice issues. He is author of *Austerity Justice* (LAG, 2012) and co-author, with Jon Robins, of *The Justice Gap* (LAG, 2009). Steve is a commissioner of The Low Commission.

Solange Valdez is a supervising solicitor and has worked at various law centres specialising in nationality, immigration and asylum law. In November 2012 Solange co-founded the Project for the Registration of Children as British Citizens (PRCBC) that assists children with their complex registration applications. In 2014, she was shortlisted for immigration lawyer of the year at the LALYs. Solange regularly trains and lectures on immigration and legal aid issues.

Contents

Table of cases

Table of statutes

Table of statutory instruments

Table of European and international legislation

Abbreviations

ABH	Actual bodily harm
AIT	Asylum and Immigration Tribunal
ASU	Asylum Screening Unit
BACS	Bankers' Automated Clearing Service
CBAM	Criminal Bills Assessment Manual
CCFS	Care Case Fee Scheme
CCMS	Client and Cost Management System
CCRC	Criminal Cases Review Commission
CCU	Complex Crime Unit
CFA	Conditional Fee Agreement
CLA	Community legal advice
CLR	Controlled legal representation
CMRF	Consolidated matter report form
CMRH	Case management review hearing
DSCC	Defence Solicitor Call Centre
DWP	Department for Works and Pensions
ECHR	European Convention for the Protection of Human Rights and Fundamental Freedoms
ESA	Employment and Support Allowance
FAQs	Frequently asked questions
FILEX	Fellow of the Institute of Legal Executives
GF	Graduated fee
GFS	Graduated Fee Scheme
HMCTS	Her Majesty's Courts & Tribunals Service
HMRC	Her Majesty's Revenue and Customs
IAAS	Immigration and Asylum Accreditation Scheme
IALS	Institute of Advanced Legal Studies
IFA	Independent Funding Adjudicator
KPI	Key performance indicator
LAA	Legal Aid Agency
LASPO	Legal Aid, Sentencing and Punishment of Offenders Act 2012
LEXCEL	Law Society's Quality Standard
LSC	Legal Services Commission
MHT	Mental Health Tribunal
MOU	Memorandum of understanding
MPAs	Multi-party actions

NASS	National Asylum Support Service
NfP	Not-for-profit
PACE	Police and Criminal Evidence Act 1984
POA	Payment on account
POP	Point of principle of general importance
RDCO	Recovery of Defence Costs Order
RSS	Really simple syndication
SAAC	Self-Assessment Audit Checklist
SCU	Special Cases Unit
SMOD	Subject matter of dispute
SMP	Standard monthly payment
SQM	Specialist Quality Mark
SWL	Social welfare law
UASC	Unaccompanied asylum-seeking children
UFN	Unique file number
VHCC	Very high cost case
VMP	Variable monthly payment

Glossary

Account Manager	Former job title – see Relationship Manager below.
Advice and Assistance	Funding for advice short of representation in criminal cases, granted by the supplier under contract with the LAA
CMRF	Consolidated Matter Report Form, the monthly Civil Contract claim submitted to the LAA online.
Community Legal Service	An arm of the LAA, which directly funds civil cases, and through the Quality Marks and partnerships attempts to plan coverage and ensure provision of competent service across a range of advice and information sectors and agencies.
Contract Compliance Audit	An audit assessing whether, based on a sample of files, an organisation is complying with the requirements of civil or criminal contracts.
Controlled Legal Representation	Representation before the Mental Health Review Tribunal, or in the Immigration Appellate Authority, granted by the supplier under contract with the LAA
Controlled Work	Legal Help, Help at Court and Controlled Legal Representation – funding granted by the supplier
Corrective Action	Action agreed with an LAA auditor to rectify a breach of a QM or contract requirement.
Criminal Defence Service	Criminal advice and representation funded by the LAA, through private practice and the Public Defender Service.
Devolved Power	A power (eg to grant a Representation Certificate) that may be exercised on the LAA's behalf by the supplier in certain defined circumstances

Financial Stewardship audit	Type of audit conducted by a Relationship Manager on a provider's premises, focussing on financial issues.
Franchise Representative	See Liaison Manager.
Funding Code	The criteria by which the LAA decide whether to grant all levels of civil funding
Help at Court	An adjunct to Legal Help, which allows representation at particular hearings in defined cases
Individual Case Contract	A separate contract between the LAA and a supplier on a particular case, usually because of high costs
Inter partes costs	Costs agreed between the parties when cases are settled between them rather than by Court Order. The rates are higher than Legal Aid rates.
Lead Assessor	An official of the LAA, responsible for Quality Mark audits.
Legal Aid	Legal advice and representation funded by the central government through the LAA and the Courts.
Legal Help	Advice short of representation, granted by the supplier under contract with the LAA
Liaison Manager	A member of the organisation's staff designated as the person responsible for quality and contract compliance and the main point of contact for the LAA. This role was previously known as the Quality Representative or Franchise Representative.
Licensed Work	Civil representation certificates – funding granted by the LAA or under devolved powers by suppliers
Matter Start	Also known as a 'new matter start' or NMS, a Matter start is a case started under Legal Help, or Controlled Legal Representation where there has been no previous Legal Help
McKenzie Adviser	A person who is present at a hearing to advise and assist, but not represent, a party.
Prior Authority	A certificate that the LAA considers a disbursement to be reasonable, and therefore that the costs will be paid at the end of the case. May also allow a payment on account.

Peer review	An assessment of the quality of legal work carried out by independent lawyers working under contract with the LAA.
Pro bono	Free legal advice and/or representation.
Procurement area	Geographical area for competitive bidding, usually based on a top tier local authority area.
Provider	Term used by the LAA to describe any type of organisation with which it has a contract to deliver services.
Provider Assurance	New department of the LAA, which carries out data analysis and audits to support Relationship Managers.
Public Defender Service	Solicitors employed by the LAA to do criminal work, in competition with private practice. 4 offices in England and Wales
Quality Concern	A failure to meet a requirement of a Quality Mark. Critical Concerns are more serious than General Concerns. The organisation will be required to put corrective action in place, or in particularly serious cases, will be at risk of contract termination.
Quality Mark	An accreditation scheme regulating conduct and quality of legal services. There are various levels of QM, awarded to different types of service provider. Compliance may be audited by the LAA or authorised third party.
Quality Representative	See Liaison Manager.
Regional Director	Head of an LAA Regional Office, responsible for all funding, policy and partnership issues in the region. This role has been phased out as part of LAA restructuring.
Regional Office	Historically, an office of the LAA dealing with all funding and local policy matters within its region. In future, regional offices will act as processing centres as part of the LAA's restructuring programme.
Relationship Manager	An official of the LAA with responsibility for the entire commercial relationship with a provider. They will be based as close to the provider's lead office as feasible.
Representation Certificate	Funding for representation in civil and family cases, granted by the LAA or in emergencies by the supplier

Representation Order	Funding for representation in criminal cases, granted by the Courts
Schedule payment limit	The total amount payable to an organisation under a contract
Special Cases Unit	Department of the LAA, dealing with individual case contracts in high cost civil cases.
Specialist Quality Mark	The highest level Quality Mark, held by solicitors and NfPs which are eligible for funding by the LAA.
Standard monthly payment	The monthly payment to an organisation under contract – usually one twelfth of the schedule payment limit (subject to variation during the year)
Statutory Charge	A charge held by the LAA over property recovered or preserved in funded civil proceedings, intended to allow the LAA to recover the costs of funding the case.
Tolerance work	A case taken on by an organisation in a category in which it does not have a QM or contract.
Transaction Criteria	An audit tool, consisting of checklists used to assess whether a file contains required information. Now superseded by peer review.
Very High Cost Cases Panel	A panel of organisations accredited by the LAA to conduct VHCC crime cases. Only accredited organisations may do these cases.

Legal aid advice and litigation

CHAPTER 1

Read this before you start!

Introduction

1.1   This chapter's title is probably a counsel of perfection, and will be an unfulfilled aspiration for most caseworkers! However, the point we are trying to make is that there are lots of rules and guidance about doing publicly funded work; you need to be aware of what they are, and consult them where necessary. This is particularly important following the serious cuts in the scope of legal aid from April 2013, leaving it very tightly defined.

1.2   If you don't ensure you are aware of the statutes, regulations, rules and guidance, you may have applications or bills rejected by the Legal Aid Agency (LAA) for technical errors (and there is a contract key performance indicator that limits rejects to five per cent as part of the schedule), or refused because you have not explained your client's case in an appropriate way, or you may have claims for payment disallowed. All these things are important because they may cause your client unnecessary delay, waste your time, and could even threaten the financial viability of your organisation. If you are not sure what to do, look it up and discuss the issue with your supervisor.

The LAA Manual

1.3   The then Legal Services Commission's approach to the LSC Manual was that it should be comprehensive and contain as much as possible relating to the operation of the legal aid scheme, from legislation through regulations to guidance. The new approach is that legislation and regulations can easily be found by lawyers on various websites, and so the LAA's own manual will only contain information that cannot be found elsewhere. The LAA's contracts require all contracted providers to subscribe to the Legal Aid Agency Manual.[1] The LAA withdrew this requirement from 31 August 2015.[2]

1.4   In this book, wherever possible, we tell you where you can download a document from the LAA's website. We have given website addresses to help you locate what you need, although these are subject to change. Many of the documents are also linked to from our website at www.legalaidhandbook.com/laspo-resources, and we will keep links updated there.

---

1 See, for example, Standard Contract 2013 standard terms, clause 7.10.

2 www.gov.uk/government/news/civilcrime-news-providers-no-longer-need-to-buy-legal-aid-manual/.

The Legal Aid Agency website

1.5   Legal aid changes quickly, as the LAA changes its approach to issues and as challenges to the various cuts are played out in the courts. Everyone involved with legal aid funding needs to keep up with the latest developments. The LAA is sending out less and less information on paper, and relying on you far more to check what is on its website. You wouldn't want to miss an opportunity to tender, or find that you were using out-of-date forms, or running a case that was out of scope, for example. So what's the best way of keeping up to date?

1.6   You can sign up to the LAA's email newsletter, which will provide you with updates, announcements and changes. The updates give you a brief summary of the issue, and a link to further information. They make keeping up much easier. You can subscribe through the legal aid website at http://lscupdate.org.uk/sign-up/4P-WQ9-F49T4PQVB9/sign_up_form.aspx. However, if you are really interested in keeping up to date, you cannot beat checking the website, and even particular pages, on a weekly basis, as the LAA does not always alert people to changes.

1.7   The legal aid website is part of the gov.uk network and so follows the standard gov.uk layout and contents structure. This means that it can be hard to find what you need and the search function is often a good place to start, though only if you know the name of the document or page you need.

1.8   Our website has a resources page at www.legalaidhandbook.com/laspo-resources, which contains links to the various regulations, contracts and most of the guidance documents on the LAA site, so that can be a good place to start if you don't know the location of the item you are looking for.

1.9   It is also well worth bookmarking the key pages within the LAA site – such as the forms, contracts and billing pages – so that they are easy to return to.

1.10   One useful feature of the LAA site is the 'latest' section on the front page, which is automatically updated whenever any document or page on the LAA site is added or amended. The 'see all' link[3] contains an RSS feed which can be added to a feed reader to alert you to any changes or newly published material on the LAA site. Our Twitter account (@legalaidhbk) is set to automatically tweet any new news items or content, so following it is another way of staying up to date.

---

3 www.gov.uk/government/latest?departments%5B%5D=legal-aid-agency.

1.11   There is also a public information website on legal aid: www.gov.
uk/legal-aid. Other useful public information sites are Advicenow:
www.advicenow.org.uk and Adviceguide from Citizens Advice: www.
adviceguide.org.uk.

Civil and family – key documentation

The Standard Contract 2013, 2014 or 2015

1.12   Most civil legal aid providers operate under one of three versions of
the LAA's Standard Civil Contract.

1.13   The 2013 Standard Contract applies to family, immigration and
asylum and housing and debt. The 2014 Standard Contract applies
to mental health and community care, and the 2015 Standard Contract applies to actions against the police etc, clinical negligence and
public law. Family mediation is still covered by the 2010 Standard
Contract (for which see the 2011/12 edition of this book).

1.14   There are also three further contracts – two for welfare benefits
providers and one for providers of the Civil Legal Advice telephone
service, but as there are only a very small number of holders of these
contracts, they are not dealt with in any detail in this book.

1.15   The contracts contain many detailed provisions concerning the
way you work with clients, as well as setting out the formal relationship between your organisation and the LAA. You can download the
applicable contract from the legal aid website at www.gov.uk/govern-
ment/collections/legal-aid-agency-current-contracts. You then select
the appropriate contract.

1.16   Part A of this book sets out where you can find the main provisions in relation to casework; see Part C: 'Managing legal aid work'
for more information on the contractual relationship with the LAA.

The Standard Contract Specifications

1.17   The section of your particular contract that you will need to be familiar
with is the Standard Civil Contract Specification. The specifications
can be downloaded from the webpage noted above – follow the link
to your contract and then to the specification. All the specifications
have the same broad structure. They are split into general rules and
category-specific rules; where the two conflict, the category-specific

rules take precedence.[4] The Specification rules are discussed in detail in chapters 3–11 of this book.

1.18　　The Specification contains an introduction to the main workings of the various funding schemes. Section 1 contains general provisions; for example, it explains how to apply regulations and guidance, what is in your contract schedule and rules concerning additional matter starts. Section 2 gives information about service standards, where work can or must be done, supervisor standards, and, crucially, key performance indicators (KPIs), compliance with which may be taken into account in future tendering exercises. Section 3 explains the scope of controlled work and rules applying to it. Section 4 explains how controlled work is paid for. Sections 5 and 6 discuss the scope and main rules applying to licensed work, payment arrangements and the statutory charge (although rates of payment are shown in the Civil Legal Aid (Remuneration) Regulations 2013 and the various regulations amending them – see www.legalaidhandbook.com/laspo-resources for all the regulations).

1.19　　The remaining sections are category-specific, and each specification has its own sections depending on which contract it is part of. Each category specific section begins with supervisor standards, and then moves on to any additional rules that apply to that category:

- 2013 Contract: Section 7 – family; Section 8 – immigration; Section 10 – housing and debt (note – there is no section 9)
- 2014 Contract: Section 7 – mental health; Section 8 – community care
- 2015 Contract: Section 7 – clinical negligence; actions against the police etc; public law – all contained in one section which only deals with supervisor standards.

Guidance

1.20　　The LAA has created a series of training modules which cover changes in legal aid. They can be accessed on its website.[5] The LAA also provided some answers to frequently asked questions and guidance in respect of family, immigration, social welfare law and mental health schemes when the LASPO scheme first came in. They are useful because they deal with a number of queries that arise in day-to-day practice, and may well provide the answer to the particular

---

4　See for example Standard Contract 2013 Specification para 1.2.
5　http://legalaidtraining.justice.gov.uk.

question you have. Unfortunately they are no longer available on the LAA website, but a copy can be found on our website.[6]

1.21   The Lord Chancellor and the Director of Legal Aid Casework have issued a series of guidance documents using their LASPO statutory powers, including:

- Lord Chancellor's Guidance on Civil Legal Aid
- Lord Chancellor's Guidance on Exceptional Funding – there are two, one for inquest cases and one for other cases
- Director's Guidance on Evidence Requirements for Private Family Law Matters.

There is a series of guides and manuals covering general subjects such as financial eligibility and costs assessment, as well as category specific matters like family mediation and housing court duty schemes.

1.22   Links to all guidance documents, as well as other guides and manuals, can be found at legalaidhandbook.com/laspo-resources.

Eligibility guidance

1.23   The legal aid website: www.gov.uk/civil-legal-aid-means-testing has links to guidance materials and the eligibility calculator. See chapter 3 of this book for more information about eligibility.

Regulations and guidance

1.24   The regulations create a set of rules that govern whether an individual's case can be funded under legal aid. The key regulations are the Civil Legal Aid (Merits Criteria) Regulations 2013, the Civil Legal Aid (Procedure) Regulations 2012, the Civil Legal Aid (Remuneration) Regulations 2013 and the Civil Legal Aid (Financial Resources and Payment for Services) Regulations 2013. Many of these regulations have been amended, and so you should always check the amendment regulations as well as the original ones, as the LAA does not issue updated regulations incorporating the amendments and nor does www.legislation.gov.uk.

1.25   In addition the LAA has issued the Lord Chancellor's Guidance on Civil Legal Aid on the way the regulations should operate. It is a key reference document, whether you are granting legal aid yourself, as controlled work, or under delegated functions (previously known

---

6 http://legalaidhandbook.files.wordpress.com/2013/04/legal-aid-reform-faq-v3.pdf.

as devolved powers), or whether you are submitting an application for the LAA to decide.

1.26 Links to the regulations and guidance can be found at www. legalaidhandbook.com/laspo-resources.

Costs assessment guidance

1.27 Many caseworkers focus so hard on achieving the best possible job for their clients that they lose sight of the financial side of the case. This is not sustainable, so it is important to be aware of the rules that govern what you can and cannot claim for.

1.28 The LAA has guidance on claiming, which can be downloaded from www.gov.uk/funding-and-costs-assessment-for-civil-and-crime-matters. See chapters 13 and 14 of this book for more information about getting paid. There is also a summary of the costs assessment guidance at appendix H.

Fee exemption and remission

1.29 The fee exemption and remission scheme is administered by HM Courts & Tribunals Service (HMCTS) and is not part of legal aid funding. Court fees are a recoverable disbursement under a full legal aid representation certificate, but not under Legal Help or Controlled Legal Representation. Legally aided clients are not automatically exempt from fees, but may apply for exemption or remission on grounds of means where they are not a recoverable disbursement. For more information, see HMCTS leaflet EX160A 'Court fees – Do you have to pay them?' It can be downloaded from www.justice.gov. uk/courts/fees.

Criminal defence – key documentation

The 2015 Crime Contracts

1.30 The 2015 Crime Contracts are expected to come into effect on 11 January 2016. There are two contracts, one for all firms regulating own client work, and a further contract for those firms authorised to do duty solicitor work. The Own Client Crime Contract 2015 and Duty Provider Crime Contract 2015 can be downloaded from www. gov.uk/legal-aid-for-providers/contracts.

1.31   Part A of this book sets out where you can find the main provisions in relation to casework; see Part C: 'Managing legal aid work' for more information on the contractual relationship with the LAA.

The Crime Specifications

1.32   The sections of the contracts that caseworkers will need to be familiar with are the respective specifications. They can also be downloaded from www.gov.uk/legal-aid-for-providers/contracts.

1.33   The Own Client Contract Specification covers general rules, among other things: definitions, service standards, qualifying criteria, carrying out and claiming for work, as well as specific provisions for very high cost cases, prison law, appeals and associated civil work. It also provides information about claims assessment and review procedures (although this is not the main source document, see below).

1.34   The Duty Contract Specification covers criteria and service standards for duty work, duty scheme rules, and carrying out and claiming for work.

1.35   The crime fees are set out in the Civil and Criminal Legal Aid (Remuneration) (Amendment) Regulations 2015.

Eligibility guidance

1.36   Advice in the police station is not means tested.

1.37   Representation in the magistrates' court is means tested. There is an eligibility calculator on the legal aid website: www.gov.uk/criminal-legal-aid-means-testing. Clients who are not eligible for legal aid in the magistrates' court and pay for their defence privately can apply to reclaim their costs from Central Funds if they are subsequently acquitted.

1.38   Representation in the Crown Court is also means tested. If clients are found not guilty, their contributions will be repaid. Clients who are not eligible for legal aid in the Crown Court and pay for their defence privately can apply to reclaim their costs from Central Funds if they are subsequently acquitted. The rules and forms can be found at www.gov.uk/claim-back-costs-from-cases-in-the-criminal-courts.

Costs assessment guidance

1.39   Ensuring that you will be paid is as important in criminal defence work as in civil and family, mentioned above.

1.40   The Criminal Bills Assessment Manual (CBAM) elaborates many of the principles in the contract. It can be found at www.gov.uk/funding-and-costs-assessment-for-civil-and-crime-matters.

Logos

1.41   The former Community Legal Service and Criminal Defence Service logos were withdrawn in 2013 and organisations are no longer permitted to use them, but you can use the strapline 'Contracted with the Legal Aid Agency'. If you do not have a contract but do hold the SQM, you can use the descriptor 'Specialist Quality Mark Holder'.

This handbook

1.42   We will keep the *LAG legal aid handbook 2015/16* updated via its supporting website www.legalaidhandbook.com where you can subscribe to receive email alerts of changes to the scheme and other news and developments. You can also follow us on Twitter @legalaidhbk for news and updates. Our Twitter feed also automatically tweets all announcements, additions and amendments to the LAA website.

The legal aid framework

2.1   This chapter briefly sets out how the legal aid scheme was developed, and how the new scheme was arrived at. It also sets out the legislative framework that underpins legal aid. For more detailed information on the history of legal aid and on the passage of the Legal Aid, Sentencing and Punishment of Offenders (LASPO) Act 2012, see the LAG publications *The Justice Gap* and *Austerity Justice*.[1]

The development of exclusivity

2.2   From its inception as a relatively widely available state funded public service in 1948 up to the mid-1990s, the culture of legal aid was that any solicitor who wanted to do so could do legal aid work. Many high street firms offered small amounts of legal aid work, perhaps for divorce or personal injury, alongside their conveyancing and will-writing work.

2.3   As legal aid expanded in the 1960s and 1970s, both in scope and budget, specialist legal aid firms, and legal aid departments in larger firms, came into being. At the same time, the Law Centres movement was growing and other agencies and voluntary sector groups expanded the provision of advice services.

2.4   By the early 1990s, government policy was changing. Legal aid had moved from being administered by the Law Society to a specialist quasi-governmental body, the Legal Aid Board (LAB). Alongside that, the not-for-profit sector was becoming more significant and taking up a larger share of the overall budget. The LAB wanted to encourage the move to specialisation and introduced a franchise system. The purpose of franchising was to develop a network of specialists accredited as being experts in their type of law, and to ensure that public money was only spent on those who were providing a service of sufficient quality.

2.5   However, the LAB did not have the tools to measure legal quality or competency. It did develop the franchise standard, which was a series of criteria concerned with the management and running of a firm, but not with an assessment of the quality of the work done. Firms that applied for a franchise had to demonstrate that they met the standard, and in return were allowed to describe themselves as franchised and charge a slightly higher hourly rate for the work that

---

1   Jon Robins and Steve Hynes, *The Justice Gap: whatever happened to legal aid*, Legal Action Group, 2009; Steve Hynes, *Austerity Justice*, Legal Action Group, 2012.

they did. However, the franchise system was voluntary, and many firms simply did not apply, and in any event it offered little insight into the quality of work done.

2.6 Meanwhile, despite periodic attempts to restrict it, expenditure on legal aid was increasing steadily. By the late 1990s, the new Labour government took the view that radical reform was needed and adopted the recommendations of a report commissioned by the previous government and carried out by Sir Peter Middleton.

2.7 The result was a complete overhaul of the system. The Legal Aid Board was abolished and replaced by the Legal Services Commission (LSC), and the entire legislative basis of legal aid was re-written.

2.8 The base of the revised scheme was the Access to Justice Act 1999. The Act created the LSC, and created two separate funds – the Community Legal Service (CLS) fund for civil work and the Criminal Defence Service (CDS) for crime. Both funds were administered by the LSC and in practice there was one single legal aid budget with no ring-fencing of either fund (though many called for them to be separated, as criminal and family expenditure took an ever larger share).

2.9 The Access to Justice Act 1999 empowered the LSC to commission and procure legal aid services in such a way as to ensure that they were available to those who needed services in almost any way the LSC considered most appropriate. In practice, the LSC chose to fund services by exclusive contract, and that model continues into the post-LASPO scheme.

2.10 The franchise standard was replaced by the Specialist Quality Mark (SQM), and made compulsory. Legal aid is funded by contract – without a contract you cannot do legal aid work – and having the SQM or Lexcel is mandatory for being awarded a contract. See chapter 18 for details on the contract award process.

2.11 Therefore, since 2000 (for civil) and 2001 (for crime), legal aid work has been the exclusive preserve of organisations the LSC, subsequently the LAA, has contracted with to procure services.

2.12 Over the years since the mid-1990s, budgetary control was achieved by holding down eligibility levels and payment rates. The proportion of the population eligible for legal aid steadily shrank, and hourly rates stagnated; the lack of inflationary rises meant an effective cut of around 40 per cent by the time of the LASPO cuts.

The road to LASPO

2.13   When the government changed in 2010, it was the outcome of an election held against the backdrop of a global economic crisis. A coalition of Conservative and Liberal Democrat ministers took power on the basis that the appropriate response to the crisis, and to public expenditure deficits and government debt at home, was a programme of cuts and austerity which would impact on almost all government departments. The Ministry of Justice, by now also including prisons and probation within its remit, was no exception and was required to find savings of about £2 billion annually from its budget. It was decided that the legal aid scheme would have to be cut by about £350 million.

2.14   A consultation paper was issued, to which over 5,000 (overwhelmingly negative) responses were received, proposing drastic cuts focussed primarily on civil and family legal aid. Fees would be cut, the LSC abolished and whole areas of law removed from scope.

2.15   The result of the consultation was very little movement in government policy, and the Legal Aid, Sentencing and Punishment of Offenders Bill (soon to be universally known as LASPO) was published in June 2011. For the full detail of the content of the bill and the government's policy proposals at the time, see www.legalaidhandbook. com/2011/07/05/legal-aid-reform-overview.

2.16   The passage of the bill was marked by campaigning and lobbying across the legal aid sector and well beyond (a leading voice being the Women's Institute, for example), together with vigorous debate particularly in the House of Lords, which met with almost total government intransigence. Some concessions were made, but LASPO was passed largely intact despite the government losing a record number of votes in the Lords.

Legal Aid, Sentencing and Punishment of Offenders Act 2012

2.17   LASPO repealed the Access to Justice Act 1999, insofar as it dealt with legal aid, and established an entirely new statutory regime. Cases *started before* 1 April 2013 continue to be subject to the Access to Justice Act 1999 regime, and cases *started from* 1 April 2013 are subject to LASPO. Cases under the LASPO regime are covered in this book. Cases started the Access to Justice Act 1999 are dealt with in a previous edition of this work.[2]

2.18   LASPO is in many parts, and covers several aspects of justice policy. The key parts for legal aid are Part 1 (which contains the enabling powers for the new scheme) and Schedule 1 (which sets out what civil work is in scope).

2.19   The Act required the Lord Chancellor to make legal aid available in certain categories of case, defines what those cases are, created the Legal Aid Agency (and abolished the Legal Services Commission) to administer legal aid and empowers the passing of regulations to govern the detail of the scheme.

2.20   In practice, the abolition of the LSC and its replacement with the LAA did not make much difference. Constitutionally, there is a difference since the LSC was an arm's-length body and the LAA is an agency of the Ministry of Justice. This means that the staff are civil servants and the chief executive is more directly accountable to ministers. There was some concern during the passage of the Act that this risked potential political interference in LAA decision-making in respect of individual cases. Although there are safeguards in the Act, it remains to be seen how effective they are in practice.

2.21   Practitioners carrying out their day-to-day work did not see significant change. There are still caseworkers to assess applications for legal aid (although the LAA aspires to introduce a software driven system as soon as it can), auditors to conduct audits, and contract managers to manage contracts.

2.22   The Access to Justice Act 1999 created two separate funds for administering legal aid, the Community Legal Service and the Criminal Defence Service. Each had their own branding to be used by practitioners as well as the LSC. These were removed, so that now the Legal Aid Agency simply administers a single legal aid fund. There are no longer two separate funds, and there are no specific branding or logos for civil or criminal work. Many practitioners still display the CLS and CDS logos but this is strictly incorrect as these have been withdrawn. The LAA suggests they can state 'contracted with the Legal Aid Agency' instead.[3]

2.23   LASPO vests most of the decision-making powers in respect of legal aid in an official called the Director of Legal Aid Casework. This is the Chief Executive of the Legal Aid Agency, Matthew Coats. For

2 *LAG legal aid handbook 2011/12* is still in print and available from Legal Action Group.
3 See para 1.35 above.

practical purposes, his powers and responsibilities are delegated to LAA and Court Service staff who make decisions in respect of individual cases.

Life after LASPO

2.24   The first full financial year after the implementation of LASPO saw a fall in civil expenditure of £150 million. But that did not tell the whole story. Many of the cases paid and so included in the expenditure figures will have been Access to Justice Act cases pre-dating the LASPO cuts – future years are likely to see equally steep falls in expenditure if the other first year figures are any guide. They show:[4]

- 50 per cent fewer Legal Help cases were started in the year after LASPO compared to the year before;
- 30 per cent fewer legal aid certificates issued;

In addition to the headline figures, category based data showed that social welfare cases fell by 80 per cent, housing by 45 per cent, family by 60 per cent and mediation by 40 per cent. This means there were steep drops even in areas that stayed in scope. Even crime was not immune, showing year on year falls in both case numbers and expenditure. Most stark of all, the total number of civil providers had halved over five years – and the number of not-for-profit agencies doing legal aid work fell by 90 per cent overnight when LASPO came in.

2.25   At the same time, those practitioners who remained in the system reported greater difficulties in getting funding even when work remained in scope, through a combination of falling demand (perhaps because clients believed all legal aid had been abolished) and ever tighter bureaucratic requirements – implemented by the LAA, some felt, in an arbitrary and heavy-handed way.

2.26   Having steered LASPO through Parliament, Ken Clarke was replaced as Lord Chancellor by Chris Grayling. Soon after taking office, in April 2013, Grayling announced[5] further cuts to both crime and civil work. He proposed removing a further £200 million from

---

4   For a more detailed discussion of the figures, see our article in the July/August 2014 issue of *Legal Action*.

5   See http://legalaidhandbook.com/2013/04/09/government-consults-on-further-legal-aid-cuts/ for a full list. of the original proposals, and http://legalaidhandbook.com/2013/09/05/transforming-legal-aid-what-the-government-now-propose/ for what emerged from consultation.

the crime budget through a combination of fee cuts and restructur-ing of the market. He also proposed further cuts to civil legal aid – this time aimed not at cutting expenditure but 'restoring public confidence'. The measures included restrictions on judicial review, the introduction of a residence test as a qualification for legal aid and removing funding from 'borderline' cases, as well as removing the bulk of prison law from scope. Fees in child care cases, and for all non-family civil barristers, as well as experts, were to be cut.

2.27　　The subsequent two years have seen the professions fight these further cuts, with varying degrees of success. The proposed fee cuts have all been implemented (with the exception of cuts to advocacy fees in the Crown Court). But the government has dropped propos-als for price competitive tendering and abolishing client choice in crime[6], and has been forced to abandon the introduction of the resi-dence test by the courts.[7] Other legal challenges to the cuts have had mixed success, with the guidance on exceptional funding declared unlawful,[8] but challenges to cuts to prison law[9], the implementation of the domestic violence gateway[10] and the reduction in numbers of duty crime contracts[11] all failing. Most recently, the High Court has upheld a challenge to the exceptional funding regime, brought by the Public Law Project.[12] See chapter 4 for more on that case.

2.28　　The impact on litigants and the courts has been considerable, with a sharp rise in litigants in person, especially in family cases.

6　http://legalaidhandbook.com/2013/09/05/transforming-legal-aid-what-the-government-now-propose/.

7　*R (Public Law Project) v The Secretary of State for Justice* [2014] EWHC 2365 (Admin).

8　*R (Letts) v The Lord Chancellor* [2015] EWHC 402 (Admin) (inquests) and *R (Gudanaviciene and others) v The Director of Legal Aid Casework and The Lord Chancellor* [2014] EWCA Civ 1622 (non-inquests, with particular focus on immigration).

9　*R (The Howard League for Penal Reform and Prisoners' Advice Service) v The Lord Chancellor* [2014] EWHC 709 (Admin). The Court of Appeal has given permission to appeal on a limited basis: see [2015] EWCA 819.

10　*R (Rights of Women) v The Lord Chancellor and Secretary of State for Justice* [2015] EWHC 35 (Admin).

11　*R (London Criminal Courts Solicitors Association and others) v The Lord Chancellor* [2015] EWHC 295 (Admin) and *R (The Law Society, The London Criminal Courts Solicitors Association and others) v The Lord Chancellor* [2015] EWCA Civ 230.

12　*IS (by the Official Solicitor as Litigation Friend) v The Director of Legal Casework and The Lord Chancellor* [2015] EWHC 1965 (Admin).

This has led to a series of expressions of judicial displeasure.[13] One senior judge, the President of the Family Division Sir James Munby, even tried to create a shadow legal aid scheme by directing the Court Service to fund the representation of some litigants in person[14], but the Court of Appeal made very clear that there was no power to do so.[15] Munby P has accepted that there is no such power. But he does appear to be contemplating requiring the local authority to fund representation of an otherwise unrepresented parent.[16]

2.29   Elsewhere, two major Parliamentary reports were critical of the implementation and effects of LASPO[17], but the government remained unmoved.

2.30   So, two years on, it is clear that LASPO marked not the end of the cuts and reform programme, but only the beginning (or perhaps the middle, given the cuts to crime in particular the previous Labour government had made). The intervening period has seen relations between the government and the professions fall to a new low. But the professions themselves have hardly presented a united front as the various criminal representative bodies, The Law Society and The Bar Council have taken very different positions. Those positions have not always even been consistent within organisations as officers have changed over time.

2.31   We write shortly after the 2015 general election campaign, which resulted in the end of the coalition government and its replacement with a Conservative majority government. Chris Grayling was replaced as Lord Chancellor by Michael Gove. But it is unlikely that there will be any significant change in policy. The first ministerial statement of the new regime merely continued the policy of the old.[18]

13 See, for example, http://legalaidhandbook.com/2015/03/10/justice-has-had-to-be-sacrificed-on-the-altar-of-public-debt/ and http://legalaidhandbook.com/2015/03/02/legal-aid-in-mental-health-cases/.

14 *Q v Q; Re B; Re C* [2014] EWFC 31.

15 *Re K and H (Children)* [2015] EWCA Civ 543.

16 *M (A Child), Re* [2015] EWFC 71 para 12, citing *D (A Child), Re* [2014] EWFC 39.

17 Impact of changes to civil legal aid under Part 1 of the Legal Aid, Sentencing and Punishment of Offenders Act 2012, House of Commons Justice Committee, HC 311, March 2015; The UK's compliance with the UN Convention on the Rights of the Child; Human Rights Joint Committee, March 2015.

18 www.parliament.uk/business/publications/written-questions-answers-statements/written-statement/Commons/2015-06-10/HCWS22/ which confirmed that the second crime litigator fee cut and the duty tender process would go ahead, and also confirmed no further cuts to Crown Court advocacy fees.

See chapter 21 for more on the current political environment and likely future developments.

Regulation of civil work

The statutory foundation

2.32   Civil legal aid, or strictly under the Act, 'civil legal services', is defined by LASPO as only that which is included in Schedule 1 of the Act. In contrast to the Access to Justice Act 1999, which provided that work was in scope unless specifically excluded by the Act, LASPO says that only work explicitly included in Schedule 1 is in scope.

2.33   LASPO s8 defines what civil legal aid is. It includes:

- providing advice as to how the law applies in particular circumstances;
- providing advice and assistance in relation to legal proceedings;
- providing advice and assistance in relation to the prevention settlement or resolution of legal disputes;
- providing advice and assistance in relation to the enforcement of decisions in legal proceedings or other decisions by which disputes are resolved.

2.34   Advice and assistance includes both representation and mediation and other dispute resolution.

2.35   LASPO s9 provides that only areas of law expressly listed in Schedule 1 are in scope and can be funded under legal aid. If work is not listed in Schedule 1, it will not be covered by legal aid and you will not be paid for doing it.

2.36   LASPO s10 makes provision for what are known as 'exceptional cases'. Where cases are not covered by the scope rules in Schedule 1 but certain conditions are satisfied, an application may be made to the Director to fund the case even though it is otherwise out of scope. See chapter 4 for more on exceptional cases. Note that these cases should not be confused with Legal Help cases where costs exceed three times the fixed fee. Such cases were previously known as exceptional cases under the Access to Justice Act regime but are now called escape fee cases.

2.37   LASPO ss11 and 21 provide that legal aid will only be awarded if merits and financial criteria respectively are satisfied. Sections 25 and 26 create the statutory charge and give costs protection and section 27 enables the establishment of the mandatory telephone gateway. It is under these sections that the relevant regulations are made.

The regulations

2.38   Regulations set out the detail of the scheme. Key ones are:

- Civil Legal Aid (Procedure) Regulations 2012;
- Civil Legal Aid (Merits Criteria) Regulations 2013;
- Civil Legal Aid (Financial Resources and Payment for Services) Regulations 2013;
- Civil Legal Aid (Costs) Regulations 2013;
- Civil Legal Aid (Remuneration) Regulations 2013;
- Civil Legal Aid (Statutory Charge) Regulations 2013.

Several of the regulations have since been amended. A full list of regulations, together with amendments, can be found at www.legalaidhandbook.com/laspo-resources listed on a single page for easy retrieval. Each has a brief description as some regulation titles are more intuitive than others, and amendment regulations are listed with the regulations they amend to facilitate cross-referencing.

2.39   Regulations deal with the terms on which funding can be granted. They set out the detail of the various means and merits tests to be applied, how costs are dealt with through the statutory charge and cost protection, and not least with the rate you are paid for doing the work.

2.40   The Funding Code made under the Access to Justice Act 1999 was abolished and not replaced. Most of the equivalent provisions are now in the Merits and Procedure Regulations and the Funding Code Guidance has been replaced by the Lord Chancellor's Guidance.[19] The Procedure Regulations define the various levels of funding, and set out the form of the application, together with appeal procedures against refusal. They also define the terms on which the telephone gateway operates. See chapter 3 for more on the gateway.

The contracts

2.41   The Standard Civil Contracts 2010, 2013, 2014 and 2015 govern the relationship between the LAA and organisations holding contracts. The LAA calls such organisations 'providers'. They set out your duties and responsibilities, together with any powers delegated to you. They also govern some of the detail of the operation of individual cases building on what is in the regulations. Unless you have a contract, you will not be permitted to carry out legal aid work.

---

19 See www.gov.uk/government/uploads/system/uploads/attachment_data/
file/332795/legal-aid-lord-chancellors-guidance.pdf.

2.42 A contract consists of three main sections:

- The standard terms govern the relationship between the organisation and the LAA and Lord Chancellor and your obligations as an organisation. See chapter 16.
- The schedule sets out the types of work you are permitted to do, and in the case of Legal Help, Help with Family Mediation and Controlled Legal Representation (CLR), the maximum numbers of matters you are allowed to start per year. It will also specify any additional requirements (such as presence requirements), and will include any commitments you made as part of your tender for the contract (against the selection criteria, for example). Breach of any provision of your schedule, including any commitment you made in your tender, is a breach of contract subject to sanction in the usual way (see chapter 19).
- The specification deals with how you should conduct individual cases, and is dealt with in subsequent chapters.

2.43 Other documents which are referred to in the contract, and which you should follow or take account of (though not technically part of the contract) include:

- Specialist Quality Mark or Lexcel if that is your chosen quality standard;
- Equality and Diversity Guidance;
- Category Definitions (see appendices D–G);
- Standard Monthly Payment (SMP) Reconciliation Protocol (see appendix J);
- Independent Peer Review Process;
- Key Performance Indicator (KPI) Outcome Codes;
- Data Security Requirements.

All of these documents are available on the LAA website: www.gov. uk/legal-aid-for-providers/contracts – follow the link to your particular contract.

Regulation of criminal work

2.44 The scope of criminal work is defined by LASPO as advice to individuals arrested and held in custody (section 13), involved in investigations which may lead to criminal proceedings, before a court or tribunal in criminal proceedings, or who have been the subject of criminal proceedings (section 15).

2.45   LASPO s14 defines criminal proceedings as:

- proceedings before a court for an individual accused of an offence;
- proceedings before a court for dealing with an individual conicted of an offence, including proceedings in respect of a sentence or order;
- proceedings or dealing with an individual under the Extradition Act 2003;
- bind-overs;
- deals with the appellant is deceased;
- references under section 36 of the Criminal Justice Act 1972;
- contempt;
- such other proceedings as may be prescribed.

2.46   Under regulation 9 of the Criminal Legal Aid (General) Regulations 2013,[20] the following have been prescribed as criminal:

(a) civil proceedings in a magistrates' court arising from a failure to pay a sum due or to obey an order of that court where such failure carries the risk of imprisonment;

(b) proceedings under sections 14B, 14D, 14G, 14H, 21B and 21D of the Football Spectators Act 1989 in relation to banning orders and references to a court;

(c) proceedings under section 5A of the Protection from Harassment Act 1997 in relation to restraining orders on acquittal;

(d), (e) [Revoked.]

(f) proceedings in relation to parenting orders made under section 8(1)(b) of the Crime and Disorder Act 1998 where an order under section 22 of the Anti-social Behaviour, Crime and Policing Act 2014 or a sexual harm prevention order under section 103A of the Sexual Offences Act 2003 is made;

(g) proceedings under section 8(1)(c) of the Crime and Disorder Act 1998 in relation to parenting orders made on the conviction of a child;

(h) proceedings under section 9(5) of the Crime and Disorder Act 1998 to discharge or vary a parenting order made as set out in sub-paragraph (f) or (g);

(i) proceedings under section 10 of the Crime and Disorder Act 1998 in relation to an appeal against a parenting order made as set out in sub-paragraph (f) or (g);

(j) proceedings under Part 1A of Schedule 1 to the Powers of Criminal Courts (Sentencing) Act 2000 in relation to parenting orders for failure to comply with orders under section 20 of that Act;

20 As amended by the Criminal Legal Aid (General) (Amendment) Regulations 2015 and the Civil and Criminal Legal Aid (Amendment) Regulations 2015.

(ja) proceedings, in a youth court, in relation to a breach or potential breach of a provision in an injunction under Part 1 of the Anti-social Behaviour, Crime and Policing Act 2014 where the person subject to the injunction is under 14.

(k) proceedings under sections 80, 82, 83 and 84 of the Anti-social Behaviour, Crime and Policing Act 2014 in relation to closure orders made under section 80(5)(a) of that Act where a person has engaged in, or is likely to engage in behaviour that constitutes a criminal offence on the premises;

(ka) proceedings under paragraph 3 of Schedule 2 to the Female Genital Mutilation Act 2003 in relation to female genital mutilation protection orders made other than on conviction and related appeals;

(kb) proceedings under paragraph 6 of Schedule 2 to the Female Genital Mutilation Act 2003 in relation to female genital mutilation protection orders made under paragraph 3 of that Schedule;

(l) proceedings under sections 20, 22, 26 and 28 of the Anti-social Behaviour Act 2003 in relation to parenting orders–
  (i) in cases of exclusion from school; or
  (ii) in respect of criminal conduct and anti-social behaviour;

(m) proceedings under sections 97, 100 and 101 of the Sexual Offences Act 2003 in relation to notification orders and interim notification orders;

(n) proceedings under sections 103A, 103E, 103F and 103H of the Sexual Offences Act 2003 in relation to sexual harm prevention order;

(o) [Revoked.]

(p) proceedings under sections 122A, 122D, 122E and 122G of the Sexual Offences Act 2003 in relation to sexual risk orders;

(q) [Revoked.]

(r) proceedings under section 13 of the Tribunals, Courts and Enforcement Act 2007 on appeal against a decision of the Upper Tribunal in proceedings in respect of–
  (i) a decision of the Financial Conduct Authority;
  (ia) a decision of the Prudential Regulation Authority;
  (ii) a decision of the Bank of England; or
  (iii) a decision of a person in relation to the assessment of any compensation or consideration under the Banking (Special Provisions) Act 2008 or the Banking Act 2009;

(s) proceedings before the Crown Court or the Court of Appeal in relation to serious crime prevention orders under sections 19, 20, 21 and 24 of the Serious Crime Act 2007;

(t) proceedings under sections 100, 101, 103, 104 and 106 of the Criminal Justice and Immigration Act 2008 in relation to violent offender orders and interim violent offender orders;

(u) proceedings under sections 26, 27 and 29 of the Crime and Security Act 2010 in relation to–

    (i)   domestic violence protection notices; or

    (ii) domestic violence protection orders;

(ua) proceedings under sections 14(1)(b) and (c), 15 and 20 to 22 of the Modern Slavery Act 2015 in relation to slavery and trafficking prevention orders;

(ub) proceedings under sections 23 and 27 to 29 of the Modern Slavery Act 2015 in relation to slavery and trafficking risk orders, and

 (v) any other proceedings that involve the determination of a criminal charge for the purposes of Article 6(1) of the European Convention on Human Rights.

Sub-paragraph (v) includes contempt other than in the face of the court in the High Court (*King's Lynn and West Norfolk Borough Council v Bunning*[21]) and county court (*Brown v London Borough of Haringey*[22]).

2.47   LASPO s19 says that determinations about grants of legal aid in criminal proceedings are made by the court. Section 18 says that all other determinations made by the Director, though the contract delegates some of these decisions to you.

2.48   LASPO s17 says that, in determining whether an individual qualifies for legal aid for criminal proceedings, account must be taken of their financial resources and of the interests of justice test. Section 27 gives a right for clients to select a representative of their choice, but that right may be limited and qualified by regulation. This empowers the LAA to, for example, restrict criminal legal aid to those who hold contracts, or provide that certain offences may only receive telephone advice at the police station.

The regulations

2.49   Regulations set out the detail of the scheme. Key ones are:

- Criminal Legal Aid (General) Regulations 2013;
- Criminal Legal Aid (Remuneration) Regulations 2013.

The contracts

2.50   There are two contracts expected to apply to criminal work from January 2016 – the Own Client Crime Contract (OCCC) and the Duty Provider Crime Contract (DPCC). They replace the single Criminal Contract 2010. Each contract consists of three parts:

21 [2013] EWHC 3390 (QB).
22 [2015] EWCA Civ 483.

- The standard terms govern the management of the firm and its relationship with the LAA, and is dealt with in chapter 18.
- The schedule sets out the monthly payment the LAA will make and the types of work the organisation can carry out (also see chapter 18).
- The Specification sets out the rules on conduct of and payment for individual cases, and is dealt with in chapters 12, 14 and 17.

2.51 Other documents which are referred to in the contract, and which you should follow or take account of (though not technically part of the contract) include:

- Equality and Diversity Guidance and Policy;
- Category Definitions;
- Guidance on Category Definitions;
- SMP Reconciliation Protocol (see appendix J);
- Independent Peer Review Process (the peer review process can be downloaded from www.gov.uk/guidance/legal-aid-agency-audits# peer-review/);
- Duty Solicitor Arrangements;
- Data Security Requirements.

The majority of these documents are available on the LAA website; but you need to search for them using your normal search engine and using the exact title of the document.

Taking on civil and family cases

Introduction

3.1   When a client approaches you with a legal problem, there are a number of considerations to bear in mind in deciding whether you can take the case. These include:

- Is the case within the scope of the legal aid scheme?
- Must the client go through the telephone gateway?
- Is it covered by your contract?
- If you need to provide advice rather than going straight to court proceedings, do you have sufficient matter starts to be able to take it?
- Is the client financially eligible?
- Does the client's case pass the merits test?
- Is there any other reason why you cannot take it?

Only if the case passes all these tests can it be taken on.

3.2   Note that if you have a case that started pre 1 April 2013, it continues under the provisions of the Access to Justice Act (AJA) 1999 – see the 2011/12 edition of the Handbook for the operation of the AJA scheme.[1] Legal Help forms signed before 1 April 2013 and certificates where the application form was signed before 1 April 2013 and received by the LAA on or before 8 April 2013 remain AJA 1999 cases.[2]

3.3   Many organisations stopped providing legal aid in categories of law when the 2010 contracts were replaced with 2013 contracts, most obviously due to scope cuts. These are being dealt with under the remainder work provisions of the 2013 contract.[3] The contract required practitioners to confirm these cases were unlikely to continue for more than two years, which would expire at the end of March 2015, and would be adequate in most cases. Where cases have continued past the two-year point, the contract requires the LAA to consider reasonably whether further work should be authorised.

In this chapter we will mainly refer to the provisions of the 2013 contract, as that is the one that governs most civil cases. But (unless we say otherwise) there are equivalent rules in the other civil contracts.

---

1   *LAG legal aid handbook 2011/12* is available from LAG.

2   Ministry of Justice policy statement on transitional arrangements: http://webarchive.nationalarchives.gov.uk/20121207044149/http://www.legalservices.gov.uk/docs/cls_main/12_Policy_Statement_-_Transitional_Arrangements.pdf.

3   2013 Contract – Civil Standard Terms 26.11.

Scope of the scheme

3.4   Unless LASPO Sch 1 explicitly puts an issue in scope, it is out.[4] See appendix C for the text of Schedule 1.

3.5   Schedule 1 is not easy to understand and requires a certain amount of cross-referencing and double or even triple negatives to be navigated to understand whether a case is in fact in or out of scope. The schedule is in four parts; Part 1 lists types of proceedings which are in scope, but is subject to Part 2 (which excludes certain types of action) and Part 3 (which excludes certain courts and tribunals), as well as the definitions in Part 4. So in order to see whether a case is in scope, you need to check that it is included by Part 1 but not excluded by Part 2, and that your venue is included in Part 3 if you wish to provide advocacy.

3.6   The exclusions in Part 2 of Schedule 1 are:

- personal injury or death;
- negligence;
- assault, battery or false imprisonment;
- trespass to goods or land;
- damage to property;
- defamation etc;
- breach of statutory duty;
- conveyancing;
- making wills;
- trust law;
- a claim for damages for breach of human rights under Human Rights Act 1998 s7;
- company and partnership law;
- matters arising out of a business;
- welfare benefits and social security matters below Upper Tribunal level;
- criminal injuries compensation;
- change of name.

The Part 2 exclusions always override the Part 1 inclusions unless specifically disapplied.

3.7   For example, in housing cases, LASPO Sch 1 Part 1 para 33 says that services in relation to loss of a home are in scope, subject to the exclusions in Part 2, then para 15 of Part 2 says services in relation to benefit matters are out of scope. The result of this is that you can

---

4   Previously, legal aid was an inclusionary scheme; unless Schedule 2 to the Access to Justice Act 1999 explicitly put an issue out of scope, it was in scope.

advise and represent in respect of possession proceedings, but cannot make representations about housing benefit or submit an appeal even where housing benefit problems are the cause of the arrears underlying the proceedings (see chapter 11 – Housing for more information about dealing with housing cases under LASPO).

3.8   Or again, Part 1 para 19 says that services in relation to judicial review are in scope, subject to the exclusions in Part 2. Part 2 para 15 excludes any matter related to welfare benefits but para 19(2)(a) of Part 1 disapplies that exclusion. Therefore, notwithstanding the general exclusion of welfare benefits work, judicial review of welfare benefit decisions is in scope. This allows public law challenges, to the law generally and to the exercise of discretion by benefits authorities, but does not allow advice or representation on routine appeals to the Social Entitlement Chamber of the First-tier Tribunal.

3.9   For the purposes of awarding contracts (see more below) the Legal Aid Agency (LAA) divide the work up into categories. The category definitions documents[5] give a reasonable guide to work which is in scope, but for the detail, particularly in borderline or unclear cases or where the Part 2 exclusions may apply (for example in the case of housing benefit work within arrears cases, as above), it is always best to refer back to the Act itself. The category definitions can be found on the LAA website.[6] There is a category definitions document to accompany each version of the contract, see below.

3.10   The following table gives a summary of the areas of law in scope in each category.

---

5 See appendices D–G.

6 The 2014 and 2015 category definitions are on the main pages for their respective contracts, www.gov.uk/government/publications/standard-civil-contract-2014 and www.gov.uk/government/publications/standard-civil-contract-2015, but for some reason the 2013 category definitions have their own page at www.gov.uk/government/publications/legal-aid-agency-category-definitions-2013.

Category	Type of work	Comments
Actions against the police etc	Where the defendant is a public authority with the power to detain, imprison or prosecute: • abuse of a child or vulnerable adult • abuse of position or power by a public authority • significant breach of human rights • advice to victims of sexual offences	In each of these causes of action, the Part 2 exclusions around personal injury and death, negligence, assault, etc are disapplied. See *R (Sisangia) v Director of Legal Aid Casework* [2014] EWHC 3706 (Admin) for more on claims for false imprisonment and the application of para 21 of Part 1 of Sch 1.
Clinical negligence	Neurological injury to infants causing severe disablement and which happened in the womb, during birth or up to eight weeks after birth	
Community care	The provision of community care services and of facilities for disabled persons	LASPO Sch 1 Pt 1 paras 6 and 7 contain an exhaustive list of statutes and statutory provisions that are in scope; if it is not on the list, it is not in.
Debt	Mortgage arrears and possession Orders for sale of the home Involuntary bankruptcy where the home is included in the estate	What was the debt category in 2010 contracts was removed from scope pretty much in its entirety. What was previously an overlap between debt and housing in respect of arrears and possession cases was separated, with mortgage cases defined from April 2013 as debt and rent as housing. Debt is a mandatory gateway category.

Category	Type of work	Comments
Discrimination	Contravention of the Equality Act 2010 or a previous discrimination statute (a prescribed list is given at LASPO Sch 1 Pt 1 para 43(3)).	This was a new category from 2013 reflecting that employment law, with the exception of discrimination claims, was removed from scope. This category is not limited to employment cases and includes any matter where discrimination can be pleaded. If it overlaps with another category – for example, alleging discrimination in the provision of community care services – work can be done in either category, though discrimination is a mandatory gateway category.
Education	Special educational needs	All other education work was removed from scope. Education is a mandatory gateway category.
Family	Public law children work: • Child care and supervision • Secure accommodation orders • Adoption • Child abduction • Inherent jurisdiction Forced marriage protection Domestic abuse and protection from harassment Enforcement of international child maintenance Private law children work and financial provision on relationship breakdown, but only where there is domestic abuse or risk of child abuse – see chapter 5	In general, child protection work and work required by the UK's international obligations is in scope but private law work is out of scope. It can be brought back where there is domestic or child abuse, but only where particular prescribed evidence is available. See chapter 5 for more details.

Housing	Possession of a rented home (including most counter-claims in possession proceedings even if they would be out of scope as a stand-alone claim)	• Damages only unlawful eviction claims may however be caught by the 'suitability for a conditional fee agreement' test – see para 7.16 of the Lord Chancellor's Guidance on Civil Legal Aid and para 11.19 of this book.
	Unlawful eviction – both injunction and damages	• See chapter 12 of the Guidance for how applications for funding for disrepair will be dealt with.
	Homelessness	• See chapter 11 of this book for more on housing cases.
	Allocations where the client is homeless or is threatened with homelessness	
	Provision of accommodation by way of community care services (overlap with the community care category)	
	Disrepair, but only to require carrying out of repairs (solely damages claims are out of scope) and only where the disrepair causes a serious risk of harm	
	Anti-social behaviour	
	Protection from harassment	
	Accommodation and support for asylum seekers	

Category	Type of work	Comments
Immigration and asylum	Asylum Detention (but only advice on the detention and bail, not on the substantive issue unless independently in scope) and residence restrictions pending deportation Applications for leave to remain under the domestic violence rule Applications for leave by victims of trafficking Terrorism prevention and investigation measures Proceedings before the Special Immigration Appeals Commission Judicial review, but not • where the same issue has been the subject of a previous judicial review or appeal within the last year • of removal directions where the substantive decision or appeal was made in the last year • of a negative decision on an asylum application where there is no right of appeal to the tribunal	Most mainstream non-asylum immigration work has been removed from scope. LASPO Sch 1 Pt 1 para 19, which brings judicial review into scope, contains a number of specific restrictions limiting the circumstances in which a judicial review can be brought in an immigration case. See para 9.27. See chapter 9 of this book for more on immigration cases.
Mental health	Services in relation to the Mental Health Act 1983, the Mental Capacity Act 2005 and the Repatriation of Prisoners Act 1984 Sch para 5(2)	See chapter 10 of this book for more on mental health cases.

Miscellaneous	Working with children and vulnerable adults Protection from harassment where not arising from a family or housing relationship Proceeds of crime Environmental pollution Abuse of child or vulnerable adult except where in the actions against the police etc category Damages claims by victims of trafficking Gang-related violence injunctions	This is work that does not fit into any other category. Since all categories became 'exclusive' in 2013 (ie, tolerance work is not allowed), you can only take on miscellaneous cases if specifically authorised to do so by your schedule.
Public law	Human rights and public law challenges Upper Tribunal cases, cases in the Court of Appeal, Supreme Court and judicial review only.	
Welfare benefits		A small number of face to face contracts were awarded to deliver welfare benefits work from 2014. A list of providers can be downloaded from: www.gov.uk/government/uploads/system/uploads/attachment_data/file/322243/LAA-welfare-benefits-service-provision-england-and-wales-feb-2014.pdf

The telephone gateway

3.11   Clients with debt, education or discrimination problems can only seek telephone, not face to face, advice unless particular exceptions apply; this is known as the telephone gateway. Email and webcam advice is also available; when referring to telephone advice the LAA includes all remote electronic means of getting advice.

3.12   Clients are expected to have their cases dealt with in full over the telephone unless certain exceptions apply. The operation of the gateway is dealt with in Part 2 of the Civil Legal Aid (Procedure) Regulations and para 8.7 onwards of the Lord Chancellor's Guidance.

3.13   An exempt person can choose whether to go to the gateway or to a face to face provider; everyone else must go to the gateway. Exempt persons are:

- a person deprived of their liberty;
- a child (under 18);
- a previously assessed person – that is, someone who the gateway has referred to a face to face provider within the last 12 months and returns now with the same or a linked problem.

3.14   Where a client calls the gateway, an operator (who is not legally trained or a specialist caseworker) will assess their financial eligibility. As standard practice, Civil Legal Advice (CLA) operators will not make the assessment of suitability for telephone advice for eligible clients, they will instead put the client through to a CLA specialist caseworker to make the assessment.[7] Unless they are an exempt person, the client's wishes are not relevant at this point.

3.15   The specialist caseworker will only refer the client for face to face advice if:

- the client is exempted;
- the client's instructions cannot be understood or acted on;
- the client cannot understand or act on the advice;
- certificated work is required, in which case a referral should be made as soon as possible.

3.16   The contract holders for education and discrimination also hold the only contracts for face to face advice in those categories, and therefore will either refer the client to one of their own offices, or to an agent. The debt contract is for telephone advice only, and therefore the debt telephone providers will refer to face to face provision.

---

7 MOJ briefing on Suitability for Assessment dated 13 December 2012.

3.17   In the tender round for 2013 contracts, the LAA did not tender for face to face debt work. But every organisation awarded a housing contract also received a notional four debt matter starts, and therefore is also a debt provider (the supervisor standard is a joint one). Therefore, in practice, any referral for face to face advice will be to a housing provider wearing its 'debt hat' rather than a contracted debt provider.

3.18   If you, working in a face to face service with a housing and debt contract, are approached by a client with a debt problem, you must refer them to the gateway unless they are exempt. If the gateway refers a case to you, you should record the referral, including the reference number, on your file. Face to face services cannot take on debt cases, except for exempt persons or as a gateway referral, and any file opened in breach of this rule will be nil assessed. Applications for certificates may be made without going via the gateway but only when all possible Legal Help work has been done (and the application will not be funded). It appears in practice little certificate work is referred out from the gateway.[8]

3.19   In December 2014, the government published a review[9] of the operation of the gateway, which found it to be operating effectively, though with scope for improvements to be made. A later independent report by the Public Law Project was more critical.[10] It was government policy at the time of the implementation of LASPO to roll out the gateway to other areas of law, but at the time of writing no announcement on whether or when this will happen has been made.

Scope of contracts

3.20   As described above, legal aid cases are divided into categories by the contracts. At the highest level, civil and crime are treated separately, have separate contracts and different funding rules. See chapter 10 for crime.

---

8   See para 8.12 of the Lord Chancellor's Guidance.

9   The review can be found at www.gov.uk/government/publications/civil-legal-advice-mandatory-gateway-review and associated data at www.gov.uk/government/publications/civil-legal-advice-mandatory-gateway-research-findings.

10 www.publiclawproject.org.uk/resources/199/an-independent-review-of-the-mandatory-civil-legal-advice-gateway.

3.21   At the time of writing, there are four main civil contracts, plus two specifically for the small number of welfare benefits providers:

- The **Standard Civil Contract 2010**: actions against the police; clinical negligence; family mediation; public law. This will be replaced in most categories by the 2015 version (see below). The sole remaining category under 2010 provisions will then be family mediation. Note that family mediation continues to operate under an amended version of the 2010 contract following a re-tendering exercise. New contracts took effect from 1 February 2015.
- The **Standard Civil Contract 2013**: housing and debt; family; immigration and asylum.
- The **Standard Civil Contract (welfare benefits) 2013** from 1 October 2013 – welfare benefits in London and the South East, and the Midlands and the East.
- The **Standard Civil Contract (welfare benefits) 2014** from 1 February 2014 – welfare benefits advice in the North, South West and Wales.
- The **Standard Civil Contract 2014**: from 1 August 2014 – mental health; community care.
- The **Standard Civil Contract 2015**: from 1 November 2015 – actions against the police etc, clinical negligence, public law.

3.22   Discrimination and education are only available through the telephone gateway and the providers of this work and those of the debt, housing and family telephone services have a separate contract (the CLA Contract 2013).

3.23   An organisation may therefore be operating under several separate contracts simultaneously depending on the work it does and it is vitally important that you apply the correct rules to the particular category of work you are operating in.

3.24   The definitions of each category are set out in the appropriate category definitions specific to the contract which applies, so there are 2010 category definitions (as amended per LASPO), 2013 category definitions (debt, discrimination, education (SEN), family, housing, immigration and asylum, welfare benefits, miscellaneous work), 2014 category definitions (community care, mental health and miscellaneous work), 2015 category definitions (clinical negligence, actions against the police etc, public law and miscellaneous work), and in the crime contract. See appendices D–G.

Case study

We have a 2013 contract in housing. My client is a homeowner facing possession proceedings. Can I advise her under our housing contract?

Mortgage possession work is categorised as debt work and not included in the housing category. Debt work is gateway work, meaning the client must approach the telephone gateway first (unless she is an exempt person). You should therefore tell her to contact the gateway. Since proceedings have been issued, the gateway may well decide that face to face advice and representation is required, but that is a decision for the gateway, not for you or the client. If the gateway does decide that, they will refer the client for face to face advice, and if the case is referred back to you, you will be given a gateway reference number which you must record on your file in order to be paid.

The same applies if you represented the client on a Housing Possession court duty scheme; if ongoing work is required, you should refer it to the gateway not do it yourself.

3.25 An organisation can only be funded to conduct civil legal aid cases if it has a Standard Civil Contract with the LAA. The contract will specify what cases the organisation can take on.

3.26 Every contract has a schedule, which is the part specific to the organisation. In order to be allowed to take on cases, you must be permitted to work in that category by your schedule. The schedule will specify the number of matter starts of controlled work, and whether licensed work is allowed for each category. Controlled work – Legal Help, Help at Court and Controlled Legal Representation – is funding for advice granted by the organisation; licensed work, also known as legal representation or certificated work, is funding for representation in courts, mainly granted by the LAA.

3.27 The matter starts permitted in your schedule are the maximum number of new controlled work cases in that category of law you are permitted to take on during the life of the schedule (usually a year). You can only take on cases in a category in which you have a supervisor and a contract.

3.28 Licensed work is not restricted by matter starts, so there is no limit on the number of certificate applications you may make in a year, as long as you have a contract in the appropriate category.

3.29 Therefore, provided you have a contract in the relevant category, the matter is in scope and you have sufficient matter starts (where relevant), you can take on the case, if the client is eligible. In many categories of law organisations which bid for contracts in the lower lot sizes are able to self-authorise up to 50 per cent additional matter starts in the first contract year. You should check your contract schedule for details.

Exceptional cases

3.30   You may, however, take on cases that would otherwise be excluded but fall within the 'exceptional case' provisions in LASPO.[11] All decisions on exceptional cases are made by the LAA. The test is:

(a) that it is necessary to make the services available to the individual because failure to do so would be a breach of–
  (i) the individual's Convention rights (within the meaning of the Human Rights Act 1998), or
  (ii) any rights of the individual to the provision of legal services that are enforceable EU rights, or
(b) that it is appropriate to do so, in the particular circumstances of the case, having regard to any risk that failure to do so would be such a breach.

3.31   Exceptional cases are dealt with in Part 8 of the Procedure Regulations. An application should be made to the LAA, who will determine whether funding should be granted. Guidance on making exceptional applications can be found on the LAA website: www.gov.uk/ government/publications/legal-aid-exceptional-case-funding-form- and-guidance.

3.32   Legal aid can be backdated to cover making the application under regulation 68 of the Civil Legal Aid (Procedure) Regulations 2013, but only if legal aid is granted. You may have to make the application pro bono unless the client can pay privately. See chapter 4 for more information about making applications and a review of relevant case-law.

Financial eligibility

3.33   There are two significant barriers to taking on cases: the means test and the merits test. Every client must qualify financially before their case can be taken on (with very limited exceptions in the family and mental health categories; see chapters 7 and 10), and the case must pass the relevant merits test.

---

11 LASPO s10(3).

3.34   Financial eligibility is assessed on three separate criteria, all of which the client must satisfy, by being below the threshold on capital, gross income and disposable income.

3.35   The limits on each of these are set out in the Civil Legal Aid (Financial Resources and Payment for Services) Regulations 2013 which are amended periodically, usually at least once per year as benefit levels are uprated. Up to date limits can be found on the LAA website: www.gov.uk/civil-legal-aid-means-testing.

3.36   In the case of controlled work, you should ascertain the client's resources and calculate eligibility; the decision on whether the means test is met is delegated to you. For licensed work, however, the decision is made by the LAA.

3.37   The LAA has provided guides to assessing eligibility for controlled and certificated work. In relation to certificated work, see also the Means Assessment Guidance issued by the LAA's legal team in August 2014, which is helpful in more complex cases. They can all be downloaded from www.gov.uk/civil-legal-aid-means-testing.

Case study

Para 3.23 of the 2013 Civil Contract says that satisfactory evidence of the client's means must be provided before we assess eligibility. Our clients rarely bring this evidence with them to the first appointment. Is there anything we can do about this?

You need to explain clearly to clients what evidence they will need to bring with them. Many organisations now train a member of support staff to understand what is and not acceptable and ensure that clients bring what it necessary to the first appointment. This can be confirmed in a standard letter and clients can be sent a text message the day before to remind them of the appointment and what they need to bring with them.

However, if you can justify it to protect your client's position, then you can start work before the client provides evidence, and in very rare cases the LAA may accept that it is not possible for them to provide it at all (2013 Contract Specification para 3.24). However, the LAA are taking an increasingly strict approach to this provision on audit, and if they deem that it was not reasonable to rely on it, or that evidence of means should have been provided at some point later than the first appointment, the file may be nil assessed).

3.38   Where the client has a partner with whom he or she is living as a couple, you should always aggregate the means of both the client and the partner. Partner means:

- spouse or civil partner;
- person with whom the client lives or ordinarily lives as a couple,

but not where they are separated because of a relationship breakdown likely to be permanent.[12]

However, if only one partner is seeking advice at your office in person, both are not required to sign the application form. The then Legal Services Commission issued guidance which clarified the requirement for both to sign only applies to postal and telephone applications.[13]

Passporting benefits

3.39   Prior to 1 April 2013, clients directly or indirectly in receipt of income support, income-based jobseeker's allowance, income-based employment and support allowance or guarantee state pension credit were automatically eligible for all types of legal aid without the need for further assessment of either capital or income.[14] These benefits were therefore referred to as passporting benefits. A client in receipt of support under sections 4 or 95 of the Immigration and Asylum Act 1999 was similarly passported, but only for Legal Help and Controlled Legal Representation in the immigration category.[15] For all cases started on or after 1 April 2013, passporting benefits only passport clients through the income test; you must assess capital in all cases. Current income passporting benefits are:

- income support;
- income-based jobseeker's allowance;
- universal credit;
- guarantee pension credit;
- income-related employment and support allowance.

---

12 Civil Legal Aid (Financial Resources and Payment for Services) Regulations 2013 reg 2.

13 Guidance issued by the LSC in 2009. This is available at: http://webarchive. nationalarchives.gov.uk/20121207044149/http://www.LEGALSERVICES.gov. uk/docs/forms/CW1_Client_Certification_Guidance_Nov_2009(1).pdf. It is no longer available on the current LAA website; but equally, we are aware of nothing to suggest that this approach has been changed.

14 Community Legal Service (Financial) Regulations 2000 reg 4(2).

15 Civil Legal Aid (Financial Resources and Payment for Services) Regulations 2013 reg 26.

3.40   The evidence requirement for capital is the provision of three months' bank statements or similar.

Assessment of capital

3.41   Capital is 'every resource of a capital nature belonging to [the client] on the date on which the application is made',[16] either as money or as the realisable value of an asset.[17] It includes money owed to the client, whether or not recovered,[18] and also includes life insurance and endowments if their security can be borrowed upon.[19]

3.42   However, the value of household furniture and effects, clothing and tools of trade is excluded,[20] as is (in the case of controlled work) money the client could realise by selling or borrowing on the strength of any business he or she may own.[21]

3.43   Where the client owns property, the value of that property should be taken into account in the calculation. The value is the client's equity – that is, the current realisable market value[22] (The LAA Guide to determining financial eligibility for certificated work – April 2014 v1,[23] states that a deduction of three per cent should be made from the value, to allow for the cost of selling the property. This does not appear in the equivalent guidance for assessing eligibility for controlled work; but arguably, it should as the regulation is the same), less the value of any outstanding mortgage. Deduction for mortgage is capped to £100,000[24] – so where a property is worth £220,000 and the outstanding mortgage is £120,000, the client's equity should be taken as £120,000, not £100,000. The first £100,000 of equity should also be disregarded.[25]

3.44   Where any property is the subject matter of the dispute (SMOD), the value of that property may be disregarded from the calculation, depending on its value. Pre 1 April 2013, the value of property in dispute could be completely disregarded at the Legal Help level.

---

16 Reg 30.
17 Reg 31.
18 Reg 32.
19 Reg 33.
20 Reg 34.
21 Reg 36.
22 Reg 31.
23 The guides to assessing controlled and certificated work can both be downloaded from www.gov.uk/civil-legal-aid-means-testing.
24 Reg 37.
25 Reg 39.

However, for licensed work applications before 1 April 2013 the subject matter of dispute disregard was capped to £100,000. From 1 April 2013, you need to consider the value of any property that is SMOD, whether at Legal Help or licensed work levels as the £100,000 cap applies across the board.[26]

Clients over 60

3.45   Where a client is aged 60 or over, they are entitled to a further disregard on capital. The level of the disregard is on a sliding scale determined by disposable income (see below) up to a maximum of £100,000 of capital.[27] Using the online calculator[28] will allow you to ensure this is calculated correctly.

Case study

My client instructs me to advise her regarding financial matters. She qualifies for legal aid because of a history of domestic abuse, and has evidence in the form of a letter from her GP. She and her husband own (as joint tenants) a flat, which has just been valued at £550,000. She wants the flat to be transferred to her. The outstanding mortgage is £150,000. Is she eligible for a) Legal Help; b) a certificate?

The value of the property should be taken as £533,500 – that is, £550,000 minus 3% costs of sale. Disregard the mortgage, capped to £100,000 – so the equity is £433,500.

The client's share of this is £216,750, half of the equity – although the asset is in dispute, there is a presumption of equal shares for the purposes of assessment, and they are joint tenants.

Disregard the first £100,000 of equity – the client's capital is £116,750.

For Legal Help, if she had been applying prior to 1 April 2013, the entire subject matter of the dispute would have been disregarded, so her capital would have been taken as zero and she would have been eligible on capital.

---

26 Reg 38.
27 Reg 41.
28 http://civil-eligibility-calculator.justice.gov.uk/.

> For licensed work, and for Legal Help applications from 1 April 2013, only the first £100,000 of disputed property is disregarded, so her capital is taken to be £16,750. This is above the threshold of £8,000 and therefore she is not eligible on capital.

Assessment of income

3.46 Once you have found the client eligible on capital, you should proceed to the next stage, assessment of income. The client must be eligible on both gross and disposable income, and the thresholds are set on the basis of a calendar month. For example, if the client instructs you on 6 March, you should look at all money received since 7 February.

3.47 'Gross income' means total income from all sources (apart from housing benefit and some benefits and allowances, most commonly disability living allowance/personal independence payment).[29] It will include salary, benefits, maintenance, and any other income.

3.48 You should deduct the following expenses from gross income to arrive at disposable income:

- the amount payable[30] of any rent or mortgage payments, net of any housing benefit – but capped to £545 per month if the client has no dependants;[31]
- tax and National Insurance contributions on any earnings;[32]
- childcare costs, but only to the extent that they are incurred because of work or study outside the home and only where reasonable to make a deduction;[33]
- where working, a fixed cost of employment allowance of £45 (for both the client and partner if both are working);[34]

---

29 Civil Legal Aid (Financial Resources and Payment for Services) Regulations 2013 regs 21 and 24.

30 Note the amount the client is contractually liable to pay, not the amount they are actually paying. This can be important in housing cases where the client is in arrears and not paying rent. See *R (Southwark Law Centre) v Legal Services Commission; R (Dennis) v Legal Services Commission* [2007] EWHC 1715 (Admin). Although decided on the previous regulations, the same wording is used in reg 28.

31 Civil Legal Aid (Financial Resources and Payment for Services) Regulations 2013 reg 28.

32 Reg 23.

33 Reg 27.

34 Reg 27.

- any maintenance being paid in respect of a child or other dependent relative or former partner not a member of the client's household;[35] and
- fixed dependants' allowances for the partner and each other dependent relative who is a member of the household. (Note that it is a common misconception that the dependants' allowances can only be claimed in respect of the client's children, an impression not dispelled by the wording of the forms which refer to 'child'. The regulations are quite clear that the allowance is claimable for any dependent relative who is a member of the client's household.)[36]

3.49   The LAA's eligibility calculator is helpful as it always gets the arithmetic right and applies any allowances and disregards correctly. It can be used online at http://civil-eligibility-calculator.justice.gov.uk/.

Assessment of the means of a child

3.50   You are allowed to accept applications from a child.[37] When deciding on an application for Legal Help, you should assess the means of the child and those of the person(s) who have care and control or are liable to maintain the child or who usually contribute substantially to the child's maintenance. So, in effect, you will often be assessing the means of the parents, with the expectation that they should fund the case if they are able to do so.[38]

3.51   However, you should consider whether it is just and equitable to aggregate the child's means with those of the person(s) liable to maintain them, and if it is not just and equitable you should just assess the means of the child. No guidance is given as to what is 'just and equitable', although the contract says that the presumption is that there should be aggregation but that you can take into account all the circumstances, including the age and resources of the child, and that non-aggregation is more likely to be justified where there is a conflict between the child and the liable person.[39] In the absence of detailed guidance, this is a decision for you as the provider assessing eligibility for Legal Help, and you should therefore keep a detailed

---

35 Civil Legal Aid (Financial Resources and Payment for Services) Regulations 2013 reg 26.
36 Reg 25.
37 Civil Legal Aid (Procedure) Regulations 2012 reg 22.
38 Standard Civil Contract Specification 2013 para 3.27.
39 Standard Civil Contract Specification 2013 para 3.28.

file note justifying your decision, especially if it is a decision not to aggregate.

3.52 Where a child applies for a funding certificate, it is generally only the child's means that are taken into account, not those of the litigation friend or any other person liable to maintain the child, and therefore you should only include the child's finances on the MEANS form.[40] However, in family cases you should consider whether to aggregate in the same way as for Legal Help.

Legal aid available without regard to means

3.53 Legal aid for the following types of case is not means tested:[41]

- Special Children Act cases and related proceedings (see chapter 6).
- Family Help (Lower) in cases where Children Act 1989 s31 proceedings are contemplated and the client is a parent or person with parental responsibility;
- Mental Health Tribunal cases (see chapter 10);
- certificates in Mental Capacity Act 2005 s21A cases before the Court of Protection where the client is deprived of their liberty;
- terrorism prevention and investigation measure applications, notices and proceedings;
- Hague Convention and European Convention on Child Custody cases;
- various cases concerning international enforcement of child maintenance etc. under the United Kingdom's international treaties and obligations;
- mediation information and assessment meetings and mediation in Hague Convention cases.

3.54 In family cases concerning injunctions for domestic violence and forced marriage the eligibility limits – but not contributions – can be waived. See chapter 5.

3.55 In inquests (where exceptional funding is granted) multi-party actions and cross-border disputes, eligibility limits and contributions can be waived.

---

40 Civil Legal Aid (Financial Resources and Payment for Services) Regulations 2013 reg 16(3) and (4).

41 Reg 5.

Reassessment of means

3.56   The means tests are not one-off tests; if clients' circumstances change during a case, their means should be reassessed. In the case of controlled work, you should reassess means yourself, and if the client is no longer eligible, you may need to withdraw the funding. In the case of licensed work, you should report the change of circumstances to the LAA for them to reassess the means. The LAA Guide to determining financial eligibility for certificated work – April 2014 v1[42] says that it may not be appropriate to reassess the client's means unless they have improved 'dramatically', or the matter is likely to run for some time, suggested as three months or more for controlled work, though reassessment would be done for licensed work.

3.57   Regulation 20 of the Civil Legal Aid (Financial Resources and Payment for Services) Regulations 2013 provides – for all levels of service subject to means assessment – that where:

- disposable income has increased by more than £60 or decreased by more than £25;
- disposable capital has increased by more than £750; or
- the client is no longer in receipt of a passporting benefit,

a reassessment must take place unless it is inappropriate to do so having regard to the period for which legal aid is likely to continue. In the case of controlled work whether it is inappropriate will be a decision for you. In the case of licensed work for the LAA further contributions from capital may be required. See the Means Assessment Guidance issued by the LAA's legal team for more information.[43]

3.58   It is the client's duty to report any change of circumstances to you,[44] and therefore you must always advise clients of the existence of this duty at the first meeting. It should be confirmed in your standard letter.

Merits tests

3.59   Each case must satisfy, and continue to satisfy, the merits test. There are a number of different tests, depending on the nature of the case and the type of funding sought, and they are dealt with in the relevant

---

42 See www.gov.uk/civil-legal-aid-means-testing.
43 www.gov.uk/civil-legal-aid-means-testing.
44 Civil Legal Aid (Financial Resources and Payment for Services) Regulations 2013 reg 18.

sections of chapters 5–11 of this book. You should always bear in mind that each merits test should be passed at the start of the case, and should continue to be passed throughout its life. If there is insufficient merit in a particular step in the proceedings, you should not take that step; if there is not, or is no longer, sufficient merit in the case as a whole, you should refuse or withdraw funding (controlled work), or report that to the LAA (licensed work).

Other restrictions on taking on cases

Referral fees

3.60   Although referral fees have been allowed (controversially) as a matter of professional conduct for the last few years, there is an absolute prohibition on them in legal aid work. Clause 6.8 of the Standard Civil Contract Standard Terms makes clear that no payment or benefit may be made to or received from any third party.

Client has received previous advice

3.61   The Legal Help form requires the client to certify that they have not previously received advice on the same matter, and where they have done so within the last six months requires you to explain why you took on the case. This is because there are specific rules in the contract to prevent the legal aid fund paying out twice for the same matter, and therefore in order to make a claim the second time you must be able to demonstrate that the case meets one of the exceptions allowing you to do so.

3.62   Some of the exceptions apply if you are the client's original provider looking to re-open a case that has been closed; others apply if you are a second provider looking to take over a case from the original organisation.

3.63   In the case of controlled work a second matter start can only be opened on the same case as the original provider where:

   (a) at least six months has elapsed since there was a claim on the first matter; or
   (b) there has been a material development or change in the client's instructions and at least three months has elapsed since there was a claim on the first matter.[45]

---

45 Standard Civil Contract Specification 2013 para 3.40.

3.64 Where you are relying on para 3.47(b) (material development or change), you should note that:

- Giving instructions following a failure to give instructions is not a change in instructions.
- A decision or response from any third party to any correspondence, application, appeal, review or other request made in the course of the original matter is not a material development.
- A change in the law that was anticipated in the original matter is not a material development.[46]

However, you can instead re-open the original matter and make a further claim (see chapter 5) in some circumstances.

3.65 Where you are the second provider, looking to take over a case, you can only do so where:

(a) there has been a material change in relevant circumstances since the initial decision to grant Legal Help; or
(b) the client has reasonable cause to be dissatisfied with the first provider; or
(c) the client has moved a distance away from the first provider and effective communication is not practicable; or
(d) the first provider is not making a claim for the work and confirms that in writing. [47]

The contract[48] requires you to make reasonable enquiries of the client as to whether there was previous advice. Where there is a transfer, you must establish that there is good reason, and record that reason on the file.[49]

3.66 However, it is not sufficient for you to take the client's word as to the reasons for transfer. You must seek the client's authority to obtain the file from the previous provider, and must then request the file from the previous provider. You cannot start work on the case until you receive the file. Where the client refuses to give you authority, or where you obtain the file and discover that there is in fact no good reason for transfer, you may not make a claim for the case. The sole exception is where there is urgent work that is absolutely necessary to protect the client's position or meet a court deadline, in which case you can do the urgent work and claim for it, even if it later transpires there was no good reason.[50]

46 Standard Civil Contract Specification 2013 para 3.37.
47 Civil Legal Aid (Procedure) Regulations 2012 reg 23(4).
48 Standard Civil Contract Specification 2013 para 3.40.
49 Standard Civil Contract Specification 2013 para 3.44.
50 Standard Civil Contract Specification 2013 paras 3.42 and 3.43.

3.67   In the case of certificated work, there is no specific rule or guidance on transfer of solicitor. However, to transfer, the second solicitor
would have to make an application to the LAA to amend the certificate, and the LAA will consider whether the application is justified.
The second solicitor must include work done by the first solicitor on
the bill at the end of the case, and therefore the LAA (or court) will
be able to see all work done by both solicitors, and may disallow on
assessment any unjustified duplication.

Permitted work

3.68   So, if your client's case is within the scope of the scheme and your
contract, and passes the means and merits tests, you will be able
to take it on. However, there are restrictions on what work can be
done.

3.69   The Civil Legal Aid (Procedure) Regulations 2012 set out limitations on the work that can be done at each level of legal aid. The definitions in the criteria are important, as they set out in full what can
and cannot be done at each level of funding. Where the client's case
needs work that is out of the scope of the current level, you will need
to make an application for funding at the next level.

Definitions of permitted work[51]

3.70   The main types of funding common to all areas are:

- **Legal Help**, which allows the provision of advice, negotiation and
  attempts at settlement and resolution, but not acting as a mediator, issuing or conducting court proceedings, instruction of an
  advocate or advocacy;
- **Help at Court**, which authorises help and advocacy for a client at
  a particular hearing without formally being on the court record as
  acting for the client;
- **Legal representation**, which allows the provision of representation in proceedings or contemplated proceedings, including the
  conduct of litigation and advocacy.

3.71   Controlled Legal Representation is a form of legal representation at
the controlled work level – that is, which is controlled work rather
than licensed work, and therefore granted by the provider rather than

---

51   Civil Legal Aid (Procedure) Regulations 2012 regs 4–10.

the LAA. It allows you to represent clients before tribunals, but only in the mental health and immigration categories.

3.72   Family Help is a form of funding only available in the family category, and slots in between Legal Help and legal representation. Family Help (Lower) is a form of controlled work, also known as private law level 2 work, and authorises advice and assistance in attempting to resolve a family dispute through negotiation and settlement. It does not include mediation, but can include advice in support of mediation. Family Help (Higher) is licensed work covering all litigation up to but not including a final contested hearing. Final hearings can be covered by Legal Representation (see para 6.68).

3.73   Help with Mediation was a new form of funding from 1 April 2013 for legal advice for those who are in, or have participated in, mediation. It is controlled work.

3.74   Help with Family Mediation was a new form of funding from 1 April 2013 for legal advice for those who are in, or have participated in, mediation. See chapters 6 and 8.

3.75   Investigative representation is a type of licensed work that allows the LAA to issue a certificate that is limited in scope and costs, permitting the solicitor to investigate the strength of a proposed claim but not generally to issue or conduct proceedings.

3.76   More details of the types of work that can be carried out at each funding level can be found in the following chapters.

Exceptional case funding

Introduction

4.1   When LASPO was passed, the government sought to address concerns that it would result in injustice by making available exceptional case funding – that is, a discretionary power to fund cases that would otherwise be out of scope in limited circumstances.

4.2   If legal aid is not available under Schedule 1 to the Act, it may be possible to apply for funding under LASPO 2012 s10. The test for exceptional case funding under section 10 of LASPO is:

    (a) that it is necessary to make the services available to the individual because failure to do so would be a breach of–

        (i) the individual's Convention rights (within the meaning of the Human Rights Act 1998), or

        (ii) any rights of the individual to the provision of legal services that are enforceable EU rights, or

    (b) That it is appropriate to do so, in the particular circumstances of the case, having regard to any risk that failure to do so would be such a breach.

4.3   Exceptional funding is only available in civil cases where the subject matter is out of scope because of the effect of Schedule 1 to LASPO – either because it is not included in Part 1, because it is excluded by Part 2, or because representation in the particular court or tribunal is not permitted by Part 3. It is not available to clients whose case's subject matter is in scope, but who are not eligible for legal aid for some other reason.

4.4   The client must still meet financial eligibility criteria and their case must meet the merits criteria to qualify for exceptional case funding. Exceptional case applications are dealt with by the exceptional cases funding (ECF) team within the LAA's High Cost Cases section, and every individual grant must also be personally approved by both the LAA's Principal Legal Adviser and Head of High Cost Cases.[1]

4.5   In its commentary on the statistics between April and December 2013 the Ministry of Justice noted that:

> A typical family application is in private family law proceedings. In particular these concern the right of contact with and residence of the applicant's child or the division of matrimonial assets. These cases generally involve the determination of civil rights and obligations. The overarching question to consider is whether the withholding of legal aid would make the assertion of the claim practically impossible or lead to an obvious unfairness in proceedings.

---

1   Director of Legal Aid Casework Annual Report 2014–15 para 24.

Lord Chancellor's Guidance

4.6   You must have regard to the Lord Chancellor's guidance on exceptional case funding. There have however been difficulties with that guidance and both the inquests and non-inquest versions have been held to be unlawful on several occasions (see below).

4.7   The non-inquest guidance was updated on 9 June 2015 in light of the findings of the Court of Appeal. At the time of writing, no equivalent update had been made to the inquests guidance.

4.8   The guidance can be found here: www.gov.uk/funding-and-costs-assessment-for-civil-and-crime-matters. It is to be read in conjunction with the case-law, and we discuss the two principal cases below.

Guidance on non-inquest cases

4.9   When LASPO came into force, the Lord Chancellor issued guidance on exceptional funding, which made clear that he interpreted its scope very narrowly and expected very few grants. The result was that both the number of applications and the number – and proportion – of grants were very much lower than expected, and lower than the projections the government had used to reassure Parliament during the Act's passage. This led to a number of challenges to the guidance and the way the LAA implemented exceptional funding, which are discussed below.

The Gudanaviciene cases

4.10   In *R (Gudanaviciene and others) v The Director of Legal Aid Casework and The Lord Chancellor*,[2] the Court of Appeal considered the Lord Chancellor's appeal against the High Court's earlier decision[3] that the exceptional funding guidance was unlawful.

4.11   The Court of Appeal refused to follow the approach of the High Court either in *Gudanaviciene* (Collins J) or the earlier case of *M v Director of Legal Aid Casework and others*[4] (Coulson J) in construing section 10 of LASPO. Lord Dyson MR, giving the judgment of the court, set out the test to be applied:

> 31. We see no warrant for construing section 10(3)(a) as imposing a condition that an ECF determination should only be made where it can definitely be said (Coulson J's formulation) that refusal would

2 [2014] EWCA Civ 1622.
3 [2014] EWHC 1840 (Admin).
4 [2014] EWHC 1354 (Admin).

be a breach; or where there is a 'high level of probability' that refusal would be a breach (Collins J's test). There is no need to add a gloss to the wording of the statute 'would be a breach'. In deciding whether there would be a breach, the Director should apply the principles to be derived from the case-law (some of which is mentioned at para 27 of the Guidance). There is no need for elaboration. When determining whether a complaint of a breach of Convention rights has been established, the ECtHR does not ask itself whether there has definitely been a breach or whether there has been a breach to a high level of probability. It simply asks whether there has been a breach. In our view, this approach should inform the meaning of the words 'would be a breach' in section 10(3)(a). We do not consider that the word 'clearly' in the Explanatory Notes (see para 9 above) takes the argument any further. We should add that we accept the submission of Mr Chamberlain that the 'real risk of a breach' is a concept which has no part to play in the exercise envisaged by section 10(3). Section 10(3)(a) speaks of the situation where a failure to make civil legal services available would be a breach, not where there would be a real risk of a breach. The concept of real risk has no part to play in the question whether the denial of legal aid would amount to a breach of an individual's procedural rights under the Convention or under article 47 of the Charter.

32. In short, therefore, if the Director concludes that a denial of ECF would be a breach of an individual's Convention or EU rights, he must make an exceptional funding determination. But as we shall see, the application of the ECtHR and CJEU case-law is not hard-edged. It requires an assessment of the likely shape of the proposed litigation and the individual's ability to have effective access to justice in relation to it. The Director may conclude that he cannot decide whether there would be a breach of the individual's Convention or EU rights. In that event, he is not required by section 10(3)(a) to make a determination. He must then go on to consider whether it is appropriate to make a determination under section 10(3)(b). In making that decision, he should have regard to *any* risk that failure to make a determination would be a breach. These words mean exactly what they say. The greater he assesses the risk to be, the more likely it is that he will consider it to be appropriate to make a determination. That is because, if the risk eventuates, there will be a breach. But the seriousness of the risk is only one of the factors that the Director may take into account in deciding whether it is appropriate to make a determination. He should have regard to all the circumstances of the case.

4.12   In considering the Lord Chancellor's Guidance in relation to whether there would be a breach of article 6 ECHR in refusing funding, Lord Dyson said:

45. In our judgment, the cumulative effect of these passages is to misstate the effect of the ECtHR jurisprudence. As we have seen, the Guidance correctly identifies many of the particular factors that should be taken into account in deciding whether to make an exceptional case determination, but their effect is substantially neutralised by the strong steer given in the passages that we have highlighted. These passages send a clear signal to the caseworkers and the Director that the refusal of legal aid will amount to a breach of article 6(1) only in rare and extreme cases. In our judgment, there are no statements in the case-law which support this signal. For the reasons stated earlier, we do not consider that the reference in *X v UK* to 'exceptional circumstances' provides support for it.

46. The general principles established by the ECtHR are now clear. Inevitably, they are derived from cases in which the question was whether there was a breach of article 6(1) in proceedings which had already taken place. We accept the following summary of the relevant case-law given by Mr Drabble: (i) the Convention guarantees rights that are practical and effective, not theoretical and illusory in relation to the right of access to the courts (*Airey* para 24, *Steel and Morris* para 59); (ii) the question is whether the applicant's appearance before the court or tribunal in question without the assistance of a lawyer was effective, in the sense of whether he or she was able to present the case properly and satisfactorily (*Airey* para 24, *McVicar* para 48 and *Steel and Morris* para 59); (iii) it is relevant whether the proceedings taken as a whole were fair (*McVicar* para 50, *P,C and S* para 91); (iv) the importance of the appearance of fairness is also relevant: simply because an applicant can struggle through 'in the teeth of all the difficulties' does not necessarily mean that the procedure was fair (*P,C and S* para 91); and (v) equality of arms must be guaranteed to the extent that each side is afforded a reasonable opportunity to present his or her case under conditions that do not place them at a substantial disadvantage vis-à-vis their opponent (*Steel and Morris* para 62).

4.13   In making an exceptional funding determination, what is required is a consideration of all the circumstances of the case (and 'exceptional' is not a test of itself, nor does it necessarily imply that grants will be rare, contrary to what is stated in the Guidance). The Strasbourg case-law does not require representation in all but the most straightforward of cases; but nor does it only require representation in extreme cases:

> ... the critical question is whether an unrepresented litigant is able to present his case effectively and without obvious unfairness. The answer to this question requires a consideration of all the circumstances of the case, including the factors which are identified at paras 19 to 25 of the Guidance. These factors must be carefully weighed.

Thus the greater the complexity of the procedural rules and/or the substantive legal issues, the more important what is at stake and the less able the applicant may be to cope with the stress, demands and complexity of the proceedings, the more likely it is that article 6(1) will require the provision of legal services (subject always to any reasonable merits and means test). The cases demonstrate that article 6(1) does not require civil legal aid in most or even many cases. It all depends on the circumstances.[5]

4.14   The court's conclusions in respect of article 6 were held to apply with equal force to article 47(3) of the Charter of Fundamental Rights of the EU.

4.15   The court went on to consider article 8, concluding that the guidance stating that article 8 could not lead to a grant of legal aid in immigration cases was wrong. Instead, the court said that the test to be applied is:

72. Whether legal aid is required will depend on the particular facts and circumstances of each case, including (a) the importance of the issues at stake; (b) the complexity of the procedural, legal and evidential issues; and (c) the ability of the individual to represent himself without legal assistance, having regard to his age and mental capacity. The following features of immigration proceedings are relevant: (i) there are statutory restrictions on the supply of advice and assistance (see section 84 of the Immigration and Asylum Act 1999); (ii) individuals may well have language difficulties; and (iii) the law is complex and rapidly evolving (see, for example, per Jackson LJ in *Sapkota v Secretary of State for the Home Department* [2012] Imm AR 254 at para 127).

...

75. Para 59 [of the Lord Chancellor's Guidance] is plainly correct: immigration decisions do not involve the determination of civil rights and obligations. But para 60 is wrong as Mr Chamberlain has conceded. For the reasons that we have given, the *W v UK* test should be applied in immigration proceedings.

76. What guidance is it appropriate to give as to the circumstances in which article 8 requires the provision of legal aid in immigration cases? We have already set out at para 72 above some of the relevant circumstances. In addressing these, it will often be helpful to take into account the factors set out at paragraphs 19 to 24 of the Guidance in relation to article 6(1). In carrying out this exercise in relation to article 8, the decision-maker should not apply a 'very high threshold' for the reasons that we have given in rejecting such a threshold in relation to article 6(1).

5   [2014] EWCA Civ 1622 para 56.

77. Deportation cases are of particular concern. It will often be the case that a decision to deport will engage an individual's article 8 rights. Where this occurs, the individual will usually be able to say that the issues at stake for him are of great importance. This should not be regarded as a trump card which usually leads to the need for legal aid. It is no more than one of the relevant factors to be taken into account. The fact that this factor will almost invariably be present in deportation cases is not, however, a justification for giving it reduced weight.

4.16 It then considered the various individual appeals, which included family reunion, deportation and trafficking cases. Practitioners dealing with such cases will want to consider those parts of the judgment carefully, though the judgment is applicable to all exceptional cases.

4.17 The Lord Chancellor sought permission to appeal to the Supreme Court in the case of *Edgehill,* one of the cases dealt with in *Gudanaviciene* (and the one in which the Court of Appeal said that article 8 could lead to legal aid in immigration cases), but permission was refused.[6] Further appeals were sought by two other parties, *B*[7] and *LS*[8], but permission on those cases has yet to be determined as at the time of writing.[9]

4.18 Some six months after the judgment in *Gudanaviciene,* the Lord Chancellor issued revised guidance for non-inquest cases. The guidance deals with the principle articles of the ECHR (6 and 8) and with article 47 of the EU Treaty in general terms, and then briefly considers the individual categories of law in an annex.

The Lord Chancellor's new guidance – article 6 ECHR

4.19 The guidance says that there is a three-stage test that caseworkers must consider:

1) Does the case involve the determination of civil rights and obligations?
2) If yes, will withholding legal aid mean the applicant will be unable to present his or her case effectively, or lead to an obvious unfairness in the proceedings?
3) If yes, what are the minimum services required to meet the legal obligation to provide legal aid?

---

6 www.supremecourt.uk/docs/permission-to-appeal-2015-03.pdf.
7 Arguing that family reunion cases are not out of scope – see chapter 9.
8 On the issue of legal aid in trafficking cases.
9 See Meredith and Pickup, 'Grayling Stalls Over Changes to Exceptional Funding', May 2015 *Legal Action* 14, footnote 5.

4.20   It will be seen from this that the LAA's focus remains on only grant-ing exceptional legal aid where it is absolutely necessary to do so, and then only to the minimum extent possible.

4.21   Further guidance is provided on factors to be taken into account in determining whether the applicant can present his or her case effectively and without obvious unfairness. These include the import-ance of the issues at stake, the complexity of law fact and procedure, and personal characteristics of the applicant. Specific guidance for adults who lack capacity and children is given. However, some of the principles set out in *Gudanaviciene* – for example para 46, quoted above – are rather skated around.

The Lord Chancellor's new guidance – article 8 ECHR

4.22   Unlike the previous version, the new guidance acknowledges that article 8 cases can lead to a grant of legal aid. However, the discussion of article 8 in the guidance is very brief. It refers back to the factors set out in the article 6 discussion as being required to be taken into account in determining applications.

4.23   Although it will be necessary to take into account the guidance in making applications for exceptional funding, not least because it is what caseworkers will use in considering, in our view it doesn't go far enough to deal with the concerns expressed by the Court of Appeal in *Gudanaviciene*. Paragraph 6 of the guidance specifically reminds caseworkers that they must have regard to *Gudanaviciene* as well as the guidance itself. In making applications for exceptional funding where you consider that your case comes within *Gudanaviciene* but perhaps would be caught by the minimising intent of the guidance, it might be as well to emphasise that paragraph in the application. It is also likely that there will be further litigation over the terms of the guidance and whether funding should be granted in particular cases.

The IS case

4.24   IS, one of the original claimants in *Gudanaviciene*, was granted legal aid and so his case was separated. It was used to bring a challenge not directly to the Lord Chancellor's guidance, but rather to the LAA's operation of the scheme.

4.25   In *IS (by the Official Solicitor as Litigation Friend) v The Director of Legal Aid Casework and The Lord Chancellor*[10] – a lengthy, detailed and

10 [2015] EWHC 1965 (Admin).

comprehensive judgment – Collins J noted a series of problems with the scheme as it has been implemented by the LAA:

- The crucial test for whether exceptional funding should be granted, as laid down by the Court of Appeal in *Gudanaviciene*, is 'whether an unrepresented litigant is able to present his case effectively and without obvious unfairness' (para 24).
- Even after *Gudanaviciene,* the success rate for applications is very low (para 29).
- The forms are unnecessarily complex, repetitious and do not reflect the right test for whether funding should be granted (paras 56 and 80).
- The forms require legal assistance to complete. The LAA should make available a form that can be filled in by an unrepresented applicant (para 54).
- Consideration should be given to making Legal Help available for solicitors to make initial enquiries, decide whether an application is justified, and make it (para 57).
- The revised Lord Chancellor's guidance, issued in response to *Gudanaviciene*, still does not give effect to it and places too many restrictions on when funding should be granted (paras 66 to 71).
- 'The belief that because courts and tribunals have to deal with litigants in person legal representation can be refused is one which must be very carefully applied. It should only be used to refuse an application if the issues are truly relatively straightforward' (para 71).
- In cases where 'a judge seized of the material proceedings has requested' representation 'because otherwise a fair hearing will not take place ... it is difficult to see that save in a rare case to fail to comply with the judge's request [to grant exceptional funding] would be justified. It is not generally appropriate for a caseworker who is not apprised of the full circumstances to second guess the judge's view. There must be a very good reason indeed for such a refusal.' (para 72).
- The LAA's urgent applications procedure is not satisfactory and the absence of a mechanism for issuing an emergency certificate is unreasonable (para 78).
- The scheme 'is not, as it is operated, meeting its need to ensure that an unrepresented litigant can present his or her case effectively and without obvious unfairness. That extends to the need to ensure that he or she has access to assistance which may be needed, as in IS's case, to make representations to the relevant

authority to achieve a particular purpose. The same need exists as for hearings before a court or tribunal.' (para 79).

- 'The system is defective in failing to provide for a right of appeal to a judicial person against a refusal where the result would be an infringement of the very essence of the right of access to a court.' (para 93).

4.26   In a particularly useful passage for family lawyers, Collins J ran through an analysis of recent cases in which the family courts have drawn attention to the difficulty of deciding cases without legal aid, and concluded:

> 40. It is difficult to imagine a family case, particularly when there are contested issues about children, in which there would not be an interference with the Article 8 rights of either parent or the children themselves. Thus unless the party seeking legal aid could albeit unrepresented present his or her case effectively and without obvious unfairness, a grant of legal aid would be required. That does not mean that every case will require it: some may be sufficiently simple for the unrepresented party to deal with. Obviously if there is a lack of capacity even such cases may require legal aid. That issue I will have to consider in further detail later. But I am bound to say that I believe that only in rare cases, subject to means and merits if properly applied, should legal aid be denied in such cases. As it is now applied, the scheme is clearly wholly deficient in that it does not enable the family courts to be satisfied that they can do justice and give a fair hearing to an unrepresented party. While the problem may perhaps be less acute in other civil cases, I have no doubt that the difficulties I have referred to in family cases apply.

4.27   Collins J also discussed the legal aid merits tests, and concluded:

> 96. There are in my view two difficulties in the way the merits test has been applied. First, the requirement that in all cases there must be an even or greater than even chance of success is unreasonable. Secondly, the manner in which the LAA has assessed the prospects of success has been erroneous. The whole point of representation is that it will produce the chance of success which without representation will not exist. If a case involves issues of fact which will depending on the court's findings determine the outcome, it must be obvious that the ability to challenge apparently unfavourable material and to cross examine adverse witnesses effectively may turn the case in a party's favour. Accordingly, what has to be assessed is not what the present material when untested may indicate but whether if competent cross examination or legal submissions are made the result may be favourable. It is not for the LAA to carry out the exercise which the court will carry out, in effect prejudging the very issue which will be determined by the court. I recognise that there will be cases which it

will be possible to say that whatever may be achieved by competent representation the result is likely to be unfavourable. The lengthy and detailed refusals which have been exhibited by the various witnesses have tended to carry out what I regard as the impermissible approach. The removal of the borderline cases from those that can succeed on merits grounds seems to me to be unreasonable.

97. Mr Chamberlain has relied on the observation of the court in *R(G)* that 'the cases demonstrate that Article 6(1) does not require civil legal aid in most or even many cases. It all depends on the circumstances'. That may be true of the cases in which a breach of Article 6(1) or the procedural requirements of Article 8 were considered. But I do not think the court was making a judgment which would apply to all applications. As was said, the circumstances of each case will be determinative and there can in my view be no doubt that the way in which merits have been approached has been flawed.

4.28 This meant that Collins J declared unlawful the relevant sections of the Civil Legal Aid (Merits Criteria) Regulations 2013, as amended, which mean that legal aid cannot be awarded in poor or borderline cases. As this applies both to in-scope and exceptional funding, the revised merits tests that resulted are dealt with in the next chapter.

4.29 As we went to press, and despite the strong criticisms of it in the judgment, the LAA had not amended the exceptional cases application form. Nor has it instituted a mechanism for emergency applications. It is to be hoped that it does so soon, and when it does we will alert you via www.legalaidhandbook.com.

4.30 So where does that leave exceptional funding now? To make an application, you must be able to show that the criteria in LASPO s10 are met:

- that it is necessary to fund because failure to do so would be a breach of ECHR or enforceable EU rights; or
- that is appropriate to fund, having regard to any risk that failure to do so would be a breach.

4.31 Once a breach or risk of a breach – usually, but not necessarily, of articles 6 or 8 – has been shown, the test to be applied whether, unrepresented, the applicant can present their case effectively and without obvious unfairness. If so, it will not be necessary or appropriate to grant funding. But if a failure to provide representation would create unfairness or prevent the applicant presenting their case effectively, then legal aid should be granted even if the prospects of success are poor, especially if the provision of representation would create a chance of success that would not otherwise exist. It will not generally be enough for the LAA to say that a court or tribunal can assist a litigant in person, nor should a judge's request for a party to be represented be lightly refused.

Guidance on inquest cases

4.32   There is separate Lord Chancellor's guidance for inquest cases, but much of the above discussion, particularly about the process of applying for exceptional funding, will also apply in inquest cases. In *R (Letts) v The Lord Chancellor*[11] Mr Justice Green considered the Lord Chancellor's Guidance on Exceptional Funding (inquests).

4.33   After considering carefully the content of the guidance in light of the obligations of the State under article 2 ECHR, and reviewing the law relating to article 2 Green J concluded that:

> 55. ... the typical caseworker would find the conclusion that he or she had to take a decision, based on actual evidence that the State was arguably in breach as a precondition to a consideration of need, an irresistible one. References to arguability of breach as the lynchpin of the right to funding permeate the entire Guidance. There is no reference to there being any other possible test or to there being exceptions to this rule. Indeed, it is explicitly said that the procedural obligation arises (in a narrow range of circumstances) 'only' (cf para [9]) where evidence suggests an arguable breach by the state. There is hence no room on the basis of the Guidance for the possibility that the duty might arise in other circumstances not involving arguable breach.
>
> 56. Further some of the circumstances where the law, quite clearly, lays down that breach is irrelevant (eg deaths in custody) are explained and analysed in terms of the probability of the evidence leading to a conclusion of arguable breach.

4.34   He noted:

> 70. The case law thus quite clearly recognises a legal right for the next-of-kin to be involved to protect 'legitimate interests'; and the analysis of purposes and objects above informs what those interests may be. The right to legal aid flows directly from this recognition since in many cases if it were not available the right to involvement would be rendered nugatory and the purpose behind article 2 thwarted by a decision of the state.

4.35   And so:

> 94. I have set out at paragraph [54] above my analysis of the Guidance and as to the extent to which it rests upon a test of arguable breach. For the reasons that I have set out above in my judgment this contains a number of errors.

11 [2015] EWHC 402 (Admin).

95. First, the Guidance indicates that there is but one trigger for article 2, namely evidence of arguable breach by the State: See, eg para [54(iv)] above. This is incorrect in that case law identifies a variety of circumstances and types of case of real public importance and significance where the duty arises independently of the existence of evidence of arguable breach.

96. Secondly, where the Guidance refers to case types where the test may be modified (for example in the case of death in custody) it persists in articulating the test upon the basis of arguability of breach. Since these case types include cases where the law now makes clear that the duty can arise automatically the reference to the arguability test is wrong in law: See para [54(vii)] above.

97. Thirdly, and related to the first two errors, is the failure even at a broad level to acknowledge the existence of cases where the test is other than arguability.

4.36   Green J therefore concluded:

118. The test is hence: Would the Guidance if followed (i) lead to unlawful acts (ii) permit unlawful acts or (iii) encourage such unlawful acts? In my view for the reasons already given the Guidance would do all of these three things.

The 'unlawful act' being a refusal of legal aid where it was required, or a failure to consider the right legal basis for determining an application.

As we went to press, on 20 August 2015, the Lord Chancellor issued revised guidance taking account of the judgment in *Letts*.[12] The guidance sets out the situations where the Lord Chancellor believes funding should and should not be granted, but also recognises that this is a developing area of the law and says that caseworkers deciding applications should take into account case law that emerges. Funding will only be granted where article 2 ECHR duties are engaged, or where there is significant wider public interest in the applicant being represented at the inquest (LASPO s10(4)). It remains to be seen whether the guidance will survive future challenges.

Application process and forms

4.37   Practitioners cannot use delegated functions to grant exceptional case funding. All applications must be submitted to the ECF unit of the LAA.

---

12   See www.gov.uk/government/publications/legal-aid-exceptional-case-funding-form-and-guidance.

4.38   The form is the CIV ECF1, which should be submitted with a CW1 (if you are applying for Legal Help), or a CIV APP1 (civil licensed work or special case work) or CIV APP3 (for family licensed work cases) and the applicable means form if you are applying for representation.

4.39   These should be submitted to the Exceptional Cases Funding Team at Legal Aid Agency, Post Point 6.42, Sixth Floor, 102 Petty France London SW1H 9AJ or Legal Aid Agency, DX 16144 Westminster 8. Applications may also be scanned and submitted by email to the ECF team email address.

4.40   There is currently no emergency procedure for granting exceptional case funding, a situation criticised by Collins J in *IS* (see para 4.24 above). Hopefully the LAA will introduce an emergency procedure, but until then it aims to process the application within 20 working days. If you wish the application to be treated as urgent you should complete page 13 of the CIV ECF1 and provide details explaining why the case is urgent, for example an imminent date for a hearing or expiry of a limitation date or reasons why delay would cause risk of harm or prejudice to the client's case. The LAA aims to determine all cases within 20 working days from the date of receipt of the fully completed application. However, they cannot guarantee that an application will be determined before the urgent work is needed.

4.41   Details and guidance for inquest and non-inquest cases can be downloaded from: www.gov.uk/government/publications/legal-aid-exceptional-case-funding-form-and-guidance

4.42   There is no mechanism for paying you for completing unsuccessful applications, and so advising a client on the availability of exceptional funding and making an application is subject to conditional funding.

Legal Help/controlled work

4.43   Provided the application is submitted within two months of the date when the client signs the controlled work form, the LAA will backdate any successful exceptional case funding application to the date the client signed the CW1 or CW2 form.

Legal representation

4.44   Where the application is submitted within two months from the date on the CIVAPP1 or CIVAPP3 as the date of the client's first attendance/instruction on the matter, the LAA will backdate the certificate to that date.

Review process

4.45   There is no independent appeals process but you can submit an application for review of an unfavourable decision within 14 days. This is done using form APP9E, which should be completed with grounds for review and any supporting documentation to the ECF Team. The LAA aims to process the application for review within ten working days. There is no right of appeal or any further review process. Only one application for review may be submitted.

4.46   However, if an application is refused, that is a decision subject to judicial review – and a judicial review of a refusal of exceptional funding would be *in* scope because of para 19 of Part 1 of Schedule 1 to LASPO. You can therefore grant Legal Help, and apply for legal aid, to challenge a refusal of exceptional funding by way of judicial review. There is a helpful discussion of the requirements of such an application – and dealing with refusals of it – in a paper by John Halford and Francesca Allen of Bindmans LLP.[13]

Public Law Project – help and support for practitioners

4.47   One of the problems with exceptional case funding from a practitioner's point of view that you only get paid for making the application if it is successful – although some people report that clients have been granted mainstream legal aid funding by this route.

4.48   The Public Law Project has some useful resources[14] to assist in making applications. They also run a helpline to assist with queries on exceptional case funding and civil legal aid more generally – 0808 165 0170. It is open from 10 am to 11 am every weekday except Thursday.

4.49   PLP has used some of the evidence gathered through this project to support its challenge to the exceptional funding scheme, which was heard in the High Court as we were writing.[15] Once judgment is given, the online version of the Handbook will be updated.

---

13 *Physician, Heal Thyself: securing exceptional funding from the LAA to challenge its own exceptional funding refusals*, available at www.publiclawproject.org.uk/data/resources/194/JH_FA_physician_heal_thyself.pdf.

14 www.publiclawproject.org.uk/exceptional-funding-project.

15 See www.publiclawproject.org.uk/news/50/press-release-high-court-to-hear-systemic-challenge-to-the-operation-of-the-governmenteys-legal-aid-/.

Use of exceptional cases funding

4.50   During the passage of LASPO, the government said that it expected 5,000 to 7,000 applications per year, of which around 3,700 would be granted. Frequent reference to exceptional funding was made to reassure MPs and peers concerned about the impact of the cuts. But it turned out that those figures were wildly inflated.

4.51   In 2013–14, in total 1,520 ECF applications were received by the LAA. Of these applications, 69 per cent were for family or immigration cases. In 2013–14 the number of ECF applications granted was 69.

4.52   The most recent set of figures available at the time of writing, those for October to December 2014,[16] showed that only 280 applications were made in that period, a drop of three per cent compared with the same period in 2013. However, 70 were granted – showing a significant rise in the proportion of grants. The Ministry of Justice ascribes this to the impact of *Gudanaviciene* (see above) leading to a lower threshold for granting funding, and it may well be, but it is likely that it is also related to the drop in numbers of applications – with those least likely to succeed being less likely to be submitted. Most grants are for inquests, around half of the total, with immigration and family being the next most common areas.

16 www.gov.uk/government/statistics/legal-aid-statistics-october-to-december-2014.

CHAPTER 5

Conducting a civil/family case

continued

Introduction

5.1 This chapter deals with the general procedures which apply to most types of civil/family case, where the procedures are very similar. There are separate chapters on family cases (private and public law), immigration and mental health, which cover their own funding schemes and rules, as well as on housing.

5.2 In chapter 3, we saw that there are three key stages in providing legal aid services; to ensure that the matter is within scope, the client is financially eligible and the case meets the merits test. In addition, you need to ensure that forms are completed correctly and funding is obtained.

5.3 This chapter explains how these steps are taken successfully in respect of most civil work. Most references are to the 2013 Standard Civil Contract, because most cases still in scope are governed by that Contract, but there are equivalent provisions in the other civil contracts; where there are differences between contracts, we will say so.

5.4 See appendices H and I for a summary of the Legal Aid Agency's (LAA's) Costs Assessment Guidance, in respect of the most common queries raised by caseworkers.

Legal Help

Scope

5.5 At the most basic level, work must be allowed under LASPO (see chapter 2 for more information).

5.6 Legal Help allows you to provide advice and assistance in relation to a specific matter, but does not cover issuing proceedings, advocacy, or instruction of an advocate (although you may obtain counsel's opinion, where justified in a complex case, but this would be very rare). For information about clients who are outside England and Wales or who are not from England and Wales, see further 'Clients abroad' below.

Other sources of funding

5.7 The Civil Legal Aid (Merits Criteria) Regulations 2013[1] state that Legal Help may only be provided if it is reasonable to do so, having

1 Reg 32.

regard to any other sources of funding available to the client. This means that, for example, you should check whether the client has legal expenses insurance (perhaps as part of home contents cover) or is a member (or the partner of a member) of a trade union.

Forms

5.8 The form is the CW1 Legal Help, Help at Court and Family Help (Lower) form.

5.9 The assessment of means and client's details sections must be fully completed, and signed by the client, normally in the presence of someone from your organisation, before you start doing any legal work.[2]

Case study

I don't really want to stick a Legal Help form under the client's nose and ask them to sign, even before we've said 'Good morning'. Does that mean I will not be able to charge for all my time during the initial interview?

You will be covered, as the 2013 Standard Contract Specification para 3.10(i) confirms all the time in an interview will be allowed, when a client signs the CW1 form at any point.

5.10 The form must be kept on the file and is not sent to the LAA, unless requested for an assessment.[3]

What if the client cannot sign the form?

5.11 There will be occasions when your client is a child or patient, and you may not be satisfied of their capacity to sign the form and give instructions. Sometimes a client will not be physically able to attend your office. You must not use more than 10 per cent of your matter starts in any schedule period for clients who cannot attend on you personally.[4]

5.12 Whenever you grant Legal Help to a client in the circumstances described below, you should make an attendance note justifying

2 Standard Civil Contract Specification 2013 para 3.10.
3 Standard Civil Contract Specification 2013 para 3.11.
4 Standard Civil Contract Specification 2013 para 3.17. This restriction does not apply if you have accepted the case this way in order to comply with the Equality Act 2010.

what you did, and tick the appropriate box on page 5 of the Legal
Help form.

Applications on behalf of children/protected parties

5.13   You can accept an application direct from a child, if the child is entitled to bring, prosecute or defend proceedings without a litigation
friend or equivalent;[5] or there is good reason why one of the persons
listed in regulation 22(4) (see para 5.15 below) cannot apply on the
client's behalf and the adviser is satisfied that the child understands
the nature of the work and is capable of giving instructions.

5.14   An application can be accepted on behalf of a child from:

- a parent, guardian or other person responsible for the child's
  care; or
- a litigation friend or guardian ad litem; or
- if neither of the above are available, any other person (except anyone
  who works in your organisation), provided that the other person
  has sufficient knowledge of all the circumstances to act responsi-
  bly in the child's interests and to give proper instructions.

5.15   An application can be made on behalf of a protected party by:

- a person acting or proposing to act as the protected party's litigation friend; or
- any other person (who does not work for your organisation) where
  there is good reason why a litigation friend or proposed litigation
  friend cannot make the application.[6]

Applications by post

5.16   You may grant Legal Help to a client by post where there is a 'good
reason'. This is defined in Standard Civil Contract Specification 2013
para 3.14 as 'where the client requests that the application is made in
this way and it is not necessary for the interests of the client or his or
her case to attend in person'.

People resident outside the European Union

5.17   You may not grant Legal Help to a client resident outside the European Union if one of the following applies:[7]

---

5 Civil Legal Aid (Procedure) Regulations 2012 reg 22(2).
6 Civil Legal Aid (Procedure) Regulations 2012 reg 22(4).
7 Standard Civil Contract Specification 2013 para 3.15.

a) the client could, without serious disadvantage, delay their application until they had returned to the EU;

b) someone resident in the EU could apply on their behalf; or

c) it would otherwise be unreasonable to accept the application.

This facility has been particularly useful in immigration cases where clients have been refused entry to the UK, or have been removed or deported, but have a right of appeal that can be exercised from outside the UK. From April 2013 such cases are less likely to be in scope but clients abroad can apply for legal aid if the work does remain in scope, for example judical reviews and pre-action work on citizenship, passport and other immigration refusals, where there is no right of appeal and all internal administrative reviews have been exhausted.

Applications by fax

5.18   You can only accept applications by fax if that is specified in your contract schedule. If it is, you need to follow the rules set out in Standard Civil Contract Specification 2013 para 3.16.

Telephone, webcam and email advice

5.19   You can give, and claim for, advice over the telephone or by email, webcam etc if the client cannot attend your office for a 'good reason' as defined in Standard Contract Specification, 2013 para 3.14, see applications by post above, provided the client is later found to be eligible for Legal Help and signs the form. If the client subsequently fails to sign the form, you cannot claim payment.[8]

Financial eligibility

5.20   Clients must be financially eligible on both capital and income. They must inform you of any change in their means and you may have to stop work if their means change significantly (see chapter 3 for more information). However, there are no contributions to be paid in respect of Legal Help.

5.21   The Standard Civil Contract Specification 2013 para 3.23 states that you can only carry out work for clients who are financially eligible and that you must obtain satisfactory evidence of their means before assessing eligibility. In practical terms, that means, except in

---

8 Standard Civil Contract Specification 2013 para 3.20.

exceptional circumstances, you must obtain evidence of a client's means before starting work.

5.22   If it is 'not practicable to obtain it before commencing controlled work', you may start without it; but you need to show that you acted reasonably in assessing eligibility and starting work without evidence. In practice you should record on your initial attendance note:

- **why** it was reasonable to start work without evidence of means (for example, because the client needed advice urgently due to the imminent expiry of a time limit); and
- **how** you assessed eligibility (eg by making sure that the Legal Help form is properly completed, using the information the client was able to give you from their account of what they have been living on).

5.23   You must get the evidence as soon as practicable unless the client's circumstances prevent this being done at all at any point in the case, for example due to mental disability, age or homelessness.[9]

5.24   If you act reasonably in granting Legal Help to a client before obtaining evidence of their means and you do not claim any disbursement or report any time after the point where the LAA decides it would have been practicable to obtain satisfactory evidence of means, you can still claim payment for the work.

5.25   However, if the LAA decides that you could have obtained evidence of means at any stage of the case, costs will be 'nil assessed' at any audit. Having files 'nil assessed' can have very serious consequences, so it is strongly advisable to get valid evidence of means prior to starting work in all but emergency situations.

Merits test

5.26   The Legal Help merits test is known as the 'sufficient benefit test', and in full states: 'Help may only be provided where there is sufficient benefit to the client, having regard to the circumstances of the matter, including the circumstances of the individual, to justify the cost of the provision of legal help'.[10] This is not intended to be a high hurdle, at least to initial advice, but will apply to all steps in the case. See para 4.2.14 of the Lord Chancellor's Guidance:

---

9   Standard Civil Contract Specification 2013 para 3.24.
10   Civil Legal Aid (Merits Criteria) Regulations 2013 reg 32(b).

... it may well be considered worthwhile for an individual to pay for initial advice, including the advice that the case is not worth pursuing further. The more legal help is provided, however, the more that the benefits deriving from the costs incurred will need to be taken into account.[11]

Previous advice

5.27   Clients are generally only entitled to advice on a matter from one legal aid provider, so you should always ask the client whether they have taken previous advice before starting work.

5.28   The Standard Civil Contract Specification 2013 paras 3.40–3.45 set out what you must do if the client has received previous advice, whether that is from your organisation or somewhere else.

5.29   There is a list of particular circumstances in which a new matter start will not be justified at para 3.46 of the Standard Civil Contract Specification 2013. However, it is worth noting that you can open a new matter if a client faces enforcement proceedings because he or she is alleged to have breached the terms of a suspended or postponed order, or the terms on which proceedings were adjourned.[12]

5.30   You generally cannot open a new matter for a client who has received advice on the same matter within the last six months, unless an exception applies. Exceptions are listed at para 3.36 of Standard Contract 2013 Specification:

- There has been a material development or change in the client's instructions and at least three months have elapsed since the previous claim was submitted:
  - note that if the client has simply failed to give instructions, that cannot be counted as a change in instructions;
  - any change in the law that was anticipated in the original matter cannot count as a material development;
  - a decision, or other response from another party, arising from the first piece of work cannot count as a material development.
- The client has reasonable cause for dissatisfaction with the previous adviser (this must be justified dissatisfaction with the service, not because the client was unhappy about good advice they were given, or wants a second opinion).

---

11 Available at www.gov.uk/funding-and-costs-assessment-for-civil-and-crime-matters.
12 Standard Civil Contract Specification 2013 para 3.48.

- The client has moved away and has difficulty communicating with the previous adviser.
- The first adviser is no longer able to act for a good reason relating to professional conduct, eg conflict of interest.
- The first adviser has confirmed that no claim will be made.

5.31   If the client says that he or she is dissatisfied, you must request confirmation of the reasons for transfer, and a copy of the file from the previous organisation. If the client refuses consent, no advice should be given and no claim can be made.[13] No work may be done until the previous file has been received, unless absolutely necessary to protect the client's position or meet a deadline. When you receive the file, if you believe the client was unreasonable in being dissatisfied with the service, you must stop work but can still claim a fixed fee if urgent work was justified before getting the file.[14]

Case study

Can I open a new matter when the client has already received advice on the same problem from my organisation?

Legal Help forms are also known as 'new matter starts' (see chapter 3 for more information about means and merits tests for Legal Help cases).

Matter claimed	Open new matter?
Up to 3 months ago	No
3–6 months	Yes – if there is a material development or change in instructions
6+ months ago	Yes

---

13 Standard Civil Contract Specification 2013 para 3.42.
14 Standard Civil Contract Specification 2013 para 3.43.

Case study

My client says she received advice from the Civil Legal Advice telephone service last month. Can I open a new matter start?

First, check that the advice would fall within your contract (ie, family or housing).

It is mandatory for debt work to go through the telephone gateway. As a face to face provider you can only do debt work if the client is exempt (see chapter 2) or the gateway refers it to you.

The other two gateway categories, education and discrimination, are restricted further in that face to face work can only be done by the telephone providers or their agents.

Having established whether you can take it on in principle, it depends how much work they did for the client. Ask her to show you the confirmation of instructions, advice and action letter which the gateway will have sent under SQM requirement F1.1.

If the client has not signed a Legal Help form, you can open a new matter, as initial telephone advice is not 'controlled work' under the Civil Legal Aid (Procedure) Regulations 2012 reg 2.

Otherwise, you should treat advice from the Civil Legal Advice telephone service as you would advice from any other LAA provider.

Reopening a closed matter

5.32   Although you may not be able to open a new matter, you can (and may be obliged to) do more work on the original matter.[15] The disadvantage is that you cannot claim an additional fixed fee; but there are compensations:[16]

- previous work and additional work after the client comes back, can be counted together towards the escape fee threshold;
- further disbursements can be claimed.

15 Standard Civil Contract Specification 2013 para 3.35.
16 Standard Civil Contract Specification 2013 para 3.49.

Case study

What is the procedure for reporting a revived Legal Help case to the LAA?

You complete the appropriate amendment spreadsheet to the LAA (civil, crime, or mediation[1]) and send it with an email to Provider Assurance (also known as Operational Assurance) explaining what you have done: PA-ClaimAmend@legalservices.gsi.gov.uk. You should put your organisation's name and account number in the subject line. Provider Assurance will void the first claim so that you do not claim twice for the same matter. They will confirm the action they have taken and copy to your contract manager for information.

Opening more than one matter

Separate and distinct

5.33   If a client has problems that are 'separate and distinct',[18] you can open more than one matter. Opening more than one matter for a client must be carefully justified in every case if you are not to fall foul of LAA audits. If your organisation is found to have opened matters incorrectly, significant amounts of money may need to be repaid to the LAA, so it is extremely important to get this right.

5.34   It is relatively easy to justify more than one case as 'separate and distinct' if they necessarily fall under different categories of law. So, if a client has a housing problem and needs a divorce, it is likely to be justifiable to open two matters (subject to scope rules).

5.35   It is more difficult to justify opening more than one matter within one overall category of law. The first thing to remember is that the rules contained in the category specific sections of the Specification take precedence.[19] So, if you are considering whether to open more than one matter within a category, you should look up the category specific rules first.

Different causes or events

5.36   If your client's circumstances are not explicitly dealt with, it is worth applying the wording in the general Contract Specification, which states that matters are 'separate and distinct' 'typically because they

---

17   www.gov.uk/submit-a-contracted-work-and-administration-cwa-claim-online.
18   Standard Civil Contract Specification 2013 para 3.31.
19   Standard Civil Contract Specification 2013 para 1.2.

arise out of different causes or events'. So, it is a good idea to ask yourself whether the causes or events are separate. For example, if your client has a serious housing disrepair problem and a family law problem, these would be very likely to be separate and distinct.

5.37 It is more difficult if the client has 'more than one separate and distinct legal problem' within a category.[20] You must be able to demonstrate two things:

> If legal proceedings were started, or other appropriate remedies pursued, for each problem it would be appropriate for such proceedings to be both issued and heard separately.
>
> AND
>
> Each problem requires substantial legal work which does not address the other problem(s).

'Substantial legal work' is defined as at least 30 minutes' additional preparation or advice, or separate communication with other parties on legal issues.[21]

Work that does not address the other problem(s)

5.38 If you are going to satisfy the LAA that work on one issue does not address another, this has to be clear in your case recording. If you consistently deal with two or more issues together, it will be very difficult to argue that they were really 'separate and distinct'. You will need to open two separate files and keep separate attendance notes and letters relating to each issue. However, more than one problem may be discussed in one interview with a client as this may be more convenient for them. If so, separate attendance notes should be produced for each and time apportioned between the issues.

5.39 If you consider that the test is satisfied, you can ask the client to sign more than one Legal Help form at the initial meeting, or subsequently.[22]

More than one client

5.40 The LAA says that you should only use one new matter if the problem involves more than one client, unless:[23]

a) if proceedings were issued, each client would be a party to those proceedings;

20 Standard Civil Contract Specification 2013 para 3.31.
21 Standard Civil Contract Specification 2013 para 3.32.
22 Standard Civil Contract Specification 2013 paras 3.30(c) and 3.33.
23 Standard Civil Contract Specification 2013 para 3.39.

b) each client has a separate and distinct legal interest in the problem or issue; *and*

c) in considering whether there is sufficient benefit for the second or any subsequent client to receive Legal Help, you take into account the fact that Legal Help that is already being provided in relation to the same general problem.

Case study

I have a client who has been unlawfully evicted from his rented property. He doesn't want to go back there but does want to sue the landlord. He also wants to apply to the local authority as homeless. How many Legal Help forms should he sign?

This is two matter starts. They are two separate causes of action, albeit both within the housing category, and were the cases to go to court they would be separate proceedings.

Funding

Fixed fees

5.41   Legal Help is paid under fixed fees, although cases that reach the escape threshold (three times the fixed fee) can be paid in full at hourly rates. Current fees and hourly rates are found in the Civil Legal Aid (Remuneration) Regulations 2013.

5.42   Paragraph 3.31 of the Standard Contract Civil Specification states that you must not open more than one matter start for a client unless the client has more than one 'separate and distinct' legal problem – see above.

More than one fixed fee

5.43   In some circumstances, you may be able to justify opening more than one Legal Help file for a client. For more information about this, see para 5.33 above; and comments in relation to individual categories of law, below.

Housing possession schemes

5.44 You cannot ask a client to sign a Legal Help form at a court duty scheme, as this work is funded under a separate schedule, and is paid at a fixed fee per client seen.[24]

5.45 If the client's case needs further work, you can ask the client to come to your office and sign a Legal Help form (subject to the usual rules in relation to means and merits).

5.46 However, you cannot then claim a fee for advising that client under the court duty scheme.[25] It is very important that organisations have systems to prevent double-claiming in error in these circumstances. If you open a housing Legal Help case within six months of having advised the same client on the same case at a duty scheme you will not be entitled to the court duty payment for that client, so your systems will need to allow you to identify such cases and where necessary notify the LAA to rescind a payment already made against your court duty schedule.

Disbursements

5.47 You can claim disbursements in addition to the fixed fee,[26] provided that they meet the criteria set out in the contract:

- it is in the best interests of the client to incur the disbursement;
- it is reasonable to incur the disbursement for the purpose of providing controlled work, ie necessary for the purpose of giving advice to the client or progressing the case;
- the amount of the disbursement is reasonable; and
- it is not a disbursement which is specifically prohibited.[27]

Disbursements that may not be claimed under controlled work

5.48 The Standard Civil Contract Specification 2013 para 4.24 provides a non-exhaustive list of disbursements that may not be incurred in the provision of controlled work. Note that the same disbursements are

---

24 Standard Civil Contract Specification 2013 para 10.19.
25 Standard Civil Contract Specification 2013 para 10.24.
26 Standard Civil Contract Specification 2013 para 4.6.
27 Standard Civil Contract Specification 2013 para 4.21 and subject-specific sections.

prohibited for licensed work, save that court fees are an allowable disbursement under a certificate.[28] These disbursements are:

- costs of (or expenses relating to) the residential assessment of a child or treatment, therapy, training or other interventions of an educative or rehabilitative nature unless authorised by the LAA;
- Ad Valorem stamp duties;
- capital duty;
- client's travelling and accommodation expenses save in the circumstances prescribed in the Costs Assessment Guidance and unless they relate to treatment, therapy, training or other interventions of an educative or rehabilitative nature or to the residential assessment of a child;
- all fees, charges and costs of child contact centres, including assessments and reports on supervised contact, and of other professional assessments of contact between children and adults;
- court fees unless for a search/photocopies/bailiff service or as part of Controlled Legal Representation or otherwise permitted by Category Specific Rules;
- discharge of debts owed by the client, for example, rent or mortgage arrears;
- fee payable on voluntary petitions in bankruptcy;
- fee payable to implement a pension sharing order;
- fee payable to the Office of the Public Guardian;
- immigration application fees;
- mortgagees' or lessors' legal costs and disbursements;
- passport fees;
- probate fees;
- in the Family category of law only, costs of or expenses in relation to the provision of family mediation, conciliation or any other dispute resolution including family group conferences;
- in the Family category of law only, costs or expenses of risk assessments within section 16A of the Children Act 1989 (as amended) and undertaken by Cafcass officers or Welsh family proceedings officers, including assessments of the risk of harm to a child in connection with domestic abuse to the child or another person;
- in the Family category of law only, costs of or expenses relating to any activity to promote contact with a child directed by the court under sections 11A to 11G of the Children Act 1989 (as amended) – this includes all programmes, consideration of suitability under section 11E and other work to or with a view to establishing,

28 Standard Civil Contract Specification 2013 para 6.62.

maintaining or improving contact with a child or, by addressing violent behaviour, to or with a view to enabling or facilitating contact with a child;

- any administration fee charged by an expert including, but not limited to, (i) a fee in respect of office space or provision of a consultation room, (ii) a fee in respect of administrative support services, such as typing services, (iii) a fee in respect of courier services and (iv) a subsistence fee;
- any cancellation fee charged by an expert, where the notice of cancellation was given to the expert more than 72 hours before the relevant hearing or appointment.

5.49   The LAA limits what it will pay in respect of experts to 45 pence per mile for travelling costs, and £40 per hour travelling time. Substantive work by experts will be limited to the hourly rates/fixed fees for that expertise set out in the remuneration regulations (see paras 5.123 and 11.15 below for more).

5.50   Family practitioners should note the Standard Civil Contract Specification 2013 para 7.66, which states that:

> Court fees are an allowable disbursement under Family Help (Lower) only where such fees are incurred for the purpose of obtaining a consent order. In all cases, court fees may only be incurred where they are a reasonable and proportionate step which satisfies the reasonable private paying individual test (regulation 7 of the Merits Regulations).

5.51   This is slightly ambiguous, but it means that consent order fees are the only ones permitted and it must be reasonable to incur them.

5.52   This contrasts with licensed work, where court fees are an allowable disbursement, and with Legal Help, where court fees are never allowable.

Help at Court

Scope

5.53   Work must be allowed under LASPO (see chapter 3 for more information). Help at Court is help and advocacy for a client in relation to a particular hearing, without formally acting as legal representative in the proceedings.

> 'Help at court' means the provision of any of the following civil legal services at a particular hearing–
> (a) instructing an advocate;

(b) preparing to provide advocacy; or

(c) advocacy.[29]

But note that counsel may not be instructed under Help at Court.

5.54   Ongoing representation can only be provided under a legal representation certificate.

5.55   Help at Court is useful for cases where a legal representation certificate would not be available, for example where a client does not have a defence to a possession claim; but does need an experienced adviser to set out repayment proposals to the court. Help at Court can also be used to represent the client on an application for enforcement of an order where the client is the applicant.

5.56   However, it is always preferable to provide representation under a legal representation certificate wherever possible as this provides costs protection for the client (see para 5.79) and is better paid (at hourly rates in civil categories).

Financial eligibility

5.57   As Legal Help, see above.

Merits test

The sufficient benefit test (see Legal Help, above)

5.58   The nature of the proceedings and the circumstances of the hearing must be such that representation will be of real benefit to the client.[30] This means the issue(s) must be more complex than the client could have explained to the court himself or herself.

5.59   You must apply the test before every hearing and note the file with your justification. 'Sufficient benefit test met' is not an adequate justification.

Forms

5.60   The form is the CW1 Legal Help, Help at Court and Family Help (Lower) form (see Legal Help, above).

5.61   If the client has already signed a Legal Help form to cover advice and assistance, he or she does not need to sign another form in relation to Help at Court.[31]

29 Civil Legal Aid (Procedure) Regulations 2012 reg 5.
30 Civil Legal Aid (Merits Criteria) Regulations 2013 reg 33.
31 Standard Civil Contract Specification 2013 para 1.43.

Funding

5.62   Advisers without rights of audience may provide informal advocacy and claim payment under Help at Court, as long as advocacy is justified and the court agrees to hear them. Counsel may not be instructed.

5.63   There are no additional fixed fees to cover Help at Court. However, the additional work involved may make it more likely that the case will reach the escape threshold (three times the fixed fee).

5.64   Where advocacy is justified, you may claim travel and waiting to/ from and at court, as well as preparation and attendance, where appropriate. See chapter 13 for more information on payment schemes.

Help with Family Mediation

5.65   This level of controlled work was introduced from 1 April 2013 to pay for legal advice to clients who are participating, or have participated, in family mediation – see chapter 6 for more information.

Ending a case

5.66   Standard Civil Contract Specification 2013 para 3.66, sets out the circumstances in which you can close your file and claim your costs.

5.67   Most are obvious: the client decides not to proceed, or decides to take the matter forward themselves; a representation certificate is granted, or you cannot act further due to a conflict of interest or other professional conduct issue; or the matter simply reaches a logical conclusion.

5.68   One is less obvious, which is where the client fails to give instructions for three months (unless the matter is on hold, for example, because you are waiting for a third party to act or you have agreed it with the client). You have to watch out for this, because on a costs/ contract compliance audit (see chapter 19) the LAA may say that the case terminated at that point, and disallow all profit costs and disbursements after it. This is important in escape fee cases.

5.69   You cannot stop work or close a matter simply because the value of your costs is equal to, or more than, the fixed fee.[32]

5.70   You should close and claim for your case as soon as you properly can, as apart from anything else, the date of the claim is when time

32 Standard Civil Contract Specification 2013 para 3.7.

starts to run to open a new matter start if the client subsequently needs further advice.

5.71   You have to submit a claim for controlled work standard fee matters within six months of the ending of the matter.[33]

5.72   Note that claims for escape fee cases have to be submitted more quickly than standard fee cases, ie within three months.[34]

5.73   If you fail to submit claims within time limits 'persistently', you may receive a contract warning notice, which could lead to contract termination.[35]

Ending a case – monitoring

5.74   The LAA monitors organisations remotely, using the data they supply as a matter of course when applying for funding or claiming at the end of the case.

5.75   The Standard Contract 2013 includes key performance indicators (KPIs). We will deal with all the KPIs in this section for completeness, although some relate to controlled work and some to licensed work. Some KPIs apply to all categories of law and a few are category specific. Standard Civil Contract Specification 2013 paras 2.50–2.66 contains the detailed rules. Note that there are fewer KPIs than in some previous contracts. In particular the requirements to use 85 per cent of NMS has gone, as has that to achieve a substantive benefit for clients (save for Immigration/asylum CLR, see KPI 6, para 2.66).

5.76   Failure to meet KPIs can result in further audit or monitoring and could be taken into account when bidding for a new contract.[36] Therefore, it is important for caseworkers to be aware that their performance under the contract can affect the organisation as a whole.

Key performance indicators

5.77   KPIs are monitored on a rolling three-month basis, rather than on each individual case. A summary of the KPIs is as follows.

KPI 1 – Controlled work (non-fixed fee) – assessment reduction 10 per cent max

When your 'escape cases' are assessed (these are the cases that used to be called exceptional cases, where the costs on a time and item

---

33 Standard Civil Contract Specification 2013 para 4.32.
34 Standard Civil Contract Specification 2013 para 4.17.
35 Standard Contract 2013 clause 14.5.
36 Standard Contract 2013 clauses 11.4 and 11.5.

basis are 3 x the fixed fee), the costs claimed must not be reduced by more than 10 per cent. This includes disbursements but not VAT.

KPI 2 – Licensed work – assessment reduction 15 per cent max

This sets a similar target in relation to licensed work cases that are claimed on a time and item basis.

KPI 3 – Fixed fee margin – 20 per cent max

The LAA is concerned that some organisations will select clients with straightforward cases that do not require much work, in order to retain a high surplus under each fixed fee case. This KPI can only be met if the total cost of cases under fixed fees when calculated in minutes and items is at least 80 per cent of the appropriate fixed fees.

This KPI applies to controlled work cases, and Family Private and Public Law Representation Scheme cases that are paid by way of fixed fees.

KPI 4 – Rejection rates for licensed work – 5 per cent max in the schedule period

Rejections are when applications or claims are refused because of technical errors in form completion, or lack of enclosures etc. This applies to applications for legal aid (known as applications for determinations that an individual qualifies for legal aid in the post LASPO scheme), and claims for payment.

KPI 5 – Refusal rates for licensed work – 15 per cent max in the schedule period

This applies to applications for legal aid which are refused because the LAA considers that the practitioner has failed to show that they meet the applicable merits test.

KPI 6 – Immigration CLR positive outcome – 40 per cent minimum

This KPI is taken as an indicator of quality and applies to Immigration CLR work only.

Legal Aid Representation Certificates

Scope

5.78   Legal Aid Representation Certificates are also known as 'full legal aid certificates'. They authorise the conduct of litigation and the provision of advocacy and representation, and include steps preliminary and incidental to proceedings, and steps to settle or avoid proceedings.

5.79   Clients in receipt of a legal aid certificate have a high degree of protection against costs being awarded against them.[37] Failure to advise clients of their ability to seek public funding where available is a matter of professional misconduct[38] (though there is no obligation on any individual solicitor to take on a case on legal aid as opposed to privately as long as the client is aware they could have got legal aid somewhere else).

Investigative representation

5.80   This is a type of civil legal aid funding certificate (not available in family, mental health or immigration) limited to the investigation of a claim where the prospects of success are unclear without substantial investigative work; but it appears that once the investigative work is completed, the case would meet the merits test for a representation certificate[39] (see below). It is preferable to conduct investigation under this form of funding where possible rather than under Legal Help as it is paid under hourly rates and there is less uncertainty about payment than a Legal Help escape fee claim.

5.81   The Lord Chancellor's Guidance on civil legal aid[40] suggests that substantial investigative work would be at least six hours of fee earner work or disbursements (including counsel's fees) of £400 or more (ex VAT). Therefore, an application needs to be very clear about the extent of work required. It may be possible to obtain a very brief opinion pro bono from counsel to confirm that merits are not clear and counsel will need to consider the papers in full before advising on merits. It will not be necessary for counsel to give any advice on the actual details of the case itself at this stage.

---

37   LASPO s26 and Civil Legal Aid (Costs) Regulations 2013.
38   Solicitors Code of Conduct 2011 Indicative Behaviour 1.6.
39   Civil Legal Aid (Merits Criteria) Regulations 2013 reg 40.
40   Lord Chancellor's Guidance under section 4 of LASPO 2012, para 6.11.

Before you apply for a certificate

5.82 You need to ensure that the standard criteria are satisfied (see also para 5.89):

- The case must concern a matter of England and Wales (or Welsh) law, and in an area permitted by LASPO (see chapter 3).
- The client must be an individual, and a party or proposed party to the proceedings or potential proceedings.
- You must be permitted by your contract to carry out the case.
- The client must not have acted unreasonably in this or any other application, or in these or any other proceedings (for example, by concealing information or acting dishonestly to obtain funding – this criterion does not refer to a client's general character or notoriety).
- There must be no alternative funding available to the client, for example through an insurance policy or trade union membership, or through another person or organisation the client could approach to fund the case.
- There must be no alternatives to litigation, or the client must have exhausted reasonable alternatives, such as complaints and ombudsman schemes and alternative dispute resolution mechanisms.
- The application should not be premature – that is, funding under Legal Help or Help at Court would not be more appropriate at this stage.
- It must be necessary for the client to be represented in the proceedings, and funding will be refused if it is not necessary, for example if the case is straightforward and parties would ordinarily not be represented, or if the client does not need to be separately represented.
- Funding will be refused for cases allocated to the small claims track in the county court.[41]
- Representation will be refused if the case is suitable for a conditional fee agreement and the client is likely to be able to enter into a conditional fee agreement (CFA), damages-based agreement or other litigation funding agreement.[42] This test is likely to be applied strictly.[43]

---

41 Civil Legal Aid (Merits Criteria) Regulations 2013 reg 39.
42 Civil Legal Aid (Merits Criteria) Regulations 2013 reg 2.
43 See para 7.16 of the Lord Chancellor's Guidance on Civil Legal Aid.

Clients abroad

5.83   Although the case must be a matter of England and Wales (or Welsh) law, the client does not have to be resident in England or Wales to receive funding. Where clients abroad are entitled to access the courts in England and Wales, they remain eligible for legal aid subject to the usual scope, means and merits provisions. For example, legal aid is likely to be refused if any order obtained in England and Wales is likely to be ineffective, for example, if there is no reciprocal judicial protocol[44].

Clients abroad – procedures

5.84   Where the client is outside the EU (the Channel Islands and Isle of Man counting as part of the EU for these purposes), special procedures must be followed:

- The application must be made in English or French.
- If the client is not a member of UK armed forces posted outside the EU, the application must be sworn before a person authorised under local law to administer oaths or before a British consular official.
- The application must be accompanied by a sworn statement, made by a responsible person who has knowledge of the facts, certifying the client's statement of means as accurate.[45]

Clients from abroad

5.85   Under Home Office guidelines,[46] legal aid is not classed as a 'public fund' for the purposes of those with no recourse to public funds. Legal aid is available regardless of immigration status. The proposed residence test has been ruled unlawful by the High Court, though this is subject to appeal – see para 2.27.

Children

5.86   Where the client is a child, you should note that (unlike controlled work) children cannot apply for funding direct. Where children are parties to litigation in the courts, they should be represented by litigation friends, and it is the litigation friend who should make the

---

44 Civil Legal Aid (Merits) Regulations 2012 reg 66(2).
45 Civil Legal Aid (Procedure) Regulations 2012 reg 31(3).
46 See www.gov.uk/government/publications/public-funds.

application for funding on behalf of the child. However, the application should be in the name of the child. Where the court orders that the child can be a party to the proceedings without a litigation friend, you should make the application on the child's behalf as the child's solicitor.[47]

5.87   The child's own means, not those of the litigation friend, are the means to be assessed, and you should therefore put the child's means on the MEANS form.[48] In cases where others might have an interest (for example, in special educational needs and public law cases), the LAA can require them to make a financial contribution.[49] Therefore, where you are submitting an application on behalf of a child, you should make clear whether you are seeking to justify non-aggregation of means, and if so, explain why it would be inequitable to aggregate, for example because there is a conflict between the child and adult.

Financial eligibility

5.88   See chapter 3. See also para 5.141 'Funding from the client's point of view', below. Where the client declares a bank account on the MEANS form, he or she will be required to provide three months' worth of statements. Where the client is in employment, he or she will need to provide three months wage slips (and an L17 is not required unless they cannot do so).

Merits test

5.89   Funding will not be granted unless the case passes the merits test. There are a number of different merits tests depending on the type of case – for those that apply in family, immigration and housing cases, see chapters 6, 7, 9 and 11; for all others, see below. The various merits tests are set out in the Civil Legal Aid (Merits Criteria) Regulations 2013, and in each case you must satisfy both the standard criteria and the particular criteria applicable to the case.

---

47 Civil Legal Aid (Procedure) Regulations 2012 reg 30(2)(b).
48 Civil Legal Aid (Financial Resources and Payment for Services) Regulations 2013 reg 13.
49 Civil Legal Aid (Financial Resources and Payment for Services) Regulations 2013 reg 44(6).

The standard criteria

5.90   Before you apply for a certificate you need to ensure that the standard criteria are satisfied:[50]

(a) the individual does not have access to other potential sources of funding (other than a conditional fee agreement) from which it would be reasonable to fund the case;

(b) the case is unsuitable for a conditional fee agreement;[51]

(c) there is no other person other than the individual, including a person who might benefit from the proceedings, who can reasonably be expected to bring the proceedings;

(d) the individual has exhausted all reasonable alternatives to bringing proceedings including any complaints system, ombudsman scheme or other form of alternative dispute resolution;

(e) there is a need for representation in all the circumstances of the case including–

(i)   the nature and complexity of the issues;

(ii) the existence of other proceedings; and

(iii) the interests of other parties to the proceedings; and

(f) the proceedings are not likely to be allocated to the small claims track.

5.91   The first criterion requires you to consider whether the client has alternative methods of funding the case at their disposal, and you will need to explore with the client and consider whether they have, for example, trade union membership or legal expenses insurance. Many household insurance policies include legal expenses insurance and therefore if the client has a policy you will need to consider the certificates to satisfy yourself that the particular case is not covered (you will need to address this on the application form).

5.92   The LAA will ask people unconnected with the case (and possibly even unrelated to the client) to complete CIVAPP1 or CIVAPP3 forms. This has forced clients to tell people they might not wish to know, about their situation. The difficulty is that the Civil Legal Aid (Financial Resources and Payment for Services) Regulations 2013 reg 16(5) allows the LAA to take the resources of persons other than the person applying for legal aid into account if the LAA considers that they may be 'substantially maintaining' the client. However, this power is discretionary, and is there are valid reasons why it should not be applied in a particular case, the LAA should be asked to take these into account.

---

50 Civil Legal Aid (Merits Criteria) Regulations 2013 reg 39.

51 See para 7.16 of the Lord Chancellor's Guidance on Civil Legal Aid for the approach the LAA will take to suitability for a CFA. See also para 5.94 below.

5.93   For example, the LAA will want evidence about the means of adults living in a property if it appears they would benefit from defending possession proceedings and could contribute to legal costs. If they are unable to contribute due to their own circumstances, the reason should be provided in the 'extra information' section of the CIV Means2 form.

5.94   The Director of Legal Aid has to consider whether the case is 'unsuitable' for a CFA and the LAA changed the wording on the CIV-APP 1 form so that it matches the exact wording of the regulation.[52] You therefore need to make sure you tick the 'yes' box on the form to confirm the case is NOT suitable for a CFA, bearing in mind the guidance below. The Lord Chancellor's Guidance on Civil Legal Aid says:

> 7.17 The test of suitability for a CFA is an objective one, rather than a question of whether an individual provider is willing to act under a CFA (although the test cannot be met if there is evidence of a CFA in fact having been offered or put in place for the applicant). In principle a non-family case may be considered suitable for a conditional fee agreement if:
> – Prospects of success are considered at least at 60%
> – The opponent is considered able to meet any costs and/or damages (or other sum of money) that might be awarded
> – After-the-event insurance can be obtained by the applicant
>
> 7.18 An applicant without after-the-event insurance seeking services otherwise considered suitable for a CFA will be expected to provide evidence of attempts to secure such insurance. Even where evidence is provided of refusals of insurance, the Director him/herself may make enquiries of insurers to see if they would support a CFA in the individual circumstances. Moreover, it will not always be sufficient for the applicant to allege that s/he cannot afford the after-the-event premium. If the proposed claim is for damages then the applicant would need to demonstrate that it has not been possible to defer payment of the premium from any damages recovered.
>
> 7.19 If the proposed proceedings do not include a claim for damages or other money, however, particular considerations apply. An applicant for legal aid is unlikely to be able to pay an after-the-event insurance premium or success fee from his/her own resources, and the case should not generally be considered as suitable for a CFA unless both:
> • prospects of success are at least 80%, (otherwise it would be unreasonable to expect the legal representative to act at risk in relation

---

52 Civil Legal Aid (Merits Criteria) Regulations 2013 reg 39.

to costs without the prospect of a success fee or for the applicant to risk an adverse costs order); and

• the case will not involve significant expenditure on disbursements (in particular experts' fees).

Of course, if there is no likelihood of either damages or costs being awarded (for instance in seeking an injunction against an impecunious opponent) then there is no basis on which the case could be pursued under a CFA.

7.20 The fact that the applicant may wish to obtain legal aid rather than a CFA because of the potential deduction from damages in respect of a success premium or damages agreement, will not of itself prevent a case being suitable for a CFA. The test is not whether the applicant or provider would prefer legal aid to a CFA, but is, in essence, whether the case could realistically be brought under a CFA in the absence of legal aid. It will be a question of fact on the individual circumstances of the case whether the need to meet an insurance payment from the likely damages would render the proceedings futile.

5.95   You may wish to carry out a pre-emptive 'shopping around' exercise, trying to attempt obtaining ATE in a couple of typical scenarios, so that you could use those as examples of why a CFA is not available. If you are an NfP agency that does not offer CFAs, you could try asking a friendly firm whether they would accept some typical case scenarios on a CFA basis and again use their response as evidence that such cases are not commercially attractive. If you are a private firm that does offer CFAs, you could set out your criteria for accepting CFAs and why the particular case does not meet them.

5.96   Two key criteria that must be addressed are the need for representation and the likely track allocation. The effect of these is that legal aid will not be available for the most simple and straightforward cases, including those likely to be small claims.

Merits – specific cases

5.97   In addition to satisfying the standard criteria, you must be able to demonstrate that your case passes the applicable merits test for the type of work. Most merits criteria are expressed by reference to the prospects of success test. In *IS (by the Official Solicitor as Litigation Friend) v The Director of Legal Aid Casework and The Lord Chancellor*,[53] Collins J declared unlawful the part of the merits test which restricted legal aid to cases where the prospects of success were better than 50

53 [2015] EWHC 1965 (Admin).

per cent, and so the LAA revised the test with effect from 27 July 2015.

5.98   The test is set out in the Civil Legal Aid (Merits Criteria) Regulations 2013, as amended by the Civil Legal Aid (Merits Criteria) (Amendment) (No 2) Regulations 2015. Unfortunately the LAA does not make available consolidated sets of regulations, and neither does the official government site www.legislation.gov.uk. It is therefore necessary to consult and cross reference both sets of regulations in order to see the full accurate test. In our view, this is very unsatisfactory and we would encourage the LAA to make publicly available a single, definitive and up-to-date set of regulations for the whole scheme.

5.99   Regulation 5 of the 2013 regulations, as amended by regulation 2 of the 2015 regulations sets out the prospects of success – the likelihood of achieving a successful substantive outcome – and categorises them thus:

- very good – 80% or above;
- good – 60% to 80%;
- moderate – 50% to 60%;
- poor – 20% to 50%;
- very poor – less than 20%;
- borderline – it is not possible, because of disputed law, fact or expert evidence, to assign the case to another category but it cannot be categorised as 'unclear'; or
- unclear – the case cannot be assigned to any of the other categories because there are identifiable investigations to be carried out after which the prospects can be estimated.

The 'borderline' category was removed from the merits tests in 2014 by the Civil Legal Aid (Merits Criteria) (Amendment) Regulations 2014, but it remained in the definitions, and so has been reinstated to the merits tests by the 2015 amendment regulations.

5.100   The standard to be applied in assessing the prospects of success is the prospects as they would be with the assistance of competent legal representation, not the prospects on the basis of material available but untested at the time of the application. This is to ensure that cases where competent representation would turn the case in the applicant's favour are not excluded from funding:[54]

- Where prospects of success are moderate or better, the prospects of success criterion will be met and so legal aid will be granted

54   [2015] EWHC 1965 (Admin) para 96, per Collins J.

(subject to any other criteria that may apply in the individual case.

- Where prospects of success are borderline or poor but not very poor, the prospects of success criterion will only be met if it is necessary to deem it met to prevent a breach of the applicant's ECHR or enforceable EU rights, or appropriate to do so having regard to the risk that failure to do so would risk such a breach.[55]
- Where prospects of success are unclear, it will generally be more appropriate to grant Investigative Help than full representation, so that investigation can be carried out and the prospects clarified.

In addition, the value of the outcome must justify the costs. For damages claims, see below.

5.101   Besides the prospects of success test, there are other tests:

- The proportionality test[56] is met if 'the Director is satisfied that the likely benefits of the proceedings to the individual and others justify the likely costs, having regard to the prospects of success and all the other circumstances of the case'.
- The public interest test[57] is met if 'the Director is satisfied that the case is an appropriate case to realise –
  (a) real benefits to the public at large, other than those which normally flow from cases of the type in question; and
  (b) benefits for an identifiable class of individuals, other than the individual to whom civil legal services may be provided or members of that individual's family.'
- The reasonable private paying individual test is met if 'the Director is satisfied that the potential benefit to be gained from the provision of civil legal services justifies the likely costs, such that a reasonable private paying individual would be prepared to start or continue the proceedings having regard to the prospects of success and all the other circumstances of the case'.[58]

The regulations go on to set out a merits test that applies to general certificated cases, with variations for specific types of cases.

5.102   The general merits test is set out in the Civil Legal Aid (Merits Criteria) Regulations 2013 reg 41.

55 Civil Legal Aid (Merits Criteria) Regulations 2013 reg 43, as amended by Civil Legal Aid (Merits Criteria) (Amendment) (No 2) Regulations 2015 reg 2(4).
56 Civil Legal Aid (Merits Criteria) Regulations 2013 reg 8.
57 Civil Legal Aid (Merits Criteria) Regulations 2013 reg 6.
58 Civil Legal Aid (Merits Criteria) Regulations 2013 reg 6.

Damages and financial cases where there is not significant wider public interest

5.103   The cost-benefit criteria are (reg 42 of the 2013 regulations, as amended by reg 2(3) of the 2015 regulations):

- if prospects are very good, likely damages must exceed likely costs;
- if prospects are good, likely damages must exceed likely costs by a ratio of 2:1;
- if prospects are moderate, borderline or poor, the ratio must be 4:1.

5.104   The tests for specific types of cases are set out below.

Public law claims

5.105   For public law claims (defined in regulation 2 as judicial review, habeas corpus and homelessness appeals), there are additions to the standard criteria:[59]

- the act, omission or matter complained of appears to be susceptible to challenge; and
- there are no alternative proceedings before a court or tribunal which are available to challenge the act, omission or other matter, except where the Director considers that such proceedings would not provide an effective remedy.[60]

5.106   The merits test for full representation in public law claims is:[61]

- the standard criteria are met (including the additional ones above);
- unless impracticable to do so, a letter before claim has been sent and the defendant given a reasonable time to respond;
- the proportionality test is met; and
- prospects of success are:
  - moderate or better; or
  - borderline or poor, but it is necessary to determine that the prospects of success criterion is met to prevent a breach of the applicants ECHR or enforceable EU rights, or appropriate to

---

59 Civil Legal Aid (Merits Criteria) Regulations 2013 reg 53 and Civil Legal Aid (Merits Criteria) (Amendment) Regulations 2013.
60 Civil Legal Aid (Merits Criteria) Regulations 2013 reg 53(b) as amended by Civil Legal Aid (Merits Criteria) (Amendment) Regulations 2013 reg 2.
61 Civil Legal Aid (Merits Criteria) Regulations 2013 reg 56 amended by Civil Legal Aid (Merits Criteria) (Amendment) (No 2) Regulations 2015 reg 2(5).

do so in the circumstances of the case having regard to any risk that failure to do so would be such a breach.[62]

See para 7.34 of the Lord Chancellor's Guidance for detailed guidance on public law claims but note that, at the time of writing, it had not been amended to reflect the changes to the merits test made by the 2015 regulations.

Claims against public authorities

5.107   For claims against public authorities (paras 21 and 22 of Part 1 of Schedule 1 of LASPO), the test is:

- the proportionality test is met; and
- prospects of success are:
  - moderate or better; or
  - borderline or poor, but it is necessary to determine that the prospects of success criterion is met to prevent a breach of the applicants ECHR or enforceable EU rights, or appropriate to do so in the circumstances of the case having regard to any risk that failure to do so would be such a breach.[63]

Other cases

5.108   For immigration, housing, mental health and family merits tests, see the appropriate chapters of this book.

Changes to prospects of success or cost-benefit

5.109   As the case progresses, inevitably further information and evidence will come to light. If you consider that the merits test is no longer met, the case should be referred to the LAA for decision.

5.110   There is useful guidance on the difference of approach under the LASPO scheme which can be found in the Lord Chancellor's Guidance on Civil Legal Aid, which can be downloaded from www.gov.uk/funding-and-costs-assessment-for-civil-and-crime-matters.

8.35 Regulation 42 addresses the grounds and procedures for withdrawal of determinations. The grounds for withdrawal are set out at 42(1). These are expanded in comparison with those under the funding code to include the provisions in relation to the domestic violence

---

62 See chapter 5 of the Lord Chancellor's Guidance on Civil Legal Aid but note that, at the time of writing, it had not been amended to reflect the changes to the merits test made by the 2015 regulations.

63 See chapter 5 of the Lord Chancellor's Guidance on Civil Legal Aid but note that, at the time of writing, it had not been amended to reflect the changes to the merits test made by the 2015 regulations.

'gateway' to civil legal services in family proceedings no longer being satisfied 42(k) and a ground for withdrawal.

8.36 Regulation 42(3) provides for an equivalent of the 'show cause' procedure under the funding code procedures through notification of an intention to withdraw a determination. The scheme is different in that, if the determination is withdrawn as a result of this procedure, the withdrawal takes place with effect from the initial notification of intention (42(3)). That represents a difference from the position under the funding code in that:

(a) The client will not have cost protection, under the Civil Legal Aid (Costs) Regulations 2013, in the period from when the Director first notified an intention to withdraw the determination;

(b) The provider can carry out work at risk in relation to whether the withdrawal does occur, whereas no work could be carried out within the show cause period under the funding code without express permission irrespective of the ultimate outcome of the show cause.

Forms

5.111   Applications for certificates for legal representation and for Investigative Help are made to the LAA. Except in certain circumstances where urgent work is required (see below), solicitors do not have the power to grant or amend certificates directly.

5.112   Special procedures also apply in urgent cases (see below).

5.113   The LAA has announced that it intends to make its electronic Client and Cost Management System (CCMS) mandatory from 1 February 2016, a date which has been put back several times. At the time of writing it is available but remains optional. CCMS has been created in such a way that the questions asked are dependent on answers to other questions and so the electronic screens do not mirror the paper forms which they are to replace. There have been considerable difficulties with the system, so at the time of writing it remains to be seen whether it will be possible to make it mandatory as intended.

5.114   Form CIVAPP1 is completed with your client and submitted to the LAA. The form needs to be accompanied by the relevant MEANS form – MEANS 1, MEANS 2, etc – depending on the client's circumstances. Evidence of the client's means covering the last three months will also be required. See chapter 3 for details of financial eligibility.

5.115   The CIVAPP1 contains a statement of case, and this should be completed in as much detail as possible, as this is the part of the application that demonstrates that the criteria for granting a certificate are met. Don't forget that your client's statement is not the same as a statement of case! You have to explain to someone at the LAA, who has not met your client, why what the client says amounts to a cause of action and why it should be funded.

5.116   If you are applying for exceptional case funding (see chapter 4 and merits tests above), you will also need to submit an ECF1 form. See the Lord Chancellor's Guidance on exceptional funding.[64]

5.117   It is also extremely important to ensure that forms are completed correctly: historically, significant numbers of forms were rejected as they were not signed and/or dated. This wastes your time and the LAA's time, and delays the client's case. Low levels of rejects and refusals are KPIs under the Standard Contract 2013, see chapter 18 and para 5.75. The introduction of CCMS would undoubtedly resolve this issue, if the electronic system becomes an effective replacement for paper as intended.

5.118   See appendix B for an application checklist.

Refusals and appeals

5.119   A refusal of a certificate on the basis of merit can be appealed, within 14 days of the decision, first to a review by the director, then to an independent adjudicator.[65] A refusal on financial grounds cannot be appealed, though a director's review is available and a fresh application can be made if circumstances change.

Funding

5.120   Civil Legal Aid Representation Certificates are funded on an hourly rate basis. See chapter 13 for more information.

5.121   In almost every case, a funding certificate is only granted subject to two limitations:

---

64   Available at www.gov.uk/government/publications/legal-aid-exceptional-funding-form-and-guidance.

65   Civil Legal Aid (Procedure) Regulations 2012 reg 44.

- a particular step in the proceedings, such as 'all steps up to the filing of a defence and thereafter obtaining counsel's opinion', or 'all steps up to a case management conference'; and
- a costs limitation, usually £2,250. Costs limitations include profit costs (and any enhancement or uplift), counsels' fees and disbursements, but not VAT.

5.122   It is extremely important not to do work outside the scope of either limitation as you will not be paid for it. It is particularly easy to lose track of counsels' fees and disbursements, and it really helps to keep all documents relating to financial issues together in the file. One of the advantages of CCMS is that you can log on and see claims made by counsel under your certificate, helping to keep track of costs.

5.123   Limitations can be amended on application to the LAA or under delegated functions (previously called devolved powers under the AJA 1999) in urgent circumstances (see below for more information about delegated functions).

Amendments to scope and costs

5.124   Requests for amendments to either scope or costs limitations are made to the LAA, using form CIVAPP8. In making a request, the adviser will be obliged to demonstrate that the case continues to satisfy both limitations of the merits test, and state what new scope or costs limitation is required. Therefore, there must be merit not only in the case as a whole, but in each step of the proceedings.

5.125   Timing the application for an amendment has to be done with care, as the date an amendment takes effect is the date of the decision. If you leave your application until the last minute, you risk exceeding the current limitation and not being paid. On the other hand, you must justify why the work needs to be done at the particular time, as the LAA will refuse any amendment considered to be premature. They also refuse an amendment that might become redundant due to some other event taking place.

Use of counsel and amendments for a QC

5.126   A Representation certificate allows you to instruct counsel; but if the case warrants a QC, you must apply to the LAA for authority. See the LAA's Costs Assessment Guidance for more information. See also chapter 15.

Disbursements and prior authority

5.127   In many cases, disbursements can be large, and there is a risk to the organisation that they will not be allowed, or allowed in full, on assessment of the bill.

5.128   Therefore, the prior authority scheme allows an organisation to apply to the LAA for authority to incur a disbursement in advance, if it is above £100 and is not an expert fee covered by the standard rates/hours introduced from 3 October 2011 and reduced from 2 December 2013.[66] The application is made using form CIVAPP8, accompanied by a quote for the disbursement and reasons why it is necessary. The advantage of having authority is that no question as to the validity of the disbursement can be raised on assessment of the bill, unless and to the extent that it exceeds the amount or scope of the authority. Prior authority therefore gives a measure of costs protection for expensive disbursements.

5.129   You may apply for prior authority if:[67]

a) an item of costs is either unusual in its nature or is unusually large;
b) you wish to instruct a QC;
c) prior authority is required under the specification; or
d) you wish to instruct an expert at higher rates than are set out in the Civil Legal Aid (Remuneration) (Amendment) Regulations 2013.

If you do not apply for prior authority and b), c), or d) above applies, you will not be paid in full or at all for the fees incurred.

Experts' fees

5.130   Experts' fees have been codified since October 2011. The Civil Legal Aid (Remuneration) Regulations 2013 set out applicable rates for experts in different areas of expertise. The fees were reduced by 20 per cent by the Civil Legal Aid (Remuneration) (Amendment) Regulations 2013. In some cases, there are fixed fees for reports, in others

---

66 Community Legal Service (Funding) (Amendment) (No 2) Order 2011 (for AJA 1999 cases) and Civil Legal Aid (Remuneration) (Amendment) Regulations 2013 Schedule 2 (for LASPO cases) expert fees were reduced by 20% on 2 December 2013 and so the rates in Schedule 5 of the 2013 Remuneration Regulations are no longer valid for cases started after that date.

67 Standard Civil Contract Specification 2013 para 5.11 or 2010 Specification para 5.25.

hourly rates. The hourly rates are a maximum, not a fixed rate.[68] The LAA has issued some useful guidance on experts' fees.[69]

5.131   There are 'London' and 'non-London' rates; which applies is determined by the location of the expert. Where an expert has offices both in and outside London, it is the location of the solicitor that determines the rate.[70]

5.132   The rates cannot be exceeded unless the LAA has granted prior authority in advance. Prior authority will only be granted in exceptional circumstances, defined as being where:[71]

- the expert's evidence is key to the client's case and either:
  - the complexity of the material is such that an expert with a high level of seniority is required; or
  - the material is of such a specialised and unusual nature that only very few experts are available to provide the necessary evidence.

5.133   Applications for prior authority should be made on form CIVAPP8A. Prior authority cannot be granted in Legal Help cases, and so where you instruct an expert at a higher rate in a Legal Help case you should justify on the file why you have done so. It would be unusual – and risky – to do this in a Legal Help case.

5.134   Where a particular type of expert is not specified in the Remuneration Regulations and therefore there are no codified rates, the LAA will assess rates on a case-by-case basis, but will 'have regard to' the codified rates.

5.135   Where either enhanced or non-codified rates are sought, the LAA will expect to see at least two written quotes setting out the hourly rate, number of hours and total fee.

5.136   Where joint experts are instructed and all instructing parties are legally aided, the codified rates apply to the total instruction, not each party's share. Any application for prior authority need only be made by the lead solicitor.

5.137   Where joint experts are instructed by both legally aided and non-legally aided parties, the LAA will take a pro rata approach. Where

---

68 The full list of rates can be found in Civil Legal Aid (Remuneration) Regulations 2013 Sch 5 for cases started before 2 December 2013 and in Civil Legal Aid (Remuneration) (Amendment) Regulations 2013 Sch 2 for cases started after that date.

69 Guidance on the Remuneration of Expert Witnesses: www.gov.uk/expert-witnesses-in-legal-aid-cases.

70 Costs Assessment Guidance para 3.46.

71 Standard Civil Contract Specification 2013 para 6.61 or 2010 Specification para 6.62.

fixed fees are specified, the LAA will pay a share of the fee. Where an hourly rate is specified, the LAA will determine their share on the basis of hours rather than rates. They will pay – in a two party case – half the time at the codified rate.[72]

5.138   For example, a surveyor is instructed jointly on behalf of a tenant and a landlord. If he takes six hours to do his report, the LAA will pay for three hours, up to the maximum of £115 per hour (in London) – so £345. They will not pay six hours at £115 (£690) where the landlord also agrees to pay six hours at £115 – the approach is that the codified rate is the maximum the expert can charge to the fund and in a joint instruction the LAA will pay half the time taken to prepare the report. The other party can agree to pay the expert more, but that is a matter between them and the expert.

5.139   As a result of these changes, the LAA now require disbursement vouchers with a breakdown of time spent and hourly rates charged with POA1s and CLAIM1s, even those assessed by the court. If the court has assessed an hourly rate higher than the codified rates without prior authority, the LAA will reject it and it will have to go back to the court for re-assessment.[73] Other restrictions on experts' fees include:

- capping travel time to £40 per hour and costs to 45p per mile;
- ban on claiming for administration costs;
- must not claim a cancellation fee unless given less than 72 hours' notice of the cancellation;
- requiring experts to time record and itemise time spent on their invoices.

5.140   The codified rates also apply to attendance at court. Some experts have been in the habit of charging for half or full days for court attendance; now they must charge the hourly rate.

Funding from the client's point of view

Contributions

5.141   Clients on passporting benefits or with very limited means do not have to make contributions to the cost of their case during its lifetime; but they may need to make payment at the end of their case if money or property is recovered or preserved, under the statutory

---

72 Costs Assessment Guidance para 3.41.
73 See the court-assessed claim checklist at www.gov.uk/government/ publications/civ-claim1-civil-claim-form-not-fixed-fee.

charge (see below at 5.140 for more information). It is therefore easy for such clients to be lulled into feeling that their legal aid is going to be free, when it is not, and so it is even more important to ensure they understand the effect of the statutory charge and are given a costs estimate which is revised at every relevant point throughout the case.

5.142　If the client's capital is between the lower and upper thresholds, the client is required to pay a contribution. The amount of the contribution is the lower of (a) the amount by which capital exceeds the lower threshold and (b) the total estimated costs of the case.

5.143　If the client's disposable income is between the lower and upper threshold, a contribution will be payable. The amount of the contribution depends on the amount by which income is above the lower threshold, but is a fixed sum plus a percentage of the excess each month for the life of the certificate. The eligibility calculator on the LAA website will show you the level of contribution the client will have to pay.

5.144　If the client fails to pay a contribution, you will receive notification from the LAA, and although you do not have to stop work, you are at risk that legal aid will be withdrawn from the date of the notice[74] if the client does not make payment.

5.145　Should the amount paid in contributions exceed the final costs as assessed, the client will be entitled to a refund of the difference.

Changes in circumstances

5.146　Clients must be financially eligible on both capital and income. They must inform the LAA of any change in their means. A reassessment will then be carried out.

Statutory charge

5.147　The charge is governed by the Civil Legal Aid (Statutory Charge) Regulations 2013. The statutory charge under certificates operates at all levels of service, and across all categories except family mediation. It operates on both property recovered and property preserved.[75]

5.148　If a matter is funded by Legal Help *only*, the charge does not arise in any category.[76]

74　See the Civil Legal Aid (Procedure) Regulations 2012 reg 43.
75　LASPO s25.
76　Civil Legal Aid (Statutory Charge) Regulations 2013 reg 4(1).

5.149   If a case is funded initially under Legal Help, Help with Mediation or Family Help (Lower) and goes on to a certificate, if the charge arises, it also applies to those costs.[77]

5.150   If money or property is at issue in the proceedings, then the successful client is at risk of the charge. A claimant client whose claim succeeds recovers property; a defendant client who resists a claim preserves property.[78] Even if title to the property is not in issue, but possession of it is, the charge still arises.[79]

5.151   Where the proceedings result in recovery or preservation for someone other than the client, the charge arises.[80]

5.152   The charge gives the LAA first call on any money or property recovered in the proceedings. It is used to repay the costs of funding the case. You should note that even though damages in disrepair cases are out of scope under LASPO, the LAA takes the view that if the client has had the benefit of legal aid to enforce repairs, the statutory charge applies to the whole of the proceedings (see chapter 11 for more information). So, if a claimant in a housing disrepair case wins compensation of £5,000, and costs under the certificate and Legal Help were £1,500, then (assuming no costs were awarded from the other side) the charge would operate and the client would receive only £3,500 (recovery). On the other hand, if the client was defending a claim for a £5,000 share in property and won the case, if the costs were £1,500, he or she would be liable to pay £1,500 (preservation).

5.153   All monies due to a client in legal proceedings must be paid to his or her solicitor if the client is legally aided in any way.[81]

5.154   All property is caught by the charge, unless exempt by regulation. Exempt property is currently limited to:

- periodical payments of maintenance;
- sums paid under
  - Matrimonial Causes Act 1973 ss25B or 25C;
  - Inheritance (Provision for Family and Dependants) Act 1975 s5;
  - Family Law Act 1996 Part 4;
  - Civil Partnership Act 2004 Sch 5 paras 25(2) or 26;
- interim payments in Inheritance Act proceedings;
- the first 50 per cent of a redundancy award;

---

77   Reg 4(2).
78   *Hanlon v Law Society* [1980] 2 All ER 199.
79   *Parkes v Legal Aid Board* [1994] 2 FLR 850.
80   LASPO s25(1)(a).
81   Civil Legal Aid (Statutory Charge) Regulations 2013 reg 13.

- the client's clothes, household furniture or tools of the trade (except in exceptional circumstances);
- state benefits and pensions, and any other property subject to a statutory prohibition on assignment.[82]

5.155   The amount of the charge is calculated to compensate the LAA for funding the case, and is therefore the amount of costs as assessed (less any contribution paid by the client), less costs recovered from the other side. Therefore, the amount is the net amount paid to the supplier by the LAA.

5.156   If the charge arises, the client will have a financial interest in the organisation's bill of costs. Clients should be advised of the potential effect of the charge at the outset of the case, given regular costs updates, and at the end of the case be given a copy of the bill and advised of their right to make representations on the bill, including at any assessment hearing. The only elements of the bill that do not form part of the charge are the costs of assessment and costs of complying with Equality Act 2010 obligations to clients with disabilities[83] as well as any settlement fees in family cases.[84]

Recovery of money

5.157   Regulation 3 provides that all monies owing to a funded client should be paid to his or her solicitor, not to the client direct. The only exceptions are periodic payments of maintenance, and money paid into court to be invested for the client's benefit in the limited circumstances set out in reg 11. Regulation 15(1)(a) obliges the solicitor to report any recovery or preservation to the LAA straight away.

5.158   Once money is received, the solicitor may make a judgment as to whether it is exempt property. If it is, it may be paid to the client. If not, it must be paid to the LAA. In cases of doubt, the best course is to pay to the LAA, which can refund the client. If the solicitor fails to protect the LAA's charge and pays the money to the client without deducting it, the solicitor is liable.[85]

5.159   Regulation 15(3) entitles the solicitor to apply to the Regional Director for permission to pay to the client money which is not required to satisfy the charge – for example, if £10,000 is recovered

---

82 Reg 5.
83 Civil Legal Aid (Statutory Charge) Regulations 2013 reg 6.
84 Reg 4(4).
85 Standard Contract Standard Terms 2010/2013 clause 14.12; Specification para 5.37 (para 5.20 in 2013 Specification).

and costs will not exceed £5,000, an application can be made to return the extra £5,000 to the client.

5.160   Unless an application to defer the charge is being made (see below), the solicitor should send a cheque for the value of the money recovered with the final bill to the LAA. The LAA will assess the bill, pay solicitor and counsel, and return the balance to the client.

Recovery of property, and preservation cases

5.161   In such cases, money is unlikely to be paid to the solicitor. Instead, the solicitor will report recovery or preservation to the LAA. The LAA will pay the costs of solicitor and counsel, and pursue the client for the costs.

Enforcement of the charge – the LAA's powers

5.162   The LAA has no power to waive the charge altogether, except in very limited circumstances (basically, where it was recognised as a wider public interest case from the start and the LAA funded this client but not others to act as a test case: reg 9).

5.163   In certain circumstances, enforcement of the charge can be postponed under reg 22. The conditions are:

- the property is the client's (or his or her dependant's) family home; or in family cases, money to be used to purchase a home for the client or dependants; and
- the LAA is satisfied that the home will provide sufficient security for the charge; and
- it would be unreasonable for the client to repay the charge.

5.164   If the charge is postponed, simple interest at 8 per cent per annum will accrue from the date of registration. Interest is due on the lower of the value of the charge or the value of the home (reg 25). The charge must be registered at the Land Registry or equivalent steps taken.[86]

5.165   Otherwise, the charge is payable immediately unless the LAA agrees to accept payment by instalment, and the LAA can enforce the charge, if necessary, by enforcement proceedings in the courts.

5.166   The solicitor should report to the LAA using the appropriate ADMIN form.

---

86 Civil Legal Aid (Statutory Charge) Regulations 2013 reg 22(2).

Ending a case

5.167 Legal aid certificates come to an end in one of three ways: being discharged or revoked, or when a final bill is submitted at the end of the case.

Discharge

5.168 When the LAA decides that a certificate should not continue because changing circumstances indicate that funding is no longer justified on the merits, or because the client is no longer financially eligible, the certificate will be discharged. The effect of this is that the client is no longer in receipt of legal aid. If discharge is at the instigation of the LAA, there is a right to appeal to an independent adjudicator. Once the certificate is discharged, the case is at an end and the file can be billed. At the end of a case, the adviser should usually apply for the certificate to be discharged.

Revocation

5.169 The effect of revocation[87] is not simply to end the funding of a case – revocation retrospectively removes funding from the client, so that he or she never had a valid legal aid certificate at all. The LAA will only revoke a certificate when information comes to light to suggest that it should never have been issued, for example because a client concealed information about his or her resources because the client was never in fact eligible. The effect of revocation is that the client becomes liable for all costs incurred under the certificate.

Submission of final bill

5.170 See chapter 13.

Urgent cases

Scope

5.171 The LAA defines a case as urgent if it is necessary to carry out work before a substantive application could be made and determined. The LAA aims to process most substantive applications within four weeks. Therefore an emergency certificate is unlikely to be granted unless the work has to be carried out before a substantive certificate could be granted and cannot wait without serious adverse consequences to

---

87 Civil Legal Aid (Procedure) Regulations 2012 reg 42(2).

the client, for example risk to the life, liberty or physical safety of the client or the client's family or the roof over their heads; or the delay will cause a significant risk of miscarriage of justice, or unreasonable hardship to the client, or irretrievable problems in handling the case; and in either case there are no other appropriate options available to deal with the risk.

5.172   Other appropriate options could be: contacting the police where life or physical safety are at risk; seeking an adjournment of a hearing or an extension of time; dealing with the urgent work via another level of service (eg Legal Help or Help at Court); or by the client taking urgent steps in person where that was reasonable.

5.173   You should also consider whether it would be more appropriate to grant or amend a certificate under delegated functions (see para 5.184 below) before you submit an application to the LAA for decision.

Financial eligibility

5.174   See chapter 3. See also 'Funding from the client's point of view', para 5.141 above.

5.175   Emergency representation may be granted without a full means assessment. This clearly has short term advantages for the client, but it creates a financial risk for the legal aid fund.

Revocation

5.176   The client may turn out to be financially ineligible, may not co-operate with the means assessment, or may not accept an offer, should a contribution be required. In all of those circumstances the emergency certificate will be revoked (ie cancelled and the client treated as though he or she was never in receipt of legal aid).

5.177   The client will be responsible for the full costs of his or her representation. In addition he or she will not have the protection from opponents' costs provided by a representation certificate. You must therefore advise the client of this and give a costs estimate. If the certificate is revoked, you should submit a bill in the usual way; the LAA will pursue the client for the costs.

Merits test

5.178   The appropriate merits test (see para 5.89 above) must be satisfied, as well as the urgency criteria.

5.179   However, as the situation will be urgent, it may often be that only limited information is available. If so, emergency representation may be granted where it appears likely on the information available that the merits test will be satisfied.

Forms

5.180 Emergency applications for civil legal aid certificates are made on form CIVAPP6 and are submitted by fax. Emergency amendments to limitations on existing certificates are made on CIVAPP8.

5.181 The LAA must receive the substantive application within five working days of the emergency grant. If you fail to submit the application, the emergency certificate only covers work done within the first five working days, and you will not be paid for work beyond that period.

Funding

5.182 Emergency certificates will usually be limited to £1,350 (profit costs, counsels' fees and disbursements, but not VAT), though you can grant a higher limit, or amend to a higher limit, as long as you do not go above £10,000 and as long as the costs only relate to urgent work.

5.183 Emergency certificates only last for eight weeks, so you must ensure that you are covered by a substantive certificate from that date, or else you will not be paid. This time limit cannot be extended.

Delegated functions (formerly devolved powers)

Scope

5.184 The Standard Civil Contract Specification 2013 (paras 5.2–5.4) lists the delegated functions available. The LAA monitors the use of delegated functions, and may suspend or terminate them if they have been seriously misused.[88]

5.185 Certificates can be granted for full legal representation in urgent cases. You may not use delegated functions to grant a certificate where there is an outstanding certificate or application at the LAA, or where a previous application has been refused and there is no clear and relevant change of circumstances to suggest that a reapplication would be granted.

---

88 Funding Code: decision-making guidance section 12.8. Post-LASPO guidance has not been issued.

5.186   You may not use delegated functions to grant exceptional case funding under section 10 of LASPO (see para 3.30 and chapter 4 for more information), nor judicial review cases (with limited exceptions mainly for emergency homelessness cases or unless you have specific authorisation) see para 5.3 of the 2013 Contract Specification.

Steps for granting an emergency certificate

5.187   The LAA has issued guidance on the matter types, standard wordings and limitation codes you will need which can be downloaded here: www.gov.uk/government/publications/civil-legal-aid-application-forms-supporting-guidance.

   1   Select a matter type code.
   2   Identify the wording code for the allowable proceedings.
       If there is no appropriate wording code, the relevant LAA processing office must be contacted.
   3   Apply an appropriate scope limitation wording.
   4   Apply a costs limitation.
       Costs limitations include profit costs, disbursements and counsels' fees, but *not* VAT.
       In emergency applications this will generally be £1,350.
   5   Submit an application for a substantive certificate within five working days.

Amendments under delegated functions

5.188   Under the Legal Aid Civil (Procedure) Regulations 2012 reg 39(3)(b), you can amend an emergency certificate as long as the LAA has not yet granted a substantive certificate and the amendment is required because of the urgency of the situation.

Refusals under delegated functions

5.189   There is no right of appeal against the refusal to grant an emergency certificate.[89]

Financial eligibility

5.190   As 'Urgent cases', above.

Merits test

5.191   As 'Urgent cases', above.

89 Civil Legal Aid (Procedure) Regulations 2012 reg 53.

Forms

5.192   Delegated functions grants are made using CIVAPP1. Delegated functions amendments are made using CIVAPP8. MEANS6 can be emailed to the LAA for a preliminary assessment. (See para 6.105 for more information.)

5.193   A substantive application must be submitted to the LAA using CIVAPP1, or in the case of an amendment CIVAPP8, within five working days of the exercise of delegated functions.

Funding

5.194   As 'Urgent cases', above.

Very expensive cases/special case work

5.195   Civil high cost cases are called 'special case work' under LASPO and are governed under regulation 54 of the Civil Legal Aid (Procedure) Regulations 2012.

Scope

5.196   High cost civil cases are dealt with by two teams at the LAA – family and civil non-family cases. In civil cases the LAA will agree individual case contracts for cases. In family, an individual case contract can be agreed or you can opt to be paid under the 'events model' or 'Care Case Fee Scheme', which is a form of graduated/fixed fee, dependent on the number of hearing days and other events (as outlined in guidance). The benefit of the CCFS is that it avoids multiple revisions to detailed case plans, which is popular with practitioners and is often (but not always) considered preferable to an individually agreed case plan. From 1 October 2015 all single advocate care cases will be paid under CCFS unless you can show you would be paid at least 30 per cent more by claiming hourly rates with a case plan.

5.197   High cost cases fall into five types:

- individual very high-cost cases: where costs are expected to exceed £25,000, such as Children Act 1989, clinical negligence and judicial review cases;
- cases which might exceed £75,000 if they proceeded to contested trial, final hearing or the conclusion of any appeal stage before the Court of Appeal or Supreme Court;

- multi-party actions (MPAs): these range from 1,000-claimant actions to 10-claimant actions;
- exceptional funding cases: when funding is approved outside LASPO provisions;
- 'community action' cases in relation to individuals who belong to an identifiable geographic community the members of which have a common interest in the proceedings.

5.198   The LAA can treat more than one set of proceedings or certificates as a single case when deciding whether the cost thresholds are reached, for example in public law Children Act proceedings involving numerous parties.

5.199   Cases can be referred to the High Cost Case Team by the LAA's processing office at any stage if it appears that they may meet the criteria.

Financial eligibility

5.200   See chapter 3. See also 'Funding from the client's point of view', para 5.141 above. The LAA has a limited power to waive eligibility rules in relation to MPAs.[90]

Merits test

5.201   Only three types of case are automatically entitled to funding:

- special Children Act proceedings;
- proceedings in which the client's life or liberty are at risk;
- judicial review proceedings in which:
  - the court has given permission for the case to continue, and
  - the case:
    - has a significant wider interest; or
    - is of overwhelming interest to the client; or
    - raises significant human rights issues.

5.202   Cases concerning multi party actions, appeals to the Supreme Court, breaches of Convention rights (within the meaning of the Human Rights Act 1998 or a Community Action, may be subject to special controls.[91]

---

90 Civil Legal Aid (Procedure) Regulations 2012 reg 53.
91 Civil Legal Aid (Procedure) Regulations 2012 reg 58.

Forms

5.203   You need to submit:

- a statement of what the case is about;
- a statement of objectives – what is in issue and what is likely to be secured;
- a case analysis – this must include:
  - issues of law – favourable and unfavourable, setting out how any obstacles will be overcome;
  - issues of fact – favourable and unfavourable, assessing the evidence supporting each;
  - expert evidence required – and why;
  - costs in issue – eg amount of claim for damages – special rules for clinical negligence see below;
  - key events and resources required – likely costs of solicitors, counsel, experts and disbursements;
  - risk analysis – and how to deal with risks identified;
  - statement of prospects of success within the terms of the funding code;
- an assessment – addressing each relevant element of the merits criteria and stating how each is satisfied;
- case theory – a short statement (five sentences or less) explaining why the client will win the case;
- broadly costed overall case plan, including:
  - when counsel and experts will be instructed;
  - when the case management conference will be held;
  - when the trial will take place;
  - forecast of cumulative costs – at key events and appropriate intervals and at 31 March each year;
  - fully costed plan for the next stage of the case, showing an overall price for the stage – also setting out costs of all elements of work to be performed and costs to be incurred;
  - breakdown of costs to date;
  - details of any costs-sharing agreements;
- details of the person managing the case, and of the team (if any) who will be doing the work;
  - names of person managing the case and the team members;
  - what they will be doing;
  - evidence of their suitability;
  - evidence of the firm's suitability to handle the work to its conclusion.

5.204   There is more information about what to submit (including sample case plans) on the LAA's website at www.gov.uk/government/publications/high-cost-cases-non-family-civil

Funding

5.205   The LAA has produced guidance, which can be downloaded from www.gov.uk/government/publications/high-cost-cases-non-family-civil, or www.gov.uk/civil-high-cost-cases-family.

5.206   Funding is agreed as set out in the case plan. There is very little flexibility to move costs from one heading to another once they are agreed. It can also be difficult to get amendments to the case plan accepted.

5.207   For a case where inter partes costs are expected to be paid if successful, funding is provided on a risk-sharing basis. If it settles, recovery is at full inter partes rates; but if unsuccessful, the LAA will pay at specified hourly rates with no mark-up (normally £90.00 for senior counsel, £70.00 per hour for solicitors and £50.00 for junior counsel).

5.208   There are specific rates of payment for contracted cases, which vary depending on the type of case, prospects of success, and any exceptional circumstances.

5.209   Claims can be made on form CIVCLAIM1, at the hourly rates applying, for costs to date at the start of the contract, and at the end of each stage. If a stage lasts longer than six months, a claim for costs can be made every six months. These are applications for payment on account, made on form CIVPOA1.

5.210   At the end of the case, claims can be made in the same way as under an ordinary certificate (see chapter 11), though at the hourly rate agreed in the contract. If no costs were awarded, and the statutory charge does not apply, form CIVCLAIM1 should be used. Otherwise, CIVCLAIM2 and the appropriate ADMIN form are required. If costs are recovered from the other side, the LAA is entitled to the recoupment of payments on account. High cost case bills are always assessed by the LAA, not the courts.

CHAPTER 6

Conducting a family private law case

continued

Introduction

6.1   This chapter deals with conducting family private law cases, that is where the issues are between private individuals rather than involving the state (in the shape of social services). There are separate chapters on the general rules that apply to all civil cases, as well as family public law, housing, immigration and mental health, as they have their own funding schemes and rules.

6.2   In chapter 3, we saw that there are three key stages in providing publicly funded services: to ensure that (i) the matter is within scope, (ii) the client is financially eligible and (iii) the case meets the merits test. In addition, you need to ensure that applications are completed correctly and funding is obtained. The Lord Chancellor's Guidance under section 4 of LASPO has a helpful section in relation to how the Act applies: www.gov. uk/funding-and-costs-assessment-for-civil-and-crime-matters.

6.3   This chapter explains how these steps are taken successfully in respect of family private law. Where appropriate, you will be referred back to chapter 5, as that chapter sets out the general rules.

6.4   See appendices H and I for a summary of the Legal Aid Agency's (LAA's) Costs Assessment Guidance, in respect of the most common queries raised by caseworkers.

Scope

6.5   Scope is determined by LASPO. Part 1 of Schedule 1 to the Act lists the services which may generally be provided in the family category:

In scope with no need for evidence of abuse

6.6   The following types of case are within scope without the need to produce evidence of domestic abuse or evidence that a child is at risk of abuse.

Inherent jurisdiction of the High Court

6.7   Inherent jurisdiction of the High Court in relation to children and vulnerable adults (Sch 1, para 9) applications for wardship are covered by legal aid.

Unlawful removal of children

6.8　You can prevent removal from the jurisdiction but can only secure return of a child if unlawfully removed within the jurisdiction (Sch 1, para 10). Unlawfully means removed by someone who does not have authority to do so, either because they do not have parental responsibility or because of a court order.

Domestic abuse

6.9　Advice and representation in relation to home rights, occupation orders and non-molestation orders under Part 4 of the Family Law Act 1996, injunctions following assault, battery or false imprisonment, and inherent jurisdiction of the High Court to protect an adult (Sch 1, para 11) are all in scope.

6.10　It is really important to note that this paragraph is not qualified – it is not necessary for the client to show or provide evidence of any previous violence to be eligible for 'civil legal services'. Civil legal services include all forms of legal aid, so advice under Legal Help can be provided in relation to the issues concerning domestic violence itself, and say a warning letter drafted, prior to, or instead of, applying to court for an injunction.

Respondents

6.11　Legal aid is still available to respondents in some cases but it depends on the facts of the case. See below for an extract from the Lord Chancellor's Guidance.

> **Respondents**
>
> 10.31 The prospects of success criteria (Merits Regulation 67(2)(a)) and the proportionality test (Merits Regulation 67(2)(b)) are unlikely to be satisfied by a respondent to non molestation proceedings or a forced marriage protection order only, unless there are very serious allegations which are plausibly denied wholly or substantially. An exception is where there is any question of inability to defend, for example because of mental incapacity or age, in which case a grant is likely to be justified. When considering the proportionality test, the impact on the client of the order sought will be taken into account, including any impact on contact or other related family proceedings.
>
> 10.32 In cases where the allegations are less serious or are admitted to a significant extent the main issue may well be whether the respondent should give an undertaking to the court and what form that undertaking should take. Legal help will usually be more appropriate in such cases (Regulation 20 of the Merits Regulations).

Other areas within scope

6.12 These are:

- mediation (Sch 1, para 14);
- children who are parties to family proceedings (Sch 1, para 15);
- forced marriage cases (Sch 1, para 16);
- EU and international agreements concerning children (Sch 1, para 17);
- EU and international agreements concerning maintenance (Sch 1, para 18).

In scope with evidence of abuse

Other private law matters arising out a family relationship (Sch 1, para 12)

6.13 Legal aid (both advice and representation) for divorce, financial matters and arrangements for children is only available to people who can show in very specific ways (set out in regulation 33 of the Civil Legal Aid (Procedure) Regulations 2012 (as amended[1])) that they are the victims of domestic violence.

6.14 LASPO has the following wide definition of 'domestic violence':

'domestic violence' means any incident, or pattern of incidents, of controlling, coercive or threatening behaviour, violence or abuse (whether psychological, physical, sexual, financial or emotional) between individuals who are associated with each other; ...[2]

'abuse' means any incident or repeated incidents of threatening behaviour, violence or abuse (whether psychological, physical, sexual, financial or emotional, and including acts of neglect, maltreatment, exploitation or acts of omission) between adults who are or have been intimate partners or family members, regardless of gender or sexuality.

Protection of children and family matters (Sch 1, para 13)

6.15 Legal aid advice and representation is available in private family law matters where a child is at risk from an adult who is not the person receiving legal aid. Again, legal aid is only available to people who can show in very specific ways (set out in regulation 34 of the Civil Legal

---

1 Civil Legal Aid (Procedure) (Amendment) Regulations 2014.
2 Legal Aid, Sentencing and Punishment of Offenders Act 2012 (Amendment of Schedule 1) Order 2013 r4(1).

Aid (Procedure) Regulations 2012 (as amended[3]) that the child is at risk of abuse.

Evidence of domestic abuse

6.16   Acceptable evidence of abuse is listed in regulation 33(2) of the Civil Legal Aid (Procedure) Regulations 2012 and was amended to include some additional forms of evidence in April 2014.[4] Any of the following are acceptable. However, note that Legal Help is not available to assist the client to obtain the evidence or to pay the costs, eg GP's report fees, of obtaining it. The LAA has issued some standard letters which clients can ask the relevant agency to complete. It is advisable that they are used wherever possible as the regulations are tightly drafted and unless the wording precisely covers all elements of the regulation, the LAA cannot accept it. The letters can be downloaded from www.gov.uk/government/collections/legal-aid-cases-of-domestic-violence-and-child-abuse-letters-for-professionals.

6.17   You cannot grant Legal Help, nor will the client be eligible for a representation certificate for private family law services listed at LASPO Sch 1 para 12 without one of the following – see also children at risk below:

(a) an unspent conviction for a domestic violence offence;
(b) a police caution for a domestic violence offence given within the twenty four month period immediately preceding the date of the application for civil legal services;
(c) evidence of relevant criminal proceedings against the opponent for a domestic violence offence which have not concluded;
(d) a protective injunction against the opponent which is in force or which was granted within the twenty four month period immediately preceding the date of the application for civil legal services;
(e) an undertaking given by an other party in a family relationship within the twenty four month period immediately preceding the date of the application provided that a cross-undertaking was not given by your client;
(ea) evidence that the other party is on police bail for a domestic violence offence
(f) a letter from a member of a multi-agency risk assessment conference (MARAC) confirming that the client was referred to the MARAC as a victim of domestic violence; and that the MARAC has, within the twenty four month period immediately preceding

---

3 By Civil Legal Aid (Procedure) (Amendment) Regulations 2014.
4 By Civil Legal Aid (Procedure) (Amendment) Regulations 2014.

the date of the application put in place a plan to protect the client from a risk of harm by an other party in a family relationship;

(g) a copy of a finding of fact, made in within the twenty four month period immediately preceding the date of the application, that there has been domestic violence by the other party giving rise to a risk of harm to the client;

(h) a letter or report from a health professional confirming that a professional has examined the client within the twenty four month period immediately preceding the date of the application and is satisfied that the client had injuries or a condition consistent with those of a victim of domestic violence; and has no reason to believe that the client's injures or condition were not caused by domestic violence;

(i) a letter from a social services department confirming that, within the twenty four month period and immediately preceding the date of the application, the client was assessed as being, or at risk of being, a victim of domestic violence by the other party;

(j) a letter or report from a domestic violence support organisation in the United Kingdom confirming

   (i) that the client was, within the twenty four month period immediately preceding the date of the application, admitted to a refuge;

   (ii) the dates on which the client was admitted to and, where relevant, left the refuge; and

   (iii) that the client was admitted to the refuge because of allegations of domestic violence.

(k) a letter confirming the client was refused admission to a refuge because of lack of accommodation;

(l) a referral letter or report from a health professional to a domestic violence support organisation within the twenty four month period and immediately preceding the date of the application, or from the domestic violence support organisation confirming that they received such a referral;

(m) a Domestic Violence Protection Notice or Order

(n) evidence of a bind over in connection with a domestic violence offence

6.18 The Director has released detailed guidance on the operation of the evidence requirements, available at www.gov.uk/government/uploads/system/uploads/attachment_data/file/345515/legal-aid-evidence-for-private-family-law-matters.pdf. This specifies in detail what is required for each piece of evidence. It also confirms that full and satisfactory evidence must be provided *before* work starts, otherwise legal aid will be refused or the Legal Help will be nil assessed (para 2.4 of the Guidance). Where you are applying for a certificate, you should submit certified copies of the evidence and retain the originals on file (para 1.8).

6.19   Where work on a case covers work automatically in scope (eg an application for a domestic violence injunction) and work only in scope on production of evidence (eg a prohibited steps order) you can only work on the in-scope element until the evidence is obtained (whether through the initial in-scope work or separately) (para 1.5 of the Guidance).

Evidence that a child is at risk of abuse

6.20   In relation to the legal services listed in LASPO Sch 1 para 13, acceptable evidence is listed in regulation 34(2) of the Civil Legal Aid (Procedure) Regulations 2012 as amended. Any of the following are acceptable:

(a) an unspent conviction for a child abuse offence;
(b) a police caution for a child abuse offence given within the twenty four month period immediately preceding the date of the application;
(c) evidence of relevant ongoing criminal proceedings for a child abuse offence;
(d) a relevant protective injunction which is in force or which was granted within the twenty four month period immediately preceding the date of the application;
(e) a copy of a finding of fact made within the twenty four month period immediately preceding the date of the application, of abuse of a child by the other party;
(ea) evidence that the other party is on police bail for a child abuse offence;
(f) a letter from a social services department confirming that, within the twenty four month period immediately preceding the date of the application, the child was assessed as being, or at risk of being, a victim of child abuse by the other party;
(g) a letter from a social services department confirming that, within the twenty four month period immediately preceding the date of the application, a child protection plan was put in place to protect the child from abuse or a risk of abuse by the other party;
(h) an application for an injunction made with an application for a prohibited steps order against the other party.

For a full list of the work that can be done in the family category, see appendix D.

Controlled work and licensed work

6.21 Controlled work is granted by the solicitor according to rules under the Standard Contract 2013. It is called 'controlled' because the LAA controls the number of matter starts which are allowed each year. The kinds of controlled work that are relevant to family practitioners are Legal Help and Family Help (Lower). Help at Court is not available in family work.

6.22 You need a Representation certificate, sometimes known as a legal aid certificate, to represent a client in legal proceedings. This is called licensed work, as the firm has a general licence to do such work, and numbers of matter starts are not limited. Certificates may be granted by the LAA, or, in urgent circumstances, granted as a delegated function by the organisation.

Private family law – controlled work

6.23 Under LASPO much private family law was removed from scope unless the client can demonstrate that he or she is the victim of domestic violence or that a child is at risk of abuse. Check carefully that the case you intend to take on remains in scope before granting controlled work (see the section on scope, above). This is particularly important as if you grant controlled work in an out of scope case, you may be paid for it on your initial claim, as it will be submitted electronically and the LAA may not be able to identify your error through claim codes without seeing the file; but the LAA may seek to recover fees on audit and may well extrapolate the finding across all your claims. You do not want to receive a hefty bill and a contract notice.

Legal Help – level 1

6.24 Legal Help allows you to provide legal advice and assistance in relation to a specific matter, but does not cover issuing proceedings, advocacy, or instruction of an advocate (although you can obtain counsel's opinion, where justifiable). If you need to advise your client on issues arising from mediation and arbitration, see Help with Family Mediation, (which was a new level of service from 1 April 2013, below).

6.25 Representation is not available in uncontested proceedings for divorce or judicial separation, except in very limited circumstances. Straightforward divorce work, where representation at court is not required, should be done under Legal Help, where it remains in scope for people who are the victims of domestic violence (see 'Scope' at para 6.5 above for more information).

6.26   Legal Help is also known as level 1 in the family standard fees scheme.

Scope

6.27   See chapter 4 for information on the following:

- whether other funding may be available, and legal aid should therefore not be granted;
- what to do if your client has received previous advice from another organisation;
- what to do if your client has received previous advice from your organisation;
- clients from abroad or clients who are abroad;
- clients who are children.

Legal Help is designed to cover cases which complete after little work beyond the first meeting with the client, and covers the consequential letters to the client and any letters to a third party. If you do more work in relation to children or finance issues, you may be able to go on to grant Family Help (Lower) funding (see below).

Domestic violence and child abduction cases

6.28   These cases are included in the controlled work standard fee scheme as far as level 1. Level 2 is not designed to cover these cases and you will often find that you need to issue proceedings under a certificate very quickly.

6.29   For evidence of domestic violence which acts as a passport to private Family law services, see 'Scope' above.

Wills and change of name cases

6.30   These cases are no longer in scope under LASPO.

Divorce petitioner cases

6.31   There is a 'stand alone' fee which applies to divorce, nullity, judicial separation and proceedings to dissolve civil partnerships (assuming the work is brought into scope due to evidence of domestic abuse). This covers cases where the client requires advice to initiate proceedings, they are issued, and there are no children or finance issues that would justify the grant of Family Help (Lower). We will look at this in more detail later on.

Financial eligibility

6.32 See chapter 3 for more information on the following:

- passporting benefits;
- assessment of capital;
- assessment of income;
- reassessment of means.

6.33 See chapter 5 for more information on the following:

- evidence of means;
- when you can start work without evidence of means;
- reassessing the client's eligibility if their means change significantly.

Merits test

6.34 The Legal Help merits test is known as the 'sufficient benefit test', and in full states: 'there is likely to be sufficient benefit to the individual, having regard to all the circumstances of the case, including the circumstances of the individual, to justify the cost of provision of legal help'.[5] The question is whether a reasonable private paying individual of moderate means would pay for the work.[6] In most family cases remaining within scope, the test will be met.

Forms

6.35 The form is the CW1 Legal Help, Help at Court and Family Help (Lower) form. The assessment of means and client's details sections must be fully completed, and signed by the client, normally in the presence of someone from your organisation, before you start doing any legal work.[7]

How many Legal Help forms?

6.36 You can have more than one Legal Help matter open at the same time, but this is very unusual in family work. It may be permissible if your client has entirely separate family disputes.[8] The LAA gives the example of disputes in respect of different family relationships, where any potential proceedings would be separate. This would apply, for

---

5 Civil Legal Aid (Merits Criteria) Regulations 2013 reg 32(b).
6 Civil Legal Aid (Merits Criteria) Regulations 2013 reg 7.
7 Standard Civil Contract Specification 2013 para 3.10.
8 Standard Civil Contract Specification 2013 para 7.169.

example where your client was the mother of children with different fathers each of whom was applying separately for residence.

Funding

6.37   Legal Help – level 1 is paid as two different standard fees.[9] The higher fee is only applicable when your client is the petitioner in a divorce and there are no significant children or finance issues and no other form of civil legal service is provided to your client. The higher fee can be claimed three months after proceedings are issued or when the proceedings are concluded (whichever is sooner).

6.38   In all other cases, the lower level 1 fee is payable (whether or not combined with a level 2 fee).

6.39   Divorce, child abduction and domestic abuse cases that exceed three times the fixed fee when calculated at hourly rates, can be claimed in full (see chapter 11 for more information about claiming escape fee cases).

6.40   Other level 1 cases cannot be claimed as escape fee cases.

Family Help (Lower) – level 2

Scope

6.41   This covers the provision of ongoing assistance with some kinds of 'Family Dispute'.[10]

Private Family Law – conditions for level 2

6.42   Up to and including 8 May 2011, paragraph 10.55 of the then Family Contract Specification required two meetings with the client in order to justify a level 2 fee. Note also that following certification of Point of Principle CLA 54,[11] definition of 'meeting' was broadened from 20 December 2010 to include phone calls. The LSC removed the requirement for a second meeting from 9 May 2011 and instead practitioners had to show that 'substantive negotiations' had taken place. This remains the position under the 2013 Standard Contract, for cases within the new reduced scope.

---

9   Current fees and hourly rates are found in the Civil Legal Aid (Remuneration) Regulations 2013 Sch 1.

10   Standard Civil Contract Specification 2013 para 7.60.

11   See www.gov.uk/legal-aid-points-of-principle-of-general-importance-pop.

Criteria for Family Help (Lower) – meaning of 'significant family dispute' – Family Contract Specification 2013

7.60 You may only make a determination that a Client qualifies for Family Help (Lower) where all relevant criteria in the Merits Regulations, Financial Regulations and Procedure Regulations are satisfied including the criteria in Paragraph 35 of the Merits Regulations. In addition, the fee for Family Help (Lower) may only be claimed for those Family Disputes:

(a) which involve more than simply taking instructions from and advising the Client, and providing any follow up written or telephone advice; and

(b) where you are involved in substantive negotiations with a third party (either by conducting the negotiations yourself or by advice and assistance in support of mediation); and

(c) where the dispute, if unresolved, would be likely to lead to family proceedings; and

(d) which do not primarily concern processing a divorce, nullity, judicial separation or dissolution of a civil partnership; and

(e) which do not primarily concern advice relating to child support.

Family Help (Lower) – children

6.43 This covers all work up to the issue of proceedings. It is not necessary to obtain a consent order to formalise any agreement in respect of children, although if you are claiming a settlement fee (see para 6.48 below), it is advisable to record the agreement in writing, so that the LAA can see that it was a 'genuine settlement to conclude that aspect of the case'.[12]

Family Help (Lower) – finance

6.44 This covers all work including the issue of proceedings and all work required to obtain a consent order.[13]

Family Help (Lower) – children and finance

6.45 Where a case involves children and finance issues meeting the criteria set out above, both the children and finance fees may be claimed. You claim two Family Help (Lower) fees, one for children and one for finance, where the merits criteria are met[14] (see merits test at para 6.50 below).

---

12 Standard Civil Contract Specification 2013 para 7.67.
13 Standard Civil Contract Specification 2013 para 7.67.
14 Standard Civil Contract Specification 2013 para 7.61.

Forms

6.46   You do not need another CW1 Legal Help, Help at Court and Family Help (Lower) form. Simply tick the box at the bottom of page 5 of the original form to affirm that the criteria for level 2 are met.

Funding

6.47   Family Help (Lower) (level 2) is paid under standard fees, although cases that reach the escape threshold (three times the fixed fee at levels 1 and 2 combined) can be paid in full at hourly rates. For more information about claiming escape fee cases, see chapter 13.

Settlement fees

6.48   Settlement fees can be claimed for cases that conclude at this level, without the issue of proceedings (save to obtain a consent order – Standard Civil Contract Specification 2013 para 7.67). In order to be considered as 'settled', that aspect of the case (ie children or finance) must be fully resolved at that level and the client actively involved in a decision to accept a settlement. The agreement on financial issues must be recorded in writing or in a consent order. It is advisable to record the agreement in respect of children in writing as well.

6.49   If the client ceases to give instructions, dies, or the parties are reconciled, the settlement fee cannot be claimed.[15]

6.50   You must wait for 21 days after the case has been concluded before claiming the settlement fee. In relation to financial issues, if the settlement breaks down, and you become aware of the fact within six months, the settlement fee becomes repayable. In relation to children issues, the period is three months.[16]

6.51   For more information about when you can or should close a case, see chapter 4.

---

15 Standard Civil Contract Specification 2013 para 7.67(c).
16 Standard Civil Contract Specification 2013 para 7.67(b).

Case study

Mrs Brown had been married for 11 years and has two children, James and Jennifer. She came to see us about her divorce. It transpired that her husband had been very controlling, preventing Mrs Brown from contacting her family and only permitting her access to small amounts of money, which had to be fully accounted for. This had resulted in Mrs Brown suffering from anxiety and depression, about which she had consulted her GP within the last two years. She was able to obtain a GP's letter to show that she was eligible on the basis of 'domestic abuse' under LASPO.

Mr Brown refused to attend mediation; and also instructed solicitors on a private paying basis. Eventually we were able to finalise the divorce and obtain agreement to settlements in respect of the arrangements for the children and the finances.

Our office is in Salisbury. What can we claim?

You can claim:	
Legal Help level 1	£86.00
Family Help (Lower) (children)	£199.00
Family Help (Lower) (finance)	£208.00
Settlement fee (children)	£119.00
Settlement fee (finance)	£125.00
	Total £737.00

Funding from the client's point of view – the statutory charge

6.52 For information about the statutory charge,[17] see chapter 5. The statutory charge does not apply to cases completing at Legal Help (level 1), but if the case goes beyond level 1, the level 1 costs are included in the costs caught by the charge.

6.53 The home is exempt from the charge in cases completing under Legal Help, Help at Court or Family Help (Lower). It does not apply to maintenance payments. However, even where a lump sum is paid, the statutory charge does not apply to standard fee cases. This is a

17 Civil Legal Aid (Statutory Charge) Regulations 2013.

powerful incentive to clients to settle at level 2, as in most cases their legal aid will be free.

6.54 However, in escape fee cases, the charge applies, but only to costs above the escape threshold (ie, those costs over three times the standard fee).

6.55 Where the charge arises only under Legal Help, Help at Court or Family Help (Lower), it is in favour of the firm. You may apply to the LAA to waive it, if its operation would cause grave hardship or distress to the client, or where it would be unreasonably difficult to enforce.[18]

6.56 You should collect the appropriate sum from the client and claim the net costs from the LAA.

6.57 But note that at level 3 (certificated work), the charge applies in favour of the LAA and includes the fees at levels 1 and 2.[19]

Help with Family Mediation

Introduction

6.58 LASPO introduced a level of service to allow solicitors to provide legal advice to clients during and immediately following mediation. It is designed to assist the mediation process and give legal effect to any agreement reached. This covers the provision of any of the following legal services in relation to a family dispute:

(a) civil legal services provided in relation to family mediation; or
(b) civil legal services provided in relation to the issuing of proceedings to obtain a consent order following the settlement order following the settlement of the dispute following family mediation.[20]

Scope

6.59 Help with Family Mediation is controlled work.[21] Therefore, you need to use a matter start under your schedule to start a case.

6.60 Help with Family Mediation covers legal advice to a client who is undergoing or who has participated in family mediation within the last three months and can include the issuing of proceedings to

---

18 Civil Legal Aid (Statutory Charge) Regulations 2013 reg 81.
19 Civil Legal Aid (Statutory Charge) Regulations 2013 reg 4(2).
20 Civil Legal Aid (Procedure) Regulations 2012 reg 8.
21 Civil Legal Aid (Procedure) Regulations 2012 reg 21(2).

obtain a consent order following the settlement of the dispute following family mediation.[22]

Financial eligibility

6.61 See Legal Help above.

Merits test

6.62 The merits test is the sufficient benefit test, see above. You will need evidence on the file that the client is, or has been within the last three months, participating in family mediation.[23]

Forms

6.63 The form is the CW5. It has to be signed by the mediator as well as the client.

Funding

6.64 You may not claim for Help with Family Mediation if you have provided Family Help or legal representation in relation to the same family dispute within the previous six months. If a certificate is granted to a client in respect of the same family dispute within six months of your claim, your fee will be recouped.[24]

6.65 You may only claim one Help with Family Mediation fee per case, regardless of the number of clients you represented who took part in the mediation or the number of different issues covered by the mediation.[25]

6.66 There is a fixed fee of £150; but you can also claim a further £200 if you draft a consent order giving effect to a mediated agreement and which is approved by the court. There is no 'escape' from these flat fees.[26]

22 Civil Legal Aid (Procedure) Regulations 2012 reg 8.
23 Standard Civil Contract Specification 2013 para 7.69.
24 Standard Civil Contract Specification 2013 para 7.72.
25 Standard Civil Contract Specification 2013 para 7.70.
26 Standard Civil Contract Specification 2013 para 7.3.

Certificates – private family law

Scope

6.67   A Representation certificate authorises the conduct of litigation and the provision of advocacy and representation, and includes steps preliminary and incidental to proceedings, and steps to settle or avoid proceedings.

6.68   The then LSC introduced a standard fee funding scheme known as the Private Family Law Representation Scheme (PFLRS) from 9 May 2011. Under the PFLRS there are two levels of funding:

- Family Help (Higher) – Level 3: To cover all work up to the preparation for final hearing.
- Legal Representation – Level 4: To cover all work from preparation for a final hearing up to and including all work to conclude a case after the final hearing, eg application to the court of first instance for permission to appeal, and advice on the merits of an appeal against a final order.

6.69   The LSC introduced a standard fee scheme for advocacy, the Family Advocacy Scheme (FAS) from 9 May 2011. For more information on the fee schemes see chapter 13. For more on the FAS, see chapter 16.

6.70   Before you apply for a certificate, see chapter 5:

- general criteria;
- clients who are abroad;
- clients from abroad;
- clients who are children.

Mediation

6.71   The LAA expects every effort to be made to resolve issues through mediation rather than through contested proceedings. Therefore, you should encourage your client to consider mediation wherever possible. Clients must attend an intake assessment with a mediator, unless one of the following applies:

- Family proceedings are already in existence and the client is a respondent/defendant who has been notified of a court date which is within eight weeks of the date of notification.
- The client has a reasonable fear of domestic abuse from a partner or former partner (see below for more information).

- The client or other party cannot see a mediator (examples given include where bail conditions prevent contact with an ex-partner, or where the client is in custody or hospitalised, or lives more than two hours away, etc).
- The other party is unwilling to attend mediation.
- Emergency representation is required.

Domestic violence and abuse

6.72   The LAA does not consider the fact that domestic abuse or violence has taken place should automatically rule out consideration of mediation. They will accept that it is not reasonable to consider mediation if an allegation of domestic abuse has resulted in a police investigation or the issuing of civil proceedings for the protection of the applicant within the last 12 months. In other circumstances, you will need to justify why it is not appropriate to involve the police, for example where this might jeopardise the long-term financial or other interests of the family, or if you have reason to believe that the police will not be able to assist, or if they have been contacted but have failed to respond or to provide adequate assistance in the past.

6.73   It is unlikely that funding will be granted for committal proceedings if criminal proceedings have been instigated by the police. Breach of a non-molestation order became a criminal offence in 2007, and the LAA would ordinarily expect the client to report a breach to the police before seeking an amendment to the certificate for committal.

6.74   The LAA normally expects a warning letter to be sent to the respondent. However, this is not an absolute rule, for example if you can show that a warning letter might endanger the client.[27]

Final hearings

6.75   In cases where evidence of abuse has been required to bring them within scope, practitioners have reported problems moving from Family Help (Higher) to Legal Representation – in practice, amending a certificate to cover a final hearing. During 2014, the LAA started to take a strict line on the procedure regulations, that this was a new level of funding, requiring fresh evidence of abuse. Where the abuse was within two years of the start of the case but by the final

---

27 See the Lord Chancellor's Guidance on Civil Legal Aid, which can be downloaded from www.gov.uk/funding-and-costs-assessment-for-civil-and-crime-matters.

hearing was more than two years old, this meant that funding would be withdrawn.

6.76   With effect from 17 July 2005, regulation 2(5) of the Civil and Criminal Legal Aid (Amendment) (Regulations) 2015 added a new regulation 31(7A) to the Civil Legal Aid (Procedure) Regulations 2012. This had the effect of disapplying regulations 33 and 34 of the procedure regulations (the regulations which prescribe what evidence of abuse is required) for applications for representation (including amendments) where there has already been a determination (not withdrawn) that the individual qualifies for Family Help (Higher). In other words, this means that from that date it was no longer necessary to provide up to date evidence when applying to amend a certificate to cover a final hearing, and certificates should no longer be withdrawn even where the evidence is by that time outside the two-year limit. As long as the evidence met the requirements at the time of the initial determination that level 3 funding was required, that will be enough to keep the case in scope for its whole life.

Financial eligibility

6.77   See chapter 3.

Waiver in domestic abuse cases

6.78   The LAA has discretion to waive the upper disposable income and capital limits for victims of domestic abuse seeking protection from the court.[28] However, any contribution from income or capital that is applicable under the regulations cannot be waived. If granting a certificate as a delegated function, you can assume the LAA will exercise its discretion; but when you submit the substantive application, you should make clear that the case is a domestic abuse case, and that you are seeking the waiver. It is best to do this by including it in a covering letter and also by clearly marking the front of the MEANS form.

6.79   You should advise your client that, although the upper limit may be waived, the liability to pay contributions is not. The usual rules on contributions will apply, so the client's funding will be revoked in the event of non-payment. Clients with income much above the upper limit who successfully obtain a waiver can find themselves paying quite substantial contributions, so you should clearly advise

---

28 Civil Legal Aid (Financial Resources and Payment of Services) Regulations 2013 reg 12.

the client to expect that. You can provide an indication of how much this will be by using the LAA's eligibility calculator at http://civil-eligibility-calculator.justice.gov.uk/

6.80 This is particularly important in emergency cases, since if you grant an emergency certificate, and the client is then offered a full certificate with contributions and declines the offer, he or she will be liable for the full costs you incur on the emergency certificate.

Merits test – standard criteria

6.81 Before you apply for a certificate you need to ensure that the standard criteria are satisfied.[29] Those that apply in private family law cases are:

- The individual does not have access to other potential sources of funding from which it would be reasonable to fund the case.
- There is no other person besides the individual, including a person who might benefit from the proceedings, who can reasonably be expected to bring the proceedings.
- The individual has exhausted all reasonable alternatives to bringing proceedings including any complaints system, ombudsman scheme or other form of alternative dispute resolution.
- There is a need for representation in all the circumstances of the case including:
  - the nature and complexity of the issues;
  - the existence of other proceedings; and
  - the interests of other parties to the proceedings.

6.82 The first criterion requires you to consider whether the client has alternative methods of funding the case at their disposal, and you will need to explore with the client and consider whether, for example, the local authority would pay for adoption proceedings. You will need to address any potential sources which are not in fact available on the application form.

Stage 1 – Prospects of success

6.83 All cases must be put into one of the following categories according to its prospects of success:[30]

---

29 Civil Legal Aid (Merits Criteria) Regulations 2013 reg 39.
30 Civil Legal Aid (Merits Criteria) (Amendment) Regulations 2013 reg 5, amended by Civil Legal Aid (Merits Criteria) (Amendment) (No 2) Regulations 2015 reg 2.

- very good – 80% or above;
- good – 60% to 80%;
- moderate – 50% to 60%;
- poor – 20% to 50%;
- very poor – less than 20%;
- borderline – it is not possible, because of disputed law, fact or expert evidence, to assign the case to another category but it cannot be categorised as 'unclear'; or
- unclear – the case cannot be assigned to any of the other categories because there are identifiable investigations to be carried out after which the prospects can be estimated.

The 'borderline' category was removed from the merits tests in 2014 by the Civil Legal Aid (Merits Criteria) Amendment Regulations 2014, but it remained in the definitions, and has been reinstated to the merits tests by the Civil Legal Aid (Merits Criteria) (Amendment) (No 2) Regulations 2015.

6.84   The standard to be applied in assessing the prospects of success is the prospects as they would be with the assistance of competent legal representation, not the prospects on the basis of material available but untested at the time of the application. This is to ensure that cases where competent representation would turn the case in the applicant's favour are not excluded from funding:[31]

- Where prospects of success are moderate or better, the prospects of success criterion will be met and so legal aid will be granted (subject to any other criteria that may apply in the individual case).
- Where prospects of success are borderline or poor but not very poor, the prospects of success criterion will be met if it is necessary to deem it met to prevent a breach of the applicant's ECHR or enforceable EU rights, or appropriate to do so having regard to the risk that failure to do so would risk such a breach.[32]
- Where prospects of success are very poor, representation will be refused.

6.85   In *IS v The Director of Legal Casework and The Lord Chancellor*,[33] Collins J said:

---

31 See *IS (by the Official Solcitor as Litigation Friend) v The Director of Legal Aid Casework and The Lord Chancellor* [2015] EWHC 1965 para 96, per Collins J.

32 Civil Legal Aid (Merits Criteria) Regulations 2013 reg 43, as amended by Civil Legal Aid (Merits Criteria) (Amendment) (No 2) Regulations 2015 reg 2(4).

33 [2015] EWHC 1965, para 40.

It is difficult to imagine a family case, particularly when there are contested issues about children, in which there would not be an interference with the Article 8 rights of either parent or the children themselves. Thus unless the party seeking legal aid could albeit unrepresented present his or her case effectively and without obvious unfairness, a grant of legal aid would be required. That does not mean that every case will require it: some may be sufficiently simple for the unrepresented party to deal with. Obviously if there is a lack of capacity even such cases may require legal aid. That issue I will have to consider in further detail later. But I am bound to say that I believe that only in rare cases, subject to means and merits if properly applied, should legal aid be denied in such cases.

This would apply both to in-scope family cases categorised as borderline or poor, and also to applications for exceptional funding for out of scope cases (see chapter 4).

Stage 2 – Cost-benefit/successful outcome

6.86   This varies according to the type of case, see below.

Appealing refusals

6.87   A refusal of a certificate on the basis of merit can be appealed, within 14 days of the decision, to the Independent Adjudicator. A refusal on financial grounds cannot be appealed, though a fresh application can be made if circumstances change.

Private law children cases – merits test

6.88   Private law children cases are proceedings concerning contact, residence, parental responsibility, financial provision for children, and other matters under the Children Act which are not special Children Act or other public law proceedings.

6.89   You need to show that you are likely to obtain a 'successful outcome' – a significant improvement in the arrangements for children.

6.90   The merits test is as follows:

- Prospects of success are:
    - moderate or better; or
    - borderline or poor, but it is necessary to determine that the prospects of success criterion is met to prevent a breach of the applicants ECHR or enforceable EU rights, or appropriate to

do so in the circumstances of the case having regard to any risk that failure to do so would be such a breach.[34]

- Representation will be refused unless the reasonable private paying individual test is met: 'the potential benefit to be gained from the provision of civil legal services justifies the likely costs, such that a reasonable private paying individual would be prepared to start or continue the proceedings having regard to the prospects of success and all the other circumstances of the case'.[35]

Forms

6.91   As mentioned in chapter 5, the LAA intends to introduce mandatory use of its online Client and Cost Management System (CCMS) for all new applications from 1 February 2016. This would replace the paper forms explained below.

6.92   The client should attend an appointment with a mediator unless any of the exceptions apply (see above). You must complete form CIVAPP3.

6.93   Representation will be refused if no reasonable attempts to settle without recourse to litigation (whether by negotiation or otherwise) have been attempted.

6.94   Forms will be rejected if the signatures are more than two months old. See the aide-memoire at appendix A.

Financial matters – merits test

6.95   You need to show that you are likely to obtain a 'successful outcome' – a significant improvement in financial or other arrangements. The merits test is as follows:[36]

- Prospects of success are:
  - moderate or better;
  - borderline or poor, but it is necessary to determine that the prospects of success criterion is met to prevent a breach of the applicants ECHR or enforceable EU rights, or appropriate to do so in the circumstances of the case having regard to any risk that failure to do so would be such a breach;

---

34 Civil Legal Aid (Merits Criteria) Regulations 2013 reg 68, amended by Civil Legal Aid (Merits Criteria) (Amendment) (No 2) Regulations 2015 reg 2(9).

35 Civil Legal Aid (Merits Criteria) Regulations 2013 reg 7.

36 Civil Legal Aid (Merits Criteria) Regulations 2013 reg 69, amended by Civil Legal Aid (Merits Criteria) (Amendment) (No 2) Regulations 2015 reg 2(10).

    – unclear and the case is of significant wider public interest, of overwhelming importance to the client, or the substance of it relates to a breach of Convention rights.

- Representation will be refused unless the likely benefits justify the likely cost, such that the reasonable private paying individual would be prepared to take or defend the proceedings in all the circumstances.

Forms

6.96   Again, before applying for funding, the client should attend mediation (unless the exceptions apply) and to have attempted to settle, by negotiation or otherwise. Form CIVAPP3 is required, together with the appropriate MEANS form and Form FM1.

Funding

6.97   The then LSC introduced a funding scheme known as the Private Family Law Representation Scheme (PFLRS) from 9 May 2011.

6.98   It also introduced a fee scheme for advocacy, the Family Advocacy Scheme (FAS) from 9 May 2011. For more information on the fee schemes see chapter 13.

Grant and scope of a certificate

6.99   In almost every case, a certificate is only granted subject to two limitations. First, it is very rare for a certificate to be granted to cover the entirety of proceedings. Usually, it is limited to a particular step in the proceedings. Secondly, costs will be limited, usually to £2,250 plus VAT in the first instance.

6.100   Costs limitations include profit costs (and any enhancement or uplift), counsel's fees and disbursements, but not VAT. It is extremely important not to do work outside the scope of any limitation as you will not be paid for it. You should note that payments to counsel under the FAS count towards the financial limitation on certificates.[37] It is particularly easy to lose track of counsel's fees and disbursements and it really helps to keep all documents relating to financial issues together in the file. If you have delegated functions, you have the power to amend the financial limitation on an emergency (but not full) certificate up to £10,000, but only to allow you to do work that is urgent. If you exercise this power, you should inform the LAA on form APP8 that you have done so.

---

37 Standard Civil Contract Specification 2013 para 6.65.

Domestic abuse cases

6.101   Representation is available to apply for an injunction under Family Law Act 1996 Part 4. This is covered by LASPO Sch 1 para 11, therefore there is no need to produce evidence of previous domestic abuse as this only applies to services under para 12.

6.102   The merits test is as follows:[38]

- Prospects of success are:
  - moderate or better; or
  - borderline or poor, but it is necessary to determine that the prospects of success criterion is met to prevent a breach of the applicants ECHR or enforceable EU rights, or appropriate to do so in the circumstances of the case having regard to any risk that failure to do so would be such a breach.
- Representation will be refused unless the case meets the proportionality test: 'that the likely benefits of the proceedings to the individual and others justify the likely costs, having regard to the prospects of success and all the other circumstances of the case.[39]

6.103   The LAA has made detailed guidance available on its website, see the Lord Chancellor's Guidance on Civil Legal Aid, which can be downloaded from www.gov.uk/funding-and-costs-assessment-for-civil-and-crime-matters

Applying for a certificate – urgent cases

6.104   You may exercise a delegated function to grant an emergency certificate. See chapter 5 for more information about delegated functions.

6.105   If a full certificate is refused (on means or merits), or made conditional on a contribution which the client refuses, the client is liable for all costs incurred under the emergency certificate. The client must therefore be advised of this at or before the time of the grant, and given a costs estimate. In these circumstances, the solicitor should bill the certificate in the usual way; the LAA will pursue the client for the costs.

- **Merits**: Emergency representation may be granted as a matter of urgency where it appears in the interests of justice to do so.[40]

---

38 Civil Legal Aid (Merits Criteria) Regulations 2013 reg 67, amended by Civil Legal Aid (Merits Criteria) (Amendment) (No 2) Regulations 2015 reg 2(8).
39 Civil Legal Aid (Merits Criteria) Regulations 2013 reg 8.
40 Civil Legal Aid (Procedure) Regulations 2012 reg 52(1)(b).

- **Means**: Emergency representation may be provided where there has not yet been a detailed assessment of the client's resources, provided that he or she has provided sufficient financial information to demonstrate that it is likely that he or she will be found to be eligible.[41] In cases of doubt, you can email the LAA for a preliminary assessment at: contactcivil@legalaid.gsi.gov.uk. State MEANS URGENT in the header and put your client's full name. See above for the LAA's power to waive the capital and income limits in domestic abuse cases.
- **Limitations**: You must apply both a scope and a costs limitation (see the standard limitations at www.gov.uk/government/publications/civil-legal-aid-application-forms-supporting-guidance). Scope should be limited to the steps that need to be taken urgently. The initial scope limitation can be amended, provided the certificate remains limited to steps that need to be taken urgently. Costs will usually be limited to £1,350 plus VAT in the first instance, though this can be exceeded or amended where justifiable.
- **Submission of forms**: The LAA processing office must receive the substantive application within five working days of the emergency grant, and in the event of a delegated function amendment to scope or costs, must receive a CIVAPP8 within five working days of the amendment.

6.106 It is important to ensure that your emergency certificate is replaced by a substantive certificate within 56 days, as emergency certificates expire at that point and any further work would not be funded. The time limit cannot be extended.

6.107 See chapter 5 for information about:
- amendments to certificates;
- refusals and appeals;
- use of counsel and amendments for a QC;
- changes to prospects of success or cost-benefit;
- disbursements and prior authority;
- contributions;
- high-cost cases;
- ending a case;
- discharge of certificate;
- revocation of certificate.

6.108 See chapter 13 for information about getting paid in family cases.

---

41 Civil Legal Aid (Procedure) Regulations 2012 reg 52(2).

Conducting a family public law case

Introduction

7.1   This chapter deals with conducting family public law cases. There are separate chapters on the general rules that apply to all civil cases, as well as family private law, immigration and mental health, as they each have their own funding schemes and rules.

7.2   In chapter 3, we saw that there are three key stages in providing publicly funded services: to ensure that (i) the matter is within scope, (ii) the client is financially eligible and (iii) the case meets the merits test. In addition, you need to ensure that forms are completed correctly and funding is obtained. This chapter explains how these steps are taken successfully in respect of family public law.

7.3   See appendices H and I for a summary of the Legal Aid Agency's (LAA's) Costs Assessment Guidance, in respect of the most common queries raised by caseworkers.

What is public family law?

7.4   Public family law includes special Children Act proceedings and 'public law children cases'. These are defined in regulation 2 of the Civil Legal Aid (Merits Criteria) Regulations 2012. The term 'special Children Act' covers applications for funding from a child, parent or other person with parental responsibility in cases under Children Act 1989 ss31, 43, 44 and 45, and applications from a child under section 25 (use of accommodation for restricting liberty) but not appeals from final orders made in cases under those sections.

7.5   'Public law children cases' are all other matters described in paras 1 and 9 of Schedule 1 to LASPO, including care, protection and supervision matters that are not special Children Act, and High Court inherent jurisdiction cases. It also includes parties other than the child or person with parental responsibility who are joined (or want to apply to be) to special Children Act cases.

7.6   Note that special guardianship orders are private law family (under Children Act 1989 Part II), so the client would need to provide evidence to satisfy domestic violence (Procedure reg 33) or child protection requirements (Procedure reg 34) to be in scope of legal aid.

7.7   LASPO Schedule 1 para 1 brings within scope:

(a) orders under section 25 of the Children Act 1989 ('the 1989 Act') (secure accommodation);

(b) orders under Part 4 of the 1989 Act (care and supervision);

(c) orders under Part 5 of the 1989 Act (protection of children);

(d) approval by a court under paragraph 19 of Schedule 2 to the 1989 Act (arrangements to assist children to live abroad);

(e) parenting orders under section 8 of the Crime and Disorder Act 1998 ('the 1998 Act');

(f) child safety orders under section 11 of the 1998 Act;

(g) orders for contact under section 26 of the Adoption and Children Act 2002 ('the 2002 Act');

(h) applications for leave of the court to remove a child from a person's custody under section 36 of the 2002 Act;

(i) placement orders, recovery orders or adoption orders under Chapter 3 of Part 1 of the 2002 Act (see sections 21, 41 and 46 of that Act);

(j) orders under section 84 of the 2002 Act (parental responsibility prior to adoption abroad).

7.8   LASPO Schedule 1 para 9 brings within scope:

(1) Civil legal services provided in relation to the inherent jurisdiction of the High Court in relation to children ...[1]

See appendix D for a list of work that falls within the Family category under the legal aid standard contract.

7.9   Where appropriate, you will be referred back to chapter 5, as that chapter sets out the general rules.

Scope

7.10   See chapter 5 for information on the following:

- what to do if your client has received previous advice from another organisation;
- what to do if your client has received previous advice from your organisation;
- clients from abroad or clients who are abroad;
- clients who are children

For exceptional case funding for cases that are out of scope under LASPO see chapter 4.

Controlled work and licensed work

7.11   Controlled work is granted by solicitors according to rules under the Standard Contract 2013. It is called 'controlled' because the LAA controls the number of matter starts which are allowed each year. The

---

1 Vulnerable adults are also within scope but not in the family category.

kinds of controlled work that are relevant to family practitioners are Legal Help and Family Help (Lower). Help at Court is not available in family work.

7.12   You need a representation certificate, sometimes known as a legal aid certificate, to represent a client in legal proceedings. This is called licensed work, as the practice has a general licence to do such work, and numbers of matter starts are not limited. Certificates may be granted by the LAA, or, in urgent circumstances, granted as a delegated function, by the organisation.

Public family law – controlled work

Legal Help – level 1

Scope

7.13   This covers initial (ie pre-proceedings) advice and assistance in relation to any kind of public law family case, including the consequential letters to the client and any letters to a third party.

7.14   However, it is not designed to cover attending child protection conferences as a matter of course. The LAA believes that legal advice is only required in 'exceptional circumstances'.[2] If you attend a child protection conference, you will need to ensure that this is fully justified on your attendance note.

Merits test

7.15   The 'sufficient benefit test' applies to Legal Help: 'there is likely to be sufficient benefit to the individual, having regard to all the circumstances of the case, including the circumstances of the individual, to justify the cost of provision of legal help'.[3] The question is whether a reasonable private paying client of moderate means would pay for the work.[4] It is hard to think of circumstances where it would not be met in such cases.

Financial eligibility

7.16   Legal Help is means tested, even in relation to care cases.

---

2 Family Fee Scheme Guidance (excluding advocacy), February 2012 para 3.2
3 Civil Legal Aid (Merits Criteria) Regulations 2013 reg 32(b).
4 Civil Legal Aid (Merits Criteria) Regulations 2013 reg 7.

7.17 See chapter 3 for more information on the following:

- passporting benefits;
- assessment of capital;
- assessment of income;
- reassessment of means.

7.18 See chapter 5 for more information on the following:

- evidence of means;
- when you can start work without evidence of means;
- reassessing the client's eligibility if their means change significantly.

Forms

7.19 The form is the CW1 Legal Help, Help at Court and Family Help (Lower) form.

7.20 The assessment of means and client's details sections must be fully completed, and signed by the client, normally in the presence of someone from your organisation, before you start doing any legal work.[5]

How many Legal Help forms?

7.21 You can have more than one Legal Help matter open at the same time, but only if they relate to entirely separate family disputes where any proceedings would be issued and heard separately.[6] The LAA gives the example where there is a public law Legal Help matter in relation to concerns raised by the local authority and also a private law matter in relation to a divorce.[7]

Funding

7.22 Legal Help – level 1 is paid as a standard fee.[8] Cases that exceed three times the fixed fee when calculated at hourly rates can be claimed in full (see chapter 13 for more information about claiming escape cases).

---

5 Standard Civil Contract Specification 2013 para 3.10.
6 Standard Civil Contract Specification 2013 para 3.31.
7 Costs Assessment Guidance 2013 Appendix 1 'Family Fee Scheme Guidance (excluding advocacy)' para 2.4.
8 Current fees and hourly rates are found in the Civil Legal Aid (Remuneration) Regulations 2013.

Family Help (Lower) – level 2

Scope

7.23   This level of funding covers advice and other work for parents or those with parental responsibility. It is intended that the focus of work at this level is on negotiation with the local authority to resolve disputes under the President's Public Law Outline. Therefore, it covers cases where the local authority has issued a notice of its intention to issue proceedings; but no proceedings have yet been issued.

7.24   The letter before proceedings may suggest that a meeting is held between the client and the local authority to discuss the concerns raised in the letter and level 2 will cover attending this meeting (sometimes called 'a family meeting') with the client.

Extract from the Standard Civil Contract Specification 2013

7.25   The Standard Civil Contract Specification 2013 para 7.38 states:

> **Payment for Family Help (Lower)**
> 7.38 A determination that a Client qualifies for Family Help (Lower) may only be made where all criteria at Regulation 35 of the Merits Regulations are satisfied. In addition, in Public Law Work remuneration for Family Help (Lower) may only be claimed where the following conditions are satisfied:
> (a) the Local Authority has given written notice of potential s31 Care Proceedings in accordance with the DCSF/Welsh Assembly government guidance issued under the Children Act 1989 guidance and regulations, Volume 1, but no proceedings have yet been issued (application for an Emergency Protection Order does not count as issue of proceedings for this purpose);
> (b) your Client is a Parent (as defined above);
> (c) your Client requires advice and assistance with a view to avoiding the proceedings, or narrowing and resolving any issues with the Local Authority.

Merits test

7.26   Family Help (Lower) is not merits tested in public family law, as long as the requirements of para 7.38 (reproduced above) are met.

Financial eligibility

7.27   Family Help (Lower) is not means tested in public family law.

Forms

7.28 There is a separate form for level 2 in public family law – the CW1PL. It is designed to be used in relation to advice after the local authority has issued its notice of intention to issue proceedings (advice prior to this is covered under the CW1 Legal Help form). Key points are:

- It is not means tested.
- It has a box that allows you to record that the criteria for advice at level 2 were met.
- The local authority's notice of intention to issue proceedings must be attached to it.

In these cases, you tick the box at the top of page 2 of the Family Help (Lower) Public Law form, and attach a copy of the notice to show that the criteria are met.

Funding

7.29 Family Help (Lower) level 2 is paid as a standard fee. Whether you can claim it depends on the local authority issuing written notice of their intention to issue proceedings. This can be in an email, as long as the wording is unambiguous.

Exceptional cases

7.30 A case escapes the fixed fee in public law matters where the costs of all levels of advice provided at controlled work, calculated at hourly rates,[9] exceed three times the relevant fees. Therefore, where level 1 and level 2 advice has been provided, costs calculated at an hourly rate must exceed three times the level 1 and level 2 fees combined. If advice has only been provided at either level 1 or level 2, the exceptional limit will be three times the fees for that level of service.

Closing controlled work matters

7.31 For information about when you can or should close a case, see chapter 5.

---

9 Set out in the Civil Legal Aid (Remuneration) Regulations 2013.

Certificates – public law cases

Scope

7.32   A representation certificate in family public law can only be granted when the local authority issues proceedings, and is therefore usually granted initially as an emergency certificate as a delegated function. It authorises the conduct of litigation and the provision of advocacy and representation.

Certificates

7.33   An application for funding in special Children Act cases is granted automatically, without reference to means or merits. An application to extend the scope of the certificate to cover related proceedings (for example, to make an application for a residence or contact order within the care proceedings, or to include representation in any other related proceedings which are being heard together) must be made, as the usual form of the certificate only covers proceedings under Children Act 1989 ss31, 43, 44 and 45, and applications from a child under section 27.

7.34   Apart from 'related proceedings', certificates in this area are kept completely separate from all other work. Therefore, a separate application must always be made – an ordinary certificate cannot be amended to cover special Children Act proceedings, and a special Children Act certificate cannot be amended to cover anything else.

7.35   The CIVAPP5 includes a question on whether separate representation is appropriate. Once funding has been granted, you have an ongoing duty to report any new information or changes of circumstance which might affect the terms of the certificate.[10]

Financial eligibility

7.36   Certificates in special Children Act proceedings are not means tested. Certificates in other public law Children cases are means tested, including interim care orders under section 38 of the Children Act 1989.[11]

7.37   See chapter 3 for information about the means test.

---

10   Civil Legal Aid (Procedure) Regulations 2012 reg 40(1)(a).
11   Civil Legal Aid (Financial Resources and Payment for Services) Regulations 2013 Pt 2 reg 5.

Merits test

7.38   Certificates in special Children Act proceedings are not merits tested.

7.39   Certificates in other public law children cases are subject to a limited merits test:[12]

- representation will be refused if:
  - alternative funding is available (eg in adoption, where the child is placed by the local authority who consent to the adoption, it would be reasonable to expect them to bear the costs of the application);
  - not necessary (for example, because of the involvement of other parties or a professional guardian);
  - it is unreasonable to provide representation, having regard to the importance of the case to the applicant; and
- if the applicant is making or supporting an appeal or application, the prospects of success of that appeal or application are:
  - moderate or better; or
  - borderline or poor, but it is necessary to determine that the prospects of success criterion is met to prevent a breach of the applicants ECHR or enforceable EU rights, or appropriate to do so in the circumstances of the case having regard to any risk that failure to do so would be such a breach.

Forms

7.40   You use CIVAPP5 for special Children Act proceedings and CIVAPP3 in other cases.

7.41   Apart from 'related proceedings', special Children Act certificates are kept completely separate from all other work. Therefore, a separate application must always be made – an ordinary certificate cannot be amended to cover special Children Act proceedings, and a special Children Act certificate cannot be amended to cover anything else.

Funding

7.42   Representation in respect of a child, parent or joined party in care and supervision proceedings (Children Act 1989 s31) and related proceedings[13] is covered by a standard fee scheme. The fees are based

---

12 Civil Legal Aid (Merits Criteria) Regulations 2013 reg 66, amended by Civil Legal Aid (Merits Criteria) (Amendment) (No 2) Regulations 2015 reg 2(7).

13 Standard Civil Contract Specification 2013 para 7.33.

on the location of the solicitor's office and the nature and number of parties represented.

7.43   Fees refer to the LAA region where the fee earner was based during the case:

- Wales;
- London, Brighton, Reading and Bristol – all claim the 'London and South' fee;
- Birmingham, Nottingham and Cambridge – all claim the 'Midlands' fee;
- Newcastle, Leeds, Liverpool and Manchester – all claim the 'North' fee.

7.44   The standard fee scheme does not apply to other 'special Children Act proceedings', ie under section 25 (when a child is brought before the court and wishes to be separately represented), section 43 (a child assessment order), section 44 (an emergency protection order) and section 45 (extension or discharge of an emergency protection order).

7.45   It does not apply to other public law family proceedings, including appeals in special Children Act cases, and proceedings under Parts IV and V of the Children Act, as well as adoption and High Court inherent jurisdiction cases.[14]

7.46   In Children Act 1989 s31 cases, funding under the Graduated Fee Scheme for legal representation certificates covers all stages up to the conclusion of the proceedings in the first instance (including representation on any interim appeal and/or advice on the merits of an appeal against a final order). Where legal representation is granted to defend or bring an appeal against a final order, it is paid by way of hourly rates.[15]

7.47   Other public law family certificated cases are funded under hourly rates.

7.48   The rates were reduced by 10 per cent for cases started on or after 22 April 2014, and so the current hourly rates and fees are set out in the Civil Legal Aid (Remuneration) (Amendment) (No 2) Regulations 2014.

Advocacy under standard fees

7.49   The standard fees do not include advocacy. Where advocacy is provided, whether by counsel or a solicitor advocate, the claim is made

14   Standard Civil Contract Specification 2013 para 7.34.
15   Standard Civil Contract Specification 2013 para 7.51.

under the Family Advocacy Scheme (FAS), which applies to cases where the certificate was granted following an application made on or after 9 May 2011 (see chapter 16 for more information).

7.50   The LAA include the following activities under the definition of advocacy for the purposes of the FAS preparation for advocacy:

- appearances as advocate before the court;
- travel to and from court and waiting time;
- attendances by the advocate at court, including attendance at advocates meetings.

7.51   If you are a solicitor carrying out advocacy, it is helpful to keep a separate file for this aspect of the case as it helps you keep track of the advocacy fees to be charged on top of the applicable standard fee for other work. It also helps you identify when to apply for an increase in the financial limitation on the certificate as this includes all profit costs as well as disbursements, advocacy fees and VAT.

Applying for a certificate – urgent cases

7.52   Unless otherwise notified, under paragraph 7.41 of the Standard Civil Contract Specification 2013 you have a delegated function to grant legal representation in special Children Act cases. The CIVAPP5 should be completed and in addition, the delegated functions section on page 5 of that form must be completed, stating the date on which the delegated function was exercised and confirming that the criterion as to separate representation is met.

7.53   See chapter 5 for more information about delegated functions, and also about:

- amendments to certificates;
- refusals and appeals;
- use of counsel and amendments for a QC;
- changes to prospects of success or cost–benefit;
- disbursements and prior authority;
- contributions;
- high-cost cases;
- ending a case;
- discharge of certificate;
- revocation of certificate.

7.54   See chapter 13 for information about getting paid in family cases.

Family mediation

Introduction

8.1   This chapter deals with mediation; but mainly from the point of view of a lawyer, rather than a mediator or client. There is increased emphasis on resolving disputes through mediation rather than litigation, regardless of the way that cases are funded.

8.2   Used well, and complemented by legal advice, mediation helps clients find a solution to their problems in a more positive way. From April 2013, when LASPO took effect, mediation and Help with Family Mediation, (see chapter 6, para 6.57) are the only legal aid services available to clients seeking to resolve private family disputes, unless the client is the victim of domestic abuse, or likely to be so, or there is evidence of child protection concerns (see chapter 6).

Scope

8.3   There are two types of mediation that can be funded by the LAA:

- family mediation, where the LAA funds the mediator directly; and
- non-family mediation, which can be funded as a disbursement under both Legal Help and representation certificates.[1]

8.4   Family mediation has its own Specification in the Standard Contract 2010, which can be downloaded from www.gov.uk/government/publications/standard-civil-contract-2010. The Specification is dated 1 April 2013. There is a detailed guidance document at www.gov.uk/government/uploads/system/uploads/attachment_data/file/419977/mediation-guidance-manual-mar-2015.pdf.

8.5   The scheme includes the following:

- mediation information and assessment meetings (MIAMs) (which may be attended by one or both parties);
- mediation:
  - all issues mediation;
  - child mediation;
  - property and financial mediation.

8.6   The Children and Families Act 2014 was implemented on 22 April 2014. This makes it compulsory for people seeking to make applications in certain family proceedings to attend a mediation information

---

1   Civil Costs Assessment Guidance 2013 para 3.6.

and assessment meeting (MIAM) before making an application unless they are exempt. The legal requirement is for the applicant to attend, and respondents are expected to do so.

Financial eligibility

8.7   In non-family mediation, the means test is carried out as usual for the type of funding – Legal Help or a representation certificate (see chapter 3).

8.8   In family mediation, the mediator carries out the eligibility test. If one of the parties qualifies for legal aid, then the cost of the MIAM will be met by the LAA.

8.9   Family mediation is means tested; but from 3 November 2014 non-financially eligible parties were exempted from the financial means test in respect of the first mediation session where the other party is financially eligible for legal aid.[2] The LAA will pay half a single session fee for the non-eligible party.

8.10   For all subsequent mediation sessions, legal aid is only available for the party eligible for legal aid. The idea is that the free 'taster' session will encourage the non-financially eligible party to fund their own mediation from then on.

Merits test

8.11   Mediation beyond the MIAM will only be provided where the mediator is satisfied that mediation is suitable in all the circumstances of the case.[3]

Forms

8.12   Family mediation is controlled work. The application form is the CW5.

8.13   There are no forms for non-family mediation as this is claimed as a disbursement.

---

2   Civil Legal Aid (Financial Resources and Payment for Services) (Amendment) (No 2) Regulations 2014.
3   Civil Legal Aid (Merits) Regulations 2012 reg 37.

Funding

8.14   Where the parties are willing and the issues are suitable, the mediation should be able to deal with all the issues arising, including explanation of the law (but not advice), and disclosure.

8.15   From the client's point of view, family mediation is advantageous, as it is exempt from the statutory charge.

8.16   Robert Clerke, solicitor and mediator, has explained the stages of mediation in a typical family case:[4]

- setting the agenda/identification of the issues;
- disclosure;
- identification and exploration of options;
- impasse, and strategies to break through it;
- reality testing;
- recording the outcome – hopefully a memorandum of understanding (MOU) and, where appropriate, an open financial statement (OFS).

8.17   A lawyer is needed to advise on the law and draw up the consent order and statement of information for the court: see Help with Family Mediation – chapter 6, para 6.58.

4 *Carter survival handbook*, Quay Books, 2007, chapter 5.

CHAPTER 9

Conducting an immigration case

by Solange Valdez

continued

Introduction

9.1 This chapter deals with work funded under the immigration and asylum category of law. You should read it in conjunction with chapters 3, 4 and 5. Chapter 3 deals with general rules about taking on civil cases, and applies to work in immigration and asylum as it does to all other work. Chapter 4 deals with exceptional cases, many of which are immigration cases. Chapter 5 deals with the rules that apply to the conduct of all civil cases. The immigration and asylum-specific rules in this chapter usually build on, rather than replace, the general rules; where they do replace the general rules in chapters 3 and 5 we will say so.

9.2 See appendices H and I for a summary of the Legal Aid Agency's (LAA's) Costs Assessment Guidance, in respect of the most common queries raised by caseworkers.

What immigration work is in scope of legal aid?

9.3 The 2013 Category Definitions define asylum and immigration as work covered by LASPO Sch 1 Pt 1 paras 24 to 30, 32 and 45, together with any section 10 exceptional funding granted where the primary legal issue is immigration.

9.4 Save for where specific reference is made, you can advise and assist on the following issues under your legal aid immigration and asylum contract:

Asylum[1]
- Rights to enter and remain arising from:
  - the Refugee Convention;
  - articles 2 and 3 ECHR;
  - the Temporary Protection Directive;[2]
  - the Qualification Directive.[3]

9.5 The above will include:
- controlled work done on an asylum issue related to Special Immigration Appeals Commission (SIAC) proceedings;[4]

---

1 LASPO Sch 1 Part 1 para 30.
2 Council Directive 2001/55/EC.
3 Council Directive 2004/83/EC.
4 Standard Civil Contract Specification 2013 para 8.7(b).

- an application for indefinite leave to remain (ILR) under the Refugee Settlement Protection policy;
- an application for leave to remain on the basis of serious medical conditions which reaches the article 3 (ECHR) threshold.

Family reunion for refugees

9.6   The LAA had always interpreted LASPO as putting family reunion cases out of scope. However, in *Gudanaviciene and others v Director of Legal Aid Casework and The Lord Chancellor*,[5] Collins J said that it was in scope as a right arising from the Refugee Convention. That ruling was later overturned by the Court of Appeal,[6] which confirmed that family reunion was out of scope of legal aid. At the time of writing, it seems that an application for permission to appeal that point to the Supreme Court remains undecided.[7]

9.7   However, the Court of Appeal was in agreement with the High Court that the respondent's family reunion case was particularly complex and that failure to provide exceptional funding would amount to a breach of article 8 (ECHR), and so exceptional funding would be appropriate.

9.8   In response to Collins J, the LAA announced on 24 July 2014 interim arrangements pending a decision from the Court of Appeal whereby immigration matters to be opened for family reunion work.[8] Following the Court of Appeal ruling on 15 December 2014, the LAA issued a statement confirming that family reunion work could no longer be conducted under legal aid unless an application for exceptional case funding had been approved.[9] Any work done after 15 December 2014 will not be remunerated unless exceptional case funding has been granted. This includes, work done on a matter opened before that date.[10]

---

5   [2014] EWHC 1840 (Admin).
6   [2014] EWCA Civ 1622.
7   See Meredith and Pickup, 'Grayling stalls over changes to exceptional funding' May 2015 *Legal Action* 14, footnote 5.
8   http://webarchive.nationalarchives.gov.uk/20130128112038/http:/www.justice. gov.uk/legal-aid/newslatest-updates/civil-news/update-on-refugee-family-reunion-work.
9   www.gov.uk/government/news/exceptional-legal-aid-funding-for-immigration-cases).
10 See www.ilpa.org.uk/resource/30608/ilpa-to-legal-aid-agency-of-21-january-2015-re-refugee-family-reunion (ILPA members access only).

Detention, temporary admission and restrictions

9.9   You can provide advice and assistance to an individual solely in relation to detention[11] under immigration powers, such as applications for bail and temporary admission.[12] You will not be able to claim for any non-detention work as part of the case unless this is itself in scope of immigration or asylum legal aid.

9.10   You can provide advice and assistance on temporary admission to a person who has been released from detention or to a person who has been granted temporary admission and has been given restrictions and conditions, such as restriction to reside at a fixed address, reporting and employment.[13]

9.11   You can provide advice and assistance on residence and restrictions[14] to a person who has leave to enter or remain and has made an asylum claim.[15] You can also advise on residence and restrictions to a person who has been recommended for deportation by the court.[16]

9.12   In most cases, only the detention etc. issue is in scope, not the substantive immigration case. For example, a person subject to deportation following a criminal conviction is entitled to legal aid in respect of his or her detention or residence restrictions, but not in respect of deportation advice and proceedings themselves. You will need to be careful on your file to justify that work done is genuinely in relation to the in-scope aspects, such as where it is necessary to consider the immigration history or offences leading to the deportation in order to assess bail or temporary admission and restrictions.

Victims of domestic violence – applications for indefinite leave to remain

9.13   You can provide advice and assistance to a victim of domestic violence in an application for indefinite leave to remain[17] if the person has been granted leave to remain as a spouse or partner of a British or settled person in the UK and the relationship has broken down permanently due to domestic violence. This will include a person

---

11 LASPO Sch 1 Pt 1 para 25.
12 LASPO Sch 1 Pt 1 para 26.
13 See Immigration Act (IA) 1971 Sch 2 para 21 and Nationality, Immigration and Asylum Act (NIAA) 2002 s62.
14 LASPO Sch 1 Pt 1 para 27.
15 See NIAA 2002 s71.
16 See IA 1971 Sch 3 para 2(5) or 4.
17 LASPO Sch 1 Pt 1 para 28.

who has been granted leave to enter or remain outside the immigration rules as a partner or spouse of a British or settled person in the UK (eg victims with leave to enter outside the immigration rules or with discretionary leave to remain).[18] This is so long as the advice and assistance is solely in relation to an application for ILR under the domestic violence provisions.

9.14   The time you spent advising and assisting a victim with an application under the three-month Destitute Domestic Violence Concession (DDVC) can also be claimed as part of the substantive ILR application.

9.15   Other than the above, the fact that the applicant is a victim of domestic violence does **NOT** generally entitle them to legal aid for immigration advice (eg victims with partners and spouses on short term leave). You will also not be able to advise a person who has leave to remain as a partner or spouse of a person in the armed forces who has leave to remain.

Victims of domestic violence – residence cards (EEA regulations)

9.16   You can provide advice and assistance in relation to an application for a residence card[19] to a person who has ceased to be a family member on the termination of a marriage/partnership (ie only if divorced), who was a victim of domestic violence or was a family member of the victim and the violence took place during the time that the marriage was subsisting.[20]

9.17   Other than the above, the fact that the applicant is a victim of domestic violence does **NOT** generally entitled them to legal aid for immigration advice (eg those family members not divorced from their EEA spouse or those in durable relationships who were never married to EEA nationals in the first place).

---

18 Applications made under Immigration Rules appendix FM (Family Members), DVILR para 289A and appendix (Armed Forces) para 39(b)(i).

19 LASPO Sch 1 Pt 1 para 29.

20 Applications for residence cards made under regulation 17 and 16 in connection with retaining right to reside under reg 10(5)(d)(iv) of the Immigration (EEA) Regulations 2006 SI No 1003.

Definition of domestic violence under LASPO

9.18 Domestic violence means

> ... any incident, or pattern of incidents, of controlling, coercive or threatening behaviour, violence or abuse (whether psychological, physical, sexual, financial or emotional) between individuals who are associated with each other (within the meaning of section 62 of the Family Law Act 1996).[21]

Victims of trafficking in human beings

9.19 You can provide advice and assistance in relation to applications for leave to enter or remain by a victim of trafficking.[22] However, in order for you to assist there must either be a conclusive determination that the person is a victim or have 'reasonable grounds' to believe that the person is a victim and there has been no conclusive negative determination.

9.20 There is no legal aid available to assist a person in the process of ascertaining whether s/he is a victim of trafficking by way of an application to the first respondent or to the competent authority.[23]

9.21 There is no time restriction on the availability of funding to assist a person who has been determined as a victim of trafficking by the competent authority under controlled work.[24] However, in licensed work, there is a time restriction of twelve months from the date of determination that the person is a victim or before the end of any leave outside the rules granted to the victim.[25]

Where a client has been determined as a victim of trafficking and is also making an asylum claim, you will need to treat the asylum work and any 'associated' or 'additional' application for leave to

---

21 LASPO Sch 1 Pt 1 paras 28(5) and 29(4) as amended.

22 Note that only LASPO Sch 1 Pt 1 para 32(1) comes within the immigration category; the other civil claims referred to in para 32(2) and (3) are in the miscellaneous work category and therefore can only be carried out by providers whose schedule authorises miscellaneous work (see para 37 of the Category Definitions 2013).

23 *R (Gudanaviciene and others) v Director of Legal Aid Casework and The Lord Chancellor* [2014] EWCA Civ 1622.

24 Frequently asked questions, Civil Legal Aid Reforms v1.3 para 57 – no longer on the LAA website but available at http://legalaidhandbook.files.wordpress.com/2013/04/legal-aid-reform-faq-v3.pdf.

25 Civil Legal Aid (Procedure) Regulations 2012 reg 31(8).

remain on human rights grounds as one asylum matter start under the Immigration specification.[26]

Victims of slavery, servitude or forced or compulsory labour

9.22   From 31 July 2015, you can provide advice and assistance in relation to applications for leave to enter or remain by victims of slavery, servitude or forced compulsory labour.[27] Similar to victims of trafficking, in order for you to assist there must either be a conclusive determination that the person is a victim or have 'reasonable grounds' to believe that the person is a victim and there has been no conclusive determination that the person is not a such a victim. The meaning of 'slavery', 'servitude' and 'forced or compulsory labour' have the same meaning as they have for the purposes of article 4 ECHR.

Special Immigration Appeals Commission (SIAC)

9.23   Advice and assistance including representation to a person in relation to an appeal before the Special Immigration Appeals Commission (SIAC)[28] is in scope. This may normally involve controlled work under Legal Help for any initial advice and licensed work for any preparation and representation on a SIAC appeal.

Terrorism prevention and investigation measures etc

9.24   Advice, assistance and representation to a person in relation to notices and control orders proceedings under the Terrorism Prevention and Investigation Measures Act 2011 is in scope.[29]

Advocacy

9.25   Representation in immigration and asylum cases that are in scope will also be in scope for legal work before the First-tier and Upper

26 Standard Civil Contract Specification 2013 para 8.3.1, see also para 56 of Frequently asked questions, Civil Legal Aid Reforms, available at http://legalaidhandbook.files.wordpress.com/2013/04/legal-aid-reform-faq-v3.pdf.

27 LASPO Sch 1 Pt 1 para 32A. See also Standard Civil Contract Specification 2013 para 8.8 as amended in July 2015.

28 LASPO Sch 1 Pt 1 para 24.

29 LASPO Sch 1 Pt 1 para 45.

Tribunal appeals and bail hearings. Any advocacy[30] in the High Court, Court of Appeal and Supreme Court is only in scope if arising out of in scope services.[31]

9.26 Advocacy in the First-tier Tribunal and the Upper Tribunal is also available in appeals where a person is being deprived of British citizenship under section 40A of the British Nationality Act 1981 and rights of residence under regulation 26 of the Immigration (EEA) regulations 2006. However, this is only to the extent that the appeal concerns a contravention of the Equality Act 2010.

Judicial review

9.27 Judicial review is in scope by virtue of LASPO Schedule 1, Part 1, para 19(1), but there are specific restrictions in immigration cases, set out in paras 19(5) to 19(8):

> (5) The services described in sub-paragraph (1) [judicial review] do not include services provided in relation to judicial review in respect of an issue relating to immigration where–
>> (a) the same issue, or substantially the same issue, was the subject of a previous judicial review or an appeal to a court or tribunal,
>> (b) on the determination of the previous judicial review or appeal (or, if there was more than one, the latest one), the court, tribunal or other person hearing the case found against the applicant or appellant on that issue, and
>> (c) the services in relation to the new judicial review are provided before the end of the period of 1 year beginning with the day of that determination.
>
> (6) The services described in sub-paragraph (1) do not include services provided in relation to judicial review of removal directions in respect of an individual where the directions were given not more than 1 year after the latest of the following–
>> (a) the making of the decision (or, if there was more than one, the latest decision) to remove the individual from the United Kingdom by way of removal directions;
>> (b) the refusal of leave to appeal against that decision;
>> (c) the determination or withdrawal of an appeal against that decision.

9.28 Despite these restrictions, judicial review is still permitted in fresh asylum claims and other certified cases (effectively where there would be no appeal to the immigration tribunal against the decision):

---

30 LASPO Sch 1 Pt 3 paras 1, 2 and 3.
31 LASPO Sch 1 Pt 3 paras 8 and 19.

(7) Sub-paragraphs (5) and (6) do not exclude services provided to an individual in relation to–

   (a) judicial review of a negative decision in relation to an asylum application (within the meaning of the EU Procedures Directive[32]) where there is no right of appeal to the First-tier Tribunal against the decision;

   (b) judicial review of certification under section 94[33] or 96[34] of the Nationality, Immigration and Asylum Act 2002 (certificate preventing or restricting appeal of immigration decision).

(8) Sub-paragraphs (5) and (6) do not exclude services provided in relation to judicial review of removal directions in respect of an individual where prescribed conditions relating to either or both of the following are met–

   (a) the period between the individual being given notice of the removal directions and the proposed time for his or her removal;

   (b) the reasons for proposing that period.

9.29   It is important to be clear about what funding is being sought for in judicial review cases, and to ensure that the work is in scope and is not excluded under the above provisions. You will need to ensure that this is clearly spelt out in all funding applications to the LAA.

9.30   It is expected that all internal reviews and appeals are exhausted before any refusal of funding is challenged in court proceedings.[35]

Exceptional case funding

9.31   An exceptional case funding application to fund work not in scope may be made under LASPO s10, but only where you can demonstrate the test is met:

   (a) that it is necessary to make the services available to the individual ... because failure to do so would be a breach of–

      (i) the individual's Convention rights (within the meaning of the Human Rights Act 1998), or

      (ii) any rights of the individual to the provision of legal services that are enforceable EU rights, or

---

32 Council Directive 2005/85/EC of 1 December 2005 on minimum standards on procedures in Member States for granting and withdrawing refugee status.

33 Unfounded human rights or asylum claims.

34 Certification on the basis of an earlier right of appeal.

35 *Rrapaj and others v Director of Legal Aid Casework* [2013] EWHC 1837 (Admin).

(b) that it is appropriate to do so, in the particular circumstances of the case, having regard to any risk that failure to do so would be such a breach.[36]

9.32   In his original exceptional case funding guidance, the Lord Chancellor did not consider that immigration cases would come within the ambit of exceptional funding. In *R (Gudanaviciene) v Director of Legal Aid Casework*,[37] the Court of Appeal held that certain paragraphs of this guidance were incompatible with article 6(1) ECHR and with article 47 of the Charter of Fundamental Rights of the European Union and incompatible with article 8 ECHR in immigration cases.

9.33   The court in *Gudanaviciene* also held that whether funding should be granted will depend on the facts of the case, including the importance and complexity of the issues and the person's ability to act on his/her own without legal assistance and any language difficulties. Since there is no appeal (beyond review by the Director) against an exceptional case funding determination,[38] any challenge on a refusal of funding would be by way of judicial review.

9.34   Some six months after the Court of Appeal handed down its judgment, the Lord Chancellor issued new guidance[39] which was amended to take account of *Gudanaviciene*, though does so in a way that tries to minimise its impact. Before making any application for exceptional funding you should carefully consider the judgment as well as the revised guidance (see chapter 4 for more on exceptional cases).

What is an immigration or asylum matter?

9.35   Paragraphs 8.7 and 8.8 of section 8 of the Standard Civil Contract Specification 2013 divide work in the immigration category into asylum and immigration matter types.

9.36   It is important that you correctly report open and claim matters as asylum or immigration, both as part of your contractual obligation but also because the funding limits are different. The contract says:

---

36   LASPO s10(3).
37   [2014] EWCA Civ 1622.
38   Civil Legal Aid (Procedure) Regulations 2012 reg 69.
39   www.gov.uk/government/uploads/system/uploads/attachment_data/file/433486/legal-aid-chancellor-non-inquests.pdf.

Contract Work covered by this Specification

8.7 For the purposes of Controlled Work, a Matter should proceed and be reported under this Specification as an *'Asylum Matter'* where:

(a) it relates to civil legal services in respect of the rights set out in paragraph 30 of Part 1 of Schedule 1 of the Act ('Immigration: rights to enter and remain');

(b) it relates to an asylum issue and is proceeding under paragraph 24 of Part 1 of Schedule 1 to the Act ('Special Immigration Appeals Commission').

8.8 For the purposes of Controlled Work, a Matter should proceed and be reported as an *'Immigration Matter'* where it relates to civil legal services in respect of the rights mentioned in:

(a) paragraph 25 of Part 1 of Schedule 1 to the Act ('Immigration: detention');

(b) paragraph 26 of Part 1 of Schedule 1 to the Act ('Immigration: temporary admission');

(c) paragraph 27 of Part 1 of Schedule 1 to the Act ('Immigration: residence etc restrictions);

(d) paragraph 28 of Part 1 of Schedule 1 to the Act ('Immigration: victims of domestic violence and indefinite leave to remain');

(e) paragraph 29 of Part 1 of Schedule 1 to the Act ('Immigration: victims of domestic violence and residence cards');

(f) paragraph 32 of Part 1 of Schedule 1 to the Act (Victims of trafficking in human beings') insofar as civil legal services relate to an application by the individual for leave to enter, or to remain in, the United Kingdom;

(g) paragraph 24 of Part 1 of Schedule 1 to the Act ('Special Immigration Appeals Commission') where it relates to an immigration issue;

(h) paragraph 45 of Part 1 of Schedule 1 to the Act ('Terrorism prevention and investigation measures etc').

Who can do the work?

Individual caseworkers

9.37   Immigration work is unique in legal aid in being completely subject to an accreditation scheme. Other areas of legal aid also use accreditation, for example to qualify as a supervisor, and even restrict work by accreditation, for example criminal police station work, but only immigration funding is subject to a category-wide restriction.

9.38   Unless you are accredited, you cannot be paid for doing any legal aid work in the immigration category at all.[40] There are several levels of accreditation:

- Probationary;
- Level 1 accredited caseworker;
- Level 2 senior caseworker;
- Level 3 advanced caseworker;
- Accredited supervisor.

Type of contract work	Level of accreditation/other restriction
Conduct of Legal Help matters	Level 1 accredited and above
Use of delegated functions to grant Controlled Legal Representation (CLR) and conduct of CLR cases	Level 2 accredited and above
All contract work carried out for an unaccompanied asylum-seeking child	Level 2 accredited and above and must hold an enhanced Criminal Records Bureau check carried out within the last 24 months
All work carried out at an immigration removal centre under the detained fast track scheme or at an on-site surgery	Level 2 accredited and above
Acting as a designated supervisor	Accredited supervisor

9.39   What work can be done by caseworkers of each level is defined by the contract and the accreditation work restrictions.

9.40   In this context, 'conduct' means 'having responsibility and control for the progression of the case'.[41] So a level 1 fee earner can carry out tasks on an appeal conducted by a level 2 fee earner, whereas all work on the file of an unaccompanied child must be carried out by a level 2 fee earner.

9.41   In addition to that broad rule, you must comply with the work restrictions,[42] which unfortunately no longer appear on the main

40 Standard Civil Contract Specification 2013 para 8.15.
41 Standard Civil Contract Specification 2013 para 8.21.
42 Standard Civil Contract Specification 2013 para 8.15(b).

LAA website.[43] The restrictions specify tasks that are restricted by accreditation level. Probationers may only carry out the listed tasks; level 1 caseworkers cannot deal with certain types of cases, such as vulnerable clients or disputed nationality cases. Work done by level 3 caseworkers attracts an uplift of 5 per cent on the payment rates, but only on controlled work paid at hourly rates.[44]

9.42   The 2013 contract (para 8.17) requires each of your offices to maintain a ratio of at least one full-time equivalent level 2 caseworker for every two level 1 caseworkers.

Organisations

9.43   Only those organisations with a contract in immigration can do work in the category. The LAA has also restricted certain types of work to organisations that have special permission to do it – they hold an Exclusive Schedule in addition to their Standard Contract Schedule setting out the restricted work they can do. Unless your organisation has an exclusive Immigration Removal Centre contract with the LAA,[45] you will not be able to carry out any controlled work at any Immigration Removal Centre (IRC) which operates under an exclusive legal aid detention contract.[46] Regrettably, the current list of exclusive contract IRCs providers is not on the Legal Aid Agency website.[47] Providers with an exclusive detention contract have either a contract to carry out work by way of an onsite surgery or a Detention Fast Track contract or both.[48] The exclusive contract does not apply to licensed work (ie work that is in scope and that is carried out under a funding certificate in higher court proceedings).

9.44   However, you can continue to advise and assist an existing client under asylum and immigration controlled work, where you have already carried out five hours or more of work before your client was detained[49] or where the person in detention is a close family member

---

43   An archived version may be found here: http://webarchive.nationalarchives.gov.uk/20140604173139/http://www.justice.gov.uk/downloads/legal-aid/civil-categories-of-law/ias-accreditation-scheme.pdf.

44   Standard Civil Contract Specification 2013 para 8.79.

45   Standard Civil Contract Specification 2013 paras 8.46–8.48.

46   Standard Civil Contract Specification 2013 para 8.6.

47   The most up to date list is April 2014 and can be found in the LAA website archive: http://webarchive.nationalarchives.gov.uk/20140711191156/http://www.justice.gov.uk/downloads/legal-aid/civil-categories-of-law/irc-provider-list-april-2014.pdf.

48   Standard Civil Contract Specification 2013 para 8.5.

49   Standard Civil Contract Specification 2013 para 8.6(b).

of your existing client and your knowledge of the family's circumstances is material to the detainee's case. A close family member of your client is defined as a spouse, partner, sibling, parent, grandparent or grandchild.[50]

Scope

9.45 See chapter 5 for information on the following:

- whether other funding may be available, and public funding should not granted;
- what to do if your client has received previous advice from another organisation;
- what to do if your client has received previous advice from your organisation;
- clients from abroad or clients who are abroad;
- clients who are children.

Structure of immigration work

9.46 In general. immigration work can be divided into four stages:

1) advice on Home Office/entry clearance applications;
2) appeals to the First-tier Tribunal;
3) appeals to the Upper Tribunal;
4) litigation in the Upper Tribunal and higher courts.

9.47 Stage 1 is funded by Legal Help. Stages 2 and 3 are funded by Controlled Legal Representation (CLR) (though different rules apply and it helps to think of them as different types of work), and stage 4 is funded by a certificate.

9.48 The Immigration Specification does not create any additional rules for certificated work in the higher courts, and this is therefore not dealt with to any great extent in this chapter.

9.49 The various funding types are consecutive as the case progresses. For example, where a client's application is refused, you should consider whether there is merit for CLR, and if so grant it. CLR should be applied for as soon as practicable after the right to appeal has arisen, and before the appeal is lodged.

---

50 Standard Civil Contract Specification 2013 para 8.6(a).

9.50   Once CLR is granted or refused, the Legal Help comes to an end and no further Legal Help work may be done on that matter.[51] Post-appeal work will form part of the CLR.[52]

9.51   Similarly, where you take an appeal to the Court of Appeal, the issue of a certificate to conduct the appeal brings the controlled work matter to an end. If the Court of Appeal then remits the case back to the Immigration and Asylum Chamber (IAC), a new matter start will be required to do the remitted appeal, which will be paid at hourly rates.[53] If during either Stage 1 or Stages 2 or 3, it is necessary to do work under a certificate while the relevant stage remains pending, then either the Legal Help or the CLR, as the case may be, may be kept open to deal with that work.

Fee types

9.52   Some immigration work is paid as standard fees, some at hourly rates. Different rules apply to standard fee work and hourly rates work, and it is therefore important to determine at the start of the case which is which.

9.53   Paragraph 8.77 of the 2013 Standard Civil Contract Specification lists all hourly rates work:

(a) Asylum Matters opened under this Contract which relate to an Asylum application (including 'NAM' or 'Legacy'), made to the UKBA prior to 1 October 2007;

(b) a fresh claim/further application for Asylum opened under this Contract where the original Asylum application was lodged, whether concluded or not, prior to 1 October 2007;

(c) advice in relation to the merits of lodging an application for permission to appeal to the Upper Tribunal (where advice has not been received under Stage 2 of the Standard Fee);

(d) CLR in relation to an application for permission to appeal and, appeals before the Upper Tribunal – see paragraphs 8.93 to 8.98;

(e) Bail applications;

(f) advice and applying for a determination that a Client qualifies for civil legal services provided as Licensed Work, including complying with any pre-action protocol;

(g) initial advice in relation to an Asylum application prior to claiming Asylum at the Asylum Screening Unit where you then cease to be instructed. This will also apply where the Client returns after attend-

---

51 Standard Civil Contract Specification 2013 para 8.63.
52 Standard Civil Contract Specification 2013 para 8.65(g).
53 Standard Civil Contract Specification 2013 para 8.77(j).

ance at the Asylum Screening Unit but where it is confirmed that the Client will be dispersed and will not continue to instruct you;

(h) Escape Fee Cases under the Standard Fee;

(i) advice in relation to a Client who is an UASC (unaccompanied asylum-seeking child);

(j) cases remitted, reviewed or referred from the Court of Appeal to the Upper Tribunal or the Upper Tribunal to the First-tier Tribunal;

(k) in relation to a Provider who holds an exclusive Schedule, any Matters opened as a result of an On Site Surgery or for a Fast Track Client;

(l) advice in relation to Terrorism Prevention and Investigation Measures Orders;

(m) applying for a determination that an individual qualifies for civil legal services provided as Licensed Work in relation to Terrorism Prevention and Investigation Measures; and

(n) applying for a determination that an individual qualifies for civil legal services provided as Licensed Work in relation to the Special Immigration Appeals Commission.

All other work not included in paragraph 8.77 is payable as standard fees.

9.54 Where the substantive matter is standard fee, nonetheless any bail, Upper Tribunal, remittals, applications for funding certificates and pre-action work under the same matter will always be paid at hourly rates. In this situation, the hourly rates work is an additional payment. By contrast, where the substantive matter is hourly rates, bail, applications for funding certificates and pre-action work all falls under the costs limit of the substantive matter. The costs limit for Upper Tribunal and remittals work is explained later in this chapter.

9.55 You should be especially careful when dealing with the case of an unaccompanied asylum-seeking child. If the child turns 18 before CLR is granted, the CLR work on this matter will be standard fee. The Legal Help work on this matter will still all be hourly rates. If the child turns 18 after CLR is granted, then both the Legal Help and CLR work on this matter will remain at hourly rates.

Matter starts and separate matters

9.56 A 'matter' is all work done on a single case for a client. A matter can pass through Legal Help and CLR and will still be treated as the same matter.

9.57 The following explains when only one matter should be opened and when more than one matter should be opened:

- An application and subsequent appeal is one matter.[54]
- Any human rights application associated with an asylum matter should be dealt with under that asylum matter.[55]
- A fresh application for asylum is a new matter.[56]
- Work in relation to preparation for and applying for a certificate for licensed work (including compliance with any pre-action protocol) may be dealt with under the relevant existing matter or by opening a new matter.[57]
- Where a client applies to enter or remain in the UK under more than one category, or applies to switch status while the first –application remains outstanding, this will be one matter,[58] but where the first application is at appeal stage and a different *additional* application is made, the second application will be a new matter.[59]
- If you are acting for several clients in relation to the same case, this should generally be one legal matter. For example, where you have an asylum claim with a principal applicant and a family member who is dependent then this should usually be one matter. However, if there need to be separate applications or appeals for each family member, then separate matters may be opened. To determine that separate applications or appeals are needed, you must consider that each family member has a separate and distinct legal interest for which there is sufficient benefit to justify a separate matter. For example, where the family members are claiming asylum each in their own right there should normally be separate matters.[60]

9.58   A second matter start for the same client would not be justified on the same case unless at least six months have elapsed since the first matter was closed, or unless at least three months have elapsed and there has been a material development or change in the client's instructions.[61] If the client fails to give instructions and you close the file, and then the client returns, that is not a change in instructions. A decision, response, etc from a third party to an application, represen-

54 Standard Civil Contract Specification 2013 para 8.29.
55 Standard Civil Contract Specification 2013 para 8.31.
56 Standard Civil Contract Specification 2013 para 8.32.
57 Standard Civil Contract Specification 2013 para 8.33.
58 Standard Civil Contract Specification 2013 para 8.34.
59 Standard Civil Contract Specification 2013 para 8.35.
60 Standard Civil Contract Specification 2013 para 3.39.
61 Standard Civil Contract Specification 2013 para 3.36.

tations, correspondence etc made in the first matter is not a material development.[62] Where further work is justified, but you cannot start a new matter under the rule, new disbursements can be claimed, as can profit costs if the case is an hourly rate case. You may claim new disbursements and profit costs if the case is an hourly rate case, or an escape fee case if the new work plus the old work would make it an escape fee claim.[63] However, note that the previous relevant upper costs and disbursements limits will apply and you will need to apply for extensions where necessary.

9.59   See chapter 3 for further information on how to report further work on a revived case and where a new matter would be justified.

Granting Legal Help

9.60   The Legal Help means test as set out in chapter 3 must be applied. The only difference in the immigration category is that support under Immigration and Asylum Act 1999 s4 or s95 is a passporting benefit.[64] In all controlled work cases, the means of minors should not be aggregated with those of the local authority.[65] Proof of means will be required. Many asylum-seekers and migrants without leave who are not in receipt of support will be accommodated and maintained by friends and relatives. Where that is the case, you will need to get proof, usually in the form of a letter signed by the person accommodating the client and setting out the nature and extent of support being given (and quantifying it if it includes money). It is very important the letter is signed and dated and makes it clear that the support has covered the whole of the month prior to the date the form was signed.[66] Letters which do not specify a time period since the support began have not been allowed as acceptable evidence of means at audit.

9.61   The merits test is the sufficient benefit test – see chapter 3 for further information on the means test, and chapter 5 for further information on the merits test.

---

62 Standard Civil Contract Specification 2013 para 3.37.
63 Standard Civil Contract Specification 2013 para 3.38.
64 Civil Legal Aid (Financial Resources and Payments for Services) Regulations 2013 reg 6(1).
65 *Guide to determining financial eligibility for Controlled work and Family mediation* (April 2014) v1 para 9.1.2.
66 See also *LAA Guide to Determining Financial Eligibility for Controlled Work and Family Mediation* para 12.2.16.

Granting Controlled Legal Representation (CLR)

9.62   CLR is subject to the means test. The test is the same as for Legal Help, except that the capital limit for CLR is £3,000 for all non-asylum appeal work, rather than the £8,000 that applies to all other levels of civil funding.[67] We know of no good reason as to why this provision should exist, but exist it does.

9.63   CLR has its own merits test, which is set out at regulation 60 of the Civil Legal Aid (Merits Criteria) Regulations 2013 and which should be applied under Legal Help[68] and kept in mind throughout once CLR has been granted. The test is, in addition to the standard criteria[69] (see chapter 5):

- if the case is not of significant wider public interest the reasonable private paying client test is met (reg 60(2)(a));
- if the case is of significant wider public interest, the proportionality test is met (reg 60(2)(b));

and, in either case, prospects of success are (reg 60(3)):[70]

    (a) very good, good or moderate; or
    (b) borderline or poor but it is–
        (i) necessary for the Director to determine that the criterion in this paragraph is met to prevent a breach of –
        (aa) the individual's Convention rights; or
        (bb) any rights of the individual to the provision of legal services that are enforceable EU rights; or
        (ii) appropriate for the Director to determine that the criterion in this paragraph is met, in the particular circumstances of the case, having regard to any risk that a failure to make such a determination would be such a breach; or
    (c) the prospects of success are unclear, and –
        (i) the case is of significant wider public interest;
        (ii) the case is one with overwhelming importance to the individual; or

---

67 Civil Legal Aid (Financial Resources and Payments for Services) Regulations 2013 reg 8(3) – the limit is £3,000 for work in scope under LASPO Sch 1 Pt 1 paras 25–29 and 32(1)(immigration) but £8,000 for all other work, including paras 30 and 31 (asylum and asylum support).

68 Standard Civil Contract Specification 2013 paras 8.62(c)–(d) and 8.102(a)(i).

69 Civil Legal Aid (Merits Criteria) Regulations 2013 SI No 104 reg 39(a)–(e).

70 Civil Legal Aid (Merits Criteria) Regulations 2013 reg 60(3) was amended by Civil Legal Aid (Merits Criteria) (Amendment) Regulations 2014 reg 2 on 27 January 2014 to delete the 'borderline' prospects of success category. The Civil Legal Aid (Merits Criteria) (Amendment) (No 2) Regulations 2015 reinstated the 'borderline' category on 27 July 2015.

(iii) the substance of the case relates to a breach of Convention rights.

'Unclear' means where there is further work to be carried out before making a reliable assessment on the prospect of success.[71]

9.64 Regulation 7 says:

... the reasonable private paying individual test is met if the Director is satisfied that the potential benefit to be gained from the provision of civil legal services justifies the likely costs, such that a reasonable private paying individual would be prepared to start or continue the proceedings having regard to the prospects of success and all the other circumstances of the case.

9.65 Regulation 8 says:

... the proportionality test is met if the Director is satisfied that the likely benefits of the proceedings to the individual and others justify the likely costs, having regard to the prospects of success and all the other circumstances of the case.

9.66 Regulation 6(1) says:

... a case is of significant wider public interest if the Director is satisfied that the case is an appropriate case to realise–
(a) real benefits to the public at large, other than those which normally flow from cases of the type in question; and
(b) benefits for an identifiable class of individuals, other than the individual to whom civil legal services may be provided or members of that individual's family.

9.67 Regulation 2 says:

... a case with overwhelming importance to the individual' means a case which is not primarily a claim for damages or other sum of money and which relates to one or more of the following –
(a) the life, liberty or physical safety of the individual or a member of that individual's family (an individual is a member of another individual's family if the requirements of section 10(6) are met); or
(b) the immediate risk that the individual may become homeless.

9.68 The merits test applies to both First-tier and Upper Tribunal appeals.

9.69 Where you are satisfied that the merits are either very good, good or moderate, you should sign the CLR form, and it is your signature (the client having already signed the form) that effects the grant since you are making the determination on behalf of the Director.[72]

---

71 Civil Legal Aid (Merits Criteria) Regulations 2013 reg 5(2).
72 Civil Legal Aid (Merits Criteria) Regulations 2013 reg 3.

9.70   From 31 July 2015, you no longer have delegated functions to determine and grant CLR where you assess that the merits test is poor or borderline. Instead, you must submit your client's CW2 form to the LAA for the Director to determine whether to grant CLR. The same will apply if you were to re-assess the merits of a CLR as being poor or borderline at any time after having granted CLR.[73]

Refusing and withdrawing CLR

9.71   Where you believe the merits test is not, or is no longer, satisfied, you should refuse or withdraw CLR as appropriate and complete form CW4 setting out your reasons.

9.72   A copy of the form must be provided to the client within five days of your decision, and you must also advise the client of their right to appeal against your decision.

9.73   Either the client can appeal direct to the LAA, or instruct you to do so on their behalf. See paras 8.41 to 8.45 of the 2013 Specification. Again, this work is normally carried out under Legal Help.

Notifying the LAA

9.74   Under the immigration specification, you are expected to notify the LAA of all grants, refusals and withdrawals of CLR, whether in relation to a substantive appeal or bail.[74] However, this is no longer required from April 2013.[75]

Change of supplier

9.75   A person's remedy against a refusal of CLR would be to appeal to the LAA against a provider's decision to refuse or withdraw CLR. If an appeal to the Independent Funding Adjudicator (IFA) is being considered, the applicant will have 14 days by which to submit the appeal to the Director of Legal Aid Casework.[76] Where you are asked to take on a transfer following refusal of CLR, you should generally advise the client to appeal to the IFA. However, there may be occasions,

73 On 31 July 2015, the LAA confirmed this new process by way of a letter to all immigration legal aid providers, see: www.ilpa.org.uk/resource/31241/ changes-to-merits-regulations-legal-aid-agency-31-july-2015 (ILPA members only).

74 Standard Civil Contract Specification 2013 para 8.44.

75 Guidance for reporting controlled work matter starts, v15 para 3.1.

76 Civil Legal Aid (Procedure) Regulations 2012 reg 44(1).

where your specific experience and knowledge compel you to take a different view on the merits and grant CLR funding on this basis. But you will need to follow the usual rules for transfers of funding (see Chapter 5). If you re-assess and decide to grant funding, without your client having to appeal to an IFA, you will need to record details of your revised determination in section A6, paragraph 5 or 6 of the CW2 form. You may also wish to discuss your determination with a senior LAA caseworker.

Conducting the case

9.76   Once you have determined the case is in scope and Legal Help or CLR, as appropriate, has been granted (and assuming there is sufficient merit on an ongoing basis), you can conduct the case.

9.77   Generally you are permitted to take instructions, take witness statements, make applications and representations, conduct appeals, and so on.

9.78   There are rules that govern certain aspects of the conduct of cases, which we will look at in this section.

Attendance at interviews

9.79   These are excluded under LASPO unless allowed by regulations.[77] The Civil Legal Aid (Immigration Interviews) (Exceptions) Regulations 2012[78] provides for attendance at asylum screening interviews and asylum interviews where the person is a child[79], or at an asylum interview where the person is either being detained under the fast track scheme or lacks mental capacity.[80] In respect of attendance at interview of a child, a child does not include a child whose age is being disputed at the time of the interview unless the UKVI have said that they are nevertheless going to treat the person as a child for the purpose of the interview.[81]

9.80   Payment for attendance at an interview is not determined by the age of the child at the time of signing controlled work but whether the child is a still a child at the time of the actual interview.

---

77 LASPO Sch 1 Pt 1.
78 SI No 2863.
79 Reg 3 and see also explanatory statement of these regulations.
80 Reg 4.
81 Reg 2.

9.81   Where you attend in a standard fee case, you can claim the interview additional fee. In an hourly rate case, the contract says that attendance at a substantive interview is outside the relevant costs and disbursement limits.[82]

Travel to detained clients

9.82   You can claim for travel and waiting costs to visit a client in detention. However, travel time is capped to a maximum of three hours for the return journey. Travel and waiting time and associated disbursements are excluded from any applicable costs limit, and in a standard fee case payable on top of the relevant fee.[83]

Bail

9.83   Where a client is in detention, you can make a bail application where there is merit to do so.

9.84   Bail applications to the tribunal are covered by CLR funding (applications for temporary admission and chief immigration officer bail are under Legal Help).[84] If you do not already have CLR open for an appeal, you should grant CLR to cover bail. If you are already conducting an appeal, you should extend the scope of CLR to cover the bail application. The merits test for bail is the same for CLR generally, except will be specifically related to the prospects of a successful bail application.

9.85   Bail work is always paid at hourly rates.[85] See below for costs limits in bail matters.

Attendance at hearings

9.86   Appeals work is out of scope of Legal Help, but is covered by CLR. You may instruct an advocate (within or outside your organisation) to attend any hearing if CLR has been granted.

9.87   The advocate's time should be included on your claim as if it were your profit costs and it will be paid at the relevant hourly rate or as part of the standard fee – in a standard fee case, their time will count

---

82 Standard Civil Contract Specification 2013 para 8.83. See also page 84 of Guidance for reporting controlled work matters, v15, Annex J: immigration and asylum.

83 Standard Civil Contract Specification 2013 para 8.48.

84 Standard Civil Contract Specification 2013 para 8.81.

85 Standard Civil Contract Specification 2013 para 8.77.

towards exceptionality. Where an advocate is instructed, you cannot make a claim for time spent accompanying them at the hearing.[86]

9.88 You can apply to the LAA to increase the rates payable to advocates (including advocates employed by you) if the case raises an exceptionally complex or novel point of law (eg country guidance cases) or if there is a significant wider public interest (as defined above). Any enhanced rates that may be granted apply to advocacy, attendance and preparation only.[87]

9.89 Time spent instructing advocates and in conference is properly claimable if reasonable in the circumstances of the case.

Post-appeal work

9.90 The scope of Legal Help ends at the point of Home Office decision and consideration of CLR merits. Therefore, by definition, Legal Help cannot be used for post-appeal follow-up work, such as chasing of status papers and advice on status.

9.91 The CLR will cover advice on the outcome of the appeal, including on the rights conferred by a grant of status, together with any post-appeal advice and assistance that does not justify a new matter start (see above for rules on matter start boundaries).[88]

Appeals to the Upper Tribunal

9.92 Work on an application for permission to appeal to the Upper Tribunal, and if granted the appeal itself and any subsequent remittal back, is CLR work. It is payable at hourly rates.[89]

If you apply for permission to appeal and permission is refused, you may not claim any costs related to the application or appeal, but may claim any disbursements incurred, including interpreters' fees. This rule does not apply in detained fast track cases or where it is the UKVI which appeals. See paras 8.93–8.98 of the Standard Civil Contract Specification 2013.

9.93 In all new controlled work cases opened on or after 2 December 2013,[90] you are no longer able to claim an uplift on legal aid rates in

---

86 Standard Civil Contract Specification 2013 para 8.99.
87 Standard Civil Contract Specification 2013 paras 8.90–8.92.
88 Standard Civil Contract Specification 2013 para 8.65.
89 Standard Civil Contract Specification 2013 para 8.98.
90 Civil Legal Aid (Remuneration) Regulations 2013 Sch 1 Table 8(b) was revoked by Civil Legal Aid (Remuneration) (Amendment) Regulations 2013 reg 2(4)(a).

at risk appeals to the Upper Tribunal where permission is granted.[91] If permission to appeal is granted on an at risk appeal, you can only claim the standard rates.[92]

Higher courts litigation

9.94   Onward litigation will usually take the form of an appeal to the Court of Appeal against a decision of the tribunal. In this case, a full representation certificate is required. See chapter 5 for information on applying for a certificate.

9.95   For appeals to the Court of Appeal, the initial application to the Upper Tribunal for permission is funded as part of controlled work.[93] If that application is granted, or if it is refused and renewed to the Court of Appeal, a certificate will be needed to fund proceedings before the Court of Appeal, and the issue of the certificate will end the controlled work matter. Therefore, remittal back to the tribunal would be a new matter.

9.96   The main difference in the immigration category to the usual rules on certificate applications is that you do not have the delegated function to grant emergency certificates in judicial review claims unless you have specifically been granted that power by the LAA – the reverse of the position in other categories, where suppliers have the power by default. You therefore need to submit an application for emergency funding to the LAA. There are special dedicated e-mail addresses for immigration emergency applications and for out-of-hours immigration emergency funding applications.[94]

Managing costs

9.97   The amount of any costs limit depends on the stage of the case and the type of funding.

9.98   In standard fee cases, save for disbursements, only the standard fee is payable unless the matter becomes an escape fee case. There

---

91   Standard Civil Contract Specification 2013 para 8.94 will no longer apply to cases opened from 2 December 2013.
92   Set out in Civil Legal Aid (Remuneration) Regulations 2013 Sch 1 Table 8(c).
93   Standard Civil Contract Specification 2013 para 8.55.
94   LAA guidance: Applications for emergency funding in judicial review cases, processes and procedures, from April 2013: www.gov.uk/government/uploads/ system/uploads/attachment_data/file/350953/legal-aid-judicial-review-emergency-funding-process.pdf.

is a limit on disbursements. Hourly rate cases are limited by both profits costs and disbursements. Review and reconsideration cases before the Upper Tribunal are not subject to costs limits for either costs or disbursements, since they are subject to assessment on a case-by-case basis by the LAA.

9.99 These are the applicable costs limits:

- Standard fee stage 1 (Legal Help):
  - £400 disbursements;[95]
  - no profit costs limits.
- Standard fee stage 2 (CLR):
- £600 disbursements;[96]
- No profit costs limits.
- Hourly rates Legal Help:
  - £800 profit costs (asylum); £500 profit costs (non-asylum);[97]
  - £400 disbursements.[98]
- Hourly rates CLR:
  - £1,600 combined costs and disbursements (asylum)/£1,200 combined costs and disbursements (non-asylum).[99]
- Bail work:
  - £500 for all bail work, inclusive of disbursements[100] (where CLR has not already been granted for an appeal; where it has, bail work forms part of the main £1,600/£1,200 limit. If CLR has already been granted for bail, when it is granted for a substantive appeal, the costs already spent on bail count towards the £1,600/£1,200).[101]

9.100 Any of the above limits can be extended on application to the LAA. In addition, there are limits for specific case stages:

- Where a client instructs you prior to making an application at the ASU, and following attendance at the ASU you cease to be instructed – £100 including disbursements.
- Where advice is given on the merits of an appeal to the Upper Tribunal under Legal Help (usually because the case has transferred to you at this stage, otherwise such advice would be part of CLR stage 2b) – £100 including disbursements.

---

95 Standard Civil Contract Specification 2013 para 8.68.
96 Standard Civil Contract Specification 2013 para 8.68.
97 Standard Civil Contract Specification 2013 para 8.80.
98 Standard Civil Contract Specification 2013 para 8.84.
99 Standard Civil Contract Specification 2013 para 8.86.
100 Standard Civil Contract Specification 2013 para 8.86.
101 Standard Civil Contract Specification 2013 para 8.87.

- Where you provide initial advice in relation to an asylum application which the client decides not to make or ceases to provide instructions before making – £100 including disbursements.

None of these limits can be extended.[102]

9.101   For details of making claims for costs, see chapter 13.

Licensed work

9.102   For the detail of how licensed work operates, see chapter 5.

9.103   The merits tests for immigration and asylum work are the standard merits tests described in chapter 5. There are no specific tests for licensed immigration work (Civil Legal Aid (Merits Criteria) Regulations 2012 reg 60 applies to CLR before the First-tier Tribunal), and so either the standard test, or the test for judicial review/public law, will apply.

9.104   However, the general merits criteria do not apply to Dublin III judicial review, and instead the merits test is whether the Director of the Legal Aid Agency is satisfied that the case has a tangible prospect of success. [103]

---

102 Standard Civil Contract Specification 2013 paras 8.82 and 8.89.
103 Reg 56A inserted by Civil Legal Aid (Merits Criteria) (Amendment) (No 3) Regulations 2013, 1 January 2014. See also reg 2 of the Amendment Regs for definition of a Dublin III claim.

CHAPTER 10

Conducting a mental health case

by Richard Charlton

Introduction

10.1   This chapter deals with the funding of mental health cases, and should be read alongside chapters 3, 4 and 5. In this chapter we set out the rules specific to mental health work. You should note that most of those rules are in addition to and build on the general rules applicable to all civil work, set out in chapters 3 and 5. There is no specific costs guidance for mental health work, but see appendix H for a summary of costs issues applicable to all civil work.

10.2   However some issues arising from the representation of those with mental health issues may be relevant for uplift of costs[1]; and in addition the payment of examination of records, for example in Mental Capacity Act cases, may be possible notwithstanding the same examination by experts instructed.[2] Further assistance in relation to mental health billing is to be found through published guidance available through the Legal Aid Mental Health Unit[3]

10.3   Previous peer review guidance has been withdrawn whilst an update is considered by the Legal Aid Agency, however useful guidance as to attendance and appropriate work is to be found in the Law Society's Practice Note.[4]

What is mental health work?

10.4   The mental health category of law is defined as:

- Cases under LASPO Sch 1 Pt 1 para 5 – services in relation to:
  - Mental Health Act 1983;
  - Mental Capacity Act 2005;
  - Repatriation of Prisoners Act 1984 Sch para 5(2).

10.5   Court of Protection work is permitted by virtue of the inclusion of the Mental Capacity Act 2005, but LASPO Sch 1 Pt 3 para 4 says that advocacy in the Court of Protection is only permitted where the proceedings concern:

- right to life;
- liberty or physical safety;

---

1   Costs Assessment Guidance 2013 para 12.8.
2   Costs Assessment Guidance 2013 para 2.14.
3   Mental Health Common Errors – February 2015. This document was supplied as 'required reading' to all mental contract holders by John Sirodcar, Head of Contract Management, in February 2015.
4   *Representation Before Mental Health Tribunals*: www.lawsociety.org.uk/support-services/advice/practice-notes/mental-health-tribunals/.

- medical treatment;
- capacity to marry, enter a civil partnership or enter sexual relations;
- right to family life.

10.6   For any other matter, advice will be in scope but not representation. Where representation can be justified, an application for exceptional funding can be made (see chapter 4), and the category definitions confirm that that will be treated as mental health work.

10.7   Mental health work is governed by the general provisions of the 2014 Standard Civil Contract, and by section 7 of the Specification with effect from 1 August 2014. See chapters 3 and 5 of this book for the general rules. Further contract guidance is published by the LAA in *Contract Management: mental health guidance* April 2014 v2.1.[5]

Who can do the work?

10.8   Under the 2014 Standard Civil Contract Mental Health Contracts were let by procurement area.

10.9   To do any mental health work at all, you must have a schedule authorisation for at least one procurement area. All advocates before the Mental Health Tribunal must be members of the Law Society's Mental Health Accreditation Scheme.[6]

Use of matter starts

10.10   You can take on cases as you see fit, subject to means and merits tests where applicable. However, you must use at least 70 per cent of your matter starts for a procurement area on clients who were physically located in the procurement area at the time the matter start is opened.[7]

---

5   www.gov.uk/government/uploads/system/uploads/attachment_data/file/342667/laa-guidance-mental-health-august-2014.pdf.
6   Standard Civil Contract 2014 Specification para 7.6.
7   Standard Civil Contract 2014 Specification para 7.7.

Levels of funding

10.11   The following levels of funding apply to mental health work:

- Legal Help – advice and assistance, but excluding representation before the tribunal;
- Help at Court – funding for representation for victims under the Domestic Violence, Crime and Victims Act 2004;
- Controlled Legal Representation (CLR) – representation before the tribunal;
- Legal representation (certificate) – appeals to the Upper Tribunal and representation in the higher courts, including the Court of Protection.[8]

Legal Help, Help at Court and CLR granted on the same case all form part of the same matter.

10.12   Mental health work is covered by standard fees for almost all controlled (ie non-certificate) work – the sole exception being Help at Court for victims.[9]

10.13   There are four fees:[10]

- the non-MHT fee, for all work that does not go to the tribunal;
- MHT fee level 1 – initial advice;[11]
- MHT fee level 2 – negotiation and preparation once an application to the MHT has been made;[12] and
- MHT fee level 3 – representation before the MHT, and follow-up work.[13]

10.14   A fee may be claimed for each stage through which the matter passes. Any disbursements incurred are in addition to the fee, but where counsel is instructed, their fees are included in the graduated fee[14] and it is for you to negotiate with counsel which part of the fee you will pay to counsel and which part you will keep. In cases of unusual complexity you can apply to the LAA for prior authority to pay a rate higher than that set for solicitors. This cannot be retrospective.[15] Further fees are payable for adjourned/postponed/cancelled hearings[16]

---

8   Standard Civil Contract 2014 Specification para 7.3.
9   Standard Civil Contract 2014 Specification para 7.85.
10   Standard Civil Contract 2014 Specification para 7.47.
11   Standard Civil Contract 2014 Specification para 7.63.
12   Standard Civil Contract 2014 Specification para 7.65.
13   Standard Civil Contract 2014 Specification para 7.69.
14   Standard Civil Contract 2014 Specification para 7.42.
15   Standard Civil Contract 2014 Specification para 7.43.
16   Standard Civil Contract 2014 Specification para 7.70.

and for travel to any hospital that the LAA has designated on their website as a remote hospital[17] (at the time of writing, none had been designated for the 2014 contract).

10.15   See chapter 13 for more on payment.

Case study

I have granted CLR to my client. I made an application to the tribunal. I prepared the case and represented him at a manager's review, but he then decided he didn't want to proceed to a full hearing yet. What can I claim?

All work is covered by the level 2 fee. You can claim for preparation work, and for attendance at meetings and reviews, at this level. You only go on to level 3 if there is an MHT hearing.

Granting Legal Help

10.16   The general rules set out in chapter 2 and 3 apply to the granting of Legal Help in the mental health category. Where the client's condition is such that he or she will not sign the application form, and there is no other person who could sign it on their behalf, a supervisor in your organisation can sign it on their behalf.[18] The reasons should be noted on file.

Means

10.17   The usual means test for Legal Help will apply – see chapter 3 for details. Note that the guidance on evidence of means, which can be accessed on the legal aid website via the eligibility calculator,[19] states:

> It will often be impracticable to obtain evidence of income from patients with mental health problems who are in hospital (for example, those detained under the Mental Health Act). Practitioners should however attempt to obtain oral or written confirmation of the position (eg type of benefit received) from the ward manager or social worker where practicable.

---

17 Standard Civil Contract 2014 Specification para 7. 74.
18 Standard Civil Contract 2014 Specification para 7.40.
19 http://civil-eligibility-calculator.justice.gov.uk/.

10.18   However, where the client is a patient whose case is the subject of proceedings or potential proceedings before the MHT, no means test is required[20] – the client is automatically eligible. Where the case covers both MHT and non-MHT issues, it will be all one matter[21] and therefore no means test need be carried out.[22]

Merits

10.19   The usual merits test for Legal Help – the 'sufficient benefit test' – will apply. See chapter 5 for details of the sufficient benefit test.

Granting CLR

10.20   CLR is granted by your signature on a form already signed by the client (subject to the same provisions set out above for Legal Help where the client is unable or refuses to sign).[23] Since a grant of CLR is a requirement in any case that goes to the MHT (subject to merit, below), and therefore very much standard practice in most cases, it can become easy to overlook the necessity actually to sign the form and keep it on file. In our experience, some firms have suffered on costs compliance audit as a result. You may wish to consider incorporating a reminder into your file opening checklist.

Means

10.21   CLR for representation before the MHT is available without the need for a means test.[24]

Merits

10.22   The merits test applicable to CLR in the mental health category is set at a very low threshold, given that the client's liberty is at stake. The test is that the Director (in practice, you) must be satisfied that it is reasonable in the particular circumstances of the case for CLR to be

---

20   Civil Legal Aid (Financial Resources and Payment for Services) Regulations 2013 reg 5(1)(f); Standard Civil Contract 2014 Specification para 7.15.
21   Standard Civil Contract 2014 Specification para 7.19.
22   Standard Civil Contract 2014 Specification para 7.20.
23   Standard Civil Contract 2014 Specification para 7.40.
24   Civil Legal Aid (Financial Resources and Payment for Services) Regulations 2013 reg 5(1)(j) and Standard Civil Contract 2014 Specification para 7.15.

granted.[25] The contract makes clear that it would be unusual for it to be unreasonable to grant CLR.[26] However, the prospects of success will govern how much work should be done. CLR is available to the patient, and if the nearest relative is the applicant to the tribunal, to the nearest relative.[27]

Conduct of the case

Non-MHT cases

10.23   All cases that do not concern an application or potential application to the MHT are deemed to be non-MHT cases and attract the non-MHT fee.[28] Only Legal Help is available.

10.24   Where you are acting for a victim, Help at Court for representation is available and claimed at hourly rates on top of the fee.[29]

10.25   Initial advice in a Mental Capacity Act case is a non-MHT matter,[30] including making an application for a certificate for representation before the Court of Protection.

MHT cases

10.26   MHT cases divide into three fee stages.

10.27   Stage 1 is funded by Legal Help and covers initial advice to the client, including a visit to the client and follow-up work up to and including making an application to the MHT.[31]

10.28   Once it becomes clear that the case is to be considered by the MHT, you should grant CLR[32] and continue work at stage 2, but you can only go to stage 2 having passed through (and done at least 30 minutes of work at) stage 1.[33] This stage covers all work up to, but not including, the substantive hearing,[34] including preparation of the case generally and for the hearing, negotiation with third parties,

25 Civil Legal Aid (Merits Criteria) Regulations 2012 reg 51.
26 Standard Civil Contract 2014 Specification para 7.35.
27 Standard Civil Contract 2014 Specification para 7.33.
28 Standard Civil Contract 2014 Specification para 7.56.
29 Standard Civil Contract 2014 Specification para 7.85.
30 Standard Civil Contract 2014 Specification para 7.28.
31 Standard Civil Contract 2014 Specification para 7.63.
32 Standard Civil Contract 2014 Specification para 7.36.
33 Standard Civil Contract 2014 Specification para 7.66.
34 Standard Civil Contract 2014 Specification para 7.65.

attendance at managers' reviews and other meetings[35] where appropriate,[36] as well as taking instructions from the client and instructing experts.

10.29   Stage 3 covers representation at the tribunal hearing,[37] including any adjourned/cancelled/postponed hearings (for which an additional fee is or may be payable[38]). Stage 3 also includes work done in applying to the tribunal for a review of its decision under Tribunals, Courts and Enforcement Act 2007 s9, or applying for permission to appeal under section 11.[39]

10.30   Where the tribunal sets aside its decision, you are still in stage 3 but may claim an additional adjourned hearing fee.[40] However, where an appeal or review goes to the upper tribunal, you will need to apply for a certificate for representation at that stage.[41]

Separate matters

10.31   Each time a client becomes eligible to make an application to the tribunal they enter a 'period of eligibility'.[42] All work done for a client within a period of eligibility, on both MHT and non-MHT matters, forms one matter start.[43] However, where more than one set of MHT proceedings are running concurrently during a period of eligibility, you can claim separate fees for each set of proceedings.

10.32   Where you are advising an informal patient (ie not detained) on a non-MHT matter, and the patient is then sectioned, you can open a separate matter to apply to the tribunal, even if the non-MHT matter continues.[44]

10.33   When dealing with a detained client, you must start a new matter for each of the following events (where work on a legal issue is required), even if you have an existing ongoing matter:[45]

---

35 Standard Civil Contract 2014 Specification para 7.67.
36 Standard Civil Contract 2014 Specification para 7.68.
37 Standard Civil Contract 2014 Specification para 7.69.
38 Standard Civil Contract 2014 Specification para 7.70.
39 Standard Civil Contract 2014 Specification para 7.86.
40 Standard Civil Contract 2014 Specification para 7.86.
41 Standard Civil Contract 2014 Specification para 7.90.
42 Standard Civil Contract 2014 Specification para 7.57.
43 Standard Civil Contract 2014 Specification para 7.20.
44 Standard Civil Contract 2014 Specification para 7.22.
45 Standard Civil Contract 2014 Specification para 7.23.

- the client has an entitlement to a further MHT due to passage of time;
- there is a change in section type;
- the client is discharged from section;
- the client withdraws from the MHT, and within the same period of eligibility applies again.

However, note that communicating the decision of the MHT, advising the client about it and about aftercare is the same matter as the MHT.[46]

10.34   Where a Mental Capacity Act matter is open, and then the client is sectioned or otherwise requires MHT advice, a separate MHT matter should be opened.[47]

Disbursements

10.35   Disbursements may be incurred in the usual way in the mental health category.

10.36   You can make a claim for payment on account of disbursements during the life of a case, but only where the matter has been open for at least six months and, if there has been a previous application for payment on account, at least six months have elapsed since that payment was made.[48]

Use of counsel

10.37   You are entitled to instruct counsel to represent clients before the tribunal. Where you instruct counsel, you will still only be entitled to the level 3 fee, and it is a matter for you to negotiate how much of that fee to pay to counsel. Counsel is not a disbursement.[49]

10.38   In unusually complex cases, you can apply to the LAA to pay counsel at an hourly rate above the standard hourly rates in the contract.[50] The LAA will grant prior authority, specifying the hourly rate and the maximum costs limit if the case poses unusually complex evidential problems, or novel or difficult points of law. The LAA consider it

---

46 Standard Civil Contract 2014 Specification para 7.24.
47 Standard Civil Contract 2014 Specification para 7.29.
48 Standard Civil Contract 2014 Specification para 7.49.
49 Standard Civil Contract 2014 Specification para 7.41.
50 Standard Civil Contract 2010 Specification paras 7.43 and 7.44.

highly unlikely that such issues will arise at MHT level. These provisions do not appear to override the requirement that all advocacy in high security hospital cases be provided by Law Society scheme members.

Licensed work

10.39   See chapter 5 for the general principles applicable to licensed work.

10.40   The merits test for certificates to be granted for mental capacity work is:[51]

- the standard criteria apply (see chapter 5); and
- the Court of Protection has ordered, or is likely to order, an oral hearing; and
- it is necessary for the individual to be provided with full representation in the proceedings. Means free representation is, however, available for the protected person and their Responsible Person's Representative in an application under Mental Capacity Act 2005 s21A.[52]

10.41   Representation is generally only available where the proceedings concern

- right to life;
- liberty or physical safety;
- medical treatment;
- capacity to marry, enter a civil partnership or enter sexual relationships;
- right to family life.

10.42   Other matters are out of the scope of representation, and an exceptional funding application will be required (see chapter 4 and para 10.5 above).

---

51 Civil Legal Aid (Merits Criteria) Regulations 2013 reg 52.
52 Civil Legal Aid (Financial Resources and Payment for Services) Regulations 2013 reg 5(g). It should be noted that it is the current practice of the Mental Health Unit of the Legal Aid Agency to also require a copy of a current urgent or standard authorisation for a deprivation of liberty or a copy of a court order made under Mental Capacity Act 2005 s21A authorising such a deprivation.

Contact with the Legal Aid Agency

10.43 All work in the mental health category, with the exception of high cost cases, is handled by the Liverpool Office of the Legal Aid Agency. All claims, and applications, including certificate applications, together with any queries, should be directed to:

> Mental Health Unit/Immigration and Asylum
> Controlled Work and Escaped Fee Claims
> Legal Aid Agency
> Level 6, The Capital
> Union Street
> Liverpool L3 9AF
>
> Phone: 0151 235 6750 (option 3)
> Email: mhu-ec@legalaid.gsi.gov.uk

Conducting a housing case

Introduction

11.1 This chapter deals with work done in the housing category. You should read it in conjunction with chapters 3 and 5. Chapter 3 deals with general rules about taking on civil cases, and applies to work in housing as it does to all other work. Chapter 5 deals with the rules that apply to the conduct of all civil cases. The housing-specific rules in this chapter usually build on, rather than replace, the general rules; where they do replace the general rules in Chapters 3 and 5 we will say so. Out of scope housing cases may be funded as exceptional cases; see chapter 4 for more on exceptional funding.

11.2 See appendices H and I for a summary of the Legal Aid Agency's (LAA's) Costs Assessment Guidance, in respect of the most common queries raised by caseworkers.

What housing work is in the scope of legal aid?

11.3 The category definitions define housing work as:

- possession of the home, other than mortgage possession and orders for sale:[1]
- eviction, including unlawful eviction and planning eviction;
- provision of accommodation and assistance under Parts 6 and 7 Housing Act 1996 for an individual who is homeless or threatened with homelessness;
- provision of accommodation by way of community care services to an individual who is homeless or threatened with homelessness;
- housing disrepair, to the extent it is in scope;
- applications to vary or discharge an injunction under Housing Act 1996 s153A;
- injunctions under the Protection from Harassment Act 1997 arising from housing matters;
- accommodation and support for asylum seekers etc;
- exceptional funding grants on any other matter concerning the possession, status, terms of occupation, repair, improvement, eviction from, quiet enjoyment of, or payment of rent or other charges for premises (including vehicles and sites they occupy) which are occupied as a residence, including the rights of leaseholders, allocation, transfers and the provision of sites for occupation.

---

1 Mortgage possession and orders for sale are in the debt category, and as such required to go through the telephone gateway.

Possession cases

11.4   Defences to claims for possession in cases other than mortgage cases are in scope and in the housing category. Legal Help will be available for initial advice, and you can apply for a certificate for representation in court should that become necessary.

11.5   Mortgage possession claims are also in scope, but are in the debt category (as are possession claims arising out of secured second charge loans). Each housing contract is actually a housing and debt contract, and includes a notional four debt matter starts per year, as well as a licence to do debt certificated work. However, debt is a mandatory gateway category. This means that a client needing Legal Help must go through the gateway unless they are exempt (see para 3.13 above). The gateway will refer clients requiring representation to face to face providers. If you are approached by a client who needs representation, because proceedings have already been issued and the merits test is met (see below), you can apply for representation without needing to go through the gateway, though you cannot sign a Legal Help form to fund the application unless you contact the gateway and get a referral number. You can exercise delegated functions to grant a debt certificate in appropriate cases.[2]

11.6   Para 33 of Part 1, Schedule 1 to LASPO says that civil legal services in relation to court orders for possession are in scope. This does not mean that you must wait until proceedings are issued before legal aid becomes available, though there must be a real prospect of that. The LAA has said that 'formal written notification that proceedings will be issued (such as a section 8 or section 21 notice)' will be enough, although a certificate will not be granted until proceedings have been issued.[3] Prior to that, you may grant Legal Help.

11.7   Therefore, general advice on the theoretical possibility of possession proceedings, or advice on the implications of a client's rent arrears at an early stage, will be out of scope. But once the landlord has issued notification of intent to take proceedings, legal aid – in the form of Legal Help – will be available. Once proceedings have actually been issued, you can apply for a certificate, using delegated functions if necessary, if the client has a defence (or a realistic prospect of

---

2   FAQ 91, Civil Legal Aid Reform FAQs – no longer on the LAA website, but available at https://legalaidhandbook.files.wordpress.com/2013/04/legal-aid-reform-faq-v3.pdf.

3   FAQ 98, Civil Legal Aid Reform FAQs – no longer on the LAA website, but available at https://legalaidhandbook.files.wordpress.com/2013/04/legal-aid-reform-faq-v3.pdf.

arguing that possession would be unreasonable). If not, you can still attend court to offer mitigation using Help at Court.

11.8   The merits test for grant of a certificate in possession proceedings is:[4]

- the standard criteria are met (see para 5.89 above);
- the individual has a defence (including that it would be unreasonable for the court to make an order for possession in the circumstances);
- prospects of success are:
  - moderate or better; or
  - borderline or poor, but it is necessary to determine that the prospects of success criterion is met to prevent a breach of the applicants ECHR or enforceable EU rights, or appropriate to do so in the circumstances of the case having regard to any risk that failure to do so would be such a breach;
- the proportionality test is met (see para 5.101 above).

In *IS (by the Official Solicitor as litigation friend) v The Director of Legal Aid Casework and The Lord Chancellor,*[5] Collins J declared unlawful the part of the merits test which restricted legal aid to cases where the prospects of success were better than 50 per cent, and so the LAA revised the test with effect from 27 July 2015. See para 5.97 for a discussion of the revised prospects of success criteria.

The standard to be applied in assessing the prospects of success is the prospects as they would be with the assistance of competent legal representation, not the prospects on the basis of material available but untested at the time of the application. This is to ensure that cases where competent representation would turn the case in the applicant's favour are not excluded from funding.[6]

11.9   Many possession cases involving rent arrears will have, as the underlying cause or a contributor to it, problems with housing benefit. Para 33(3) of Part 1, Schedule 1 to LASPO applies the Part 2 exclusions, including the welfare benefits exclusion. The effect of this is that work done in relation to the possession proceedings is in scope, but work done in relation to housing benefit is out of scope. You

---

4   Civil Legal Aid (Merits Criteria) Regulations 2013 reg 61, amended by Civil Legal Aid (Merits Criteria) (Amendment) Regulations 2014 to provide that the prospects of success test to be applied is that in regulation 43 of the 2013 regulations. Regulation 43 of the 2013 regulations was amended by Civil Legal Aid (Merits Criteria) (Amendment) (No 2) Regulations 2015 reg 2(4) to allow for grants in the borderline and poor, but not very poor, categories.

5   [2015] EWHC 1965 (Admin).

6   [2015] EWHC 1965 (Admin) para 96.

can investigate the housing benefit position to prepare a defence to the possession matter – which may include preparing witness statements, or even summonsing housing benefits officers – and can seek an adjournment for the client to resolve the benefits matter themselves. But any work in assisting the client with that resolution will not be claimable.[7]

11.10   Judicial review of housing benefit and other local authority financial assistance is in scope, though would fall into the welfare benefits and public law categories.

11.11   Where a client does not have a full or partial defence to the proceedings (including that it would be unreasonable for the court to make an order for possession in the circumstances) it is unlikely that a certificate would be justified, though Help at Court may be granted where it is conceded that possession is justified but to argue for suspended possession.[8]

11.12   Where legal aid has been granted in possession proceedings, it will also cover work done on a counterclaim, even if the subject of the counterclaim would be out of scope as a freestanding claim. The Part 2[9] exclusions of assault, battery and false imprisonment claims, trespass to goods and trespass to land, damage to property and breach of statutory duty do not apply to counterclaims in possession proceedings, so all may be pleaded and claimed for.[10]

11.13   Possession of 'the home' includes houses, caravans, houseboats and other vehicles that are the individual's only or main residence, together with the land on which they are located.[11]

11.14   Legal aid is not available to defend possession proceedings brought against squatters – that is, where there are no grounds for arguing that the individual is occupying otherwise than as a trespasser, and no grounds for arguing that their occupation began otherwise than as a trespasser.[12]

7 FAQ 107, Civil Legal Aid Reform FAQs – no longer on the LAA website, but available at https://legalaidhandbook.files.wordpress.com/2013/04/legal-aid-reform-faq-v3.pdf.

8 Lord Chancellor's Guidance on Civil Legal Aid para 6.9. See para 5.53 of this book for more on Help at Court.

9 LASPO Sch 1 Pt 2.

10 LASPO Sch 1 Pt 1 para 33(7).

11 LASPO Sch 1 Pt 1 para 33(9) and (11).

12 LASPO Sch 1 Pt 1 para 33(10).

Homelessness and allocations

11.15   Both Legal Help and, in appropriate cases, legal representation, are available to individuals who are homeless or threatened with homelessness[13] and seeking assistance under Part 6 or 7 of the Housing Act 1996. Para 34 of Part 1, Schedule 1 of LASPO says that 'civil legal services ... in relation to the provision of accommodation and assistance for the individual' are within scope. This is relatively broad and will cover advice on entitlement and suitability of accommodation for homeless people (although legal aid is not available in relation to allocations and suitability of accommodation to people who do not fall within the definition of 'homeless', which is the same as in section 175 of the Housing Act 1996[14]), as well as assistance with making an application and any review and appeal that may follow.

11.16   Legal Help will cover initial advice, the application and any review. A certificate for legal representation will cover an appeal to the County Court, or a judicial review. The merits test for homelessness cases is the same as for public law more generally.[15] The test is:

- the standard criteria are met (see para 5.89 above);
- all administrative appeals and alternatives to court have been exhausted;
- a letter before claim has been sent (only relevant to judicial review);
- the proportionality test is met (see para 5.101);
- prospects of success are:
  - moderate or better; or
  - borderline or poor, but it is necessary to determine that the prospects of success criterion is met to prevent a breach of the applicants ECHR or enforceable EU rights, or appropriate to do so in the circumstances of the case having regard to any risk that failure to do so would be such a breach.[16]

11.17   You can use delegated functions to grant emergency legal aid in homelessness cases, and in judicial review cases involving homelessness.[17]

13 As defined in Housing Act 1996 s175.
14 LASPO Sch 1 Pt 1 para 34(3).
15 Civil Legal Aid (Merits Criteria) Regulations 2013 reg 2 – see definition of 'public law'.
16 Civil Legal Aid (Merits Criteria) Regulations 2013 reg 56, amended by Civil Legal Aid (Merits Criteria) (Amendment) (No 2) Regulations 2015 reg 2(5) to remove borderline prospects of success.
17 Standard Civil Contract 2013 Specification para 5.3.

Unlawful eviction

11.18 Legal aid is available for unlawful eviction claims.[18] In most cases, the eviction will have happened and so an emergency grant of legal aid using delegated functions will be appropriate (unless the client is simply seeking damages, not reinstatement). However, a 'reasonably alleged' threat of unlawful eviction will be in scope,[19] including by way of withdrawal of services[20], and in such a case Legal Help to advise and issue a warning letter may be more appropriate. The merits test for legal representation is:[21]

- the standard criteria are met (see para 5.90 above);
- the proportionality test is met (see para 5.101 above);
- prospects of success are:
  - moderate or better; or
  - borderline or poor, but it is necessary to determine that the prospects of success criterion is met to prevent a breach of the applicants ECHR or enforceable EU rights, or appropriate to do so in the circumstances of the case having regard to any risk that failure to do so would be such a breach;
- the landlord or other person responsible for the matter complained of has been notified of the complaint (except where this is impracticable) and, where notice has been given, has had a reasonable opportunity to resolve the matter.

11.19 Where a claim is primarily for damages rather than reinstatement, it is still in scope, but you will need to explain on the legal aid application why a conditional fee agreement is not appropriate. The Lord Chancellor's Guidance suggests a conditional fee agreement (CFA) will be considered suitable – and so legal aid refused – if:[22]

- prospects of success are over 60 per cent;

---

18 LASPO Sch 1 Pt 1 para 33.
19 FAQ 84, Civil Legal Aid Reform FAQs – no longer on the LAA website, but available at https://legalaidhandbook.files.wordpress.com/2013/04/legal-aid-reform-faq-v3.pdf.
20 FAQ 105, Civil Legal Aid Reform FAQs – no longer on the LAA website, but available at https://legalaidhandbook.files.wordpress.com/2013/04/legal-aid-reform-faq-v3.pdf.
21 Civil Legal Aid (Merits Criteria) Regulations 2013 reg 63. Note that the prospects of success criterion is contained in regulation 43, which was amended by Civil Legal Aid (Merits Criteria) (Amendment) (No 2) Regulations 2015 reg 2(4) to allow for grants in the borderline and poor, but not very poor, categories.
22 Lord Chancellor's Guidance on Civil Legal Aid para 7.17.

- the opponent is considered able to meet any costs and damages awarded;
- after the event insurance can be obtained.
- where you are relying on the non-availability of ate (after the event) insurance, you will be expected to provide evidence of having tried and failed to obtain it. (See paras 5.94–5.96 for more information.)

11.20   The Part 2[23] exclusions of assault, battery and false imprisonment claims, trespass to goods and trespass to land, damage to property and breach of statutory duty do not apply to claims for unlawful eviction, so all may be pleaded and claimed for.[24]

Housing disrepair

11.21   For legal aid purposes, disrepair cases can be put into two separate categories, each with their own distinct rules.

Freestanding disrepair claims

11.22   Disrepair claims are in scope, but only in limited circumstances. LASPO Sch 1 Pt 1 para 35 says:

(1) Civil legal services provided to an individual in relation to the removal or reduction of a serious risk of harm to the health or safety of the individual or a relevant member of the individual's family where–
(a) the risk arises from a deficiency in the individual's home,
(b) the individual's home is rented or leased from another person, and
(c) the services are provided with a view to securing that the other person makes arrangements to remove or reduce the risk.
(2) Sub-paragraph (1) is subject to–
(a) the exclusions in Part 2 of this Schedule, with the exception of paragraphs 6 and 8 of that Part, and
(b) the exclusion in Part 3 of this Schedule.
(3) For the purposes of this paragraph–
(a) a child is a relevant member of an individual's family if the individual is the child's parent or has parental responsibility for the child;
(b) an adult ('A') is a relevant member of an individual's family if–

---

23 LASPO Sch 1 Pt 2.
24 LASPO Sch 1 Pt 1 para 33(7).

(i)   they are relatives (whether of the full blood or half blood or by marriage or civil partnership) or cohabitants, and

(ii) the individual's home is also A's home.

(4) In this paragraph–

'adult' means a person aged 18 or over;

'building' includes part of a building;

'child' means a person under the age of 18;

'cohabitant' has the same meaning as in Part 4 of the Family Law Act 1996 (see section 62(1) of that Act);

'deficiency' means any deficiency, whether arising as a result of the construction of a building, an absence of maintenance or repair, or otherwise;

'harm' includes temporary harm;

'health' includes mental health;

'home', in relation to an individual, means the house, caravan, houseboat or other vehicle or structure that is the individual's only or main residence, together with any garden or ground usually occupied with it.

11.23   Therefore, legal aid is only available to remove or reduce a serious risk of harm to the client or a member of his or her family. This means that it is available to force repairs to be done, but not to claim damages.

11.24   In order to be eligible for legal aid, there must at least be a credible allegation that there is such a risk.[25] Once that threshold is crossed, Legal Help will be available to investigate further, including by obtaining expert reports. If after investigation it transpires that there was no serious risk of harm, then legal aid should be withdrawn, though the costs of the investigation will be claimable.

11.25   The costs of expert reports should be limited to the maximums set out in the remuneration regulations[26] and if they are, you cannot apply for prior authority. However, if you need to go above those levels, you can apply for prior authority to do so if working under a certificate. There is no way of applying for prior authority in Legal Help cases, and so you should make a note on the file explaining why you believe the exceptional circumstances criteria are met.[27] The criteria are that the complexity of the material is such that an expert

---

25 Lord Chancellor's Guidance on Civil Legal Aid para 12.6.

26 The current rates can be found in Civil Legal Aid (Remuneration) (Amendment) Regulations 2013 Sch 2; following the 20% reduction in rates that took place in December 2013, Civil Legal Aid (Remuneration) Regulations 2013 Sch 5 is no longer current for cases started after that date.

27 FAQ 86, Civil Legal Aid Reform FAQs – no longer on the LAA website, but available at https://legalaidhandbook.files.wordpress.com/2013/04/legal-aid-reform-faq-v3.pdf.

with a high level of seniority is required, or the material is so specialised and unusual that only very few experts are available.[28] These criteria are unlikely to be met in most housing disrepair cases.

11.26   Any expert instructed should generally be a joint expert in accordance with the Housing Disrepair Pre-Action Protocol,[29] though additional medical evidence may be necessary to show that there is a serious risk of harm in the particular client's circumstances. The LAA recognises that the risk may vary from individual to individual – the risk, for example, arising from damp is higher for a tenant with a respiratory illness than a tenant without one.[30] There is, however, no specific evidential requirement to establish a serious risk of harm.[31] If the LAA does not agree that there is a serious risk, and so considers funding not justified, there is a right to request a review by the Director, but no right of appeal to an independent funding adjudicator.[32] Any further challenge would have to be by way of judicial review.

11.27   The Lord Chancellor's Guidance says that all relevant factors will be taken into account in determining whether there is a serious risk of harm, including the following (non-exhaustive) list of examples:[33]

- whether harm has already resulted;
- whether, as a result of the deficiency, an existing health condition has been exacerbated;
- whether the individual or any family members are in a high risk group, such as the elderly or very young children;
- whether the individual or any family member is vulnerable due to a disability, either because of risk to them, or damage to medical equipment;
- whether there are relevant environmental conditions – such as broken heating in winter;
- whether there are multiple deficiencies that could, taken cumulatively, be of greater seriousness;
- whether a single deficiency poses multiple risks;
- whether a deficiency affects shared rooms or areas;

28 Civil Legal Aid (Remuneration) Regulations 2013 Sch 5 para 2.
29 Lord Chancellor's Guidance on Civil Legal Aid para 12.7.
30 Lord Chancellor's Guidance on Civil Legal Aid para 12.9.
31 FAQ 79, Civil Legal Aid Reform FAQs – no longer on the LAA website, but available at https://legalaidhandbook.files.wordpress.com/2013/04/legal-aid-reform-faq-v3.pdf.
32 FAQ 80, Civil Legal Aid Reform FAQs – no longer on the LAA website, but available at https://legalaidhandbook.files.wordpress.com/2013/04/legal-aid-reform-faq-v3.pdf.
33 Lord Chancellor's Guidance on Civil Legal Aid para 12.10.

- whether an instructed expert reports that future deterioration is likely;
- whether the local authority has identified hazards.

11.28 Damages claims are out of the scope of LASPO. Where you claim both for enforcement of repairs and for damages, you should separate the work done on the file and ensure that you do not claim any work done in respect of the damages aspect on your legal aid bill.

11.29 But you should also note that the LAA take the view that the statutory charge applies to the whole proceedings, not just the funded part.[34] So if you recover damages as part of a case for which you have legal aid, even if the damages part was out of scope and you have made no claim for work done in respect of it, your client will be required to pay the costs of the in-scope part of the case out of any damages recovered.

11.30 It may therefore be in the client's best interests to bring a claim where the damages element is more than purely nominal under a CFA. In any event, the LAA is likely to take the view that a claim involving a substantial damages element is likely to be suitable for a CFA, and so refuse a certificate on that basis. See paras 5.94–5.96 above for more on suitability for a CFA.

11.31 Statutory nuisance proceedings under Environmental Protection Act 1990 s82 are in scope.[35] However, the combined effect of para 35(2)(b) of Part 1 and Part 3 of Schedule 1 of LASPO is to exclude the provision of advocacy services in the magistrates' court.

The merits test for disrepair claims is the same as for harassment claims, see para 11.35 below.

Disrepair counterclaims

11.32 Disrepair counterclaims in possession proceedings are in scope, and unlike disrepair claims, counterclaims for damages are included.[36] The Part 2[37] exclusions of assault, battery and false imprisonment claims, trespass to goods and trespass to land, damage to property

---

34 FAQ 81, Civil Legal Aid Reform FAQs – no longer on the LAA website, but available at https://legalaidhandbook.files.wordpress.com/2013/04/legal-aid-reform-faq-v3.pdf.

35 FAQ 104, Civil Legal Aid Reform FAQs – no longer on the LAA website, but available at https://legalaidhandbook.files.wordpress.com/2013/04/legal-aid-reform-faq-v3.pdf.

36 LASPO Sch 1 Pt 1 para 33(6)(a).

37 LASPO Sch 1 Pt 2.

and breach of statutory duty do not apply to counterclaims in possession proceedings, so all may be pleaded and claimed for.[38]

11.33　However, if a tenant withholds rent in order to provoke possession proceedings, and then counterclaims for disrepair, legal aid is likely to be refused.[39] This is because legal aid will only be granted if the Director is satisfied it would be reasonable to do so in light of the applicant's conduct.[40] It appears that this provision has caused little difficulty in practice.[41]

11.34　In practice, many practitioners have found bringing a counterclaim a useful way to bring funded disrepair cases where there has previously been a possession order, even if the possession proceedings are not currently ongoing.[42]

Harassment

11.35　Legal aid is available to victims of harassment to bring an application for an order under Protection from Harassment Act 1997 ss3 or 3A, and to defend against such an application. It will only be in the housing category where the injunction arises out of a housing issue, such as harassment by a landlord or arising out of a neighbour dispute. The merits test for legal representation is:[43]

- the standard criteria are met (see para 5.89 above);
- the proportionality test is met (see para 5.101 above);
- prospects of success are:
    - moderate or better; or
    - borderline or poor, but it is necessary to determine that the prospects of success criterion is met to prevent a breach of the applicants ECHR or enforceable EU rights, or appropriate to do so in the circumstances of the case having regard to any risk that failure to do so would be such a breach, and

---

38 LASPO Sch 1 Pt 1 para 33(7).

39 Lord Chancellor's Guidance on Civil Legal Aid para 7.4(c).

40 Civil Legal Aid (Merits Criteria) Regulations 2013 reg 11(6).

41 See Jan Luba QC and Sara Stephens, 'Sorting myths from facts over housing cases' November 2014 *Legal Action* 10.

42 See http://nearlylegal.co.uk/blog/2014/04/disrepair-counterclaims-after-possession-order/ and http://nearlylegal.co.uk/blog/2014/08/more-on-post-possession-order-disrepair-counterclaims/ for a discussion of the legal basis of such counterclaims.

43 Civil Legal Aid (Merits Criteria) Regulations 2013 reg 62. Note that the prospects of success criterion is contained in reg 43, which was amended by Civil Legal Aid (Merits Criteria) (Amendment) (No 2) Regulations 2015 reg 2(4) to allow for grants in the borderline and poor, but not very poor, categories.

- the landlord or other person responsible for the matter complained of has been notified of the complaint (except where this is impracticable) and, where notice has been given, has had a reasonable opportunity to resolve the matter.

Legal Help will be available to advise prior to proceedings and to issue a warning letter.

Anti-social behaviour

11.36　Injunctions under the Anti-social Behaviour, Crime and Policing Act 2014 are in scope and, where they arise out of a housing issue, are in the housing category. Advice funded by Legal Help, and representation in the County Court or Youth Court by certificate, will be available in the usual way. Even though applications for injunctions against under 18s are dealt with in the Youth Court, they are still deemed to be civil cases for the purposes of legal aid. Where you have general authorisation to do so, you can grant an emergency certificate using delegated functions.

11.37　　Breach proceedings, although dealt with in the County Court (for adults) are deemed by the LAA to fall within the crime category and thus the provisions of the Crime Contract. Civil practitioners whose firm does not have a crime contract can apply for an individual case contract to represent an existing individual client, though in practice the LAA is likely to expect referral to a crime firm instead. This does not apply to the defence of possession proceedings brought on the grounds of anti-social behaviour, which are in scope, and civil proceedings, in the same way as possession proceedings brought on any other grounds.

Other housing work

11.38　All other housing cases are outside the scope of legal aid. However, applications for exceptional funding can be made – see chapter 4.

Housing possession court duty scheme

11.39　The Legal Aid Agency (LAA) contracts with a number of organisations to provide duty representation to individuals appearing in the County Courts in possession proceedings. There is only one provider per court, though individual contracts may allow the provider to use agents to cover some sessions. Representation at a court duty session is not means or merits tested, and will include the writing of an advice letter following the hearing. However, where a client needs further advice, that will be means and merits tested, and subject to the scope provisions, in the usual way. Where you have advised a client on a duty scheme who was in court for mortgage possession, you will need to refer the client to the telephone gateway unless they are exempt or you can go straight to full legal representation in appropriate cases. Further information about the operation of the duty schemes can be found in the LAA's housing possession court duty scheme guidance.[44]

11.40   You cannot ask a client to sign a Legal Help form for a housing case at a court duty scheme, as this work is funded under a separate schedule, and is paid at a fixed fee per client seen.[45]

11.41   If the client's case needs further work, you can ask the client to come to your office and sign a Legal Help form (subject to the usual rules in relation to means and merits).

11.42   However, you cannot then claim a fee for advising that client under the court duty scheme.[46] It is very important that you have systems to prevent double-claiming in error in these circumstances. If you open a housing Legal Help case within six months of having advised the same client on the same case at a duty scheme you will not be entitled to the court duty payment for that client, so your systems will need to allow you to identify such cases and where necessary notify the LAA to rescind a payment already made against your court duty schedule.

---

44 See www.gov.uk/government/publications/housing-possession-court-duty-schemes-hpcds.
45 Standard Civil Contract Specification 2013 para 10.19.
46 Standard Civil Contract Specification 2013 para 10.24.

CHAPTER 12

Conducting a criminal case

edited by Anthony Edwards

continued

Means testing • Applications • Assessing case costs • Effects of Crown Court means testing • The merits test • Disbursements • Prescribed proceedings in the Crown Court • Appeals to the Crown Court • Recovery of defence costs orders

Note: Rates of remuneration changed for grants made on or after 1 July 2015. Those reduced figures appear in brackets at appropriate places. It is likely that the original rates will be restored for a period from October 2015 until 11 January 2016.

Introduction

12.1   The 2010 Standard Contract Standard Terms (as amended) will govern criminal work [where representation is granted before 11 January 2016]. There is also a separate Contract Specification setting out the detailed funding rules that apply. There will then be a 2015 Own Client Crime Contract (OCCC) and a 2015 Duty Provider Crime Contract (DPCC). The latter will only apply to those who have successfully bid in any procurement area. Duty work at police stations and courts will then only be conducted by those holding a DPCC, their delivery partners and their agents.

12.2   Criminal work is divided into classes by the contract:

- investigations – work done pre-charge;
- proceedings – post-charge court work that does not fall into any other class;
- appeals and reviews – post-conviction work on appeals and reviews of convictions or sentences;
- prison law – work in relation to parole, treatment or discipline in the prison system;
- associated civil work – judicial review, habeas corpus and Proceeds of Crime Act 2002 work.[1]

In addition, VHCCs (very high cost cases) can be thought of as an extra class of work.

12.3   A case may move through several classes. For example, a client arrested and charged with burglary will start in the investigations class, then move into the proceedings class; if convicted, he or she may have further cases in the appeals and prison law classes. Each of those classes of work has separate rules and funding mechanisms, and we will look at each in turn in this chapter. We will also consider the general rules which apply to all classes of work.

---

1   Standard Crime Contract Specification 2010 para A1.5; OCCC para 1.3; DPCC para 1.3.

General rules

Unique file numbers[2]

12.4   The contract requires you to assign a unique file number (UFN) to every case. The case will retain the UFN throughout its life as it moves through the classes of work. Where you act for more than one client on the same case, each client will have their own UFN, though where you must submit a consolidated claim (see chapter 14) it will be under one 'lead' UFN. Where you act for one client on more than one case, each case will have its own UFN.

12.5   All UFNs must be in the format set out in the contract – DDMMYY/NNN, where DDMMYY is the date the client first instructed you on that matter and NNN is a unique three digit number. It does not matter what that number is, as long as no two clients or cases have the same number.

12.6   So, for example, the first client to instruct you on 1 February 2015 would have the UFN 01022015/001, the second might then be 01022015/002, and so on.

12.7   The purpose of the UFN is to allow the Legal Aid Agency (LAA) to track and, where necessary, check all work done for a particular client. You are therefore required to record the UFN on file, use it for all applications and claims to the LAA and, since the LAA will use it when communicating with you, ensure that you can search your database against it.

Disbursements

12.8   Disbursements – that is, expenses incurred in the course of a client's case – are generally permitted where it is in the best interests of the client to incur the disbursement for the purpose of giving advice, and the amount of the disbursement is reasonable.[3]

12.9   This amounts to a three-stage test:

1) Is it in the best interests of the client?
2) Is it for the purposes of giving advice or representation?
3) Is the amount is reasonable?

12.10 The client's best interests will be served by incurring expenditure that is necessary for you to conduct the case, or that will assist (or may

---

2   Standard Crime Contract Specification 2010 paras A4.39 and A4.40; OCCC paras 4.41 and 4.42; DPCC paras 4.40 and 4.41.

3   Standard Crime Contract 2010 Specification para A5.39; OCCC para 5.33; DPCC para 5.38.

assist) in achieving the best outcome. For example, travel expenses may be in the client's best interests, even though the client does not benefit directly, because it is necessary for you to incur them to get to court. An expert report may or may not assist the client's case – that would depend on what the expert says – but where it has the potential to do so it would likely be in the client's best interests to obtain it. This test should not be applied with the benefit of hindsight; the question is, what was reasonable based on what was known at the time?

12.11 'For the purpose of advice or representation' describes the nature and purpose of the expense. To use the preceding example, travel expenses to court are justifiable as being for the purpose of providing representation. A medical report to comment on a client's medical situation would be for that purpose, since it is evidence that could be put before the court, but paying for the client to see a medical expert to obtain treatment would not, since it is not necessary for the purpose of giving advice for the client to be treated, only for you to know what his or her condition is.

12.12 Finally, the amount of the disbursement must be reasonable. The rates for expert witnesses, save in defined exceptional circumstances prescribed by Schedule 5 to the Criminal Legal Aid (Remuneration) Regulations 2013, are to be found in that schedule. Although it is not mandatory to obtain prior authority to incur disbursements,[4] doing so is advisable where substantial sums are to be incurred as prior authority ensures that, unless the scope of the disbursement is not as authorised, it will be paid.[5]

12.13 Where disbursements are incurred, you should retain a receipt or invoice on file.[6] Where you incur mileage, no contract rate is now specified but it used to be 45 pence per mile; otherwise it was claimed at the rate of 25 pence per mile, unless the private travel rate of 45 pence per mile could be justified.

12.14 Witness expenses to attend court cannot generally be funded under the contract, unless the court has directed that they may not be recovered from central funds (the usual source of witness expenses,

---

4 Standard Crime Contract 2010 Specification para A5.33; OCCC para 5.32; DPCC para 5.32.

5 Standard Crime Contract 2010 Specification para A5.30; OCCC para 5.29; DPCC para 5.29.

6 Standard Crime Contract 2010 Specification para A5.41; OCCC para 5.40; DPCC para 5.39.

including fees of professional witnesses) and they are not recoverable from any other source.[7]

Work in the investigations class

12.15   Investigations work is work done pre-charge or in the police station, and covers:[8]

- police station telephone advice;
- police station attendance;
- advice and assistance outside the police station;
- advocacy assistance:
  - on a warrant of further detention;
  - on an application to a magistrates' court to vary police bail conditions;
  - at an armed forces custody hearing.

Police station cases

Scope of work

12.16   Police station work will consist of telephone advice, attendance in person at the police station, or both. It is generally available to anyone attending a police station, whether under arrest or as a volunteer, during the course of a criminal investigation.[9] The exceptions to this rule are:

- where the matter falls within the scope of the Criminal Defence Direct scheme (eg arrests for non-imprisonable offences);[10] and
- advice and assistance to a witness (which is covered in certain circumstances by the advice and assistance scheme).[11]

Police station work is not means tested.[12]

---

7 Standard Crime Contract 2010 Specification para A5.49; OCCC para 5.47; DPCC para 5.45.
8 Standard Crime Contract 2010 Specification para A1.5; OCCC para 1.3; DPCC para 1.3.
9 Standard Crime Contract 2010 Specification para B9.1; OCCC para 8.1; DPCC para 9.1.
10 Standard Crime Contract 2010 Specification para B9.9; OCCC para 8.9; DPCC para 9.7.
11 Standard Crime Contract 2010 Specification para B9.4; OCCC para 8.4; DPCC para 9.3.
12 Criminal Legal Aid (General) Regulations 2013 Part 2 and Criminal Legal Aid (Financial Resources) Regulations 2013 Part 2.

12.17   Police station work can also be carried out post-charge, for example to deal with identification procedures, arrest on warrant or for breach of bail, or for caution or re-charge following discontinuance or dismissal. However, only post-charge work carried out at the police station can be claimed under the criminal investigations class of work.[13]

12.18   For these purposes, a 'police station' is a place where a constable is present, and a 'constable' is an official with a power of arrest conferred by virtue of his or her office.[14] For example, an officer of HM Revenue and Customs (HMRC) is a constable, but a Department for Work and Pensions (DWP) benefit fraud investigator is not; therefore, a client arrested by HMRC is entitled to police station representation, but a client being interviewed by the DWP is not. However, such a client may be entitled to advice and assistance if the relevant criteria are met. See below for more on advice and assistance.

Case study

One of our clients has been invited to attend the DWP to be interviewed about an allegation that he has been working and claiming benefits. What should I do?

This will be an interview under PACE (Police and Criminal Evidence Act 1984) and so a criminal lawyer should attend. Since an officer of the DWP does not have a power of arrest, your client would not be entitled to police station legal aid. However, subject to means, your client would be entitled to advice and assistance. You should get the client to sign a CRM1 and CRM2 and provide proof of means, and then you will be funded to attend the interview with the client. You will have a costs limit of £300, but this can be extended on application to the LAA if necessary.

Sources of work

12.19   In January 2008, the LSC implemented the Defence Solicitor Call Centre (DSCC) and required all requests by detained persons to go through the centre – in its previous incarnation as the Duty Solicitor Call Centre it had only dealt with duty cases.

---

13 Standard Crime Contract 2010 Specification para B9.109; OCCC para 8.90; DPCC para 9.105.
14 Standard Crime Contract 2010 Specification para A1.13; OCCC and DPCC Standard Terms 1.

12.20   The call centre records the basic details of an alleged offence before passing the case on to the own solicitor requested, the duty solicitor or Criminal Defence Direct. Criminal Defence Direct provide telephone advice to clients detained for less serious offences such as drink-driving offences, non-imprisonable offences, breaches of bail and warrants.

12.21   Where an attendance is likely to be necessary, Criminal Defence Direct will not deal with the matter and the case will be passed to the own solicitor (if requested) or the duty solicitor.

12.22   However, you may also be contacted direct by a third party, for example the relative of a client, and requested to take on the case. You may also be contacted by a client direct, for example a client who is aware that the police are looking for him or her and wants to surrender. In such a situation you can take on the case and provide telephone advice and attendance as appropriate, but must report to the call centre that you have taken the case.[15]

Case study

My client's wife phoned to say that he has been arrested for theft, and wants me to go to the police station. Can I go?

Yes. You can attend the police station when instructed to do so by a third party. However, you must notify the DSCC that you have taken the case. You must notify them before you contact the client and obtain a reference number. You must notify the DSCC in advance for third party instructions and within 48 hours where you are at a police station and instructed direct, or where a client instructs you direct to attend a surrender or bail date.

Permitted work

12.23   Whatever the source of the case, you should consider whether or not to attend the police station. Attendance at the police station is mandatory where:

- the client has been arrested and is to be interviewed;
- there is to be an identification procedure (except a video parade, attendance at which is discretionary[16]);

---

15 Standard Crime Contract 2010 Specification para B9.20; OCCC para 8.20.
16 Standard Crime Contract 2010 Specification para B9.41; OCCC para 8.38; DPCC para 9.38.

- the client complains of serious maltreatment by the police.[17]

12.24 You cannot claim for payment for attendance at the police station where:

- the client has been arrested solely for non-imprisonable offences;
- the client has been arrested on a warrant for failure to appear or for breach of court or police bail, unless you have clear documentary evidence that would result in the client's release, eg a bail form showing that the client is not in fact in breach of a condition;
- the client has been arrested for offences under the Road Traffic Act 1988 ss4, 5, 6, 7 and 7A (driving whilst unfit, drunk in charge of a vehicle, driving with excess alcohol or failure to provide a specimen).[18]

12.25 However, attendance in a prohibited case will be permitted (or mandatory, as the case may be) if one of the exceptions apply:

- there is to be an interview or identification procedure;
- the client requires an appropriate adult;
- the client is unable to communicate over the telephone;
- the client complains of serious maltreatment by the police;
- the client is being investigated for an additional offence not covered by the above list;
- you are already at the same police station (but in this case you may only claim the Telephone Advice Fixed Fee);
- the advice relates to an indictable offence;
- the request is identified as a 'Special Request' by the DSCC.[19]

In all other cases, attendance at the police station is at your discretion, and you should consider whether the 'sufficient benefit' test is met. This is the merits test for police station work and states that work may only be done where 'there is sufficient benefit to the client, having regard to the circumstances of the matter, including the personal circumstances of the client, to justify work or further work being carried out'.[20]

---

17 Standard Crime Contract 2010 Specification para B9.39; OCCC para 8.36; DPCC para 9.36.
18 Standard Crime Contract 2010 Specification para B9.9; OCCC para 8.9; DPCC para 9.37.
19 Standard Crime Contract 2010 Specification para B9.10; OCCC para 8.10; DPCC para 9.38.
20 Standard Crime Contract 2010 Specification para A3.12; OCCC para 3.10; DPCC para 3.10.

12.26   The test would be automatically satisfied where the client has a right to advice under the Police and Criminal Evidence Act 1984 (PACE), or where the client is a volunteer, or under equivalent military legislation – but only in relation to initial advice; you must apply the test to determine the extent of advice, and particularly whether attendance (as opposed to telephone advice) is necessary.[21]

12.27   Where you intend to attend the police station, and it is not one of the mandatory attendances outlined above, you should be satisfied that the attendance is necessary for the purpose of giving advice that could not be given over the telephone, and is expected to progress the case materially. Specifically, the contract says that it might be reasonable to remain at the police station post-charge to provide advice or make representations on bail, but unless the client is particularly vulnerable it would not be reasonable to stay for photographs, fingerprints and DNA samples.[22]

Who may carry out work?

12.28   Although almost all work comes through the Defence Solicitor Call Centre, there is a distinction between own client and duty work – own client being cases where you or your firm were specifically requested, and duty work where the client requested the duty solicitor and the case was allocated to you.

12.29   In order to carry out police station work, you must be a solicitor or, for duty work,[23] accredited and registered as such by the LAA. An accredited representative is one who has passed the police station qualification, which is administered by the Law Society and consists of a two-part portfolio of cases, an oral examination known as the critical incidents test and a written examination (which need not be taken by a representative who has a legal qualification).

12.30   To become a probationary representative you must pass the written examination (if required) and part one of the portfolio; you then have one year to pass the remaining elements to become fully accredited. The accreditation process is no longer bypassed by qualification as a solicitor; everyone must be accredited to do duty solicitor police station work. To do own client work, a person must either be a

---

21 Standard Crime Contract 2010 Specification para B9.14; OCCC para 8.14; DPCC para 9.10.

22 Standard Crime Contract 2010 Specification para B9.16; OCCC para 8.16; DPCC para 9.14.

23 DPCC para 9.24.

solicitor or be accredited. The training and quality assurance of pro-bationary and accredited representatives must be documented.[24]

12.31   Probationary representatives cannot do duty cases, and cannot do cases where the offence under investigation is indictable only; fully accredited representatives can do all cases.[25] See chapter 19 for the obligations of those who manage and supervise representatives.

Starting a case

12.32   Police station work is not means tested, and the client is not required to complete any application form.

12.33   A case will be initiated when you are contacted, either by the DSCC or by the client or a third party, and requested to provide advice.

12.34   When you take on a case where the client has been arrested and is at the police station, you must make first contact with the client within 45 minutes of being notified of the case.[26] This is a target set out in the contract which should be met in at least 80 per cent of cases, and to enable monitoring of the target,[27] your file should contain a note of the time the case was accepted and the time of first contact, together with a note of why contact was not possible inside the 45 minutes, if applicable.[28]

12.35   Where a client has previously received police station advice on the same matter within the past six months from another firm, you cannot provide further advice on the same matter unless:

- there is a gap in time and a material change in circumstances between the first and second occasions; or
- the client has reasonable cause to transfer; or
- the first supplier confirms they will not make a claim.[29]

12.36   You should make reasonable enquiries of the client to see if there has been previous advice, and if there has been and the exceptions are

---

24 Standard Crime Contract 2010 Specification para B9.33; OCCC para 31; DPCC para 9.30.

25 Standard Crime Contract 2010 Specification paras B9.26–9.38; OCCC 8.26–8.35; DPCC paras 9.24–9.35.

26 Standard Crime Contract 2010 Specification para B9.23; OCCC para 8.23; DPCC para 9.21.

27 Standard Crime Contract 2010 Specification para B9.24; OCCC para 8.24; DPCC para 9.22.

28 Standard Crime Contract 2010 Specification para B9.25; OCCC para 8.25; DPCC para 9.23.

29 Standard Crime Contract 2010 Specification para B9.70; OCCC para 8.55; DPCC para 9.66.

not met, should not take the case and cannot make a claim. Reasonable cause for transfer will not be made out where the client finds sound advice unpalatable and wants a second opinion.[30] Where you take on a transfer case, you should note the reason on the file.

Conducting work

12.37 Once you have accepted a case, you can continue to do such work as is necessary and complies with the requirements above. Where the client is bailed to return to the police station, attendance at the bail to return is funded on the same basis as the initial attendance and will be included in the fixed fee – you should ensure that the sufficient benefit test is satisfied and that you are permitted to attend.

12.38 There is no costs limitation for police station work.

12.39 Police station work will come to an end at the point the client is charged or cautioned, the police decide to take no further action, or the case is otherwise ended. A bill should be submitted at that point – see chapter 14 for details of costs and the billing procedure.

Warrants of further detention

12.40 Where a client is detained and the police seek an extension to the detention under PACE 1984 ss43 or 44, or under Terrorism Act 2000 Sch 8 para 29 or para 36, you can provide advocacy assistance to represent the client at the hearing of the application.[31]

12.41 Advocacy assistance is not means tested[32] and the client is not required to sign an application form, but you should record on the file that you have granted funding.[33] The scope of advocacy assistance includes any reasonable preparation and follow-up work.[34] However, counsel may only be instructed in applications before the High Court or a senior judge.

12.42 Similar provisions apply to armed forces custody hearings.[35]

---

30 Standard Crime Contract 2010 Specification para B9.73; OCCC para 8.58; DPCC para 9.69.

31 Standard Crime Contract 2010 Specification para B9.145; OCCC para 8.126; DPCC para 9.113.

32 Criminal Legal Aid (Financial Resources) Regulations 2013 Part 2; OCCC para 8.129; DPCC para 9.116.

33 Standard Crime Contract 2010 Specification para B9.148; OCCC para 8.132; DPCC para 9.119.

34 Standard Crime Contract 2010 Specification para B9.151; OCCC para 8.133; DPCC para 9.120.

35 Standard Crime Contract 2010 Specification paras B9.158–B9.170; OCCC paras 8.139–8.151; DPCC paras 9.126–9.138.

Variation of police bail

12.43 In certain circumstances, where the police have the power to impose bail conditions (or 'street bail' conditions), a client can make an application to a magistrates' court to vary the conditions.[36]

12.44 You can grant advocacy assistance to represent such a client.[37] It is not means tested,[38] and no application form is required, though a note of the grant should be made on the file.[39] The scope of advocacy assistance includes any reasonable preparation and giving of any advice on appeal.[40] However, counsel may not be instructed.[41]

Advice and assistance

12.45 Advice and assistance can be given to a client who meets the means and merits tests, to advise and assist in respect of a criminal investigation – that is, before the client is charged, requisitioned or summoned for an offence. It will include representing the client at interviews with non-police agencies, such as the Department for Work and Pensions in a benefit fraud matter, as well as general advice, case preparation and related work.

Means test

12.46 In order to qualify for advice and assistance, the client must pass the means test.[42] There are two elements to the test – income and capital – and the client must pass both parts. You are responsible for assessing the client's means and deciding whether the test is met.

12.47 Where the client is directly or indirectly in receipt of any of the following benefits, he or she automatically qualifies for advice and assistance without the need for an assessment of income or capital:

- income support;
- income-based jobseeker's allowance;

---

36 PACE 1984 ss30CB and 47(1E).
37 Standard Crime Contract 2010 Specification para B9.171; OCCC para 8.152; DPCC para 9.139.
38 Criminal Legal Aid (Financial Resources) Regulations 2013 Part 2.
39 Standard Crime Contract 2010 Specification para B9.174; OCCC para 8.154; DPCC para 9.142.
40 Standard Crime Contract 2010 Specification para B9.176; OCCC para 8.156; DPCC para 9.144.
41 Standard Crime Contract 2010 Specification para B9.177; OCCC para 8.157; DPCC para 9.145.
42 Criminal Legal Aid (Financial Resources) Regulations 2013 reg 8.

- income-based employment and support allowance;
- guarantee pension credit;
- universal credit paid under Part 1 of the Welfare Reform Act 2012.[43]

A person is indirectly in receipt of a benefit if they are included in another person's claim, eg if a partner receives it on the basis of a couple.

12.48   'Capital' means all the client's assets and resources, excluding household furniture and effects, clothes and the tools of the client's trade. Where the client owns property, the value to be taken into account is the equity after disregarding any mortgage, though only up to the value of £100,000. The first £100,000 of any equity is also disregarded, and the remainder is the capital value.[44] Where the client has a partner, the partner's capital should also be taken into account.

Case study

My client has a flat worth £120,000, with a mortgage of £90,000. He has £650 in savings and his wife has £300 in her account. Is he eligible on capital?

The flat is worth £120,000. Disregard up to £100,000 of the mortgage – so the equity is £30,000. Disregard up to £100,000 of equity – so the capital is nil. Aggregate his and his wife's savings, so the total capital is £950, so the client is eligible on capital.

12.49   'Income' means all income from any source which the client may reasonably expect to receive within the seven days up to and including the day of his or her application,[45] with the following exceptions:

- any tax and National Insurance paid;
- any contributions paid under Part I of the Social Security Contributions and Benefits Act 1992;
- disability living allowance;
- attendance allowance;
- constant attendance allowance;
- any payment out of the social fund;

---

43   Criminal Legal Aid (Financial Resources) Regulations 2013 reg 2.
44   Criminal Legal Aid (Financial Resources) Regulations 2013 reg 13.
45   Criminal Legal Aid (Financial Resources) Regulations 2013 reg 6.

- so much of any back to work bonus received under section 26 of the Jobseekers Act 1995 as is, by virtue of that section, to be treated as payable by way of a jobseeker's allowance;
- any direct payments made under regulations made under section 57(1) of the Health and Social Care Act 2001 (direct payments), section 17A of the Children Act 1989 (direct payments) or section 8(1) of the Carers and Direct Payments Act (Northern Ireland) 2002 (direct payments);
- any reasonable living expenses provided for as an exception to a restraint order under section 41 of the Proceeds of Crime Act 2002; and
- any personal independence payment paid under Part 4 of the Welfare Reform Act 2012 Act.[46]

Where the client has a partner, the partner's income should also be taken into account.[47] Where the client has a partner or other dependant member of the household, you should deduct the standard allowance for each member.[48]

12.50   The thresholds for capital and income, and the standard dependants allowances, can be found on the keycard at www.gov.uk/criminal-legal-aid-means-testing. The levels are up-rated periodically, usually when benefit levels are increased in April each year, and you should check the website for the most up to date figures.

12.51   Evidence of the client's means will be required, and should be retained on file.[49] There is a power to assess means without evidence where it is not practicable to obtain it before the form is signed, but it should be obtained at a later stage and if it is not, any claim should be limited to the equivalent of two hours.[50] In exceptional circumstances, you may dispense with evidence altogether if the client's circumstances make it impracticable to obtain it at any point.[51]

---

46 Criminal Legal Aid (Financial Resources) Regulations 2013 reg 11.
47 Criminal Legal Aid (Financial Resources) Regulations 2013 reg 9.
48 Criminal Legal Aid (Financial Resources) Regulations 2013 reg 12.
49 Standard Crime Contract 2010 Specification para B9.119; OCCC para 3.7; DPCC para 3.7.
50 Standard Crime Contract 2010 Specification para A3.7; OCCC para 3.7; DPCC para 3.7.
51 Standard Crime Contract 2010 Specification para A3.6; OCCC para 3.6; DPCC para 3.6.

Merits test

12.52   Assuming the client qualifies on means, you should go on to consider whether there is merit. The merits test is the 'sufficient benefit' test – is there 'sufficient benefit to the client, having regard to the circumstances of the matter, including the personal circumstances of the client, to justify work or further work being carried out'.[52]

12.53   The sufficient benefit test must be applied throughout the case to determine the extent of the advice required,[53] and the provision of advice must cease if it becomes apparent that the test is no longer satisfied.[54]

The application

12.54   The client must complete and sign the application forms – CRM1 and CRM2 – and you should retain the original copies of them on file. Advice and assistance is granted by you, with no application to the LAA required, and so the presence of the signed forms on file is sufficient to effect the grant.

12.55   The usual rule is that the client comes to you to sign the forms. However, there will be situations where that is not possible, and therefore the contract allows for exceptions where certain criteria are met:

- A **postal application** can be accepted where it is reasonable to do so (for example, where there is good reason why the client cannot attend your offices). However, you cannot accept a postal application where a client is temporarily resident outside the European Union and the matter can be delayed until they return, or another person in England and Wales could apply for advice and assistance on the same matter.[55]
- Where the client cannot attend immediately but can telephone you, **telephone advice can be given before the form is signed**[56] and you can claim for that advice. In order to qualify, there has to be good reason why the client cannot attend the office, but the

---

52 Standard Crime Contract 2010 Specification para A3.10; OCCC para 3.12; DPCC para 3.12.

53 Standard Crime Contract 2010 Specification paras A3.11 and A3.15; OCCC paras 3.11 and 3.15; DPCC paras 3.11 and 3.15.

54 Standard Crime Contract 2010 Specification para A3.12; OCCC para 3.12; DPCC para 3.10.

55 Standard Crime Contract 2010 Specification para A4.30; OCCC para 4.32; DPCC para 4.31.

56 Standard Crime Contract 2010 Specification para B9.125; OCCC para 8.106.

client must later sign the form and be eligible. This power can be combined with one of the others; for example, you could give telephone advice to a client in prison and then post the form to him or her.

- Where the client lacks capacity, you can accept **an application on behalf of a child or person lacking mental capacity**[57] from another person, such as a parent, guardian, deputy or attorney, litigation friend, or any other person where there is good reason why one of the above-named persons cannot make the application. Again, the form will be signed by the authorised person but completed in the name of the client, and it will be the client's means that should be assessed and evidenced.

- You can also accept **an application from a child direct**[58] where the client is entitled to defend proceedings himself or herself (which is true of almost all criminal work), or where you are satisfied that there is good reason why none of the authorised persons in the previous paragraph can make the application and the child is old enough to give instructions and understand the nature of the advice, or where the child is seeking police station advice only.

Where a client cannot attend the office for one of the good reasons outlined above, you may claim for outward travel expenses,[59] and where the client is in custody, detention or hospital travel time[60] for travelling to see the client before the form is signed in order to get the form signed.

12.56   Where a client has received previous advice and assistance on the same matter within the last six months, there are restrictions on where you can accept a further application that would involve a change of solicitor.[61] You cannot accept such an application unless:

- there is a gap in time and a material change in circumstances; or
- the client has reasonable cause to transfer from the first supplier; or
- the first supplier confirms they are making no claim; or
- previous advice and assistance was police station advice only.

---

57 Standard Crime Contract 2010 Specification para A4.24; OCCC para 4.26; DPCC para 4.25.
58 Standard Crime Contract 2010 Specification para A4.27; OCCC para 4.29; DPCC para 4.28.
59 Standard Crime Contract 2010 Specification para B9.126; OCCC para 8.107.
60 Standard Crime Contract 2010 Specification para B9.127; OCCC para 8.108.
61 Standard Crime Contract 2010 Specification para B9.129; OCCC para 8.110.

You should make reasonable enquiries of the client to find out whether there has been previous advice and assistance. If so, and if you can justify the change of solicitor, there should be a clear note to that effect on the file.

Conducting work

12.57   Once you have confirmed that the client is eligible and the form has been signed, you can proceed to work on the client's case.

12.58   Advice and assistance covers all necessary work (other than work in the police station) up to the point at which the client is charged with or summoned for an offence. It will cover you for attendance and advice to the client, case preparation, taking witness statements with a view to preserving memory or avoiding charge, and so on. It will also cover attendance at interviews with non-police agencies.

12.59   Costs are limited to £300, though an application may be made to the LAA to extend that limit. The limit includes both time and disbursements. Where advice and assistance runs alongside police station work, you may not make a separate claim for the advice and assistance; all work pre-charge is covered by the police station fixed fee. However, the costs limit will continue to apply and you will need to be within the limit or have a granted extension for advice and assistance costs to count towards exceptionality. See chapter 14 for more on getting paid for criminal work.

Separate matters

12.60   All work for a client that constitutes one matter will require one application and will lead to one claim. Where, however, work is a genuinely separate matter then a separate application and a separate claim will be required.

12.61   All work in respect of a single investigation constitutes one matter and therefore one claim for costs, even if the investigation is subsequently extended to cover other offences. However, work may be treated as a separate matter if it amounts to a generally separate problem requiring separate advice,[62] unless the client requires advice on one occasion only.[63]

---

62 Standard Crime Contract 2010 Specification para A4.42; OCCC para 4.44; DPCC para 4.43.
63 Standard Crime Contract 2010 Specification para A4.45; OCCC para 4.47; DPCC para 4.46.

Case study

I had a client who was arrested for theft and taken to the police station, where it was found he was also wanted for a separate incident of criminal damage, and he was further arrested for that. Is that one matter or two?

It depends on the outcome of the case. If he were charged with both offences and bailed to the same court date, that would be one matter and one claim. This is because the two allegations required advice on one occasion only. However, if he were charged with theft and bailed to return on the criminal damage, that would constitute two matters, if you could reasonably attend on the bail to return, since they would require separate advice on more than one occasion.

Work in the proceedings class

12.62   The proceedings class runs from the point of charge/summons and now includes all magistrates' court work and most Crown Court proceedings. The main funding types in the proceedings class are:

- advice and assistance/advocacy assistance as court duty solicitor;
- representation orders.

Court duty solicitor work

12.63   A duty solicitor is a solicitor who has been grandparented under earlier contracts[64] or has passed both the police station qualification and magistrates' court qualification, and has registered as a duty solicitor with the LAA.

12.64   Duty solicitors whose firms have successfully bid in a procurement area will be allocated sessions as a duty solicitor whose role is to advise and assist otherwise unrepresented defendants.

12.65   Technically speaking, two different funding types are available to a court duty solicitor – advice and assistance and advocacy assistance, to advise the client outside court and represent the client in court respectively. In practice, however, there is no real distinction and a single consolidated claim is made for all work done for all clients on a duty day.

---

64 DPCC 1.

12.66   Court duty advice is available to clients whose cases qualify for assistance without regard to their means, and no application form is needed. However, a file note of the details of the client and the case will be needed.

12.67   However, clients can only be represented where their case comes within the scope of the scheme:

- The duty solicitor must:[65]
  - advise any client who requests it who is in custody;
  - make a bail application where a client in custody requires a bail application and such an application has not previously been made by a duty solicitor;
  - advise a client before the court in connection with 'prescribed proceedings' that civil orders deemed to be criminal for legal aid purposes. The full list of prescribed proceedings appears below at para 12.69.[66]
  - cross-examine under Youth Justice and Criminal Evidence Act 1999 s38 if a designated fee earner is appointed by the court.[67]
- The duty solicitor may:[68]
  - advise and represent any client who is in custody on a plea of guilty and wishes the case to be concluded that day;
  - advise and represent any client before the court for failure to pay a fine or other sum or to obey an order of the court, and such failure may lead to the client being at risk of imprisonment;
  - advise and represent a client not in custody in connection with an imprisonable offence;
  - help a client in making an application for a representation order, whether the nominated solicitor is the duty solicitor or another solicitor;
  - advise and represent a client seeking to vary police-imposed bail conditions pre-charge.
- The duty solicitor must not:
  - represent in committal proceedings (note that although committals have been abolished, the specification has not been amended at the date of writing);

---

65 Standard Crime Contract 2010 Specification para B10.7; DPCC para 10.7.
66 DPCC para 10.7 and Criminal Legal Aid (General) Regulations 2013 reg 9.
67 DPCC 10.32.
68 Standard Crime Contract 2010 Specification para B10.8; DPCC 10.8.

- represent at a not guilty trial or in relation to a non-imprisonable offence unless within the provision above;[69]
- advise or represent a client who has had the services of a duty solicitor at a previous hearing in the proceedings (except where they are before the court this time as a result of failure to pay a fine or other sum or comply with an order imposed previously).[70]

As duty solicitor, with the client's permission you are entitled to take on the case and apply for a representation order. However, you should not apply for a representation order where the case concludes on the day of the duty.[71]

Representation orders – magistrates' court

Scope

12.68 A representation order is the main method of funding proceedings in the magistrates' court.

12.69 It covers representation to clients charged or summoned for criminal offences, and also covers proceedings deemed to be criminal for the purpose of legal aid funding, as set out in Criminal Legal Aid (General) Regulations 2013 reg 9:[72]

    (a) civil proceedings in a magistrates' court arising from a failure to pay a sum due or to obey an order of that court where such failure carries the risk of imprisonment;

    (b) proceedings under sections 14B, 14D, 14G, 14H, 21B and 21D of the Football Spectators Act 1989 in relation to banning orders and references to a court;

    (c) proceedings under section 5A of the Protection from Harassment Act 1997 in relation to restraining orders on acquittal;

    (d), (e) [Revoked.]

    (f) proceedings in relation to parenting orders made under section 8(1)(b) of the Crime and Disorder Act 1998 where an order under section 22 of the Anti-social Behaviour, Crime and Policing Act 2014 or a sexual harm prevention order under section 103A of the Sexual Offences Act 2003 is made;

    (g) proceedings under section 8(1)(c) of the Crime and Disorder Act

---

69 Standard Crime Contract 2010 Specification para B10.9; DPCC para 10.9.
70 Standard Crime Contract 2010 Specification para B10.10; DPCC para 10.10.
71 Standard Crime Contract 2010 Specification para B10.14; DPCC para 10.14.
72 As amended by the Criminal Legal Aid (General) (Amendment) Regulations 2015 and the Civil and Criminal Legal Aid (Amendment) Regulations 2015.

1998 in relation to parenting orders made on the conviction of a child;

(h) proceedings under section 9(5) of the Crime and Disorder Act 1998 to discharge or vary a parenting order made as set out in sub-paragraph (f) or (g);

(i) proceedings under section 10 of the Crime and Disorder Act 1998 in relation to an appeal against a parenting order made as set out in sub-paragraph (f) or (g);

(j) proceedings under Part 1A of Schedule 1 to the Powers of Criminal Courts (Sentencing) Act 2000 in relation to parenting orders for failure to comply with orders under section 20 of that Act;

(ja) proceedings, in a youth court, in relation to a breach or potential breach of a provision in an injunction under Part 1 of the Anti-social Behaviour, Crime and Policing Act 2014 where the person subject to the injunction is under 14.

(k) proceedings under sections 80, 82, 83 and 84 of the Anti-social Behaviour, Crime and Policing Act 2014 where a person has engaged in or is likely to engage in behaviour that constitutes a criminal offence on the premises;

(ka) proceedings under paragraph 3 of Schedule 2 to the Female Genital Mutilation Act 2003 in relation to female genital mutilation protection orders made other than on conviction and related appeals;

(kb) proceedings under paragraph 6 of Schedule 2 to the Female Genital Mutilation Act 2003 in relation to female genital mutilation protection orders made under paragraph 3 of that Schedule;

(l) proceedings under sections 20, 22, 26 and 28 of the Anti-social Behaviour Act 2003 in relation to parenting orders–
   (i)   in cases of exclusion from school; or
   (ii) in respect of criminal conduct and anti-social behaviour;

(m) proceedings under sections 97, 100 and 101 of the Sexual Offences Act 2003 in relation to notification orders and interim notification orders;

(n) proceedings under sections 103A, 103E, 103F and 103H of the Sexual Offences Act 2003 in relation to sexual harm offences prevention orders and interim sexual harm offences prevention orders;

(o) [Revoked.]

(p) proceedings under sections 122A, 122D, 122E and 122G of the Sexual Offences Act 2003 in relation to sexual risk orders;

(q) [Revoked.]

(r) proceedings under section 13 of the Tribunals, Courts and Enforcement Act 2007 on appeal against a decision of the Upper Tribunal in proceedings in respect of–
   (i)   a decision of the Financial Conduct Authority;
   (ia) a decision of the Prudential Regulation Authority;
   (ii) a decision of the Bank of England; or

(iii) a decision of a person in relation to the assessment of any compensation or consideration under the Banking (Special Provisions) Act 2008 or the Banking Act 2009;

(s) proceedings before the Crown Court or the Court of Appeal in relation to serious crime prevention orders under sections 19, 20, 21 and 24 of the Serious Crime Act 2007;

(t) proceedings under sections 100, 101, 103, 104 and 106 of the Criminal Justice and Immigration Act 2008 in relation to violent offender orders and interim violent offender orders;

(u) proceedings under sections 26, 27 and 29 of the Crime and Security Act 2010 in relation to–
    (i) domestic violence protection notices; or
    (ii) domestic violence protection orders;

(ua) proceedings under sections 14(1)(b) and (c), 15 and 20 to 22 of the Modern Slavery Act 2015 in relation to slavery and trafficking prevention orders;

(ub) proceedings under sections 23 and 27 to 29 of the Modern Slavery Act 2015 in relation to slavery and trafficking risk orders, and

(v) any other proceedings that involve the determination of a criminal charge for the purposes of Article 6(1) of the European Convention on Human Rights.

Sub-paragraph (v) includes contempt other than in the face of the court in the High Court (*King's Lynn and West Norfolk Borough Council v Bunning*[73]) and county court (*Brown v London Borough of Haringey*[74]).

Case study

My client is in arrears on council tax. She has been summoned to appear at the magistrates' court. I cannot represent her. Can I advise her to see the court duty solicitor?

She is in principle eligible to see the duty solicitor, since she is before the court for failure to pay a sum due. Whether she can use the duty depends on whether she is at risk of imprisonment, which is the merits test. That will depend on the facts of her case and is more likely if she is in wilful default.

12.70 An order also covers advice on appeal, and any related bail proceedings in the Crown Court or High Court.[75]

---

73 [2013] EWHC 3390 (QB).

74 [2015] EWCA Civ 483.

75 Standard Crime Contract 2010 Specification para B10.35; OCCC para 9.14; DPCC para 10.36.

Financial eligibility

12.71   Representation orders are means tested. Therefore a full application for a representation order (including means information) must be completed in all cases.

12.72   Applications for representation orders are made to the LAA which will apply the means test to decide whether the client is eligible. However, you will need an understanding of the test in order to advise clients whether they are likely to be eligible.

12.73   The details of the test, together with the eligibility limits applying from time to time can be found in the Criminal Legal Aid (Financial Resources) Regulations 2013. The eligibility limits are amended every so often, usually in April, and the discussion that follows is based on the limits applying in June 2015. There is guidance in the Criminal Legal Aid Manual and on the LAA website at www.gov.uk/criminal-legal-aid-means-testing.

12.74   Eligibility for a representation order is based solely on income – capital is not taken into account except where there is a conviction at the Crown Court. There are three stages to the test:

1) Is the client under the age of 18, or directly or indirectly in receipt of a passport benefit?
2) If not, is the client's gross income below the initial test threshold?
3) If not, is the client's disposable income below the full means test threshold?

If the answer to all three questions is no, the client is automatically not eligible.

12.75   The means of the client's partner should always be taken into account, unless the partner has a contrary interest in the proceedings (for example, is a victim or prosecution witness), together with the resources of any other person which have been or are likely to be made available to the client.[76]

12.76   The passporting benefits are:[77]

- income support;
- income-based jobseeker's allowance;
- guarantee state pension credit;
- income-related employment and support allowance (ESA);
- universal credit.

---

76 Criminal Legal Aid (Financial Resources) Regulations 2013 reg 19.
77 Criminal Legal Aid (Financial Resources) Regulations 2013 reg 2.

If the client is directly or indirectly in receipt of any of these, he or she will automatically be eligible for legal aid. Indirectly in receipt means that the client is included as a dependant on another person's claim.

12.77 If the client is not passported, you will need to proceed to the two-stage means test. If gross income is below the initial threshold, currently £12,457, then he or she is eligible. If gross income is over £22,325, he or she is not eligible.[78] If gross income is between those two figures, then a full means test to determine disposable income will be required. Following that test, if disposable income is less than £3,398 the client will be eligible. All figures are annual.

12.78 'Gross income' is all income from all sources, excluding certain benefits:[79]

- attendance allowance;
- severe disablement allowance;
- carer's allowance;
- disability living allowance;
- constant attendance allowance;
- housing benefit;
- council tax benefit;
- payments out of the social fund;
- direct payments under the Community Care, Services for Carers and Children's Services (Direct Payments) Regulations;
- exceptionally severe disablement allowance;
- service pensions paid under the Naval Military and Air Forces Etc (Disablement and Death) Service Pensions Order 2006;
- independent living funds payments;
- financial support paid for the foster care of a child;
- reasonable living expenses provided for as an exception to a restraint order under section 41 of the Proceeds of Crime Act 2002.

12.79 Where the client has a partner or children in the same household, the gross income threshold increases according to the following weighting:[80]

---

78 Criminal Legal Aid (Financial Resources) Regulations 2013 reg 18.
79 Criminal Legal Aid (Financial Resources) Regulations 2013 reg 20.
80 Criminal Legal Aid (Financial Resources) Regulations 2013 reg 20 and Schedule.

Person	Weighting
Partner	0.64
Child 0–1 years	0.15
Child 2–4 years	0.30
Child 5–7 years	0.34
Child 8–10 years	0.38
Child 11–12 years	0.41
Child 13–15 years	0.44
Child 16–18 years	0.59

12.80   To calculate the weighting, add the relevant factors to 1 and divide household income by the result.

> **Case study**
>
> *My client earns £25,000 per year. He lives with his partner and their children, aged 6 and 3. Is he eligible for a representation order?*
>
> The client has a partner and two children, so the weighting is 1 + 0.64 + 0.30 + 0.34 = 2.28. Weighted income = £25,000 divided by 2.28 = £10,964.91. The gross income threshold is £12,457 and the weighted income is below that, so your client is eligible.

12.81   Where the client is not eligible on gross income, but the (weighted) household income is below the upper threshold, you will need to consider whether the client is eligible on disposable income.[81]

12.82   'Disposable income' is gross income minus:

- tax and National Insurance paid;
- council tax paid;
- rent, mortgage, etc;
- childcare costs;
- maintenance payments;
- living expenses allowance.

12.83   The living expenses allowance is a notional cost of living allowance, currently £5,676 per year. Where the client has a partner and/ or children, the allowance is increased using the scale in the table

81 Criminal Legal Aid (Financial Resources) Regulations 2013 reg 18.

above – so, in the case study, the allowance would be £5,676 x 2.28 = £12,941.28.

12.84   Proof of means will always be required to accompany the application, except where the client is in custody, in which case a statement of truth (now incorporated within form CRM15) should be signed instead, or unless the client's sole income is state benefits, in which case the courts can use their direct computer link with the Department for Work and Pensions to check against the client's National Insurance number that the means information is correct.

12.85   Where the client is not financially eligible, but can demonstrate that to pay privately would cause him or her real hardship, an application can be made for hardship funding. This application is made on form CRM16 to the LAA, and whether to grant is at the LAA's discretion.

Merits test

12.86   The merits test for the grant of representation orders is the 'interests of justice' test. The test is set out in LASPO s17(2), which says:

> In deciding what the interests of justice consist of [in relation to any individual], the following factors must be taken into account–
>
> (a) whether, if any matter arising in the proceedings is decided against the individual, the individual would be likely to lose his or her liberty or livelihood or suffer serious damage to his or her reputation,
>
> (b) whether the determination of any matter arising in the proceedings may involve consideration of a substantial question of law,
>
> (c) whether the individual may be unable to understand the proceedings or to state his or her own case,
>
> (d) whether the proceedings may involve the tracing, interviewing or expert cross-examination of witnesses on behalf of the individual, and
>
> (e) whether it is in the interests of another person that the individual be represented.

Note that this list is not exhaustive, merely examples of what can be taken into account. Guidance on the merits test as applied by the courts contains helpful information about factors that are considered. It is available at www.gov.uk/government/uploads/system/uploads/attachment_data/file/314453/LAA-guidance-consideration-defence-representation-order-applications.pdf.

12.87   Applications for representation orders should be made to the LAA, preferably electronically. Forms CRM14 and CRM15 (where required) should be completed and submitted. Where your client is not in custody, full evidence of means will be required. Where the client is in custody, the declaration in form CRM15 can be signed instead – this is a statement of truth that the information regarding means is accurate.

12.88   An application should be submitted as soon as possible after charge. Orders are deemed to be granted on the date a properly completed application was received, which will be immediate if submitted electronically.[82]

12.89   Where an application is granted, funding for the magistrates' court element of the case is in place and preparation can begin.

12.90   Where the application is refused on means, there is no right of appeal, although applicants can ask for a recalculation if they believe an error has been made, and a fresh application can be submitted at any time (if, for example, there is a change of circumstances). Where the application is refused on the merits, there is a right of appeal to the magistrates' court, who will either confirm the original decision or grant an order.[83]

Funding in the absence of an order

12.91   Advocacy assistance is available for work conducted in a virtual court, whether the work is done at the police station or in a court.[84] There is no merits and financial test.[85] Basic information must be recorded.[86] Claims can be made if the case concludes at the first hearing or if the solicitor's representation ends at that hearing.[87]

12.92   The general rule is that no work can be done and no costs claimed until such time as a representation order has been granted.

12.93   However, an order can be backdated so that a claim can be made for pre-order work where:[88]

- urgent work was required (defined as being a hearing within ten working days of taking initial instructions);
- there was no undue delay in making the application (that is, it was submitted no more than five working days after taking initial instructions);
- an order is subsequently granted.

82 Criminal Legal Aid (General) Regulations 2013 reg 23.
83 Criminal Legal Aid (General) Regulations 2013 reg 29.
84 OCCC paras 9.1–9.2; DPCC paras 10.21–10.22.
85 OCCC paras 9.3–9.4; DPCC paras 10.23–10.24.
86 OCCC para 9.6; DPCC para 10.26.
87 OCCC para 9.8; DPCC para 10.28.
88 Standard Crime Contract 2010 Specification para B10.39; OCCC para 9.18; DPCC para 10.40.

If all these conditions are granted, you are able to claim for work done from the time of initial instructions onwards – where you acted for a client in the investigations stage, from the point of charge onwards.

12.94   Where an order is subsequently refused, you can nevertheless make a claim for work done in certain circumstances:

- Where the application is refused on means, an Early Cover[89] fixed fee of £75 may be claimed if:
  - the application was submitted by 9 am on the sixth working day following initial instructions;
  - you have taken all reasonable steps to assist the client to complete the forms and provide appropriate evidence;
  - no decision had been made on the application by the first hearing;
  - you represent the client at the first hearing, and that hearing moves the case forward and any adjournment is justified; and
  - the eventual decision is that the case passes the interests of justice test but the client fails the means test.
- Where the application has been refused on the merits, a Pre-Order Cover[90] claim, limited to one hour's work at preparation rates, may be made if:
  - a qualified solicitor documents on file why it was believed the interests of justice test was passed; and
  - no claim for early cover is made.[91]
- You can claim a means test form completion[92] fixed fee of £25 where:
  - you complete an application for representation on behalf of the client, whether or not it is actually submitted;
  - you advise the client that although the interests of justice test is in all probability satisfied, the client would fail the means test and the file is marked accordingly;
  - such advice was given within ten working days of charge or summons;
  - the client does not go on to instruct you privately; and
  - you do not make a claim for early cover or pre-order cover.

---

89 Standard Crime Contract 2010 Specification para B10.124; OCCC para 9.100.
90 Standard Crime Contract 2010 Specification para B10.117; OCCC para 9.93.
91 Standard Crime Contract 2010 Specification para B10.118; OCCC para 9.94.
92 Standard Crime Contract 2010 Specification para B10.126; OCCC para 9.102.

Disbursements and prior authority

12.95   Disbursements can be incurred in accordance with the general rules – see above. When you are considering large expenditure, you can apply to the LAA for prior authority to incur the disbursement.[93] The effect of prior authority is that, provided the expenditure does not exceed the terms or amount of the authority, no question can normally be raised as to it on assessment – in other words, you are generally guaranteed to be paid.[94] If authority is refused by the LAA, or not granted in full, the application automatically goes before a Costs Assessor, but beyond that there is no appeal – though there is nothing to stop you making a further application at any time.[95]

12.96   If authority is refused, that does not prevent you from incurring the disbursement, it merely means that you do not have the security of knowing it will be paid on assessment.

12.97   Prior authority will be refused, and so will the disbursement if incurred, where it is a disbursement that should have come out of central funds, for example a court ordered report in consideration of a Mental Health Act disposal.[96]

12.98   Where an application for prior authority has been made and refused, and the client nevertheless instructs you to incur the expense, you may accept payment from the client or a third party for that expense.[97] This is an exception to the rule that legal aid is complete remuneration for the case and no additional charge may be made to the client or a third party.[98]

Counsel

12.99   A representation order for work in the magistrates' court is usually limited to representation by solicitor only. This does not mean that you cannot instruct counsel at all, it just means that counsel is not assigned by the order and therefore the rules regarding unassigned

---

93 Standard Crime Contract 2010 Specification para A5.28; OCCC para 5.27; DPCC para 5.27.

94 Standard Crime Contract 2010 Specification para A5.30; OCCC para 5.29; DPCC para 5.29.

95 Standard Crime Contract 2010 Specification para A5.29; OCCC para 5.28; DPCC para 5.28.

96 Standard Crime Contract 2010 Specification para A5.36(a); OCCC para 5.35(a); DPCC para 5.35(a).

97 Standard Crime Contract 2010 Specification para A8.52; OCCC para 7.43; DPCC para 8.43.

98 Standard Crime Contract 2010 Specification para A8.50; OCCC para 7.41; DPCC para 8.41.

counsel apply. Essentially this means that you are responsible for agreeing and paying counsel's fees.

12.100   In more serious cases, you can apply to the court for counsel (or an independent solicitor advocate) to be assigned. Where counsel is assigned, they are entitled to be paid directly by the LAA at the rates prescribed in the contract, though you should submit their bill with your own – see chapter 14.

12.101   Whether or not counsel is assigned, you must provide them with the UFN and a copy of the representation order when briefing them.[99]

12.102   For more details on the instruction of counsel, please refer to chapter 15.

Separate matters

12.103   All work done in the proceedings class is described by the LAA as a case. Only one bill can be submitted per case.[100] A case is all work done for all clients in respect of:

- one offence; or
- more than one offence where the charges are laid at the same time; or
- more than one offence where the charges are founded on the same facts; or
- more than one offence where the charges form a series of offences.[101]

12.104   'Founded on the same facts' covers situations where one charge is withdrawn and replaced by another, or where two charges are laid as alternatives.

12.105   'Series of offences' means offences of a similar nature. For example, where a client is charged with two separate offences which could be tried together, that would constitute one case. Similarly, where two clients are charged with the same offence (assuming you act for both), that would also be one case. There is no hard and fast rule here; the contract does not offer definitive guidance and it is a

---

99 Standard Crime Contract 2010 Specification para B10.42; OCCC para 9.21; DPCC para 10.43.

100 Standard Crime Contract 2010 Specification para B10.58; OCCC para 9.37; DPCC para 10.59.

101 Standard Crime Contract 2010 Specification para B10.68; OCCC para 9.47; DPCC para 10.69.

matter for your judgment whether you decide there is one case or two.[102]

Co-defendants and conflict of interest

12.106 Note that the regulations say that 'where an individual who is granted a right to representation is one of two or more co-defendants whose cases are to be heard together, that individual must select the same litigator as a co-defendant unless there is, or is likely to be, a conflict of interest'.[103] Therefore, if you are making an application for a representation order on behalf of a client whose co-defendant is separately represented, you should ensure that you demonstrate on the application form why there is a potential conflict requiring separate representation.

12.107 There is a practice note on the Law Society's website,[104] which deals with many examples of possible conflict in criminal cases. Although the 2007 Code of Conduct has been superseded, the guidance to the old rule 3, may still be helpful. It stated:

> ... the regulations are not intended to put solicitors in a position where they are asked by the court to act contrary to their professional responsibilities. If asked by the court for your reasons why you cannot act for both defendants, you must not give information which would breach your duty of confidentiality to your client(s). This will normally mean that you can say no more than that it would be unprofessional for you to continue to act.

12.108 Therefore, you do not have to disclose reasons why a potential conflict of interest exists which prevents you from acting for more than one defendant. However, where such a reason exists you should make clear on the application that there is a (potential) conflict, to avoid you being appointed for both defendants, or to avoid delay while the court makes further enquiries.

---

102 Standard Crime Contract 2010 Specification para B10.71; OCCC para 9.50; DPCC para 10.72.

103 Criminal Legal Aid (Determinations by a Court and Choice of Representative) Regulations 2013 reg 13.

104 http://www.lawsociety.org.uk/support-services/advice/practice-notes/conflict-of-interests-criminal/.

Transfer cases

12.109   Just as the court grants a representation order, where the client wants to transfer from one solicitor to another, the court must agree to the transfer of the order.

12.110   Transfers are governed by regulation, not by the contract. The regulations say that the court may grant an application to transfer where:

- the solicitor appointed under the order considers himself or herself under a professional duty to withdraw;
- there is breakdown in the relationship between solicitor and client such that effective representation can no longer be provided;
- through circumstances beyond his or her control, the authorised solicitor can no longer represent the client;
- there is some other substantial compelling reason.[105]

12.111   Note that any explanation will be strenuously tested by the courts. As a matter of administrative convenience the LAA asks that applications for transfers in the magistrates' courts be directed to the court through the LAA. Solicitors must exercise a proper and independent judgment when considering the applicant's grounds.[106]

Matter ends

12.112   A matter ends, and a bill must be submitted, when the case comes to an end in the proceedings class. This will happen when:

- the case has concluded (for example, by acquittal, sentence or committal);
- it is known that no further work will be needed (eg where the client has transferred);
- it is unclear whether further work will be required but at least one month has elapsed since the last work was done;[107]
- the LAA notify you that the case is a VHCC (very high costs case); or
- the representation order is withdrawn.[108]

---

105 Criminal Legal Aid (Determinations by a Court and Choice of Representative) Regulations 2013 reg 14.
106 *R (Sanjari) v Birmingham Crown Court* [2015] EWHC 2037 (Admin).
107 Standard Crime Contract 2010 Specification para B10.61; OCCC para 9.40; DPCC para 10.62.
108 Standard Crime Contract 2010 Specification para B10.55; OCCC para 9.34; DPCC para 10.56.

Representation in the Crown Court

12.113   Cases in the Crown Court are generally funded by representation orders.

Means testing

12.114   Representation orders in the Crown Court are means tested. However, the means test is a slightly different one from that applied in the magistrates' court and takes into account both a client's income and capital.

12.115   The starting point is that all clients who submit a complete legal aid application will be granted a representation order (the merits test is met in relation to any cases on indictment). However, depending on their means, clients may be required to make payments towards the cost of their representation either immediately or following the conclusion of their case, if they are convicted.

12.116   Certain clients are still passported. These are the same clients who would be passported in the magistrates' court, ie those under 18 or in receipt of income support, income-based jobseeker's allowance, guaranteed state pension credit or income-related employment and support allowance (ESA) or universal credit.

12.117   For those who are not passported, the client's means must be considered. In the Crown Court, unlike in the magistrates' court, this involves assessment of the client's capital as well as income. The means test can be considered in two stages, as follows.

Income

12.118   When the case becomes a Crown Court case, the client may be required to make monthly contributions towards the cost of their representation for the first five months after the case is transferred to the Crown Court. This will apply to clients who have an annual household disposable income of more than £3,398. The income threshold is the same as that in the magistrates' court, so those who passed the means test in the magistrates' court will not be required to pay any contributions from income in the Crown Court.

12.119   For those who are required to pay contributions, their annual disposable income will be divided by 12 and they will be asked to pay 90 per cent of the monthly figure each month for the first five months. Alternatively they can pay all five payments up-front in one lump sum.

12.120 Late payment of any of the five monthly contributions will result in an additional month's payment, ie the client will have to pay the same amount again for a sixth month.

12.121 There is a cap on income contributions which is determined by the type of offence. If a client's contributions reach the maximum level they will be notified and they will not be required to make any further income contributions.

12.122 If a client's case concludes within the first five months of being transferred to the Crown Court, they will not be required to continue paying income contributions. However, if they have been convicted they may become liable for payments from their capital if their income contributions do not cover the full costs of their representation (see below).

12.123 Assuming the case continues beyond five (or six) months from transfer to the Crown Court, the client will not be required to make any further contributions until the conclusion of their case.

12.124 If the client is acquitted, they will not be required to make any further payments at all and their income contributions will be refunded in full with interest (currently set at a rate of 2 per cent annual compound interest). (Note that any costs associated with late payment may be deducted, and very occasionally a client may be required to make a contribution towards their defence costs where, for example, they have misled the prosecution or the court or brought the prosecution on themselves by their conduct. This would be a matter for the judge to decide.)

12.125 However, if the client is convicted, their position will depend on the costs of their case. If the client's income contributions have exceeded the actual costs of their case, the overpayment will be refunded with interest (again subject to any deduction associated with late payment). However, if the income contributions are less than the actual costs incurred, the client's capital will then be considered.

Capital

12.126 A client will only be required to contribute from their capital at the conclusion of his or her case if:

- the client is convicted;
- any payments already made from income do not cover the client's defence costs; and
- the client has more than £30,000 of assets (eg savings, equity in property, shares or Premium Bonds).

12.127   A client with less than £30,000 worth of assets will not be required to make any further contribution even if the client's income contributions have not covered his or her defence costs. (Note, however, that this threshold may be removed if evidence of the client's assets has not been provided.)

12.128   A client with more than £30,000 worth of assets whose income contributions have not accounted for the full costs, will be required to make up the shortfall from their assets. The costs may be recovered in various ways. For example, the LAA may apply an interest-bearing or non-interest-bearing charge to a property or, as a last resort, apply for an order for sale.

Applications

12.129   Crown Court means testing means that a complete application for a representation order (forms CRM14 and CRM15 when appropriate) must be submitted for every non-passported client, even if the application is made after the case has been transferred to the Crown Court. The application should be submitted to the LAA.

12.130   The same rules apply in the Crown Court as in the magistrates' court regarding applications from children and vulnerable adults.

12.131   There are important new rules on the provision of evidence of means with an application. A major difference between applications for funding in the magistrates' court and in the Crown Court, is that clients who are in custody cannot self-declare as to their means when their case is in the Crown Court.

12.132   This does not mean that all evidence (payslips, bank statements, tax returns, share certificates and so on) must be provided with the initial application, although the CRM15 must contain all of the required information. Provided the completed forms have been submitted, a representation order will be issued. The client then has 14 days in which to provide the required documentary evidence. If the required documents are not provided in this time, sanctions may be imposed with respect to both income and capital:

• If evidence of income is not provided, the client's monthly contribution could increase to £900 or 100 per cent of the client's monthly disposable income, whichever is higher.

• If evidence of capital is not provided (or the information provided is subsequently found to be incorrect), the LAA may remove the £30,000 capital threshold and require a client who has less than this amount in capital to pay towards the costs of their defence.

12.133   Where the evidence required is over and above what would normally be required for a magistrates' court legal aid application, you may be able to claim an evidence provision fee for helping the client to provide this evidence. For standard applications a fee of £45 plus VAT can be claimed. For more complex applications involving five or more pieces of evidence, or a self-employed client whose application is referred to the National Courts Team, a fee of £90 plus VAT can be claimed.

12.134   When the completed application has been assessed, the client will be issued with a Contribution Notice or Order alongside the representation order, detailing how much they will be required to pay and the sanctions for late or non-payment.

12.135   A client can also apply for a review on the grounds of hardship if they feel they have higher than usual outgoings or would suffer financial hardship as a result of the means assessment. A completed form CRM16 must be submitted. This can be submitted either at the same time as the CRM14 and CRM15 forms, or afterwards.

Assessing case costs

12.136   Case costs in the Crown Court will vary considerably, depending on the type of case, the volume of evidence, the need for expert witnesses and so on. Therefore at the outset of a case it may be difficult to foresee whether a client's contributions will match the actual case costs.

12.137   The cap imposed on income contributions is intended to prevent clients from paying substantially more than the likely case costs up front, although it should be noted that according to the LAA figures, the cap is well above the average cost to trial in all categories of cases.

12.138   The actual case costs will be calculated at the end of the case and will include the total litigator and advocate fees and any payments to expert witnesses. At the end of the case this amount will be compared with the amount the client has already paid in income contributions: if the client has already paid more than the actual costs, the difference will be refunded with interest; if the client has paid less, they may be required to contribute further from capital as described above. The Collection and Enforcement Agency will notify the client of the position and any amount they owe once the full costs have been established at the end of the case.

Effects of Crown Court means testing

12.139   Because of the potentially high costs of Crown Court cases and the obligation to keep the client informed of the potential costs (Code of Conduct 2011, O1.13) it is essential that the cost implications of any step in the proceedings are thoroughly considered. This will be particularly important in cases where, for example, expert evidence is required: the client should be advised of the cost implications prior to the instruction of any expert and cost considerations may have an impact on the conduct of the case.

12.140   Clients may also be more reluctant to instruct a solicitor at all, and therefore it will be important to advise clients at the outset as to the potential costs (given the type of case), the advantages of being represented and, if appropriate, the possibility of a hardship application. Such an application takes account of the potential private client rates to see if the applicant has sufficient funds to meet them.

12.141   Finally, the supporting evidence requirements for a Crown Court legal aid application are more onerous than those in the magistrates' court. Therefore where a case is sent to the Crown Court and evidence has not already been provided, it is essential that this evidence is obtained as quickly as possible, as failure to provide this evidence within 14 days may have serious financial consequences for the client (see above).

The merits test

12.142   The merits test for a Crown Court representation order is the interests of justice test, just as in the magistrates' court – see above. All cases that have been sent to the Crown Court will automatically satisfy the test.[109]

12.143   Where a case goes from the magistrates' to the Crown Court, except on appeal, the magistrates' court representation order will automatically continue into the Crown Court,[110] and no application to extend or amend the order is required (although additional supporting evidence as to means may have to be provided). Even if counsel were not assigned under the order in the magistrates' court, once the case goes to the Crown Court the order is deemed to include rep-

---

109 Standard Crime Contract 2010 Specification para B10.146; OCCC para 9.121; DPCC para 10.124.
110 Criminal Legal Aid (General) Regulations 2013 reg 24.

resentation by one junior advocate (that is, any advocate other than a QC) automatically.[111]

12.144   For more information on the instruction of advocates in the Crown Court, see chapter 17.

Disbursements

12.145 Disbursements may be incurred in exactly the same way as in the magistrates' court. The test as to whether they are justified is the same, and applications for prior authority may be made.[112] The process is exactly the same as for magistrates' court cases: applications are made directly to the LAA.

12.146   Where the disbursement exceeds £100, you have prior authority and have in fact incurred the disbursement, you can make an application for payment on account of that disbursement at any time. Provided that the amount and scope of the prior authority have not been exceeded, payment should be made.[113]

12.147   See also chapter 14.

Prescribed proceedings in the Crown Court

12.148 Some civil proceedings have been deemed to be criminal for the purposes of legal aid[114] (designated 'prescribed proceedings'), and indeed where orders are imposed in the magistrates' court, the appeal lies to the Crown Court. Examples include stand-alone parenting orders, football banning orders, and Sexual Offences Act orders. The full list is given above in the section covering magistrates' court work.

12.149   Where orders are sought on conviction, dealing with the application for an order (or the appeal against its imposition by the magistrates' court) will be done in the usual way on a representation order.

12.150   Where a stand-alone order is made by the magistrates' court, and the client wants to appeal it to the Crown Court, this will also now be funded on an application by way of a representation order.

12.151   As for other representation orders in the Crown Court, funding for such cases is means tested and therefore the client will need to

---

111 Criminal Legal Aid (General) Regulations 2013 reg 18.
112 Criminal Legal Aid (Remuneration) Regulations 2013 reg 13.
113 Criminal Legal Aid (Remuneration) Regulations 2013 reg 14.
114 Criminal Legal Aid (General) Regulations 2013 reg 9 as amended; see para 12.69 for the full list.

submit completed forms CRM14 and, if appropriate, CRM15 (if non-passported).

12.152　　There is an upper limit to the costs that can be claimed for such work. Unless extended, this is £1,368.75 (£1,237.50).

Appeals to the Crown Court

12.153　Appeals to the Crown Court from the magistrates' court, whether against conviction, sentence or order (ie prescribed proceedings), require a fresh application for funding. The means test is similar to that applied in the magistrates' court.

12.154　　Clients who are passported or pass the means test will not be required to pay any contribution towards the cost of their appeal.

12.155　　Clients who do not pass the means test will be required to pay a defined contribution in the following appeals:

- £500 if an appeal against conviction is dismissed or abandoned;
- £250 if an appeal against conviction is dismissed but sentence is reduced;
- £250 if an appeal against sentence or order is dismissed or abandoned.

12.156　All applications for funding will also be subject to the interests of justice test.

Recovery of defence costs orders

12.157　Prior to the introduction of Crown Court means testing, Recovery of Defence Costs Orders (RDCOs) were the mechanism used to recover the costs paid out to wealthy defendants who were convicted. RDCOs no longer apply in cases where funding is subject to the Crown Court means testing rules (ie all new cases).

12.158　　However, in cases that started prior to the introduction of Crown Court means testing, RCDOs may still be imposed to recover defence costs as they may in the High Court, including the Court of Appeal.

Appeals and reviews

Scope

12.159　Work in the appeals and reviews class covers representation in the High Court on an appeal by way of case stated, advice on an application to the Criminal Cases Review Commission, and advice on appeals to the Court of Appeal.

Case stated

12.160 Where the client seeks an appeal to the High Court by way of case stated, the appeal is funded by representation order. The original order in the magistrates' court (or as the case may be, the Crown Court) covers advice on appeal,[115] including the application to the magistrates' court to state a case.[116]

12.161 Once the case is lodged at the High Court, an application for representation in the appeal should be made to the High Court.[117] It is an application for a criminal representation order. There is no means test, and the merits test is the interests of justice test.

12.162 Where disbursements are needed, you can make an application to the LAA for prior authority.[118] Counsel may be instructed under the order.[119]

Advice and assistance in the appeals class

12.163 Advice and assistance may be granted to assist a client with an application to the Criminal Cases Review Commission, or to appeal against conviction and/or sentence.

12.164 The representation order in the magistrates' or Crown Court includes the provision of advice on appeal,[120] up to the point where an appeal is lodged, and therefore where you represented a client in the magistrates' or Crown Court under legal aid, the advice on appeal should be done under the order. It would not be appropriate to grant advice and assistance for that.

12.165 Similarly, where a representation order is available from the Court of Appeal, advice and assistance should not be used as an alternative to, or to supplement, the Court of Appeal's powers to grant a representation order where only counsel has been authorised.[121]

12.166 Therefore, the primary use of advice and assistance is in cases where the client was not represented, or was represented and seeks a second opinion on the appeal. This would apply whether the client is entitled to go direct to the Court of Appeal or would make an application to the Criminal Cases Review Commission.

---

115 Standard Crime Contract 2010 Specification para B11.3; OCCC para 10.3.
116 Standard Crime Contract 2010 Specification para B11.46; OCCC para 10.44.
117 Standard Crime Contract 2010 Specification para B11.49; OCCC para 10.49.
118 Standard Crime Contract 2010 Specification para B11.59; OCCC para 10.59.
119 Standard Crime Contract 2010 Specification para B11.52; OCCC para 10.50.
120 Standard Crime Contract 2010 Specification para B11.3; OCCC para 10.3.
121 Standard Crime Contract 2010 Specification para B11.7; OCCC para 10.7.

12.167   The general rules on advice and assistance (see the investigations class, above) will apply. The work is means tested[122] and subject to the sufficient benefit test.[123] Costs are limited to £273.75 (£247.50) (£456.25 (£412.50) in the case of a Criminal Cases Review Commission (CCRC) application) but may be extended on application to the LAA.[124]

12.168 When you are dealing with a CCRC case, the LAA recognise that substantial work may be required, particularly where you are not the solicitor who acted at the trial. This may include obtaining the prosecution and defence files, considering transcripts,[125] commissioning further expert evidence and conducting further investigations. However, you should screen the case at as early a stage as possible, and where there is no reasonable prospect it will meet the CCRC's criteria, refuse to carry out further work.[126]

Representation orders in the Court of Appeal

12.169 The Court of Appeal has the power to grant a representation order, but not until leave to appeal has been granted, or until the application to appeal has been submitted.[127]

12.170   The court can grant a representation order to an advocate alone,[128] and indeed this is usual practice. Applications for litigators will usually only be granted to undertake some specific step in the proceedings, such as to interview a witness, rather than for the appeal as a whole.

12.171   Court of Appeal representation orders are subject to the interests of justice test. There is no means test, but Recovery of Defence Costs Orders may be made.

---

122 Standard Crime Contract 2010 Specification para B11.9; OCCC para 10.9.

123 Standard Crime Contract 2010 Specification para B11.8; OCCC para 10.8.

124 Standard Crime Contract 2010 Specification para B11.42 and Criminal Legal Aid (Remuneration) Regulations 2013 Sch 4.

125 Standard Crime Contract 2010 Specification para B11.23; OCCC para 10.23.

126 Standard Crime Contract 2010 Specification para B11.22; OCCC para 10.22.

127 The earlier Criminal Defence Service (General) (No 2) Regulations 2001 reg 10(5) was so interpreted in *Revenue and Customs Prosecution Office v The Stokoe Partnership* [2007] EWHC 1588 (Admin): now the Criminal Legal Aid (Determinations by a Court and Choice of Representative) Regulations 2013 reg 8.

128 Criminal Legal Aid (Determinations by a Court and Choice of Representative) Regulations 2013 reg 18.

Prison law work

12.172 Work in the prison law class is divided into two funding types: (i) advice and assistance and (ii) advocacy assistance.

12.173 Assistance under these two categories may be provided to prisoners (including those on remand and those released on licence or parole where appropriate) in the following types of cases:

- sentence cases;
- disciplinary cases;
- Parole Board Cases.[129]

12.174 The general rules on advice and assistance apply (see above in the investigations class), including the means test[130] and the sufficient benefit test.[131] There are complex rules on the number of matters that may be opened.[132]

12.175 There are restrictive rules on when and how much travel and waiting time can be claimed[133] and a requirement to obtain prior authority to incur a disbursement in excess of £500.[134] There is specific authority to use agents, subject to the rules set out in standard crime contract 2010[135] a practice followed by many firms. If counsel is used to give advice and assistance there are specific rules on how their fees are to be claimed.[136]

12.176 Advice and assistance is limited to a fixed fee of £200.75 (£181.50) unless effective and waiting time costs (calculated at specified hourly rates) exceed £602.25 (£544.50), in which case the costs will be assessed.[137]

12.177 Advocacy assistance for disciplinary cases and Parole Board cases is paid under a standard fee scheme. This is similar to the fee scheme for magistrates' court cases, in that you may claim a lower standard fee, a higher standard fee or a non-standard fee depending on

---

129 Standard Crime Contract 2010 Specification para B12.4; OCCC para 1.3.
130 Standard Crime Contract 2010 Specification para B12.14; OCCC para 11.13.
131 Standard Crime Contract 2010 Specification para B12.6; OCCC para 11.5.
132 Standard Crime Contract 2010 Specification paras B12.33–12.41; OCCC paras 11.23–11.31.
133 Standard Crime Contract 2010 Specification paras B12.42–12.47; OCCC paras 11.32–11.37.
134 Standard Crime Contract 2010 Specification para B12.48; OCCC para 11.38.
135 Standard Crime Contract 2010 Specification para B12.50; OCCC para 11.40.
136 Standard Crime Contract 2010 Specification paras B12.51–12.54; OCCC paras 11.41–11.44.
137 Standard Crime Contract 2010 Specification para B10.75 and Criminal Legal Aid (Remuneration) Regulations 2013 Sch 4; OCCC para 11.65.

whether your profit and waiting time costs (but not travel) fall below, between or above two standard fee limits.[138] Details of the limits are given in the amended Remuneration Regulations at Schedule 4.

12.178   Both advice and assistance and advocacy assistance are granted by you, rather than by application to the LAA.

12.179   The client must complete the relevant forms (CRM1 and CRM2 or CRM3), and must pass the means test. Means are limited by both capital and disposable income, and the eligibility levels can be found on the Legal Aid website at www.gov.uk/criminal-legal-aid-means-testing in the latest keycard. 'Disposable income' means all income received by the client and his or her partner, less tax, National Insurance and the dependants allowances set out on the keycard. The limits and allowances are amended periodically, usually when benefits levels change.

12.180   The sufficient benefit test must be satisfied in all cases, and in addition advocacy assistance may only be provided in Disciplinary cases where:

- it appears unreasonable to grant in the particular circumstances of the case; or
- (where required) permission to be legally represented has not been granted.[139]

12.181   In all cases you should record on the file how the merits test has been and continues to be met.[140]

12.182   Counsel may be instructed under advocacy assistance, but you may not claim for accompanying them to a hearing.[141] If you instruct counsel, you are responsible for agreeing a fee with them and paying them directly. Any fee must not exceed the hourly rate payable to a solicitor.

Scope of prison law work

12.183   With the effect from 4 November 2013, the scope of prison law was reduced.

12.184   Regulation 4 of the Criminal Legal Aid (General) (Amendment) Regulations 2013 says that advice and representation may only be provided in sentence cases where the case is about the calculation

---

138 Standard Crime Contract 2010 Specification para B12.76; OCCC para 11.65.
139 Standard Crime Contract 2010 Specification para B12.116; OCCC para 11.28.
140 Standard Crime Contract 2010 Specification para B12.7; OCCC para 11.6.
141 Standard Crime Contract 2010 Specification para B12.57; OCCC para 11.47.

of the total time to be served before a prison is eligible for automatic release or for consideration of release by the Parole Board.

12.185　Advice and Representation is only available in Parole Board cases where the Parole Board has the power to direct the prisoner's release. Advice and representation is only available in disciplinary cases that involve the determination of a criminal charge for the purposes of article 6(1) ECHR, or where the Governor has exercised the discretion to allow advice and assistance.

12.186　The Court of Appeal has given limited leave to challenge the above scope cuts.[142]

Associated civil work

12.187　Associated civil work is civil work arising out of criminal proceedings, for example judicial review or habeas corpus, or civil work under the Proceeds of Crime Act (POCA) 2002. Although you are permitted to do this work if you have an OCCC or DPCC, even if you don't have a Civil Contract, it is fundamentally civil work and the usual civil rules apply.[143] See chapters 3 and 5 for more details of civil funding.

12.188　Criminal offences under POCA 2002 are dealt with in the same way as all other criminal offences. Confiscation as part of criminal proceedings forms part of the criminal case, so where confiscation is sought against a defendant you can deal with that under the representation order.

12.189　Where confiscation is sought as part of criminal proceedings but which affects a third party (for example, someone who jointly owns property with a defendant), that party can apply for civil legal aid to be represented in the confiscation, notwithstanding that it is part of criminal proceedings in the Crown Court.

12.190　The availability of legal aid is now defined by the Legal Aid, Sentencing and Punishment of Offenders Act 2012 Sch 1 para 40.

142　*R (Howard League for Penal Reform and Prisoners' Advice Service) v The Lord Chancellor* [2015] EWCA Civ 819. See also www.howardleague.org/legal-aid-for-prisoners/.

143　Standard Crime Contract 2010 Specification paras B13.2 and B13.19; OCCC para 12.3; DPCC para 11.3.

Very high cost cases (VHCC)

12.191   Criminal proceedings in which a representation order was granted on or after 3 October 2011 and, if the case were to proceed to trial, would likely last more than 25 days may qualify as very high cost cases (VHCC).

12.192   VHCCs are subject to individual case contracts. If you have such a case, you are obliged to report it to the LAA Complex Crime Unit within five working days of the Plea and Case Management Hearing, or becoming aware that it would be a VHCC.

12.193   You can only continue with the case if you enter into a contract with the LAA in relation to the individual case.

12.194   Further information on the arrangements for VHCCs can be found in the standard contract terms and the 2010 VHCC Guidance document, all published on the legal aid website at www.gov.uk/government/publications/high-cost-case-arrangements-and-contract-documents.

CHAPTER 13

Getting paid for civil and family work

continued

Introduction

13.1 This chapter deals with billing and payment for civil and family work. You should refer to chapters 2–12 for information on conducting cases.

13.2 This chapter does not deal with contract management (which is covered in part C), but with the rules and processes for billing individual cases.

13.3 See appendices H and I for a summary of the Legal Aid Agency's (LAA's) Costs Assessment Guidance, in respect of the most common queries raised by caseworkers.

13.4 Most payment rates under the 2013, 2014 and 2015 contracts are to be found in the Civil Legal Aid (Remuneration) Regulations 2013. Some of the rates have been amended and so the latest rates are in the following instead:

- Civil Legal Aid (Remuneration) (Amendment) Regulations 2013 – reduced fees for experts, and for non-family counsel, from 2 December 2013.
- Civil Legal Aid (Remuneration) (Amendment) Regulations 2014 set rates for welfare benefits work under 2014 contracts.
- Civil Legal Aid (Remuneration) (Amendment) (No 2) Regulations 2014 implemented remuneration changes arising from the introduction of the single Family Court.
- Civil Legal Aid (Remuneration) (Amendment) (No 4) Regulations 2014 implemented changes to court bundle payments in FAS from 31 July 2014.
- Civil and Criminal Legal Aid (Remuneration) (Amendment) Regulations 2015 amended the regulations to prescribe payment rates for orders under the Anti-Social Behaviour, Crime and Policing Act 2014.
- Civil Legal Aid (Remuneration) (Amendment) Regulations 2015 implemented conditional payment for judicial review work done pre-permission for all certificates granted on or after 27 March 2015.

Controlled work

13.5 Controlled work cases are billed individually, but they are paid by way of a monthly payment from the LAA. Each month, the organisation submits claims and receives a monthly payment (known as a standard monthly payment (SMP)), with the aim that bills and pay-ments balance each other out over the course of the financial year, or a variable monthly payment (VMP) based on what it has billed that month. See chapter 20 of this book for more information on this process (known as reconciliation) and on the management of Civil Contracts generally. Organisations can opt for the payment system which suits them best.

13.6   Standard fees are paid for controlled work. These are shown net of VAT and disbursements which may be claimed in addition. Stand-ard fees are claimed by submitting an online claim within 20 days of the end of each month.

13.7   Escape fee cases (known under the 2010 Standard Contract and its predecessors as 'exceptional cases', defined as those where costs exceed three times the fixed fee) may be claimed in full.

13.8   In escape cases, you need to submit an EC1 claim form with your file in order to be credited with the balance above the fixed fee. Under the Standard Civil Contract Specification 2013 para 4.17, you must submit claims for escape fee cases within three months of the end of the case.

13.9   If costs are reduced on assessment, you can appeal (see costs appeals, paras 13.26–13.30 below).

13.10   Although the basic systems for claiming immigration/asylum and mental health controlled work fees are the same as other civil and family work, they have more complex fee schemes. Family cases also have their own schemes. There is more information about these below.

13.11   The fixed fees and underlying hourly rates for all civil and fam-ily work are set out in the Standard Contract 2010 for cases opened before 1 April 2013, and cases in categories where the 2010 contract still applies.

Legal aid representation certificates

Payments on account

13.12   The Standard Contract[1] allows you to claim on account profit costs incurred not earlier than three months after the issue of a legal aid representation certificate. Thereafter, you can apply for further

---

1   Standard Contract 2010 Specification (civil); Standard Contract 2013 Specification (family) para 6.24; Standard Contract 2013 Specification para 6.22.

payments on account, provided that you make no more than two applications in any 12-month period. The application is made using form CIVPOA1, or it can be submitted electronically using the LAA's online facility: www.gov.uk/submit-a-contracted-work-and-adminis-tration-cwa-claim-online. Cases where the certificate was applied for through CCMS have to be claimed through CCMS. You will be paid the amount to bring the total payments on account made to 75 per cent of your profit costs to date.

13.13   See below for information about payments on account under the family law fee schemes.

Prior authority and payment on account for disbursements

13.14   You can apply to the LAA for authority to incur a disbursement in advance, if it is above £100 and is not covered by the standard rates/hours for experts introduced from 3 October 2011.[2] The LAA has set out guidance for the number of hours it considers reasonable for different types of expert reports, and will only consider a prior authority application if it is for more hours than in the guidance, or of a type not included.[3] The application must include a quote for the disbursement and set out the reasons why it is necessary. The application is made using form CIVAPP8A.

13.15   You may apply for prior authority if:[4]

a) an item of costs is either unusual in its nature or is unusually large – this means that it is outside the guidance referred to above;
b) you wish to instruct a QC;
c) prior authority is required under the specification; or
d) you wish to instruct an expert at higher rates than are set out in the Remuneration Regulations.

If you do not apply for prior authority and b), c), or d) above applies, you may not be paid in full or at all for the fees incurred.

13.16   Payments on account of disbursements can be claimed at any time, subject to disbursements being individually or cumulatively above £100. The form is the POA1, as for profit costs above. It can

---

2 Community Legal Service (Funding) (Amendment) (No 2) Order 2011, now in the Civil Legal Aid (Remuneration) (Amendment) Regulations 2013.
3 See Guidance on the Remuneration of Expert Witnesses: www.gov.uk/government/uploads/system/uploads/attachment_data/file/420106/expert-witnesses-fees-guidance.pdf.
4 Standard Civil Contract Specification 2013 para 5.11.

be submitted as a paper form, or as an e-form, using the legal aid online facility. The latter is recommended, not least because payment is made more quickly. See www.gov.uk/legal-aid-eforms. An invoice showing the hourly rate and number of hours claimed must accompany the claim.

Assessment of the final bill

13.17   Once a case has concluded, the final bill should be submitted to the court or LAA for assessment, as appropriate (see below). It should be noted that both the LAA and the court require authority to assess the bill. The authority to assess is either a discharged certificate, or a final order requiring costs to be assessed. Therefore, if the final order makes no mention of costs, a discharge should be sought before submitting the bill.

13.18   For civil licensed work, where the court is responsible for assessment, you must first submit your claim for assessment by the court; and when that is complete, make a claim for payment from the LAA within three months of the final assessment certificate being received from the court.

13.19   Where the LAA is responsible for assessment you must submit a claim within three months of the right to claim accruing.[5] Frequent submission of late claims may lead to contract sanctions, even termination.[6]

Enhanced rates

13.20   In certain circumstances, you can apply for payment at an enhanced rate. The LAA will consider whether enhancement is justified, and if so will increase the hourly rates for some or all of the work done on the case. It would be very unusual for enhanced rates to be allowed on routine items such as travel and waiting (where payable) or letters and telephone calls.

13.21   The test for enhancement is that:

- the work was done with exceptional competence, skill or expertise; or
- the work was done with exceptional dispatch; or
- the case involved exceptional circumstances or complexity,

compared with the generality of proceedings.

5   Standard Civil Contract 2010 and 2013 Specifications paras 6.34–6.36.
6   Standard Civil Contract 2010 and 2013 clause 14.5.

13.22   Where the test is met, the LAA will allow a percentage increase
to the relevant hourly rate not exceeding 50 per cent, or in cases in
the Upper Tribunal or the High Court or above 100 per cent.[7] The
amount of the percentage increase will be determined by having
regard to:

- the degree of responsibility accepted;
- the care, speed and economy with which the case was prepared;
- the novelty, weight and complexity of the case.

Conditional payment for judicial review

13.23   For cases started on or after 22 April 2014, payment for work done
between issue of proceedings and grant of permission in judicial
review cases was made conditional on either:[8]

- the court granting permission; or
- notwithstanding that no permission was granted, the LAA agreeing to discretionary payment.

The LAA would only agree to payment of pre-permission work in
cases where permission was not granted if:

- the court neither granted nor refused permission, and it considers that it is reasonable to pay remuneration in the circumstances
  of the case, taking into account, in particular–
  (i) the reason why the provider did not obtain a costs order or
      costs agreement in favour of the legally aided person;
  (ii) the extent to which, and the reason why, the legally aided per-
      son obtained the outcome sought in the proceedings; and
  (iii) the strength of the application for permission at the time it
      was filed, based on the law and on the facts which the pro-
      vider knew or ought to have known at that time.

Disbursements – including court fees – will always be payable, but
the above provisions affect both solicitor and counsel fees. Payment
on account applications may be made in the usual way, but will be
recouped if payment is not authorised.

However, on 3 March 2015 the High Court found the regulations
to be irrational in the case of *R (Ben Hoare Bell Solicitors and others)
v The Lord Chancellor*.[9] The regulations were quashed on 24 March
2015, meaning that the above amendments to the remuneration reg-

---

7 Civil Legal Aid (Remuneration) Regulations 2013 reg 6(3).
8 Civil Legal Aid (Remuneration) (Amendment) (No 3) Regulations 2014.
9 [2015] EWHC 523 (Admin).

ulations were of no effect. Therefore, payment was once again available in all judicial review cases started since 22 April 2014, and if you haven't already done so you should submit or re-submit claims on certificates granted after that date.

Rather than appeal the judgment, the Lord Chancellor accepted it but immediately laid new regulations that affected all certificates granted on or after 27 March 2015, which effectively reinstated the quashed regulations with some amendments aimed at alleviating the grounds on which the Court found against them.

The Civil Legal Aid (Remuneration) (Amendment) Regulations 2015[10] provide that, for all certificates applied for on or after 27 March 2015, payment for judicial review work done pre-permission is conditional on one of the following:

- the court giving permission;
- the defendant withdrawing the decision to which the application for judicial review relates, resulting in the court refusing permission or making no decision on permission;
- the court ordering an oral permission hearing or an oral hearing of an appeal against a refusal of permission;
- the court ordering a rolled up hearing; or
- the court neither granting nor refusing permission but the Lord Chancellor considers it reasonable to pay remuneration in the circumstances of the case, taking into account, in particular:
  - the reason why no costs order or agreement was obtained;
  - the extent to which, and why, the outcome sought was achieved; and
  - the strength of the application for permission at the time it was filed, based on the law and on facts which the provider knew or ought to have known at the time.

Existing certificates granted before, but to which new judicial review proceedings are added on or after, 27 March 2015 will also be subject to the new rules.

Assessment of costs by the LAA

13.24   Assessment of costs is governed by the 2010 or 2013 Contract, the Remuneration Regulations 2013 (as amended) and the Civil Procedure Rules.

---

10 SI No 898. Reg 2 inserts regulation 5A in to the Civil Legal Aid (Remuneration) Regulations 2013.

Where proceedings have been issued, the LAA assesses all bills where profit costs are up to £2,500 (excluding VAT). Bills in excess of £2,500 are assessed by the court. The exception to this is where there is an element of costs between the parties, where the bill is assessed by the court regardless of the size of the claim. There is provision in the Standard Contract for the LAA to take over assessment of all claims, but there is no definite date for this.

13.25   Claims to the LAA are made on form CIV CLAIM1, which must be completed in full and accompanied by the certificate, fee notes and invoices, orders and the full file of papers. There is a useful checklist to ensure the claim is correctly submitted at: www. gov.uk/government/uploads/system/uploads/attachment_data/file/421687/lc1-laa-assessed-claim1-checklist.pdf.

Costs appeals

13.26   If costs for exceptional controlled work or licensed work are reduced on assessment, you can appeal. You may want to do this, even if the effort of preparing the appeal seems disproportionate to the reduction in fees, if a successful appeal would improve your key performance indicators (see chapter 20).

13.27   Appeals must be made in writing and accompanied by the file. An LAA Internal Reviewer will carry out a formal and detailed review of the original decision. If dissatisfied, there is a further right of appeal to an Independent Costs Assessor. The Independent Costs Assessor is an experienced solicitor in private practice, and not a member of the LAA's staff. The Independent Costs Assessor may confirm, increase or decrease the amount assessed.

13.28   Any appeal to an Independent Costs Assessor is considered on paper, although in exceptional circumstances either party can apply to the Assessor for an oral hearing. Such requests are rarely granted.

13.29   See the Standard Civil Contract 2010 Specification, paras 6.68–6.87 or Standard Civil Contract 2013 Specification paras 6.67–6.86 for more information on costs appeals.

Points of principle of general importance[11]

13.30   At any point after the submitting of an appeal to the Assessor, but not later than 21 days after receipt of the final decision, the LAA or the provider can seek clarification on the costs rules and provisions. This is done by applying for a certificate of a point of principle of

11   There is no right to apply for POPs under the 2014 or 2015 contracts.

general importance (POP). POPs are the LAA's equivalent of costs case-law, and are binding on regional offices and Independent Costs Assessors when assessing bills. They are not binding on the courts. Applications can be made to the LAA or direct to an Assessor if one has been appointed. The application must set out the exact wording of the POP sought. The LAA will decide whether the matter should progress to the Costs Appeals Committee, which will decide whether a POP should be certified. The text of current POPs, and the procedure for applying for one, are set out in the POP Manual.[12]

Assessment of costs by the courts – legal aid only

13.31   Bills to be assessed by the courts must be drawn up in the form prescribed by the Civil Procedure Rules and the Senior Court Costs Office Guide. A costs draftsman's fee can be claimed on the bill. The bill should then be submitted to the court using the appropriate notice, and accompanied by the relevant fee. Each court and costs office has its own local practices; some will require just the bill, certificate, orders and fee notes and invoices, others the full file of papers.

13.32   The forms to be used, the Guide, and a list of fees for different types of case, are available on the Justice website at www.justice. gov.uk/courts/rcj-rolls-building/senior-courts-costs-office. Unless a hearing before a district judge or costs officer is requested, assessment will be on the papers. On receipt of the returned assessed bill, the time limit for appealing the assessment begins to run. Solicitors should notify counsel of reductions to their costs within seven days, and all appeals should be submitted within 14 days. Solicitors appeal on behalf of counsel.

13.33   For full detail of the procedure, see the Senior Court Costs Office Guide (available on the Justice website: www.justice.gov.uk/courts/ rcj-rolls-building/senior-courts-costs-office/guidance) and the Civil Procedure Rules parts 47 and 52.

13.34   Once the assessment process is completed, you should draft the Costs Certificate, and return to the court for sealing with the appropriate fee. The sealed Costs Certificate, the assessed bill, the funding certificate, and fee notes should then be sent to the LAA with form CIV CLAIM1 for payment.

---

12 See www.gov.uk/legal-aid-points-of-principle-of-general-importance-pop.

Assessment of costs by the courts – inter partes, and legal aid where the client has an interest in the assessment

13.35   Where the bill is entirely inter partes, or mixed inter partes and legal aid, the bill must be served on the other side before assessment proceedings begin. The other side has three weeks to accept the bill or serve points of dispute, to which you should respond. If agreement cannot be reached, the bill should be sent to the court for assessment. In disputed cases, a hearing before a district judge or costs officer is usual. The procedure then follows that outlined above.

13.36   The client has an interest in the assessment if the statutory charge arises, or if a contribution has been paid. The client has the same right to dispute the bill, and to be represented on the assessment, as any other paying party. If the client does not respond, or chooses not to exercise that right, the solicitor should certify accordingly on the bill.

13.37   Following assessment, the sealed Costs Certificate should be submitted to the LAA as above, but using form CIV CLAIM2, which is used to report to the LAA in all cases where another party is liable for all or part of the costs. If the other party cannot or will not pay, the solicitor can either take enforcement proceedings, or assign the costs to the LAA. In this scenario, the LAA will pay the costs, but only at prescribed rates, not inter partes rates, and then pursue the paying party for the costs.

13.38   For full details, see the Senior Court Costs Office Guide and the LAA's Civil Costs Assessment Guidance (the latter can be found at: www.gov.uk/funding-and-costs-assessment-for-civil-and-crime-matters).

Inter partes costs and legal aid only costs

13.39   In cases where inter partes costs are possible, it is not uncommon for costs to be ordered or negotiated on the basis of payment of part of the costs of the case. If so, it is important that you are clear as to the terms of the order or agreement, as in some cases but not others you may be able to claim the balance from the legal aid fund. The Standard Civil Contract allows you to claim from the legal aid fund any costs not payable by another party (legal aid only costs), but only if certain conditions are met.[13]

---

13   Standard Civil Contract Specification 2010 paras 6.52–6.53; Standard Civil Contract Specification 2013 paras 6.51–6.52.

13.40   The Specification defines 'legal aid only' costs – costs that can be claimed from the legal aid fund even where inter partes costs are recovered – as:

- costs of completing legal aid forms and communicating with the LAA;
- certain limited types of costs disallowed or not agreed;
- costs of work not covered by a costs order or agreement.

13.41   Where a costs order or agreement specifies that another party should pay a proportion of the client's costs (but not a fixed sum), the same proportion of the total work that is not covered is legal aid only costs.

13.42   To take a practical example, say total costs on the case are £2,000 at legal aid rates and £4,000 at inter partes rates. If the other side agree to pay your costs in the sum of £2,000, that could be expressed in one of three ways:

- £2,000 as the total agreed costs of the case;
- agreement to pay costs between x and y dates, totalling £2,000; or
- agreement to pay 50 per cent of the costs, being £2,000.

In each case, you receive £2,000 from the other side. In the first case, that £2,000 represents the total costs of the case, so there are no legal aid costs (apart perhaps from £100 or so for filling in the APP1 and so on). In the second case, costs outside the agreed dates are not subject to the costs order, so you can claim those costs from the LAA in addition to the inter partes costs you have received. In the third case, the other side have agreed to pay 50 per cent of your costs, so the other 50 per cent are legal aid only costs, so you can claim £1,000 (50 per cent of £2,000 at legal aid rates) from the LAA, in addition to the £2,000 from the other side.

Family

Controlled work

13.43   Claims for Legal Help and Family Help (Lower) in both private and public family schemes, and Help with Family Mediation claims are paid and claimed as other civil categories, described above.

Family – controlled work escape fee cases

13.44 The escape threshold for Legal Help and Family Help (Lower) in both private and public Family schemes is that profit costs calculated on an hourly rate basis must exceed three times the fixed fee.

Licensed work

13.45 The general rules and procedures for claiming licensed work costs are described above.

13.46 Standard fee claims are submitted to the LAA as above.

13.47 In cases where proceedings have not been issued, the LAA assesses the costs.

13.48 Where proceedings have been issued the LAA assesses bills where profit costs are up to £2,500 (excluding VAT). The £2,500 refers to assessable costs – that is, as costs that are claimed under legal aid other than by way of any Standard or Graduated Fee, ie disbursements, solicitor advocacy, escape fee claims and costs otherwise falling outside the Higher Standard Fee Scheme.

13.49 Bills in excess of £2,500 are assessed by the court. The exception to this is where there is an element of costs between the parties, where the bill is assessed by the court regardless of the size of the claim.

13.50 Claims for advocacy under the FAS must be made on an appropriately completed Advocates Attendance Form (EX506). If such form(s) are not submitted the claim(s) will only be paid at the unit 1 rate.

13.51 Claims covered by family standard fees are made on CIV CLAIM1A.

Family – public law standard fee scheme: escape fee[14] cases

13.52 The escape threshold for Family Help (Higher) in the public family scheme is that profit costs calculated on an hourly rate basis must exceed twice the fixed fee. Don't forget that advocacy is claimed separately and in addition to the fixed fee, so advocacy costs do not count towards reaching the escape threshold.

---

14 Cases that escape the standard fees and are paid by way of hourly rates were known as 'exceptional cases' under the Standard Contracts 2010 and 2012, but are known as 'escape fee' cases in the Standard Contract 2013 and the amended 2010 contract. The rules are the same in both contracts.

Family – private law standard fee scheme: escape fee cases

13.53   The escape threshold for Family Help (Higher) in the private family scheme is that profit costs calculated on an hourly rate basis must exceed three times the fixed fee. As above, advocacy is excluded when calculating the escape threshold.

Family – public and private law standard fee schemes: enhancement of hourly rates

13.54   At level 3 – Family Help (Higher), you cannot take any enhancement of hourly rates into account in deciding whether a case escapes from the standard fee, including the 15 per cent uplift that would otherwise be available for panel membership.[15]

13.55   If the case escapes when calculated at the normal hourly rate, you can apply for an enhancement where justified. An enhancement may be justified where the work was done with exceptional competence, skill or expertise; the work was done with exceptional speed; or the case involved exceptional circumstances or complexity.[16] However, an enhancement may never exceed 100 per cent for cases in the High Court or above (or in the Family Court in front of a High Court – in all other cases the maximum is 50 per cent).

13.56   In escape cases, you can claim an enhancement of 15 per cent for membership of the following panels:

- the Resolution Accredited Specialist Panel;
- for work done under a Certificate which includes proceedings relating to children, the Law Society's Children Panel; or
- the Law Society's Family Law Panel Advanced.

Family – public and private law standard fee schemes: client transfers

13.57   If your fees on an hourly rates basis are equal to or greater than the standard fee, you claim the standard fee.[17] If your fees on an hourly rates basis are less than the standard fee, you claim half the standard fee.

13.58   If you are instructed for less than 24 hours, where you are instructed at the same time as another solicitor, or where your client's

---

15   Standard Civil Contract Specification 2013 para 7.21.
16   Section 12 of the LAA's Costs Assessment Guidance.
17   Standard Civil Contract 2012 Specification para 7.17; Standard Civil Contract 2013 Specification para 7.18.

application to be joined to proceedings is refused, you will be paid by way of hourly rates.[18]

Family – public law standard fee scheme: advocacy

13.59   The standard fees for care proceedings under Children Act 1989 s31 do not include advocacy. The LAA defines 'advocacy' to include not only appearances as advocate before the court, but also any associated travel and waiting time and attendance as advocate at advocates meetings in public law children matters, as well as preparation for advocacy.

13.60   See chapter 16 for information on the Family Advocacy Scheme.

Family – very high cost cases

13.61   From 1 October 2015 all single advocate care cases will be paid under Care Case Fee Scheme (CCFS) unless you can show you would be paid at least 30 per cent more by claiming hourly rates with a case plan. You can find out more information at www.gov.uk/civil-high-cost-cases-family. The CCFS model is used in family cases to avoid multiple revisions to detailed case plans. It is a form of graduated/fixed fee, dependent on the number of hearing days and other events.

13.62   A series of fixed amounts are applied to each event based on the predicted timetable. At the end of the case, the final costs are adjusted to reflect the actual timetable. The fee applied to each event is based on detailed analysis of the average costs and hours in these types of expensive/complex cases.

13.63   The benefit of the CCFS is that it avoids multiple revisions to detailed case plans, which is popular with practitioners and is often (but not always) considered preferable to an individually agreed case plan.

13.64   All very high cost cases are assessed by the LAA.

Immigration and asylum

13.65   This section describes payment for Legal Help and CLR cases. For licensed work in the immigration category, see the general principles above.

---

18 Standard Civil Contract 2012 Specification para 7.18; Standard Civil Contract 2013 Specification para 7.19.

Standard fee cases

13.66   The scope of the standard fee scheme is not defined in the contract, except by exclusion. Paragraph 8.77 of the Specification simply lists hourly rates cases, all others being standard fees. Therefore, standard fees apply to all cases other than:

(a) work in relation to an asylum application (including 'NAM' or 'Legacy'), which was made prior to 1 October 2007;

(b) a fresh asylum application where the original asylum application was lodged, whether concluded or not, prior to 1 October 2007;

(c) advice in relation to the merits of lodging an application for permission to appeal to the Upper Tribunal (where advice has not been received under a stage 2 standard fee);

(d) Controlled Legal Representation in relation to an application for permission to appeal and, where granted, the subsequent appeal before the Upper Tribunal;

(e) bail applications;

(f) advice and applying for a Certificate for Licensed Work, including complying with the pre-action protocol;

(g) initial advice in relation to an Asylum application prior to claiming asylum eg at the Asylum Screening Unit (ASU) where you then cease to be instructed. This will also apply where the client returns after attendance at the ASU but where it is confirmed that the client will be dispersed and will not continue to instruct you;

(h) Escape fee cases[19] under the Graduated Fee Scheme;

(i) advice in relation to a client who is an unaccompanied asylum seeking child;

(j) cases remitted from the Court of Appeal to the Upper Tribunal or Upper Tribunal to the First-tier Tribunal;

(k) where you hold an exclusive schedule, any matters opened as a result of an on-site surgery at an IRC or for a fast track client.;

(l) advice in relation to terrorism prevention and investigation measure orders (TPIMs);

(m) applying for a certificate in relation to TPIMs;

(n) applying for a certificate for Special Immigration Appeals Commission work.

Exceptional cases are paid at hourly rates rather than through the standard fee scheme.

---

19 These are the cases described under the 2010 contract as exceptional fee cases; exceptional cases under the new contract are those out of scope but funded under LASPO s10.

Immigration and asylum fee stages[20]

13.67   Fees are split into three main stages: 1, 2a and 2b. Different fees apply at each stage in asylum and non-asylum matters, but the stages are the same for both. The fees include travel and waiting.

13.68   There are additional fees on top of the basic fee for extra work at each stage (see below).

13.69   Stage 1 covers the Legal Help stage of the case, and ends when Controlled Legal Representation (CLR) is granted or refused, or when the matter ends, whichever is earlier.

13.70   Stage 2 covers the CLR stage of the matter. Either – but not both – the 2a or 2b fee will be payable, depending on the point at which the matter ends. The 2a fee will be payable where the case does not proceed to – or, at least, representation is not provided at – a substantive hearing; 2b is payable where the case does proceed to a substantive hearing. Stage 2 will end when CLR is granted or refused to lodge an application to the Upper Tribunal, or when the matter ends, whichever is earlier. Where CLR is granted for an application to the Upper Tribunal, the case will be paid at hourly rates from that point onwards.

13.71   See the Standard Civil Contract 2013 Specification paras 8.62–8.66 for full definitions of each stage and examples of what work is included.

13.72   A claim for stage 1, and either stage 2a or stage 2b, must be submitted within six months of the end of each stage.[21]

Immigration and asylum – additional fees[22]

13.73   Additional fixed fees are payable on top of the relevant graduated fee in the following circumstances:

- attendance at a Home Office interview where permitted (see chapter 9);
- representation at a Case Management Review Hearing (CMRH) – different fees are payable depending on whether it is an oral or telephone hearing;
- representation at a substantive tribunal hearing;
- representation at a part-heard or relisted hearing.

---

20   Remuneration Regulations 2013 Sch 1 table 4(a).
21   Standard Civil Contract 2013 Specification para 8.60.
22   Remuneration Regulations 2013 Sch 1 table 4(b), (c).

Immigration and asylum – counsel

13.74 Where counsel is instructed for representation at a hearing, the relevant additional fee for representation will be added to the graduated fee paid to the solicitor and it will be for the solicitor to pay counsel.

Immigration and asylum – disbursements

13.75 All disbursements, including interpreters and travel expenses, are payable on top of the graduated fee, subject to the relevant disbursement limits. Disbursements at the Legal Help stage should not exceed £400.[23] Where the case is a graduated fee, disbursements for the CLR should not exceed £600;[24] where the case is payable at hourly rates, costs and disbursements together should not exceed £1,600 (asylum) £1,200 (immigration) or £500 (bail only).[25]

13.76 An application may be made to the LAA to extend any or all of these limits for matters opened from 10 November 2010. Save for the costs of waiting time where 'there is a significant delay on the day of a hearing, which is no fault of yours or your Client, provided you apply for an extension to the Cost Limit as soon as practicable thereafter',[26] costs limits cannot be extended retrospectively. You must apply for extension on the relevant extension forms (CW3A/CW3B).[27]

13.77 A claim can be made in respect of unpaid disbursements. This claim can be made if at least six months have elapsed since the start of the matter and, if you have become entitled to make a Controlled Work claim or have previously applied for payment under this paragraph, at least six months have elapsed since that entitlement arose or application was made.[28]

Immigration and asylum – escape fee cases[29]

13.78 The calculation for determining whether escape fee payments can be made is relatively complicated. The calculation is made at the end of the case, and covers costs for the whole case – Legal Help plus

---

23 Standard Civil Contract 2013 Specification para 8.68 (a).
24 Standard Civil Contract 2013 Specification para 8.68 (b).
25 Standard Civil Contract 2013 Specification para 8.86.
26 Standard Civil Contract 2013 Specification para 8.88.
27 www.gov.uk/government/publications/cw3-extension-of-upper-cost-limit-in-controlled-work-cases.
28 Standard Civil Contract 2013 Specification para 8.104.
29 Standard Civil Contract 2013 Specification para 8.72.

CLR. Where total profit costs at hourly rates, minus any additional payments made, are more than three times the graduated fee, then an exceptional case payment may be claimed. The amount of the exceptional payment is total profit costs, minus additional payments, minus standard fee already paid.[30]

13.79   Claims for exceptional cases should be made at the end of the case – that is, following the completion of both the Legal Help and CLR, where relevant. When making a claim for an exceptional payment, any previous claims under the standard fee scheme should be reconciled against the payment sought.[31] A claim for escape fee payment must be made at the end of the case once all costs are known and certainly within three months of the case being reported as a completed matter.[32] These claims are subject to an individual costs assessment and submitted on an EC-Claim 1 IMM form.[33]

Immigration and asylum – hourly rates cases

13.80   All cases excluded from the standard fee scheme (see above) are payable by hourly rates.

13.81   In hourly rates cases (except those that become hourly rates cases by escaping from the standard fee scheme) there are costs limitations which may be extended on application to the LAA.

13.82   For Legal Help, the limit (excluding VAT and disbursements) is £800 in asylum cases and £500 in non-asylum cases.[34]

13.83   For CLR, the limit (excluding VAT, but including disbursements[35] and counsel) is £1,600 for asylum cases, £1,200 for non-asylum cases and £500 for stand-alone bail applications (where a substantive appeal includes a bail application, bail is included in the £1,600/£1,200).[36]

13.84   Legal Help claims must be submitted within six months of submission of a fresh application for asylum (fresh claim cases only), or within six months of the Home Office decision (all other cases), and then within six months of the end of the case. CLR claims should be submitted within six months of the first tribunal decision, and then within six months of the end of the case.[37]

---

30 Standard Civil Contract 2013 Specification para 8.74.
31 Standard Civil Contract 2013 Specification para 8.75.
32 Standard Civil Contract 2013 Specification para 4.17.
33 www.gov.uk/government/publications/escape-fee-case-claim-forms.
34 Standard Civil Contract 2013 Specification para 8.80.
35 Standard Civil Contract 2013 Specification para 8.86.
36 Standard Civil Contract 2013 Specification para 8.87.
37 Standard Civil Contract 2013 Specification para 8.102.

Upper Tribunal cases

13.85   Upper Tribunal cases are not subject to costs limits, either in respect of costs or disbursements. Instead 'reasonable costs'[38] will be allowed, though may be assessed. Where the application for review was made by the Home Office, or the client is detained under fast track procedures, you may always claim your costs. The rates set out in table 8(a) of Schedule 1 to the Civil Legal Aid (Remuneration) Regulations 2013 should be claimed.

13.86   In all other cases, no claim for costs may be made if permission to appeal is refused (Specification para 8.93). Therefore, costs in these cases are at risk, and the higher rates set out in table 8(b) of Schedule 1 to the Civil Legal Aid (Remuneration) Regulations 2013 may be claimed for all cases opened before 2 December 2013. For cases started on or after that date, the higher rates were removed and the rates in Table 8(a) will apply.[39] Disbursements will always be claimable (Specification para 8.96).

Mental health

13.87   This section relates to work done before the tribunal under CLR. For licensed work in the mental health category, see the general principles above.

Mental health fee scheme

13.88   The mental health fee scheme applies to all controlled work in the mental health category of law, except for Help at Court for Victims (which is paid at hourly rates), and is divided into:

- a fee for all non-MHT (Mental Health Tribunal) matters ('non-MHT fee'); and
- three fees for MHT matters ('MHT fees') as follows:
  - MHT fee level 1 (initial advice);
  - MHT fee level 2 (negotiation and preparation); and
  - MHT fee level 3 (representation before the Mental Health Tribunal).

---

38   Standard Civil Contract 2013 Specification para 8.94.
39   Table 8(b) revoked by Civil Legal Aid (Remuneration) (Amendment) Regulations 2013 SI No 2877 on 2 December 2013.

You cannot claim both the non-MHT fee and any level of MHT fee in the same matter for a client.

13.89   Help at Court for Victims[40] is not remunerated under the mental health fee scheme but is paid at hourly rates.

Mental health – disbursements

13.90   In general, the cost of all time spent in travel and waiting is included in the fees payable. However, the LAA intends to designate some hospitals as 'remote', and where work is done at these hospitals a remote travel payment will be claimable. Payment of remote travel payments will be generated by completing the appropriate box on the Consolidated Matter Report form (CMRF). At the time of writing, no hospitals had been so designated.

13.91   Other disbursements are paid in addition to the fees.

Mental health – transfers

13.92   Where a client transfers his or her case to you, you are entitled to claim the full mental health fee for each of the levels of work you undertake, including initial advice and negotiation/preparation.[41]

Mental health – adjourned hearing fees

13.93   When a hearing is adjourned or is postponed or cancelled on the day at the request of the tribunal or Responsible Medical Officer, or in circumstances where you make a request to adjourn, postpone or cancel, and where you could not have otherwise reasonably avoided making such a request, and you have actually attended the place of the tribunal, you can claim this fee for each additional hearing that is adjourned on the day.[42]

Mental health – escape fee cases

13.94   Where the amount of any claim as calculated on the basis of hourly rates exceeds three times the mental health fee(s) payable, it becomes an escape fee case and is paid at hourly rates.

---

40 Help at Court – funding for representation for victims under the Domestic Violence, Crime and Victims Act 2004. See Standard Civil Contract 2014 Specification para 7.85.
41 Standard Civil Contract 2014 Specification para 7.84.
42 Standard Civil Contract 2014 Specification para 7.70.

13.95   For work covered by the non-MHT fee or the MHT fee level 1, the relevant hourly rate is that for Legal Help.

13.96   For work covered by MHT fee Level 2 and MHT fee level 3, the relevant hourly rate is that for CLR.

13.97   When calculating whether a matter or case qualifies as an escape fee case, if the case qualifies for remote travel payment(s) and/or adjourned hearing fee(s), then in order for it to become exceptional its costs need to exceed the total of three times the total of all fee levels payable *plus* the total of all additional payments payable.[43]

13.98   The LAA provides the following example:

> In an MHT case with work at levels 1, 2 and 3 and two adjourned hearings, in order to escape the costs would need to be greater than:
>
> (3 x (Level 1 Fee + Level 2 Fee + Level 3 Fee)) + (2 x Adjourned Hearing Fee).[44]

13.99   Escape fee cases will be remunerated on the basis of the relevant hourly rates. These rates will apply to work carried out by either solicitor or counsel.

Mental health – counsel's fees

13.100 Counsel's fees do not count as a disbursement and you are responsible for agreeing and paying counsel's fees.

13.101 In an unusually complex case you may request prior authority from the LAA for a higher hourly rate. The LAA says this will be highly unusual in MHT cases. Where it is allowed, an hourly rate and a maximum cost limit will be specified. These may not be exceeded without further authority (which will not be granted retrospectively). Where authority is granted but the matter start does not qualify as an exceptional case, then the LAA will pay an additional sum equal to the difference between counsel's fees as authorised by the prior authority and the applicable fees which would have been payable.

---

43 Standard Civil Contract 2014 Specification para 7.79.
44 Standard Civil Contract 2014 Specification para 7.81.

CHAPTER 14

Getting paid for criminal work

edited by Anthony Edwards

continued

Figures in brackets apply for cases where the grant of advice and assistance, advocacy assistance or representation was made on or after 1 July 2015. New rules apply in many cases of grants on or after 11 January 2016.[1] It is likely that the original rates will be restored for a period from October 2015 until 11 January 2016.

Introduction

14.1   This chapter deals with billing and payment for criminal work. See appendix H for a summary of the Legal Aid Agency's (LAA's) Costs Assessment Guidance, in respect of the most common queries raised by caseworkers.

14.2   Most criminal work is paid for through the monthly contract payment, the biggest exception being work done in the Crown Court.[2]

14.3   Although contract cases are billed individually, they are not directly paid. Instead, each firm, or office, has a fixed monthly payment set by the Legal Aid Agency (LAA). Each month, the firm submits bills which are offset against the payment, with the aim that bills and payments balance each other out over the course of the financial year. See chapter 20 for more information on this process (known as reconciliation) and on the management of Criminal Contracts generally. Crown Court bills in cases funded by representation orders are individually paid.[3]

This chapter does not deal with contract management (which is covered in part C), but with the rules and processes for billing individual cases. For information about conducting criminal cases, see chapter 12.

Remuneration regulations

14.4   Remuneration rates are set out in the Criminal Legal Aid (Remuneration) Regulations 2013. These have been amended as follows:

- Criminal Legal Aid (Remuneration) (Amendment) Regulations 2013 codified VHCC rates and reduced expert fees for cases started on or after 2 December 2013;

---

1 Both fee changes made by the Criminal Legal Aid (Remuneration etc) (Amendment) Regulations 2015.

2 Standard Crime Contract Standard Terms para 14.8 and Specification 2010 (hereafter 'the Specification') para A5.21; OCCC paras 20.5–20.14; DPCC paras 5.20–5.24.

3 Specification para A5.26; OCCC para 5.25; DPCC para 5.25.

- Criminal Legal Aid (Remuneration) (Amendment) Regulations 2014 reduced most rates (the main exception being Advocates Graduated Fee Scheme (AGFS) rates) by 8.75 per cent from 20 March 2014;
- Civil and Criminal Legal Aid (Remuneration) (Amendment) Regulations 2015 prescribed rates for Anti-social Behaviour, Crime and Policing Act 2014 cases;
- Criminal Legal Aid (Remuneration etc) (Amendment) Regulations 2015 imposed a further 8.75 per cent cut (again except in AGFS cases) from 1 July 2015 and made amendments to the fee structures applying form 11 January 2016.

It is therefore not always easy to work out which rates apply to which cases. You should start with the main 2013 Regulations and then check later Regulations to see if there have been amendments relevant to your particular case. Unfortunately no single consolidated set of rates exists.

Investigations class work

14.5   A bill should be submitted at the end of the investigations class, even if the case continues into proceedings. One bill should be submitted for all work done in the class (subject to the exceptions set out below).

Police station telephone advice only

14.6   Where a client is at the police station and you provide telephone advice but do not attend, you can claim the telephone advice fee.[4]

14.7   The fee is not claimable in a case in which Criminal Defence Direct were involved,[5] and is triggered by a telephone call during which you speak to the client. Only one fee is payable per investigation.[6]

14.8   The value of the fee is set out in the Remuneration Regulations, and is currently £27.60 (from 11 January 2016: £24.96) (£28.70 (from 11 January 2016: £25.95) for London firms).

Advice and assistance

14.9   In cases where you provide advice and assistance to a client outside the police station, but do not attend the police station with the client,

---

4   Specification para B9.115; OCCC para 8.96; DPCC para 9.111.
5   Specification para B9.114; OCCC para 8.95; DPCC para 9.110.
6   Specification para B9.116; OCCC para 8.97; DPCC para 9.112.

you can claim for the costs of the advice and assistance at the hourly rates set out in the contract. Where the case also involves attendance at the police station, the costs of advice and assistance are included within the police station fixed fee.[7]

14.10   A single claim for all work done (except advocacy assistance, which should be claimed separately) in the investigations class should be submitted when:

- the investigation has concluded, whether by charge, summons or other disposal; or
- it is known no further investigations work will be undertaken for the client; or
- it is unclear whether further work will be required but at least one month has elapsed since the last work (unless the client has an outstanding bail back); or
- post-charge work at the police station has been undertaken (in circumstances in which such work is not otherwise funded).[8]

14.11   Where you have acted for more than one client in the same investigation, you should make a separate claim for each client, apportioning the work between them if necessary.[9]

14.12   The hourly rates applicable to this work are set out in the Remuneration Regulations. You should apply the rates to all work done, subject to any costs limit. The costs limit for advice and assistance is £273.75 (from 11 January 2016: £247.50) for both profit costs and disbursements; this limit can be extended on application to the LAA.[10]

Police station attendance

14.13   All work done at the police station is subject to fixed fees. The fee is triggered whenever there is attendance upon the client at the police station. However, it does not include attendance for an ineffective bail to return if you did not check whether it would be effective prior to attending.[11]

14.14   Where triggered, the fee will cover all work done in the investigations class including advocacy assistance. Therefore, where, for example, you carry out advice and assistance outside the police station

---

7   Specification para B9.139; OCCC para 8.120.
8   Specification paras B9.108 and B9.140; OCCC paras 8.99, 8.135, 8.148 and 8.159; DPCC paras 9.104, 9.135 and 9.147.
9   Specification paras B9.112, B9.141; OCCC para 8.71; DPCC para 9.81.
10   Specification para B9.143; OCCC para 8.124; DPCC para 9.137.
11   Specification para B9.2; OCCC para 8.2; DPCC para 9.2.

for eligible clients, such as between bails to return, that work will also be covered by the fixed fee.

14.15   There is a separate fee for each duty scheme area (from January 2016, these are replaced with London and non-London fees), and the fees are set out in the Remuneration Regulations. Only one fee is payable per client per case (even if you attend the police station on more than one occasion).[12] Where, however, work is a genuinely separate matter then a separate claim may be made, if you attend the client at the police station on a separate occasion in relation to one of the matters after another has concluded. It will be a separate matter if the client has genuinely separate legal problems requiring separate advice[13] on more than one occasion. If, for example, the client is charged with one offence and you reasonably attend on the bail to return to the police station on another, separate fees could be claimed in relation to each offence.[14]

14.16   A file note should be made setting out any justification for claiming more than one fixed fee[15] and separate Defence Solicitor Call Centre (DSCC) reference numbers should be obtained.

Case study

I had a client who was arrested for theft and taken to the police station, where it was found he was also wanted for a separate incident of criminal damage, and he was further arrested for that. Is that one matter or two?

It depends on the outcome of the case. If he were charged with both offences and bailed to the same court date, that would be one matter and one claim. This is because the two allegations required advice on one occasion only, and resulted in one set of proceedings.

However, if he were charged with theft and you reasonably attended on the bail to return on the criminal damage, that would constitute two matters since they require separate advice on more than one occasion.

---

12 Specification para B9.89; OCCC para 8.88; DPCC para 9.85.
13 Specification para B9.83; OCCC paras 8.67–8.71; DPCC paras 9.77–9.81.
14 Specification para B9.85; OCCC para 8.70; DPCC para 9.80.
15 Specification para B9.83; OCCC para 8.68; DPCC para 9.78.

Payment rates and exceptionality[16]

14.17 Although police station work is payable by fixed fee, you should record all the time spent on the case and report the value of that time at the appropriate hourly rates to the LAA. The applicable rates are set out in the Remuneration Regulations. Where the value of the case at hourly rates exceeds the Exceptional Threshold fee for the appropriate area, the case is deemed to be exceptional, and you can apply to the LAA for an additional payment.

14.18 The categories of rates for attendance are:

- own or duty solicitor;
- duty solicitor unsocial hours;
- duty solicitor serious offence social hours;
- duty solicitor serious offence unsocial hours.

Similar categories (except those for serious offences) apply for travel and waiting time.

14.19 For these purposes, social hours are between 9.30 am and 5.30 pm on a business day – that is, any day other than Saturday, Sunday, Christmas Day, Good Friday or any bank holiday.[17]

14.20 Serious offences are:[18]

- treason;
- murder;
- manslaughter;
- causing death by dangerous driving;
- rape;
- assault by penetration;
- rape of a child under 13;
- assault of a child under 13 by penetration;
- robbery;
- assault with intent to rob;
- arson;
- perverting the course of justice;
- conspiracy to defraud;
- kidnapping;
- wounding/GBH – both sections 18 and 20 of the Offences Against the Persons Act 1861;

---

16 Specification paras B9.98–B9.100; OCCC paras 8.83–8.85; DPCC paras 9.94–9.97.
17 Specification para A1.13; OCCC para 1.2 (unsocial hours); DPCC para 9.2.
18 Specification para B9.102(a); DPCC para 9.98.

- conspiracy, solicitation, incitement or attempt of any of the above;
- any offence if the client is also accused of possession of a firearm, shotgun or imitation firearm;
- any offence if the client is detained under Terrorism Act 2000 s41.

14.21   In order to claim duty rates, the case must be a duty case – that is, referred as a duty case by the call centre or done during a duty period, and the work done by an accredited fee earner.[19] To claim serious offences rates, the work must be done by a duty solicitor,[20] and you must not be a confirmed category 3 firm in relation to your crime contract.[21]

14.22   To calculate whether the case is exceptional, you calculate the value of all time spent at the appropriate hourly rate. This will include any advice and assistance outside the police station. You should also include a telephone advice fixed fee[22] or a Criminal Defence Direct acceptance fee[23] (where a former Criminal Defence Direct matter was referred to you for police station attendance). This will give you a total value for the case. If the total value is more than the relevant Exceptional Threshold set out in the Remuneration Regulations, then you can make an application to the LAA to treat it as an exceptional case.[24]

14.23   In order to do that, you should complete the form (form CRM18) and submit it to the LAA Nottingham office (see www.gov.uk/government/collections/legal-aid-crime-claim-forms). The LAA will assess the claim, and if following assessment it is confirmed that the case is worth more than the Exceptional Threshold, the case will be treated as exceptional.

14.24   However, you will still not be paid the full value of the case. Instead, you will only be paid the fixed fee, plus the amount by which the case exceeds the threshold.[25]

---

19 Specification para B9.101; DPCC para 9.97.
20 Specification para B9.102; DPCC para 9.97 (when any duty lawyer may do the work).
21 Specification para B9.103; DPCC para 9.99.
22 Specification para B9.87; OCCC para 8.72; DPCC para 9.82.
23 Specification para B9.97; OCCC para 8.82; DPCC para 9.93.
24 Specification para B9.98; OCCC para 8.83; DPCC para 9.94.
25 Specification paras B9.99–B9.100; OCCC paras 8.84–8.85; DPCC paras 9.95–9.96.

Case study

For the purposes of this example the rates for cases that commenced before 1 July 2015 have been used. The same principles will apply to the changing regimes; with figures reduced by a further 8.75 per cent after 1 July. For case commencing after 11 January 2106 a much simplified fixed fee scheme is introduced with a single London rate and a single out of London rate.

I represented a client at West End Central Police Station on a case of murder over a weekend. It was a duty case, and I spent in total 15 unsocial hours in attendance at the police station, plus six hours' travel and waiting (all unsocial). I also incurred a telephone fee. What will I be paid?

West End Central is on the Central London scheme, so the fixed fee is £237.25 plus VAT. It was a duty case and a weekend so London duty unsocial serious case rates apply: £73 per hour for attendance and £63.01 for travel and waiting, and Criminal Defence Direct fee of £7.30.

Your time is worth £(73 x 15) + £(63.01 x 6) + £7.30 = £1,480.36. The fixed fee is £237.25, and the threshold is £803.78. Therefore you are over the threshold and the case is exceptional.

You will be paid (subject to assessment) the value of the fixed fee plus the amount by which the threshold is exceeded: £237.25 + (£1,480.36 − £803.78) = £913.83.

You should send your exceptional claim to the LAA who will assess the bill.

14.25 Exceptional cases will not be paid direct. Instead, the value allowed on assessment will count towards your contract claims.

Advocacy assistance

14.26 Advocacy assistance – of whatever type – is the exception to the rule that all investigations work be billed together. Any claim for advocacy assistance should be submitted separately. This work is not subject to fixed fees, and the hourly rates set out in the contract will apply subject to a Costs Limit of £1,369.75 (£1,237.50). A single claim for all advocacy assistance on a case should be made[26] at the end of the

26 Specification paras B9.153, B9.166 and B9.178; OCCC paras 8.134, 8.147 and 8.158; DPCC paras 9.121, 9.134 and 9.146.

investigations stage.[27] Where police station advice and assistance, or free-standing advice and assistance, has already been provided, the same unique file number (UFN) must be used, although the work must be claimed separately.[28]

Proceedings class work

Virtual court claims

14.27   Rate of remuneration are specified in the Criminal Legal Aid (Remuneration) Regulations 2013 Sch 4 as amended.

Court duty claims

14.28   You should claim any work done as court duty solicitor at the end of the duty session. You should make one claim per session, rather than one claim per client.[29] The applicable payment rates are set out in the Remuneration Regulations.

14.29   You cannot claim for travel time or expenses to get to court, except where you are acting on a non-business day (eg a Saturday or bank holiday sitting), or where you are called to court having not been on the rota or having attended on a rota and been released and then asked to return.

Representation orders

14.30   See chapter 12 for details on conducting work under a representation order.

14.31   Magistrates' court work should be billed at the end of the magistrates' court stage of the case. No fee is payable if the case is sent to the Crown Court for trial. There is no provision for interim payments, so the bill will be submitted when one of the defined end points occurs:

- The case has concluded.
- It is known that no further work will be required.

---

27 Specification paras B9.154, B9.167 and B9.179; OCCC paras 8.135, 8.148 and 8.159; DPCC paras 9.122, 9.135 and 9.147.

28 Specification paras B9.168 and B9.180; OCCC paras 8.149 and 8.160; DPCC paras 9.136 and 9.148.

29 Specification para B10.17; DPCC para 10.18.

- It is unclear whether further work will be required and at least a month has elapsed since the last work was undertaken.[30]
- A warrant of arrest was issued and at least six weeks, but not more than 19 weeks, have elapsed since.[31]

14.32 The exception to this is where sentence is deferred; you may submit a bill when sentence is deferred and another when the client returns to be sentenced.[32] Bills must be submitted within three months of the end of the case.

14.33 Where you act for more than one client in a case, you should submit a single bill covering work done for all clients,[33] though you will need a separate representation order for each one.[34]

Standard fees – pre and post new crime contracts

14.34 Until the government's new proposals take effect for orders granted on or after 11 January 2016,[35] most magistrates' court work is covered by the standard fee regime. Following the abolition of committal proceedings there are three categories of fee – 1A, 1B and 2 – and in each category a lower and a higher standard fee. Under the 2016 regime there will be a single standard fee for the whole country in each category

14.35 Until the 2016 regime takes effect there are two types of fee:

- If your office is in an area specified by the contract, or if it is not but the court is, you should claim the designated area standard fee.[36]
- If not, you should claim the undesignated area standard fee.[37]

14.36 The designated areas[38] are:

- Greater Manchester, London, West Midlands and Merseyside criminal justice areas;
- the local authority areas of:

---

30 Specification para B10.61.
31 Specification para B10.66.
32 Specification para B10.65.
33 Specification para B10.59.
34 Specification para B10.64.
35 See for outline OCCC 5 and DPCC 5.
36 Specification para B10.78.
37 Specification para B10.79.
38 Specification para A1.13.

- Brighton and Hove;
- Bristol;
- Cardiff;
- Derby and Erewash;
- Kingston upon Hull;
- Leeds and Bradford;
- Leicester;
- Nottingham;
- Portsmouth;
- Newcastle-upon-Tyne and Sunderland;
- Sheffield;
- Southampton.

The difference between the two is that in a designated area, the fees are slightly higher but you cannot claim for any travel and waiting time,[39] whereas in an undesignated area you can claim travel and waiting[40] but the standard fees are lower. Even if you cannot claim travel and waiting, you are still required to record the waiting time (though need not record travel).[41] Travel, except for duty solicitors in exceptional circumstances, and waiting are not payable under the 2016 regime.

14.37   In either case, the structure of the fees is the same. Whatever the category of your case, you calculate your core costs (all profit costs except travel and waiting time).[42] If the core costs are below the lower limit for the category of case, you claim the lower standard fee. If core costs are between the lower and higher limits, you claim the higher standard fee. If core costs are above the higher limit, you claim a non-standard fee – that is, you claim your costs in full as incurred.[43]

14.38   You should decide which category of fee to claim based on the nature and outcome of the case:

- Category 1A[44] is:
  - either way guilty pleas (including thefts from a shop of goods valued at under £200);
  - indictable only cases heard in the Youth Court;

---

39   Specification paras B10.81 and B10.86; OCCC paras 9.60 and 9.62, DPCC paras 10.82 and 10.84.
40   Specification para B10.84; OCCC paras 9.60 and 9.62, DPCC paras 10.82 and 10.84.
41   Specification para B10.88; OCCC para 9.64; DPCC para 10.86.
42   Specification para B10.80.
43   Specification para B10.89; OCCC para 5.8; DPCC para 5.8.
44   Criminal Legal Aid (Remuneration) Regulations 2013 Sch 4 para 5.

- proceedings (other than committal proceedings) relating to either way offences which are discontinued or withdrawn or where the prosecution offer no evidence; and
- proceedings (other than committal proceedings) relating to either way offences which result in a bind over.

- Category 1B[45] is:
  - summary only guilty pleas;
  - uncontested proceedings arising out of a breach of an order of a magistrates' court;
  - proceedings (other than committal proceedings) relating to summary offences which are discontinued or withdrawn or where the prosecution offer no evidence;
  - proceedings (other than committal proceedings) relating to summary offences which result in a bind over;
  - proceedings arising out of a deferment of sentence (including any subsequent sentence hearing) under section 1 of the Powers of Criminal Courts (Sentencing) Act 2000;
  - proceedings prescribed under regulation 9 of the Criminal Legal Aid (General) Regulations 2013 (see para 12.69), except where the case was listed and fully prepared for a contested hearing to decide whether an order should be made; and
  - proceedings relating to either way offences which must be tried in a magistrates' court in accordance with section 22 of the Magistrates' Courts Act 1980.

- Category 2[46] is:
  - contested trials;
  - proceedings which were listed and fully prepared for trial in a magistrates' court but are disposed of by a guilty plea on the day of trial before the opening of the prosecution case;
  - proceedings which were listed and fully prepared for trial in a magistrates' court but are discontinued or withdrawn or where the prosecution offers no evidence or which result in a bind over on the day of trial before the opening of the prosecution case;
  - contested proceedings relating to a breach of an order of a magistrates' court (including proceedings relating to a breach of a Crown Court community rehabilitation order, community punishment order or suspended sentence);
  - proceedings where mixed pleas are entered; and

---

45 Criminal Legal Aid (Remuneration) Regulations 2013 Sch 4 para 5.
46 Criminal Legal Aid (Remuneration) Regulations 2013 Sch 4 para 5.

– proceedings prescribed under regulation 9 of the Criminal Legal Aid (General) Regulations 2013 where the case was listed and fully prepared for a contested hearing to decide whether an order should be made. (see para 12.69).

14.39   Note that cases sent to the Crown Court under Crime and Disorder Act 1998 s51 are treated as being Crown Court cases from charge – all work should be claimed on the Crown Court bill and no magistrates' court claim can be made (except in the event of a remittal back).[47]

14.40   Where proceedings have not concluded but a warrant of arrest has been issued, the proceedings will be treated as category 1 proceedings.[48]

14.41   Bail applications (including to the Crown Court) and appeals against bail are included in the standard fee of the substantive case.[49]

14.42   Where more than one category is possible, you should select the one that will pay the highest fee.[50]

14.43   On a change of solicitor, the old firm should claim a category 1 fee, and the new firm should claim in the usual way. The exception to this is where the conducting solicitor moves firms and takes the case – if this happens, only the new firm can claim, but should claim for both firms.[51]

14.44   Where you have claimed a fee and then a further claim is required – for example, claimed a category 1 fee when a client absconds and a warrant is issued, and then continued to represent the client following arrest on the warrant – you should calculate the total costs due for the whole of the case, deduct the amount previously claimed, and claim the balance.[52]

47 Specification para B10.75; OCCC para 9.54; DPCC para 10.76.
48 Specification para B10.95; OCCC para 9.71; DPCC para 10.92.
49 Specification para B10.72; OCCC para 9.72; DPCC para 10.93.
50 Specification para B10.92; OCCC para 9.68; DPCC para 10.89.
51 Specification paras B10.93 and B10.94; OCCC paras 9.69–9.70; DPCC paras 10.90–10.91.
52 Specification para B10.98.

Case study

My office is in Manchester. My client was charged with theft, indicated a not guilty plea and elected summary trial. He was convicted following trial, and sentencing was deferred for six months. What should I claim?

Manchester is in a designated area, so you should be claiming the designated area standard fee. Your client took the case to a trial, so the case is in category 2. You should calculate your core costs (all time excluding travel and waiting) to see whether a lower, higher or non-standard fee is claimable.

When your client comes back to be sentenced in six months' time, you can claim a further category 1B standard fee.

For cases where the representation order is granted on or after 11 January 2016, the location of the office is not relevant and there is a single level of standard fee.

Counsel

14.45   Unassigned counsel are treated as you are, and you should include their times on your bill as if they were your profit costs.

14.46   Where counsel is assigned, their costs are separate from yours. Rates for assigned counsel are set out in the Remuneration Regulations, and counsel should prepare a bill at those rates.[53] They will be paid direct by the LAA, but you should submit their bill alongside yours.[54]

Separate matters

14.47   One standard fee is payable per case. A case consists of all work for all clients in respect of:

- one offence; or
- more than one offence, where:
    - they are charged at the same time; or
    - they are founded on the same facts; or
    - they form part of a series of offences.[55]

---

53 Specification para B10.43; OCCC para 9.22; DPCC para 10.44.
54 Specification para B10.44; OCCC para 9.22; DPCC para 10.44.
55 Specification para B10.68; OCCC para 9.47; DPCC para 10.69.

14.48   Offences 'charged at the same time' is a straightforward test. 'Founded on the same facts' is intended to cover situations where two charges are brought as alternatives, or where one charge is substituted for another – common examples include theft and handling stolen goods, or ABH and common assault.

14.49   A 'series of offences' refers to offences which have similarities or form a pattern of offending, that could be tried together. Each potential series of offences has to be considered on its own facts and definitive guidance cannot be given. However, there is a useful discussion at section 6.6 of the Criminal Bills Assessment Manual (2013). The key principle is that the offences are sufficiently related. For example, offences that are based on a system of conduct, are similar in nature, or where evidence of one is admissible at the trial of another, may all form part of a series. Even though some hearings may be held at different times, or in different courts, that would not prevent a series being established.

Enhanced rates

14.50   In certain circumstances, you can apply for payment at an enhanced rate. The LAA will consider whether enhancement is justified, and if so will increase the hourly rates for some or all of the work done on the case. It would be very unusual for enhanced rates to be allowed on routine items such as travel and waiting (where payable) or letters and telephone calls.

14.51   The test for enhancement is that:

- the work was done with exceptional competence, skill or expertise; or
- the work was done with exceptional dispatch; or
- the case involved exceptional circumstances or complexity,

compared with the generality of proceedings.[56]

14.52   Where the test is met, the LAA will allow a percentage increase to the relevant hourly rate not exceeding 100 per cent,[57] or in the case of serious fraud 200 per cent.[58] The amount of the percentage increase will be determined by having regard to:

- the degree of responsibility accepted;

---

56   Specification para B10.100; OCCC para 9.76; DPCC para 10.97.
57   Specification para B10.103; OCCC para 9.79; DPCC para 10.100.
58   Specification para B10.104; OCCC para 9.80; DPCC para 10.101.

- the care, speed and economy with which the case was prepared;
- the novelty, weight and complexity of the case.[59]

14.53   Enhancement of the hourly rates takes the case out of the standard fee regime, so you should submit an individual bill to the LAA, accompanied by a note setting out why you believe the criteria for enhancement are met and justifying the percentage sought. It is important to remember that what seems obvious to you may not be so to an assessor. So, for example, you should not assume that because the court granted a certificate for counsel that you will automatically get an uplift, having decided to do the advocacy yourself. You will need to address the criteria explicitly and show how your advocacy was exceptional.

Other contract work

14.54   Advice and assistance in the appeals and prison law classes is claimed under the contract in the same way as free-standing advice and assistance in the investigations class (see above, and see also sections B11 and B12 of the contract),[60] as is advocacy assistance in the prison law class (see section B12 of the contract).[61] The Remuneration Regulations provide details of the fixed fees and standard fees applicable to prison law cases.

14.55   Representation in judicial review or habeas corpus proceedings, or civil proceedings under the Proceeds of Crime Act 2002, is claimed as all other civil legal aid; see chapter 13. See section B13 of the Standard Contract.[62]

14.56   Representation in other civil proceedings associated with criminal proceedings (eg where papers from a civil case are relevant to a criminal case) is funded by representation order and requires prior authority. However, it is claimed under the same remuneration provisions as apply to Civil Legal Representation. See sections B10.152–B10.163 of the Standard Contract.[63]

14.57   Representation on an appeal by way of case stated is funded by representation order (issued by the High Court) and claimed in the same way as in the proceedings class, except that there are no standard fees. See section B11 of the Standard Contract.

---

59 Specification para B10.102; OCCC para 9.78; DPCC para 10.99.
60 OCCC 10 and 11.
61 OCCC 11.
62 OCCC 12.
63 OCCC paras 9.128–9.139; DPCC paras 10.131–10.142.

The claiming process

14.58   Contract work is claimed by submitting details of the bills to the LAA. With the exception of magistrates' court non-standard fees, you do not need to send in the file of papers and bills will not be individually assessed.

14.59   Each month, you should submit form CRM6 to the LAA using the legal aid online portal: https://lsconlinesso.legalservices.gov. uk. Each line on the CRM6 represents one bill. There is a series of codes you should use to differentiate between different types of cases, different offences and scheme areas (for police station fee purposes). The LAA then set off each bill against your contract payments, with the overall aim being that payments match claims, within acceptable reconciliation boundaries – see chapter 19. The codes can be found on the legal aid website at www.gov. uk/government/publications/cwa-codes-guidance.

14.60   Non-standard fees in the magistrates' court are subject to individual assessment by the LAA. You should complete form CRM7 with details of the case and the amount claimed, plus justification for the costs, and send it to your LAA processing office with your file of papers.[64] The LAA will assess the bill and return the file to you with details of the amount allowed, which will be credited to your contract account rather than paid to you direct. CRM7 can also be submitted as an e-form through LAA online: https://lsconlinesso.legalservices. gov.uk.

14.61   If you disagree with the assessment, there is a right of appeal to an Independent Costs Assessor, who is a solicitor independent of the LAA. The Assessor will consider the file, the LAA assessment and your representations and will reduce, confirm or increase the amount allowed by the LAA. There is a 28-day time limit to appeal, and appeals will generally be dealt with on the papers. Full details of the appeal process are set out in the contract.[65]

14.62   There is no right of appeal beyond the Assessor, unless you can show a point of principle of general importance (POP). These are very rarely established. See section A8 of the Specification. There is no right to apply for a POP under the OCCC or DPCC contracts.

---

64   Specification para B10.73; OCCC para 9.52; DPCC para 10.74.
65   Specification section A8; OCCC 7; DPCC 8.

Crown Court – litigator fees

14.63 Although all Crown Court work is included within the scope of the contract, the payment rates and rules are governed by the Criminal Legal Aid (Remuneration) Regulations 2013 as amended.

14.64 From January 2008, the previous system of payment by hourly rates was abolished and replaced with a graduated fee scheme. It was intended to be a transitional scheme, with the ultimate aim of introducing a combined single fee scheme for all work, both litigation and advocacy. However, at the time of writing the schemes remain separate.

14.65 The scheme makes a distinction between fixed fees and graduated fees. There are fixed fees for cases that involve either way offences when the magistrates' court accepted jurisdiction but the defendant elected trial on indictment; and for cases that do not involve trial on indictment, such as committal for sentence, breaches and appeals. For cases where representation is granted on or after 11 January 2016 a new fixed fees scheme will apply to other cases where there are less than 500 pages of prosecution evidence. Graduated fees apply to all other cases heard on indictment.

14.66 Graduated fees are determined by a number of factors:

- the classification of the offence – offences are classified into 11 classes (A–K);
- the outcome – whether a guilty plea (plea entered before or at plea and case management hearing), a cracked trial (guilty plea entered after plea and case management hearing) or trial (including Newton hearings); discontinuances are paid at the same rate as guilty pleas;
- the length of the main hearing – the trial or hearing at which pleas were entered;
- the number of pages of prosecution evidence (excluding unused material) served;
- the number of defendants represented by you.

To calculate the fee, you should first categorise your case by the offence. Where there is more than one charge on the indictment, select the one which would result in the higher fee.

14.67 For each outcome type, there is a basic fee which varies depending on the classification of the offence, and to which an uplift is added depending on the number of pages of evidence and the length of the main hearing.

14.68   As a result, there are thousands of variables and the tables set out in Schedule 2 to the Remuneration Regulations 2013 and amendments thereto are lengthy and complex. However, the LAA has made available a spreadsheet into which the classification, trial length, page count and outcome can be entered, and which then calculates the appropriate fee – see www.gov.uk/government/publications/graduated-fee-calculators

14.69   All work done on a case is covered by the graduated fee; the exceptions are work done in connection with confiscation following conviction, and work classified as 'special preparation' (for instance considering more than 10,000 pages of evidence or exhibits) which is payable at hourly rates in addition to the fee.

14.70   Claims for litigator fees can be made through the LAA online billing system, and if you use it to submit claims the website will also calculate the relevant fee.

14.71   Claims are assessed item by item by the LAA, who will compare the information on your claim with that held by the Court Service.

14.72   There is a right of appeal against assessment provided for in regulation 28 of the Remuneration Regulations 2013. Appeals must be made in writing within 21 days of receipt of the assessment. You cannot challenge the fee scheme itself, but can challenge the calculation in any individual case, such as by appealing the classification of the offence or the allowed page count. On redetermination, the fee may be confirmed, reduced or increased.

14.73   If you remain dissatisfied with the assessment, you can apply for written reasons within 21 days, and then within 21 days of receipt of the reasons request a hearing before a costs judge.

Payments on account

14.74   Where you have been granted prior authority by the LAA and have incurred a disbursement of more than £100 you can apply for a payment on account of the disbursement at any time.[66]

14.75   Where a representation order is dated on or after 2 October 2014 a litigator may make a claim for an interim payment of profit costs at one or both of two stages in proceedings.[67] The rules are refined for

---

66 Criminal Legal Aid (Remuneration) Regulations 2013 reg 14.
67 See Criminal Legal Aid (Remuneration) (Amendment) (No 2) Regulations 2014.

post 11 January 2016 orders to allow for cases with under 500 pages of prosecution evidence.[68]

14.76   The first stage is where a not guilty plea is entered following a plea and case management hearing (unless it was on a defence election), or alternatively, where a retrial is ordered and representation has been transferred to a new litigator. The interim payment at PCMH stage of proceedings is set at 75 per cent of the cracked trial rate plus any uplifts. Where a retrial is ordered and representation transferred to a new litigator, the payment is set at 50 per cent. The determination of the cracked trial rate will depend on the number of pages of prosecution evidence served on the court and the classification of the offence into which the case falls.

14.77   The second stage is where a trial has commenced that is expected to last for ten or more days. Either the basic or the final fee calculated in accordance with Schedule is payable. The trial is presumed to last one day.

14.78   There is no other provision for payment on account of profit costs unless you can show financial hardship, and even then only if it has been at least six months since the start of the case and it is unlikely that payment will be received for at least three more months. You will have to provide evidence of hardship, usually in the form of a bank statement or letter from your bank.[69]

Crown Court – advocates' fees

14.79   The scheme for advocates is similar to that applying to litigators. The applicable rules and fees are set out in Schedule 1 to the Remuneration Regulations 2013.

14.80   Each case will have a trial advocate, who is responsible for claiming fees on behalf of all advocates instructed in the case. Payment will be made to the trial advocate.

14.81   The scheme provides for a basic fee based on the classification of the offence to which is added uplifts for pages of evidence, length of trial, number of witnesses and additional fees for features such as conferences. There is a higher basic fee for a trial and a lower for a guilty plea case. The basic fee includes payment for attendance at a

---

68   See Civil and Criminal Legal Aid (Remuneration) (Amendment) Regulations 2015 Sch 4.
69   Criminal Legal Aid (Remuneration) Regulations 2013 reg 21.

plea and case management hearing and four other hearings during the case; additional fees can be claimed for other hearings.

Very high cost cases

14.82   Cases accepted by the LAA as very high cost cases (VHCC) (ie, cases in which a representation order was granted on or after 3 October 2011 and, if the case were to proceed to trial, would likely last more than 25 days (60 for advocates)) may be subject to individual case contracts. The rates will depend on the category of case (seriousness) and the level of fee earner (dependent on experience). Standard rates for each category and level of fee earner are set out in the Specification to the VHCC Standard Contract.

14.83   For further information refer to the legal aid website at www. gov.uk/government/publications/high-cost-case-arrangements-and-contract-documents.

Legal aid advocacy

CHAPTER 15

Advocacy in civil cases

Introduction

15.1   This chapter deals with the conduct of and payment for advocacy in civil cases and the general rules applying to both civil and family cases.

15.2   In general, we use the term 'advocate' to refer to anyone who has a right of audience to appear in the relevant court or who the court is willing to hear where the scheme makes no distinction between solicitor and counsel. Where there is a difference according to whether advocacy is conducted by solicitor or by counsel, we will use the terms 'solicitor' and 'counsel' as appropriate.

15.3   This chapter only deals with the advocacy aspects of cases. For more information on the conduct of litigation, see Part A of this book. For information on the particular rules applying in family and criminal cases, see chapters 16 and 17.

General principles

15.4   Advocacy can only be conducted under the following levels of service:

- Help at Court;
- Controlled Legal Representation (CLR) (immigration and mental health only);
- legal representation (certificated work);
- specific contracts, such as a housing court duty possession scheme contract.

Advocacy can only be carried out by a person who has a general right of audience or who has been given permission to be heard by the court in the specific case.

15.5   Advocacy funded by legal aid can only be carried out in matters before a court and before certain limited tribunals. The full list is set out in LASPO Sch 1 Pt 3.

Help at Court

Scope

15.6   Work must be allowed within scope of the scheme (see chapter 3 and appendix G for more information).

15.7   Help at Court is help and advocacy for a client in relation to a particular hearing, without formally acting as legal representative in the proceedings or being on the record at the court (Civil Legal Aid (Procedure) Regulations 2012). Help at Court only covers informal advocacy, usually by way of mitigation at individual court hearings. Ongoing representation can only be provided under a legal representation certificate.

15.8   Help at Court is particularly useful for cases where a legal representation certificate would not be available, for example where a client does not have a defence to a possession claim, but does need an experienced adviser to set out repayment proposals to the court Note however that if it would be unreasonable for the court to make an order for possession in the circumstances, it can be treated as a defence to the a claim for possession and a certificate should, assuming means and merits tests are met, be available. Help at Court can also be used to represent the client on an application for enforcement of an order where the client is the applicant. It is not a stand-alone level of funding, but can only be granted as an add-on to a pre-existing Legal Help matter.

Merits test

The sufficient benefit test

15.9   The merits test is that:

- it is reasonable to provide funding, taking into account the availability of alternative (ie non-legal aid) funding;
- there is likely to be sufficient benefit, having regard to all the circumstances of the case, including the circumstances of the client, to justify the costs; and
- the nature and circumstances of the client, the proceedings and the particular hearing are such that advocacy is appropriate and would be of real benefit.[1]

This means the issue(s) must be more complex than the client could have explained to the court himself or herself.

15.10   You must apply the test before every hearing and note the file with your justification. 'Sufficient benefit test met' is not an adequate justification.

15.11   There are no additional fixed fees to cover Help at Court. However, the additional work involved may make it more likely that the

---

1 Civil Legal Aid (Merits Criteria) Regulations 2013 reg 33.

case will reach the Legal Help escape threshold (three times the fixed fee).

15.12　　Where advocacy is justified, you may claim travel and waiting to/ from and at court, as well as preparation and attendance, where appropriate. See chapter 13 for more information on payment schemes.

Specific areas of work

Housing cases

15.13　The Funding Code Guidance, at section 19.3, provided specific guidance on the use of Help at Court in housing cases. You may still find it helpful to consult it if your organisation has a pre-LASPO copy of the LSC Manual (eg that dated December 2012, vol 3). An online version is available in the archived version of the old LSC website.[2]

15.14　　Before making an application for a full certificate, you should consider the availability of Help at Court, and if it is more appropriate a certificate may be refused. Help at Court may be more appropriate where the client has no defence but seeks to influence the discretion of the court in relation to postponing possession or suspending eviction.[3] Help at Court should not be used in any case where a certificate would be more appropriate (unless one has been applied for and refused) – in the above, for example, where the client does have a substantive defence to the possession proceedings, or where there is a substantial issue of fact or law or where the client should be formally represented in the proceedings.

15.15　　Neither should Help at Court be used where it is not justified, for example because it would achieve no more than would explaining to the client what steps they could take themselves or writing a letter on their behalf under Legal Help.

15.16　　See chapter 11 for more on housing cases.

Who can provide advocacy?

15.17　Solicitors can attend court under Help at Court in circumstances where they have rights of audience – since it will almost always be the county court, that will be most cases. Advisers without rights of audience may provide advocacy and claim payment under Help at

2　http://webarchive.nationalarchives.gov.uk/20130403152321/http://www. justice.gov.uk/legal-aid/funding/funding-code/non-family-guidance.

3　Lord Chancellor's Guidance on Civil Legal Aid para 6.9(b).

Court, as long as advocacy is justified and the court agrees to hear them. Counsel may not be instructed under Help at Court.[4]

Payment for advocacy services

15.18 Advocacy under Help at Court – and associated preparation, attendance, travel and waiting – is claimable as part of the main Legal Help matter. The costs are included within the fixed fee, and may be taken into account in determining whether the case becomes an escape fee case – if it does, the costs will be payable at hourly rates.

Controlled Legal Representation

15.19 CLR is only available in the immigration and mental health categories, and advocacy under those levels of service is dealt with in chapters 9 and 10, and payment in chapter 15.

Representation certificates

15.20 Where a certificate is issued to a solicitor covering proceedings before a court, it will in principle be possible to provide and claim for advocacy services under the certificate at all hearings in the case, though like every other step in the proceedings attendance at hearings is subject to there being merit in taking that step. You should also make sure that the particular hearing is within the scope of the certificate; final hearings, for example, are generally not within scope of a certificate as first issued.

15.21 Advocacy under a certificate can be undertaken by a solicitor (subject to rights of audience in the higher courts) or by counsel. An advocate can be employed by your organisation or be in independent practice.

15.22 There is general authority to instruct one junior advocate under a certificate;[5] the instruction of more than one junior, or of Queen's Counsel acting as such, requires an application for prior authority to be made.[6] Unless the authority is granted, no claim can be made by a second advocate appearing at any hearing or by Queen's Counsel for

---

4 2010 Specification para 3.78; 2013 Specification para 3.62.
5 2010 Specification para 5.27; 2013 Specification para 5.13.
6 2010 Specification para 5.25; 2013 Specification para 5.11.

acting as such (it is always open to Queen's Counsel to accept instructions to appear as a junior and to be paid on that basis).[7] In a case where the statutory charge applies, you also require the informed consent of your client to the incurring of the extra costs of instructing QC or second counsel,[8] and costs officers will be looking to see that on your file.[9]

15.23   Where you instruct counsel, the brief must include a copy of the certificate and a copy of any prior authority to instruct counsel.[10] Where the certificate has not yet been issued, you should provide counsel with a copy within 14 days of receipt.[11]

15.24   You can instruct a solicitor not employed by your organisation to provide advocacy services.[12]

Payment for advocacy services

Work done by a solicitor

15.25   Advocacy work, and associated preparation, attendance, travel and waiting, done by a solicitor is payable at the hourly rates set out in the Civil Legal Aid (Remuneration) Regulations 2013. This is true whether the solicitor is employed by your firm or whether they are acting as an independent solicitor-advocate. Their times should be included on your bill along with all other profit costs and will be assessed in the usual way. See chapter 13 for details of the assessment process. The fact that a solicitor has undertaken the advocacy themselves rather than instruct counsel, especially in a complex case, will assist in justifying an enhancement to the hourly rates.

Work done by counsel – cases started prior to 2 December 2013

15.26   Barristers' fees are codified in all cases started on or after 3 October 2011. For cases started after that date, but before 2 December 2013, there are hourly rates applicable in all courts and for three categories of barrister – QCs and senior and junior counsel (respectively, ten

---

7   2010 Specification para 6.61(d); 2013 Specification para 6.60(d).
8   *Re Solicitors: Taxation of Costs* [1982] 2 All ER 683.
9   Civil Costs Assessment Guidance para 13.8.
10   2010 Specification para 5.28; 2013 Specification para 5.14.
11   2010 Specification para 5.29; 2013 Specification para 5.15.
12   2010 Specification para 2.7; 2013 Specification para 2.5.

years' call or more and less than ten years' call). The location of chambers, not the court, determines whether the London or non-London rate should be claimed (only junior counsel in the County Court have separate London and non-London rates)[13]. See Schedule 2 to the Civil Legal Aid (Remuneration) Regulations 2013 for the rates. They apply to barristers in independent practice but not solicitor advocates or barristers employed by solicitor firms, both of which claim at solicitor rates.

15.27   There is a discretion for junior counsel in the County Court to be paid at higher rates than those set out in the Remuneration Regulations. The regulations merely say that the LAA can do so if it is 'reasonable' to do so. The Costs Assessment Guidance[14] goes on to say that the decision lies with the LAA, even if the court has assessed fees at the higher rate, and that factors to be taken into account include:

- the complexity of case – for example, the gravity of the case, points of law or contested evidence;
- novel areas of law – a case requiring unusually specialised knowledge or skill or that is likely to set a precedent or have a wider impact;
- where an opponent has instructed a QC;
- a case requiring considerable amount of out-of-hours work;
- where a client has mental health problems, learning difficulties, social impairment or language difficulties that may impact on the approach taken;
- where the case involves an unusually large number of parties represented at a contested final hearing;
- where a hearing requires the cross-examination of more than one expert on technical issues, for example in clinical negligence cases;
- a fully contested hearing lasting more than two days.

Work done by counsel – cases started on or after 2 December 2013

15.28   For cases started on or after 2 December 2013, payment rates for counsel were reduced, in most cases, to the rates applicable to solicitors doing the same work where the case is in the High Court or below, or in a tribunal. There are separate rates for counsel appearing in the Court of Appeal and Supreme Court, which depend on the

13 Costs Assessment Guidance para 13.11.
14 Costs Assessment Guidance para 13.12.

level of counsel's seniority. Those rates also apply to Queen's Counsel acting as such and appearing in any court (assuming authority for QC has been granted). The rates are set out in Schedule 1 to the Civil Legal Aid (Remuneration) (Amendment) Regulations 2013.

Payment on account of counsel's fees

15.29   Counsel can apply direct to the LAA on form CLSPOA1 for a payment on account of their costs.[15] An application can be made on each anniversary of the issue of the certificate, with a window of two months before and four months after the relevant date.

15.30   An application can also be made at any point if:

- the proceedings have continued for more than 12 months;
- it appears unlikely that an order will be made for the costs of the case to be assessed within the next 12 months; and
- delay in the assessment will cause hardship to counsel.

15.31   An application can also be made if:

- the proceedings have concluded or counsel is otherwise entitled to payment; and
- six months have elapsed since then and counsel has not been paid.

On application, the LAA will pay up to 75 per cent of counsel's reasonable fees. If the final payment is less than the amount of any payments on account, the outstanding balance will be recouped from counsel.[16]

---

15 Civil Legal Aid (Remuneration) Regulations 2013 reg 11.
16 Civil Legal Aid (Remuneration) Regulations 2013 reg 12.

Case study

I am instructed in a case where my solicitor's certificate was issued on 1 April 2015 and the case is still ongoing. When can I make a payment on account application?

You can apply on the anniversary of the issue of the certificate, but there is a window either side to allow some flexibility – two months before and two months after the date. So you could have applied for a payment on account at any point between 1 February and 1 June 2016. If the case continues into 2017, you can apply again at any time between 1 February 2017 and 1 June 2017, and so on into 2018 if applicable.

At any time, you should put your total costs to date on the POA1, and the LAA will pay 75 per cent of that (subject to reasonableness), less any payment you have already received. So, for example, if you were paid £1,000 on account in 2015 and by 1 February 2016 your costs have reached £5,000, you should put £5,000 on the form and will be paid £2,750 (75 per cent of £5,000 = £3,750, less £1,000 already received).

15.32　These provisions do not apply to family proceedings where FAS applies – see chapter 16 for FAS.

High cost civil cases

15.33　Where the case is a high cost case (see chapter 5), any advocacy work will also be part of the individual case contract.

15.34　　Any contract will be with the solicitor, but where an external advocate is instructed, they will need to agree to the payment rates and case/stage plans.

15.35　　The rates payable to counsel depend on the classification of the case. Where there is a possibility that, if successful, inter partes costs will be recovered, the case is deemed to be 'at risk' and the rates will be £50 per hour for junior counsel and £90 per hour for senior counsel. Where prospects of success are only borderline but the case is nonetheless being funded because of its overwhelming importance to the client, wider public interest or significant human rights issues, the rates will be £65 and £117 respectively. Where there is no prospect of inter partes costs, standard remuneration rates will apply.[17]

17　Available at www.gov.uk/government/publications/high-cost-cases-non-family-civil.

The first £5,000 of counsel's fees will always be paid at standard rates rather than high cost case contract rates.

15.36   See chapter 13 for claiming costs in high cost civil cases.

Unpaid fees

15.37   Counsel can only claim fees through solicitors. In certificated cases, solicitors must include counsel's fees in the bill and must submit the bill to the court or LAA for assessment within the three-month time limit. See chapter 13 of Part A for details of the process.

15.38   Where the solicitor fails to submit the bill, counsel will not be paid. There is no direct remedy, since there is no provision for counsel to bill the LAA directly. Barristers can place solicitors on the List of Defaulting Solicitors, and can complain, through the Bar Council, to the SRA. Note that the new Bar Council Standard Terms of Business, released in February 2013, do not apply to legal aid work.

15.39   So counsel cannot directly enforce costs against solicitors who fail to submit bills for payment. Counsel can to some extent protect themselves by using the payment on account scheme to recover 75 per cent of their costs.

15.40   It is a term of the Standard Civil Contract that bills be submitted within the three-month time limit; failure to do so is a breach of contract, and repeated failure may lead to sanctions up to and including termination. Counsel may wish to draw a solicitor's failure to submit a bill to the attention of the LAA.

Inter partes costs and legal aid only costs

15.41   In cases where inter partes costs are possible, it is not uncommon for costs to be ordered or negotiated on the basis of payment of part of the costs of the case. If that is the case, it is important that you are clear as to the terms of the order or agreement, as in some cases but not others you may be able to claim the balance from the legal aid fund. The Standard Civil Contract allows you to claim from the legal aid fund any costs not payable by another party (legal aid only costs), but only if certain conditions are met – see paras 6.52 and 6.53 of the 2010 Specification or paras 6.51 and 6.52 of the 2013 Specification.

15.42   The Specification defines 'legal aid only' costs – costs that can be claimed from the legal aid fund even where inter partes costs are recovered – as:

- costs of completing legal aid forms and communicating with the LAA;
- certain limited types of costs disallowed or not agreed;
- costs of work not covered by a costs order or agreement.

Where a costs order or agreement specifies that another party should pay a proportion of the client's costs (but not a fixed sum), the same proportion of the total work that is not covered is legal aid only costs.

15.43   To take a practical example, say total costs on the case are £2,000 at legal aid rates and £4,000 at inter partes rates. If the other side agree to pay your costs in the sum of £2,000, that could be expressed in one of three ways:

- £2,000 as the total agreed costs of the case;
- agreement to pay costs between x and y dates, totalling £2,000; or
- agreement to pay 50 per cent of the costs, being £2,000.

In each case, you receive £2,000 from the other side. In the first case, that £2,000 represents the total costs of the case, so there are no legal aid costs (apart perhaps from £100 or so for filling in the APP1 and so on). In the second case, costs outside the agreed dates are not subject to the costs order, so you can claim those costs in addition to the inter partes costs you have received. In the third case, the other side has agreed to pay 50 per cent of your costs, so the other 50 per cent are legal aid only costs, so you can claim £1,000 (50 per cent of £2,000 at legal aid rates) from the LAA in addition to the £2,000 from the other side.

Advocacy in family cases

Introduction

16.1   This chapter deals with the particular rules that apply to conduct of and payment for advocacy in family cases. See chapter 15 for the general rules applying to both civil and family cases.

16.2   Advocacy can only be conducted under legal representation certificates in family work as Help at Court and Controlled Legal Representation (CLR) are not available in the family category.

16.3   In general, we use the term 'advocate' to refer to anyone who has a right of audience to appear in the relevant court or whom the court is willing to hear, where the scheme does not make a distinction between solicitor and counsel. Where there is a difference according to whether advocacy is conducted by solicitor or by counsel, we will use the terms 'solicitor' and 'counsel' as appropriate.

16.4   This chapter only deals with the advocacy aspects of family cases. For more information on the conduct of litigation, see Part A of this book. For information on the rules applying in criminal cases, see chapter 17, and chapter 15 for other civil cases.

Merits test

16.5   See chapter 5 for the merits tests relevant to legal representation.

Family cases started prior to 9 May 2011

16.6   The Family Graduated Fee Scheme (FGS) continues to apply to these cases. The provisions of the scheme are set out in the Community Legal Service (Funding) (Counsel in Family Proceedings) Order 2001 as amended.

Scope of the FGS

16.7   The FGS applies only to counsel. Solicitor advocates claim under the appropriate standard fee or hourly rate scheme, depending on whether the case is public or private law, and whether the case started prior to 1 October 2007.

16.8   Payments under the FGS are essentially fixed or standard fee payments with a range of base fees for different pieces of work. These fees are set according to the nature of the proceedings, the work to be done, whether junior or leading counsel is employed, and venue.

There is also a range of additional payments that may be added to the fee due, to reflect special features and complexity. The permutation of possible payments is quite complex. There is a short section in the Civil Costs Assessment Guidance[1] and a helpful guidance paper on the national archives website at http://webarchive.nationalarchives. gov.uk/20130128112038/http://www.justice.gov.uk/downloads/ legal-aid/fee-schemes/fgfsrevisedguidance-august2009.pdf

Family cases started on or after 9 May 2011

16.9   The Family Advocacy Scheme (FAS) applies to cases where the certificate was granted following an application made on or after 9 May 2011. The provisions of the scheme are set out in the Civil Legal Aid (Remuneration) Regulations 2013 Sch 3 and in section 7 of the 2013 Standard Civil Contract Specification.

Scope of the FAS

16.10   The fees apply to most advocacy, and the majority of fees can be claimed equally by solicitors or counsel, although the fees for providing opinions or advising in conference can only be claimed by counsel. The scheme uses the term 'advocate' when any advocate can claim a payment and 'counsel', when only the latter (or a self-employed solicitor or FILEX equivalent) can claim:

> 'Counsel' means either a barrister in independent practice; or a solicitor or Fellow of the Institute of Legal Executives who does not work in a partnership and does not hold a contract with us.[2]

16.11   Solicitors claim payment from the LAA in the usual way, and if you instruct a solicitor advocate freelancer or from another firm, they act as an agent and you are responsible for their fees. Counsel claim fees from the LAA direct.[3]

16.12   The advocacy fee includes all preparation for a hearing, travel to and waiting at court and time spent in advocacy itself. The advocacy fee can only be claimed by the legal representative providing advocacy

---

1   www.gov.uk/government/uploads/system/uploads/attachment_data/ file/427309/legal-aid-costs-assessment-guidance-2013-2014.pdf.

2   Civil legal aid cost assessment guidance para 2.1, appendix 2. www.gov.uk/ government/uploads/system/uploads/attachment_data/file/427309/legal-aid-costs-assessment-guidance-2013-2014.pdf.

3   Standard Civil Contract 2013 Specification para 7.109.

at a hearing. If a solicitor's representative attends with an advocate, he or she cannot also claim the fee.

16.13   Some types of advocacy are paid under hourly rates because they do not fall under the FAS scheme:[4]

- Proceedings excluded from the FAS:[5]
    (a) Child Abduction Proceedings;
    (b) proceedings under the Inheritance (Provision for Family and Dependants) Act 1975;
    (c) proceedings under the Trusts of Land and Appointment of Trustees Act 1996;
    (d) proceedings in which you provide separate representation of a Child in proceedings which are neither Specified Proceedings (as defined in section 41(6) of the Children Act 1989) nor proceedings which are being heard together with Specified Proceedings;
    (e) applications for Forced Marriage Protection Orders under the Forced Marriage (Civil Protection) Act 2007;
    (f) defended proceedings for divorce, judicial separation, dissolution of a civil partnership or for the legal separation of civil partners;
    (g) nullity proceedings (including proceedings for annulment of a civil partnership);
    (h) proceedings under the inherent jurisdiction of the High Court in relation to the children;
    (i) applications for Parental Orders under the Human Fertilisation and Embryology Act 2008.
- The following are also excluded;
    – advocacy in relation to final appeals;
    – advocacy provided under a high costs case contract issued by the LAA's Special Cases unit;
    – advocacy by QCs;
    – advocacy before the Court of Appeal or Supreme Court.

16.14   The scheme is split into five categories of case:

1) care and supervision proceedings;
2) other public law cases;
3) private law children proceedings;
4) finance cases;
5) domestic abuse cases.

---

4   Standard Civil Contract 2013 Specification para 7.101.
5   Standard Civil Contract 2013 Specification para 7.109.

Escape fee cases

16.15   There are no escape fee cases or uplifts payable under the FAS. This is because the payments are based on time periods.

Mixed categories

16.16   Where work covers more than one of the categories above within a single set of proceedings, the advocate can choose which fee to claim:[6]

- In family cases, the certificate will often either be issued to cover a number of proceedings or be subsequently amended to add or substitute proceedings during the life of the certificate.
- When the continuing proceedings fall within more than one category, an advocate must, for the purpose of payment under the FAS, choose under which single category they would wish to be paid for all the Advocacy Services performed when making a claim for payment. Usually, an advocate will claim at the category that pays the highest rate. For example, in a residence/contact application that subsequently involves allegations of abuse to a degree that the local authority issues care proceedings, at the point at which a new certificate is issued, an advocate can claim all future work (including issues as to contact) at the higher care proceedings rate[7].
- Where an Advocacy Service includes work from two categories but it falls within a single set of proceedings only one fee will be paid eg if a single hearing covers both private law children and financial issues then only one hearing fee will be payable and the advocate can choose which hearing fee to claim.

Hearing fees

16.17   Fees vary according to whether a hearing is interim or final:[8]

Interim and Final Hearings

7.129 A Final Hearing is any hearing which the court has listed for the purpose of making a final determination, either of the whole case or of all issues relating to an Aspect of the case (Domestic Abuse, Children or Finance). Subject to paragraph 7.130, there can only be one Final Hearing per Aspect and a hearing listed only to determine

---

6   Civil legal aid cost assessment guidance appendix 2 para 12.3.
7   Civil legal aid cost assessment guidance appendix 2 para 12.2.
8   Standard Civil Contract 2013 Specification para 7.129.

particular facts or issues is not a Final Hearing. A hearing listed with a view to the issues being dealt with under a consent order, or which is otherwise not expected to be effective or contested, is not a Final Hearing. Any hearing which is not a Final Hearing is an Interim Hearing.

7.130 The following hearings are also deemed to be Final Hearings for the purposes of the FAS only:

(a) In Public Law proceedings, if a case is concluded at an Issues Resolution Hearing and therefore does not proceed further, the Issues Resolution Hearing will be treated as a Final Hearing;

(b) Subject to Paragraph 7.129, in Private Law Children proceedings, a hearing listed for the purpose of findings of fact pursuant to the Practice Direction dated 14 January 2009 (Residence and Contact Orders: Domestic Violence and Harm).

7.131 If a Final Hearing is listed for a split hearing in a Public Law matter with certain issues being heard and/or determined in advance of other issues, this must be claimed as a Final Hearing, rather than as an Interim Hearing plus a Final Hearing.

7.132 It is possible for more than one Final Hearing fee to be claimed under a single certificate. In particular this can occur where a Final Hearing has taken place but subsequent enforcement proceedings are listed at first instance. Provided the enforcement issues are listed to be finally determined at the further hearing, an additional Final Hearing fee may be justified.

Interim hearing units

16.18   The fee payable depends on the length of the hearing. There are two interim hearing units:

- hearing unit 1: one hour or less;
- hearing unit 2: one hour or more but less than or equal to 2.5 hours.

If a hearing exceeds 2.5 hours, multiples of unit 2 fees will be paid (rounded up).

16.19   The applicable hearing time is the time at which the hearing is listed to start (unless the court specifically directs the advocate to attend earlier) until the time the hearing concludes:[9]

7.133 The fee payable under FAS for an Interim Hearing depends on its length. For this purpose the length of hearing is measured from the time that the hearing is listed at court to start (or such earlier time as the court specifically directs the advocate to attend) to the time that the hearing concludes, disregarding any period in which the court is

9 Standard Civil Contract 2013 Specification para 7.133.

adjourned overnight or for a lunch break. Time spent when a hearing or resumed hearing is delayed because the court is dealing with other business may however be taken into account. In the case of an Interim Hearing taking place by telephone or video link, time only runs from the time the call is made. If for an emergency hearing the court has not listed a time for the hearing or a time for the advocate to attend and the papers were only issued by the court on the day of the proposed hearing (so that the advocate must wait at court to be heard in the matter), the length of hearing may be measured from the time that the papers were issued.'

16.20   Hearing unit fees include all preparation for the hearing, travel to court (but see bolt-ons below), waiting and advocacy.

16.21   There is additional guidance in relation to interim hearings:[10]

14.6 ... Where for an emergency hearing the court has not listed a time for the hearing and the papers are only issued by the court on the day of the proposed hearing so that the advocate must wait at court to be heard the length of the hearing will be measured from the time that the papers were issued. If the application is issued and the hearing is then not heard until the next day the hearing time for that day will end when the advocate is informed of this and will start again at the time that they are told to attend for the following day.

14.7 Where a court directs a party to adjourn for further discussions at court then that time will be included in the calculation of the interim hearing fee

14.8 A hearing may take place by any method directed by the court eg by either video or telephone conference without attendance at court. If the court directs an alternative method of hearing then the advocate will receive the appropriate fee as if the hearing had taken place at court. However, in these cases the hearing time will start from the time that the telephone call/video conference is first attempted rather than the time that the hearing was listed. Bolt-ons may be claimed for telephone/video hearings if appropriate although due to the nature of these hearings bolt-ons are less likely to be applicable. It is unlikely, for example, that the criteria for the expert bolt-on would be met. As there will be no Advocates Attendance Form detailed notes of the hearing will need to be recorded and the claim justified on the CLAIM 1A or CLAIM 5A.

14.9 Where a case is resolved at an Issues Resolution Hearing held under the Public Law Outline (PLO) and no further hearings take place then this hearing will be paid as a final hearing.

---

10 Civil legal aid cost assessment guidance appendix 2.

Final hearings

16.22   Final hearings are paid under daily rates. A full daily fee is payable, regardless of the length of the hearing on that day.[11]

16.23   Finding of fact hearings will be paid for as final hearings. Issues Resolution hearings in public law cases will be paid for as final hearings (if the case concludes at that hearing).[12]

16.24   There is some additional guidance in relation to final hearings:[13]

14.11 In care proceedings, the main hearing would be the hearing at which the court determines whether or not a section 31 order is made. If a final hearing is listed for a split hearing with certain issues being heard and/or determined in advance of other issues (for example, findings of fact and/or threshold criteria), this must be claimed as a final hearing rather than an interim hearing plus a final hearing. In ancillary relief proceedings, it is likely to be the hearing at which the court determines the form of relief entitlement and in family injunctions, the on notice hearing which will determine the form and continuation of the without notice injunction order made. The definition includes all preparation or incidental work relating to the hearing including preparation, travel to court and waiting at court as well as the advocacy within the hearing itself.

16.25   See also Civil legal aid cost assessment guidance appendix 2:

15.9 A directions hearing that concludes the case does not make the hearing a 'final hearing'.

15.10 On the making of an order the court may decide to review the position after an interval of some months. That subsequent review is not a continuation of the final hearing but an interim hearing. The court may make further directions, continue or vary the order. None of these circumstances turn that later hearing into either the continuation of the final hearing or a new final hearing.

15.11 It is possible in certain circumstances for more than one final hearing fee to be paid in a case. In particular this can occur where a final hearing has taken place but subsequent enforcement proceedings are issued which are required to be finally determined or where an earlier fact finding hearing has taken place.

---

11 Standard Civil Contract 2013 Specification para 7.135.
12 Standard Civil Contract 2013 Specification para 7.130.
13 Civil legal aid cost assessment guidance appendix 2.

Cancelled hearings

16.26   Only counsel may claim a fee for cancelled hearings. Counsel must have done at least 30 minutes' preparation in order to claim a hearing unit 1 fee.[14]

Bolt-ons

16.27   Additional bolt-on fees are available for more complex cases in public and private law children cases. Claims must be verified by the judge, magistrate or legal adviser at the hearing on the Advocates Attendance form (AAF). Bolt-on fees cannot be claimed for cancelled hearings. Bolt-ons are not available in finance cases and domestic abuse cases, apart from court bundles in finance cases and exceptional travel in both finance and domestic abuse cases where applicable.[15]

Public law

16.28   In public law cases bolt-ons are claimable where:

- you are acting for a parent or others against whom allegations of serious harm to a child are made by the local authority;
- the client has difficulty giving instructions/understanding advice;
- expert/s has/have to be cross-examined.

Client – allegations of significant harm

16.29   Paragraph 7.147 of the Specification states:

This Bolt-on Fee is claimable only where your Client is facing allegations that he or she has caused significant harm to a Child. It applies only so long as those allegations remain a live issue in the proceedings. For this purpose only the following conditions constitute significant harm:
(a) death,
(b) significant head and/or fracture injuries,
(c) burns or scalds,
(d) fabricated illness,
(e) extensive bruising involving more than one part of the body,
(f) multiple injuries of different kinds,
(g) other significant ill-treatment (such as suffocation or starvation) likely to endanger life,
(h) sexual abuse.

---

14 Standard Civil Contract 2013 Specification para 7.136.
15 Standard Civil Contract 2013 Specification para 7.146.

Client – lack of understanding etc

16.30   Paragraph 7.149 of the Specification states:

> This Bolt-on applies to hearings in Public Law proceedings where:
> (a) your Client has difficulty in giving instructions or understanding advice,
> (b) this is attributable to a mental disorder (as defined in section 1(2) of the Mental Health Act 1983) or to a significant impairment of intelligence or social functioning, and
> (c) the Client's condition is verified by a medical report from either a psychologist or psychiatrist.

Advocates' meetings

16.31   In public law cases, a separate fee is available for advocates attending an advocates' meeting, where such a meeting is directed by the court in accordance with the Public Law Outline. Where in section 31 care proceedings, advocates are able to discuss all relevant matters without the need for an advocates' meeting, half the standard fee is payable (without any bolt-ons).[16]

16.32   There is additional guidance in relation to advocates' meetings:[17]

> 14.18 Although it would usually be expected that two advocates' meetings would take place in accordance with the PLO, provided that the advocates' meeting is held as directed by the court and in accordance with the PLO there is no limit to the number of these fees that may be claimed. No fees for advocates' meetings will be payable in Private Law Children cases.

> 14.19 The definition of Advocates' Meeting includes meetings held by video conference, webcam or telephone where this is appropriate in the circumstances.

Private law

16.33   In private law children cases, bolt-ons are claimable where:

- you are acting for a parent or others against whom allegations of significant harm to a child are made;[18]
- expert/s has/have to be substantially challenged in court.

16.34   In private law finance cases an early resolution fee can be claimed for cases which settle at the first appointment or Financial Dispute Resolution (FDR) Hearing, as long as the advocate materially assisted in

---

16   Standard Civil Contract 2013 Specification para 7.138.

17   Civil legal aid cost assessment guidance appendix 2.

18   See Standard Civil Contract 2013 Specification para 7.147, quoted above, for the definition.

the settlement, it is recorded in a consent order and it lasts for six months (as far as you are aware).[19]

Early Resolution Fee

7.154 This Bolt-on Fee is claimable only in Private Law Finance cases which settle at the first appointment or Financial Dispute Resolution ('FDR') hearing. It may only be claimed by an advocate who is entitled to the Hearing fee for that hearing but only if the following conditions are satisfied:

(a) the Finance Aspect of the case has been fully concluded at the first appointment or FDR hearing;

(b) the advocate attending that hearing materially assisted in the settlement;

(c) the Finance Aspect of the case does not proceed further to a new Level of Service within six months of the settlement, either with you or, so far as you are aware, another Provider;

(d) there has been a genuine settlement to conclude that Aspect of the case, rather than, for example, a reconciliation between the parties or one party dying or disengaging from the case;

(e) the settlement is recorded in a form of a Consent Order approved by the Court, either at the hearing itself or subsequently.

Court bundles

16.35 The Standard Contract Specification states that additional fees may be claimed for court bundles:[20]

- CBP 1 – over 350 pages;
- CBP 2 – over 700 pages;
- CBP 3 – over 1,400 pages (final hearings only).

16.36 At the time of writing the Specification has not been amended to reflect changes in Family Court procedure from 31 July 2014. Practice Direction 27A (PD27A) sets out the content and format of the court bundle in family proceedings and introduced a maximum 350-page limit on the size of the court bundle in family cases. From that date, the LAA amended the regulations[21] so that bundle payments were claimed by reference to the advocate's bundle rather than the court bundle.

---

19 Standard Civil Contract 2013 Specification para 7.154.

20 Standard Civil Contract 2013 Specification para 7.150.

21 Civil Legal Aid (Remuneration) (Amendment) (No 4) Regulations 2014 amended Civil Legal Aid (Remuneration) Regulations 2013 and equivalent amendments to Community Legal Service (Funding) Order 2014, through Community Legal Service (Funding) (Amendment) Order 2007, to cover cases continuing under Access to Justice Act 1999.

16.37   The amended regulations set out that the advocate's bundle may only include:

- those documents relevant to the case which have been served by the parties to the proceedings to which the hearing relates;
- notes of contact visits if included in the court bundle; and
- a paginated index agreed by the parties to those proceedings.

Advocates must also include a written explanation of how the documents included in the bundle are relevant and necessary to the case.

16.38   There are restrictions on the circumstances and number of times within a set of proceedings that a court bundle payment may be claimed for Interim Hearings:[22]

> 7.151 ... In Public Law proceedings, court bundle payments may be claimed for no more than two Interim Hearings and each of these must be either a Case Management Conference, an Issues Resolution Hearing or otherwise a hearing which is listed for the hearing of contested evidence. A court bundle payment may never be claimed more than once per hearing.
>
> 7.152 In Private Law proceedings court bundle payments may only be claimed at one Interim Hearing per case. For this purpose the Children and Finance Aspects of a case will be treated separately.
>
> 7.153 Court bundle payments may not be claimed in Domestic Abuse proceedings, either for Interim or Final Hearings.

An advocate taking on a case part way through must satisfy themselves as to whether the advocate's bundle payment/s have already been claimed or are intended to be claimed by an advocate at an earlier hearing.[23]

16.39   There is some additional guidance in relation to court bundles (see above for change in definition from 31 July 2014): Also note that although the Contract Specification had not been updated at the time of writing, the Civil Costs Assessment Guidance had been:[24]

> 14.46 The advocate's bundle will consist of those served documents relevant and necessary to the case, including a paginated index of the contents. The advocate's bundle may include the documents listed in paragraphs 4.2 and 4.3 of PD27A (and which may be included in the court bundle) and other documents relevant to the case which have been served by the parties to the proceedings to which the hearing relates. Notes of contact visits will only be included in the advocate's bundle for the purposes of the FAS if they have been included in the court bundle.

---

22   Standard Civil Contract 2013 Specification para 7.133.
23   Civil legal aid cost assessment guidance appendix 2 para 14.52.
24   Civil legal aid cost assessment guidance appendix 2 paras as set out above.

14.47 Verification of the size of the advocate's bundle will be carried out by the judge or person before whom the case is heard by way of a paginated index of documents served in the case that the advocate would be expected to have agreed with the other parties, as appropriate. Additionally, the advocate will need to provide an explanation of why any documents included in the paginated index which do not fall within paragraphs 4.2 and 4.3 of PD27A are relevant and necessary to the case.

14.51 An advocate must obtain certification of the relevant number of pages of the advocate's bundle on the Advocates Attendance Form in order to claim this payment. The Agency may request copies of both the agreed paginated list and the explanation of why additional documents not referred to in paragraphs 4.2 and 4.3 of PD27A are included either before or after payment is made.

16.40 At the time the changes were implemented, practitioners' representative groups asked the LAA for clarification about what they would require from providers on making claims for bolt on payments relating to advocates' bundles. The advice received by Resolution from the LAA is set out in italics below:

> *You should get certification of the relevant number of pages of the advocate's bundle on the Advocates Attendance Form. You are advised to have available for the judge the agreed paginated index and reasons for why any documents which do not fall within paras 4.2 and 4.3 of PD27A are relevant and necessary.*

16.41 Although there is no requirement to do so, some practitioners are seeking to ensure this is covered on the face of the order.

> *Whilst the LAA may ask for a copy of the agreed paginated index with an explanation of why any additional documents were included, there is no intention to do so as a matter of course, the certified AAF will usually be sufficient. Should the LAA make such a request, you would be expected to present the documentation prepared for the judge, but there is no expectation that the judge will have signed anything except the AAF.*

We understand that LAA caseworkers have been instructed not to refuse claims for payment for advocate's bundles with a completed and certified AAF unless there is an unexpected and unusual pattern of claims for payments.

Exceptional travel

16.42 Advocates may claim payments for exceptional travel (more than 25 miles each way), as long as it was reasonable for them to be instructed in all the circumstances, rather than someone more local to the court.[25]

---

25 Standard Civil Contract 2013 Specification para 7.156.

16.43   All advocates will need to justify the payment either on the CLAIM 1A for solicitors or on the CLAIM 5A for counsel. Counsel should also supply a copy of their brief or instructions with the claim.

Payments for counsel only

16.44   Counsel's fees may be claimed under the FAS:

- for conferences, up to a maximum of two per set of proceedings;[26]
- for opinions, up to a maximum of two per set of proceedings, unless the opinion relates to a proposed appeal against a final order:[27]
  - in private law, counsel may claim two opinions for both the children and finance aspects of a case;
  - no opinion fee may be claimed in domestic abuse proceedings.

16.45   The Costs Assessment Guidance says this about what constitutes a single set of proceedings:[28]

13.1 For particular Advocacy Services only two fees can be claimed per case. In order to determine what is or is not a 'case' for the purposes of determining appropriate claiming, applications to the court constitute a single set of proceedings, irrespective of whether they are made separately or together, where they are heard together or consecutively or are treated by the court as a single set of proceedings. In private law proceedings each aspect of the case, e.g. children and finance, counts as a separate case for the purposes of claiming opinions and conferences.

Conference fees

16.46   There is some additional guidance in relation to conference fees:[29]

14.25 A conference fee is paid for all work carried out in connection with a conference. This can include conferences by telephone or video link or webcam where this is appropriate in the circumstances. Conference fees may only be claimed by Counsel. No bolt-ons may be claimed for conferences.

14.26 Up to two conference fees may be claimed in each single set of proceedings. As for opinions in private law proceedings, if there are separate children and finance proceedings these will be considered separately for these purposes. However, no conference fee may be claimed under FAS in Domestic Abuse proceedings.

---

26 Standard Civil Contract 2013 Specification para 7.143.
27 Standard Civil Contract 2013 Specification para 7.140.
28 Civil legal aid cost assessment guidance appendix 2.
29 Civil legal aid cost assessment guidance appendix 2.

14.27 As only two conference fees may be claimed Counsel will need to designate the conferences for which he or she seeks payment under the FAS.

14.28 No conference fee may be claimed for any conference held on the same day as a Final hearing. Any discussions or negotiations taking place on any day of a final hearing will be covered by the fee for advocacy at that hearing.

14.29 A conference fee may be claimed for a conference that takes place on the same day as an interim hearing, only if the conference takes place outside of any time period that is taken into account in calculating the fee for the interim hearing. Therefore no conference fee may be claimed for a conference that takes place between the time that the hearing is listed to start and the time that hearing actually starts as this will be claimed as part of the Hearing Unit.

14.30 Where different Counsel is subsequently instructed and the allowable conference fees have already been claimed, no further claims for conference fees can be made. This is so even in circumstances where the later conference was more substantial. Where one Counsel has replaced another, Counsel must make enquiries as to whether the conference fees payments have been claimed from either the outgoing Counsel or instructing solicitors.

Opinion fees

16.47 Only counsel (see definition in para 16.10 above) may claim opinion fees.[30] There is some additional guidance in relation to opinion fees:[31]

14.22 Up to two opinion fees may be claimed in each single set of proceedings. If there are separate children and finance proceedings these will be considered separately for these purposes. No opinion fee may claimed under the FAS in Domestic Abuse proceedings.

14.23 In addition to the two opinions claimed per set of proceedings a further opinion may be claimed in relation to any a proposed appeal against a final order.

14.24 An opinion may include providing advice or drafting pleadings/ affidavits after the issue of proceedings.

Assessment

16.48 The LAA assesses all fees due to counsel under the FAS. Solicitors' profit costs and disbursements are assessed in the usual way, through

---

30 Standard Civil Contract 2013 Specification para 7.139.
31 Guidance on the FAS, February 2012 para 3.2.

assessment either by the LAA or the court. See chapter 13 for more information.

Forms

16.49　Different forms are submitted depending on whether the claim falls under the Family Graduated Fee Scheme (cases started pre 9 May 2011) or the Family Advocacy Scheme (cases started after 9 May 2011). The forms, and accompanying guidance on how to fill them out, can be downloaded from www.gov.uk/government/publications/family-graduated-fee-and-family-advocacy-claim-forms

16.50　For FAS claims, counsel claim on form CIVCLAIM5A and solicitors claim on form CIVCLAIM1A. Claims for advocacy under the FAS must be made on an appropriately completed Advocates attendance form (EX506[32]). If such form(s) are not submitted the advocacy claim will be limited to a level 1 hearing unit.

FAS in high cost cases

16.51　In Family, cases where the costs are anticipated to, or actually do, exceed £25,000 (including all profit costs with enhancement, disbursements and any counsel's fees but excluding VAT) fall under the Special Case Work provisions of the Civil Legal Aid (Procedure) Regulations 2012 (see chapter 5 for more information on Special Case Work). They are referred to the LAA's Very High Cost Case Team in South Tyneside.

16.52　The team will refer to the rates that would have been paid under FAS (if applicable) and if the FAS is not applicable then they may make reference to the rates set out in table 1 of the guidance on VHCC Payments to Counsel in Family Cases[33] or they will consider the fees paid under the VHCC Care Case Fee Scheme.

32　This is considered to be a HMCTS form and so is available via HMCTS form finder rather than on the LAA web pages http://hmctsformfinder.justice.gov.uk/HMCTS/GetForms.do?court_forms_num=EX506&court_forms_title=&court_forms_category=.

33　www.gov.uk/government/publications/family-high-cost-cases-forms-and-guidance.

CHAPTER 17

Advocacy in criminal cases

edited by Anthony Edwards

Introduction

17.1   This chapter deals with the conduct of and payment for advocacy in criminal cases. See appendix H for a summary of the Legal Aid Agency's (LAA's) Costs Assessment Guidance, in respect of the most common queries raised by caseworkers. In criminal proceedings, advocacy can be conducted under:

- advocacy assistance;
- representation order.

Advocacy may arise at all stages of criminal proceedings, including the investigations stage, where advocacy may arise due to an application for a warrant of further detention or where a client wishes to apply to vary police bail conditions.

17.2   In general, we use the term 'advocate' to refer to anyone who has a right of audience to appear in the relevant court or whom the court is willing to hear where the scheme makes no distinction between solicitor and counsel. Where there is a difference according to whether advocacy is conducted by solicitor or by counsel, we will use the terms 'solicitor' and 'counsel' as appropriate.

17.3   Who is entitled to conduct advocacy, and the payment arrangements, will depend on the type of hearing and the stage of the case.

17.4   All qualified solicitors may represent a client at a hearing in the magistrates' court, as may counsel. However, whether or not counsel may be instructed will depend on the type of hearing and whether it is funded by advocacy assistance or a representation order.

17.5   In general, advocacy at Crown Court hearings and above may only be provided by counsel or a solicitor who has higher rights of audience.

QASA

17.6   The Quality Assurance Scheme for Advocates (QASA) has been developed by the Joint Advocacy Group (JAG), which includes the three main regulators of advocacy: the Solicitors' Regulation Authority, Bar Standards Board and ILEX Professional Standards (IPS). The scheme has been controversial and as a result the precise start date has been delayed and is unknown at the time of writing.

17.7   Under QASA a common set of standards will apply to all advocates regardless of their route to qualification. There are four levels in the scheme, from level one, which covers cases in the magistrates' courts, up to level four, which covers the most complex cases in the Crown Court. Standards and performance indicators have been spelt out for each of the four levels.

17.8   Advocates can choose to progress through the levels or to remain at a particular level (in which case they will be required to be re-accredited every five years). Solicitors meet level one on qualification, but will need to be reaccredited after five years, (unless they progress to level two or above). Initially, advocates will self assess their level of competence, and will subsequently be required to prove their competence at that level through assessment. Progression is achieved through judicial evaluation.

Funding

17.9   In general, advocacy in a criminal case is funded by a representation order, which will cover all of the hearings from the first appearance in the magistrates' court up to the final sentencing hearing. A representation order will also generally be required for advocacy in appeals.

17.10   The main stage at which advocacy is not covered by a representation order is the investigations stage. At this stage, funding is provided by advocacy assistance. Advocacy assistance is also available to fund representation by the duty solicitor and representation at prison disciplinary and parole board hearings.

Advocacy assistance – investigations stage

Clients detained in custody

17.11   A client who is detained in police (or military) custody may require representation at court if there is an application to extend the custody time limit under Police and Criminal Evidence Act 1984 (PACE) s43 or s44, Terrorism Act 2000 Sch 8 para 29 or para 36, or the relevant military legislation.[1]

---

1 Standard Crime Contract 2010 Specification (hereafter 'the Specification'), paras B9.145 and B9.158; OCCC paras 8.126 and 8.139; DPCC paras 9.113 and 9.126.

17.12   The funding for such hearings is subject to the 'sufficient bene-fit' test, however the test is automatically deemed satisfied by the circumstances.[2]

17.13   There is no means test[3] and the client is not required to sign any application form.[4] However, you are required to record on the file:

- the client's name and address;
- the unique file number (UFN);
- the date, time and venue of the court appearance; and
- details of the relevant unit of work (as defined by the contract) and how the work falls within the scope of that unit.[5]

These details should be recorded either before the advocacy assistance is provided or as soon as practicable after, if the advocacy is required at short notice.[6]

17.14   Reasonable preparation and follow-up work will be included within the scope of advocacy assistance, as will travel and waiting costs. However there is an extendable costs limit of £1,368.75 (£1,237.50 for grants on or after 1 July 2015).

17.15   There are no fixed fees for this type of work so, subject to the costs limit above, work will be claimed at the hourly rates set out in the Remuneration Regulations. These vary depending on whether the hearing is before a magistrates' court or judicial authority, or before a High Court or senior judge. There are also different rates for own and duty solicitors, and for unsociable hours.

17.16   Counsel may only be instructed where the application is before the High Court or a senior judge.[7]

---

2 Specification paras B9.146 and B9.160; OCCC paras 8.127 and 8.141; DPCC paras 9.114 and 9.128.
3 Specification paras B9.147 and B9.161; OCCC paras 8.127, 8.141 and 8.153; DPCC paras 9.114, 9.128 and 9.141.
4 Specification paras B9.148 and B9.162; OCCC paras 8.129, 8.143 and 8.154; DPCC paras 9.116, 9.130 and 9.142.
5 Specification paras B9.150 and B9.163; OCCC paras 8.131, 8.144 and 8.155; DPCC paras 9.118, 9.131 and 9.143.
6 Specification paras B9.148 and B9.162; OCCC paras 8.129, 8.143 and 8.154; DPCC paras 9.116, 9.130 and 9.142.
7 Specification para B9.152; OCCC para 8.133; DPCC para 9.120.

Bail variations

17.17 A client who is not detained in custody may also require representation at court if there is an application to vary police bail conditions (including 'street bail' conditions).[8]

17.18 In this situation there are no qualifying criteria to be met and there is no means test.[9] As above, the client is not required to sign an application form but you must record the same required information on the file.[10]

17.19 Advocacy assistance in this situation includes reasonable preparation, travel, waiting and advocacy at the hearing, and the provision of advice on appeal.

17.20 The same extendable costs limit applies, and the rules on claiming are the same. The applicable fees are set out in the Remuneration Regulations.

17.21 You cannot instruct counsel in this case,[11] and you may not claim under this unit of work if you are acting as duty solicitor.[12] However, you can claim under advocacy assistance if you represented the client as duty solicitor at the police station and you are subsequently instructed in the bail variation.

Advocacy assistance – court duty solicitor

17.22 Advocacy assistance is available to cover the representation of clients by the court duty solicitor at the magistrates' court. In practice it will be claimed together with advice and assistance, which covers the provision of advice to such clients outside court. The two forms of assistance will be claimed together in a single claim at the end of the duty day.[13]

17.23 Advocacy assistance under this unit of work may only be provided by a qualified duty solicitor (ie one who has been grandparented under previous contracts or who has passed both the police station qualification and the magistrates' court qualification and has registered as a duty solicitor with the Legal Aid Agency (LAA).

---

8 Specification para B9.171; OCCC para 8.152; DPCC para 9.139.
9 Specification para B9.173; OCCC para 8.153; DPCC para 9.141.
10 Specification paras B9.174 and B9.175; OCCC para 8.155; DPCC para 9.143.
11 Specification para B9.177; OCCC para 8.157; DPCC para 9.145.
12 Specification para B9.172; DPCC para 9.140.
13 Specification para B10.17; DPCC para 10.18.

17.24   To qualify for advocacy assistance under this scheme, the client's case must come within the scope of the scheme:

- The duty solicitor must:[14]
  - advise any client who requests it who is in custody;
  - make a bail application where a client in custody requires a bail application and such an application has not previously been made by a duty solicitor;
  - advise a client before the court in connection with 'prescribed proceedings' that is civil orders deemed to be criminal for legal aid purposes (the full list appears at para 12.69):[15]
    - parenting orders;[16]
    - football banning orders;[17]
    - closure orders;[18]
    - sexual offences notification orders;[19]
    - sexual harm prevention orders;[20]
    - sexual risk orders;[21]
    - restraining orders under section 5A of the Protection from Harassment Act 1997 in relation to a restraining order on acquittal.
    - domestic violence protection orders;
    - female genital mutilation protection orders;[22]
    - slavery and trafficking prevention orders;[23]
    - slavery and trafficking risk orders;[24]
    - proceedings in any youth court in relation to the breach of a provision in an injunction under Part 1 of the Anti-social Behaviour, Crime and Policing Act 2014 where the person subject to the injunction is under 14.

---

14 Specification para B10.7; DPCC para 10.7.
15 Criminal Legal Aid (General) Regulations 2013 reg 9.
16 Crime and Disorder Act 1998 ss8, 9 and 10; Anti-social Behaviour Act 2003 ss20, 22, 26 and 28; Powers of Criminal Courts (Sentencing) Act 2000 Sch 1 Part 1A.
17 Football Spectators Act 1989 ss14B, 14D, 14G, 14H, 21B and 21D.
18 Anti-social Behaviour, Crime and Policing Act 2014 ss80, 82, 83 and 84 where a person has engaged or is likely to engage in behaviour that constitutes a criminal offence on the premises.
19 Sexual Offences Act 2003 ss97, 100 and 101.
20 Sexual Offences Act 2003 ss103A, 103E, 103F and 103H.
21 Sexual Offences Act 2003 ss122A, 122D, 122E and 122G.
22 Femal Genital Mutilation Act 2003 Sch 2 paras 3, 6.
23 Modern Slavery Act 2015 ss14, 15, 20–22.
24 Modern Slavery Act 2015 ss23, 27–29.

- under the DPCC, cross-examine under Youth Justice and Criminal Evidence Act 1999 s28 if a designated fee earner is appointed by the court.[25]
- The duty solicitor may:[26]
  - advise and represent any client who is in custody on a plea of guilty and wishes the case to be concluded that day;
  - advise and represent any client before the court for failure to pay a fine or other sum or to obey an order of the court, and such failure may lead to the client being at risk of imprisonment;
  - advise and represent a client not in custody in connection with an imprisonable offence;
  - help a client in making an application for a representation order, whether the nominated solicitor is the duty solicitor or another solicitor;
  - advise and represent a client seeking to vary police-imposed bail conditions pre-charge.
- The duty solicitor must not:
  - represent in committal proceedings;[27]
  - represent at a not guilty trial or in relation to a non-imprisonable offence unless with the provisions above;[28]
  - advise or represent a client who has had the services of a duty solicitor at a previous hearing in the proceedings (except where they are before the court this time as a result of failure to pay a fine or other sum or comply with an order imposed previously).[29]

17.25　The sufficient benefit test applies to representation by the duty solicitor (both under advocacy assistance and advice and assistance),[30] but there is no means test and clients are not required to complete an application form.[31] However, you are required to record on the file:

- the client's name and address;
- details of the relevant unit of work;

25　DPCC para 10.32.
26　Specification para B10.8; DPCC 10.8.
27　Note that, although committal proceedings have been abolished, the specification has not been amended at the time of writing.
28　Specification para B10.9; DPCC para 10.9.
29　Specification para B10.10; DPCC para 10.10.
30　Specification para B10.2; DPCC para 10.2.
31　Specification para B10.4; DPCC para 10.4.

- whether the client is in custody or charged with an imprisonable offence; and
- the date, time and venue of the court appearance.[32]

These details should be recorded either before the advocacy assistance is provided or as soon as practicable after, if the advocacy is required at short notice.[33]

17.26   The scope of the scheme is limited in terms of the work covered. In addition to the advocacy, you may only claim for reasonable advice and preparation provided during the duty session. This can include advice on the consequences of the outcome and the giving of any notice of appeal or making an application for a case to be stated.[34]

17.27   Claiming for duty solicitor advocacy is done as part of a single claim submitted for the duty session. Hourly rates are set out in the Remuneration Regulations and there is a standard hourly rate for both attendance and waiting. An enhanced rate applies to sessions on non-business days.

17.28   Under the duty solicitor scheme, you cannot claim for travel time other than on a non-business day, unless you are called out having not been on the rota or having been released but then asked to return.

Advocacy under a representation order

17.29   All representation orders granted for criminal cases in the magistrates' court and the Crown Court will include the provision of advocacy services. This will include representation at all hearings in the case including bail proceedings in the Crown Court or High Court.

17.30   Representation orders in both the magistrates' court and the Crown Court are granted subject to a means test. There is a merits test unless the case is tried in the Crown Court or on indictment. For a full discussion of these tests see chapter 12.

17.31   Advocacy under a representation order may be carried out either by a solicitor or by counsel, subject to the requirement for higher rights for advocacy in the Crown Court and above.

---

32 Specification para B10.6; DPCC para 10.6.
33 Specification para B10.4; DPCC para 10.4.
34 Specification para B10.16; DPCC para 10.17.

Magistrates' court

17.32   A representation order for a magistrates' court case will generally only cover advocacy provided by a solicitor.[35] Payment for advocacy services provided by a solicitor will be claimed within the magistrates' court standard fee regime.

17.33   Advocacy is claimed at the hourly rate prescribed in the Remuneration Regulations, in the same way as all other types of work provided under the representation order. New rules on the calculation of standard fees take effect for orders granted on or after 11 January 2016.

17.34   Travelling and waiting time can only be claimed if neither the court nor your office is in a 'designated area'. Entirely new rules take effect for orders granted on or after 11 January 2016. Designated areas will cease to exist and only duty solicitors in exceptional circumstances will be able to claim for travel. The designated areas[36] (until those orders take effect) are:

- Greater Manchester, London, West Midlands and Merseyside Criminal Justice Areas;
- the local authority areas of:
  - Brighton and Hove;
  - Bristol;
  - Cardiff;
  - Derby and Erewash;
  - Kingston upon Hull;
  - Leeds and Bradford;
  - Leicester;
  - Nottingham;
  - Portsmouth;
  - Newcastle-upon-Tyne and Sunderland;
  - Sheffield;
  - Southampton.

Note that you are still required to record the waiting time (but not travel), even if you cannot claim for it.[37]

17.35   The total core costs will then be compared against fee limits for the particular category of case (determined by outcome) and this will determine whether the standard fee or a non-standard fee is payable.

35 See Criminal Legal Aid (Determinations by a Court and Choice of Representative) Regulations 2013 reg 16.
36 Specification para A1.13.
37 Specification para B10.88.

For orders granted on or after 11 January 2016 there will only be a single standard fee and fee limit before a non standard fee is payable.

17.36   For details of the fee structure under representation orders in the magistrates' court, see chapter 14.

Counsel in the magistrates' court

17.37   Although the representation order will usually only provide for advocacy by a solicitor,[38] this does not mean that counsel cannot be instructed in the magistrates' court. It simply means that counsel is usually unassigned and cannot claim their costs from the court or the LAA. Therefore you are responsible for agreeing a fee with counsel and paying that fee promptly out of your costs. If you fail to pay within 30 days, counsel can apply to the LAA for payment and that payment will be deducted from your monthly payment.[39]

17.38   Unassigned counsel are treated like solicitor agents. From the point of view of the LAA, their work is treated as your work. Their time should be recorded on your bill as if you had done the work, and counts towards the calculation of the appropriate fee.[40] As for solicitors, counsel's travel and waiting time can only be claimed for cases in 'undesignated areas',[41] and not at all for orders granted on or after 11 January 2016.

17.39   You must provide counsel with the UFN and a copy of the representation order when briefing them.[42]

Assigned counsel

17.40   In more serious cases, you can apply to the court for counsel (or an independent solicitor advocate) to be assigned.

17.41   The regulations say that counsel may be assigned in any case where the charge is an indictable offence (that is, an offence capable of being tried on indictment, including either way offences, not just indictable only offences) or where the case is an extradition matter.[43]

---

38 See Criminal Legal Aid (Determinations by a Court and Choice of Representative) Regulations 2013 reg 16.
39 Specification paras B10.53 and B10.54; OCCC para 9.32; DPCC para 10.54.
40 Specification para B10.47; OCCC para 9.36; DPCC para 10.48.
41 Specification para B10.84; OCCC para 9.24; DPCC para 10.46.
42 Specification para B10.42.
43 Criminal Legal Aid (Determinations by a Court and Choice of Representative) Regulations 2013 reg 16.

17.42   Indictable only cases involving adults will be sent directly to the Crown Court, so in practice counsel can be assigned in adult either way cases, youth cases where the charge, whether summary or indictable, has not been sent, and extraditions.

17.43   In order to have counsel assigned, you must persuade the court that, because of circumstances which make the case unusually grave or difficult, representation by solicitor and advocate would be desirable.

17.44   In extradition proceedings, you can apply for more than one advocate, or for a QC, to be assigned where you can persuade the court that the defendant cannot be adequately represented except by QC or more than one advocate.[44]

17.45   Where counsel is assigned, they are entitled to be paid directly by the LAA at the rates prescribed in the Remuneration Regulations, though you should submit their bill with your own – see chapter 14.

Crown Court

17.46   Advocacy in the Crown Court must generally be conducted by counsel or a solicitor with higher rights of audience.

17.47   Crown Court representation orders automatically allow the instruction of a single junior advocate. Even if counsel was not assigned under the order in the magistrates' court, once the case goes to the Crown Court the order is deemed to include representation by one junior advocate (that is, any advocate other than a QC).[45]

17.48   In more serious and complex cases, an application may be made to the court to amend the order to allow for the instruction of QC or more than one advocate. The court can order representation by:

- QC alone;
- two advocates:
  - QC with junior;
  - QC with noting junior;
  - two juniors;
  - junior and noting junior; or
- where three advocates are justified, any of the above plus an additional junior or noting junior.[46]

44   Criminal Legal Aid (Determinations by a Court and Choice of Representative) Regulations 2013 regs 16 and 17.
45   Criminal Legal Aid (Determinations by a Court and Choice of Representative) Regulations 2013 reg 18.
46   Criminal Legal Aid (Determinations by a Court and Choice of Representative) Regulations 2013 reg 18.

17.49   In order to persuade the court to make an order for senior or more than one advocate, you must demonstrate that the relevant test is met:

- For QC alone:[47]
    - the case involves substantial novel or complex issues of law or fact which could not be adequately presented except by a QC; and
    - either:
        - the prosecution has instructed QC or senior Treasury counsel; or
        - the case for the defence is exceptional compared with the generality of cases involving similar offences.
- For two junior advocates:[48]
    - the case involves substantial novel or complex issues of law or fact which could not be adequately presented by a single advocate; and
    - either:
        - the prosecution have instructed two or more advocates;
        - the case for the defence is exceptional compared with the generality of cases involving similar offences;
        - the number of prosecution witnesses exceeds 80; or
        - the number of pages of prosecution evidence exceeds 1,000.
- For QC plus junior or noting junior:[49]
    - the case involves substantial novel or complex issues of law or fact which could not be adequately presented except by a QC assisted by a junior advocate; and
    - either:
        - the prosecution has instructed QC or senior Treasury counsel and two or more advocates have been instructed by the prosecution; the number of prosecution witnesses exceeds 80; the number of pages of prosecution evidence exceeds 1,000; or
        - the case for the defence is exceptional compared with the generality of cases involving similar offences.

---

47 Criminal Legal Aid (Determinations by a Court and Choice of Representative) Regulations 2013 reg 18(2).
48 Criminal Legal Aid (Determinations by a Court and Choice of Representative) Regulations 2013 reg 18(3).
49 Criminal Legal Aid (Determinations by a Court and Choice of Representative) Regulations 2013 reg 18(4).

- For three advocates:[50]
  - the case is being prosecuted by the Serious Fraud Office;
  - the court considers three advocates are required; and
  - the conditions for two juniors or QC plus junior are satisfied (as appropriate).

Only defined judges may make the relevant decisions.[51]

17.50 The payment of advocates' fees in the Crown Court is governed by the Advocates Graduated Fee Scheme. This is a similar regime to the Litigator Graduated Fee Scheme that determines payments to solicitors in Crown Court cases. The rules and fees applicable to the Advocates Graduated Fee Scheme are set out in Schedule 1 to the Criminal Legal Aid (Remuneration) Regulations 2013. This scheme applies to all advocates in the Crown Court, whether they are counsel or solicitor advocates.

17.51 Each case will have a trial advocate, who is the advocate responsible for claiming fees on behalf of all advocates instructed in the case.

17.52 The scheme provides for a basic fee based on the classification of the offence to which is added uplifts for pages of evidence, length of trial, number of witnesses and additional fees for features such as conferences. There is a higher basic fee for a trial and a lower for a guilty plea case. The basic fee includes payment for attendance at a plea and case management hearing and four other hearings during the case; additional fees can be claimed for other hearings.

17.53 The full details are set out in Schedule 1 to the Remuneration Regulations.[52]

Appeals

17.54 Although advice on appeals can, in some circumstances, be provided under the advice and assistance scheme, advocacy in appeal proceedings can now only be provided under a representation order.

17.55 Representation in appeal proceedings will require a representation order granted by the court in which the appeal is to be heard, be that the High Court (for appeals by way of case stated), the Crown

---

50 Criminal Legal Aid (Determinations by a Court and Choice of Representative) Regulations 2013 reg 18(5) and (6).

51 Criminal Legal Aid (Determinations by a Court and Choice of Representative) Regulations 2013 reg 19.

52 Criminal Legal Aid (Remuneration) Regulations 2013 Sch 1.

Court or the Court of Appeal. It is usual for representation orders granted by the Court of Appeal to be granted to an advocate alone.[53]

Advocacy assistance – prison law

17.56   Advocacy in prison law cases may be provided under the advocacy assistance scheme. Representation may be provided in disciplinary cases and in parole board cases, but see chapter 12 for scope.

17.57   You may only represent a client at hearings in these matters if the sufficient benefit test is satisfied, and the contract notes specifically that the LAA would not expect to fund a matter which did not raise a significant legal or human rights issue.[54] In addition advocacy assistance must not be provided in disciplinary cases where:

- it appears unreasonable to grant in the particular circumstances of the case; or
- (where required) permission to be legally represented has not been granted.[55]

In all cases you should record on the file how the merits test has been and continues to be met.[56]

17.58   In addition there is a financial eligibility test for both advice and assistance and advocacy assistance in prison law cases. The client must complete the relevant forms (CRM1 and CRM2 or CRM3), and must pass the means test. Means are limited by both capital and disposable income, and the eligibility levels can be found on the Legal Aid website at www.gov.uk/criminal-legal-aid-means-testing. The completed application forms must be retained on your file.[57]

17.59   Advocacy under this scheme is paid under a system of standard fees.[58] There are two standard fees for each type of case, and two corresponding standard fee limits. If your costs fall below either limit, you will be paid the respective standard fee. If your costs fall above the higher limit, you will be paid a non-standard fee for which your costs will be assessed by the LAA. See the Remuneration Regulations for details of the fees and limits.

53 Criminal Legal Aid (Determinations by a Court and Choice of Representative) Regulations 2013 reg 8.
54 Specification para B12.11; OCCC paras 11.5, 11.71–11.72, 11.85 and 11.98.
55 Specification para B12.116; OCCC para 11.86.
56 Specification para B12.7; OCCC para 11.6.
57 Specification para B12.16; OCCC paras 11.13–11.14 and 11.15.
58 Specification para B12.76; OCCC para 11.45.

17.60   Under this form of advocacy assistance, advocacy may be provided by either a solicitor or counsel. However, counsel is effectively 'unassigned' in that they are not able to claim payment directly from the LAA. Counsel's fees must be agreed and paid by the instructing solicitor from the standard fee.[59]

---

59 Specification paras B12.55 and B12.58; OCCC paras 11.41 and 11.45.

Managing legal aid work

Legal aid contracts

Introduction

18.1 This chapter explains the contract documentation, standard terms and obligations imposed by the Standard Contract and the Civil and Crime Specifications. It also covers how to get additional work under an existing contract and how to get a new contract with the Legal Aid Agency (LAA).

18.2 It also refers to some of the other contracts offered by the LAA, such as those for telephone triage and advice (CLA contracts) and Immigration Removal Centre contracts.

18.3 It is extremely important to become familiar with what your contract allows you to do and prohibits you from doing, since if you overlook something, you could find yourself served with a contract notice. Clause 24 of the Standard Contract allows for termination in relation to 'persistent breaches', that is three breaches of the same term in a 24-month period (or six different breaches), so it is very important to be aware of what you must and must not do.

Civil Standard Contracts

18.4 The civil contracts are very similar.

18.5
- The **Standard Civil Contract 2010** applies to: actions against the police; clinical negligence; family mediation; public law. For everything but family mediation this will be replaced by the 2015 version of the contract from November 2015 (see below).
- The **Standard Contract 2013** applies to housing and debt; family; immigration and Asylum.
- The **Standard Civil Contract (welfare benefits) 2013** from 1 October 2013 – welfare benefits in London and the South-east, and the Midlands and the East.
- The **Standard Civil Contract (welfare benefits) 2014** from 1 February 2014 – welfare benefits advice in the North, South-west and Wales.
- The **Standard Civil Contract 2014** from 1 August 2014 – mental health; community care.
- The **Standard Civil Contract 2015** from 1 November 2015 – actions against the police etc; clinical negligence; public law.

Crime Standard Contracts

18.6 The **Standard Crime Contract 2010** applies until 10 January 2016.

18.7 The **Own Client Crime Contract 2015** will apply from 11 January 2016. It authorises firms to undertake criminal investigations, proceedings, appeal/reviews, associated civil work, and prison law work under the contract for 'own clients' anywhere in England and Wales. The 2015 Own Client Standard Terms define an 'own client' as follows:

> 'Own Client' means an individual who selects you, at the point of request, anywhere in England and Wales and who does not fall within the arrangements under the 2015 Duty Provider Crime Contract.

18.8 The **2015 Duty Provider Crime Contract** will apply from 11 January 2016 for those successful in bidding for duty work in specified procurement areas, and will additionally authorise contract holders to do duty work in police stations and magistrates' courts.

Elements of the contract

18.9 The contracts are divided into the following sections:

a) Contract for Signature, Key Information, Tables and Annexes;
b) Office Schedule;
c) Standard Terms;
d) Specification, split into:
 – general rules and category-specific rules (in the Civil Contract);
 – general rules and specific rules on classes and units of work (in the Crime Contract).

All of the above documents form part of the contract, and you are bound by each and every part of them.

Contract for signature

18.10 As the name suggests, this is the part of the contract that is signed by the organisation and counter-signed by the LAA.

18.11 The contract covers the whole organisation (although it specifies the work that can be done at each office through an Office Schedule). This means that a breach at any office would jeopardise the whole contract, whereas in the past it was possible to withdraw a single office or category of law if it failed to meet the LAA's requirements. It is now only possible for the provider to serve notice on the LAA for the whole contract. If a provider wishes to withdraw from an office or category of law, that can only be done with the LAA's agreement. The contract for signature also includes any conditions that the LAA has imposed, the office schedules which have been issued, the applicable Quality Standard you must hold (the SQM (Specialist Quality Mark) or Lexcel), and contact details which the LAA will use to deal with you.

18.12   The Crime Contract sets out the types of criminal defence work the organisation is allowed to do, for example, police station and magistrates' court work, Crown Court work, prison law, etc. The 2015 Duty Provider Contract will also set out the Procurement Area(s) and the name(s) of any delivery partners.

Office Schedule

18.13   In civil and family, the Office Schedule sets out the details of the work you are allowed to do, including the number of matter starts in each category of work and the monthly controlled work payment.

18.14   The schedule will set out the number of new matter starts allowed, by category.

18.15   Civil Schedules contain the following tables:

- Table 1 gives the start and end dates.
- Table 2 gives the numbers of matter starts you are allowed by category and categories in which you may do licensed work.
- Table 3 sets out the maximum amount of money the LAA will pay you while the schedule is in force and the amount of your monthly payment.
- Table 4 sets out exactly what type of service and where you must provide services, by procurement area and access point, the number of any IRC rota weeks and slots. It also shows whether you are able to self-authorise up to an additional 50% of your matter starts.
- Table 5 shows if you have been authorised to carry out work at outreaches.

18.16   In the Crime Specification, numbers of cases are not specified and depend on the interests of justice test being met, as defined in the contract (see chapter 12 for more information about conducting criminal cases).

18.17   If you do work outside that authorised under your schedule, you will not be paid for it.

Supplementary matter starts

18.18   If you run out of matter starts during the lifetime of the schedule, you can ask the LAA for supplementary matter starts. If there is an urgent need or a general increase in demand[1] the LAA may issue more; but only if your allocation would be less than 50 per cent of the total in that procurement area for the category at the start of the schedule. The LAA changed its guidance in 2015 so that whether another organisation in the procurement area had NMS left was no longer a relevant issue.[2] We understand that this has made it much easier for organisations to obtain additional NMS when needed.

18.19   If you bid in one of the smaller lot sizes and your schedule allows it you will be able to self-grant up to 50 per cent additional matter starts. You will need to monitor how many NMS you have self-authorised in this way.

Standard Terms 2013

18.20   The Standard Terms apply to family, immigration and asylum and housing and debt. Key clauses are summarised below:

- **Clause 2**: You must appoint a Contract Liaison Manager and notify the LAA within five business days if the person is changed. You must monitor the email address which you have given to the LAA 'frequently each business day' and communicate with the LAA electronically where stipulated.
- **Clause 3**: You cannot subcontract, novate or otherwise delegate any of your obligations under the contract without the LAA's prior written consent. However, you can appoint agents to work for you as long as their work is properly supervised.

    If an approved third party, agent, counsel or a subcontractor ceases providing services to you, you are responsible for ensuring that you continue to fulfil the obligations under the contract.

    Note that under clause 3.7, if the fees payable by you exceed £250 per matter or case, you must require agents, counsel or sub-contractors in connection with contract work, to keep accurate

---

1   See Standard Contract 2013 Specification para 1.22.
2   See www.gov.uk/government/uploads/system/uploads/attachment_data/file/397501/supplementary-matter-starts-guidance.pdf.

records of the time they spend on the work you have appointed them to do and of the work done. They must also permit the LAA to audit the records.

This clause contains consortium provisions, although the 2013 contract tender did not in general allow for consortium bids. This is a provision which the LAA may find helpful if it needs to arrange for contracts to be delivered this way.

- **Clause 4**: Accounts must be audited or examined as required by law or professional regulation. You must notify the LAA within 14 days if your accounts are qualified.
- **Clause 5**: You must comply with the equality and diversity requirements, and you must have an Equality and Diversity Training Plan.
- **Clause 6**: Restrictions on marketing your services. It is clear that you can neither pay nor receive referral fees nor any other benefit, to any third party for the referral or introduction (directly or indirectly) of any client or potential client.
- **Clause 7**: You must monitor your performance and compliance with the contract and take corrective action if there are problems.

  This states that you must have access to the LAA Manual; but the LAA withdrew this requirement from 31 August 2015.[3]

  You must have indemnity insurance. This clause also lists much of the other regulation and legislation you must comply with. It also requires you to have a Business Continuity Plan and specifies what your IT system must be able to do. This is set at a level which would be regarded by most practices as necessary in any event. You must have an account for the LAA's online system for submitting claims (see chapter 13 for more information). The LAA also intends that at some point applications for legal aid and payments will also be made online.
- **Clause 8**: Requires you to record all the information required by the contract. You are required to keep closed client files (or copies of them) for six years. This is a prudent policy in case the LAA wants to carry out costs audits on closed files.
- **Clause 9**: Concerns access to your premises and information you must provide. Note that you must inform the LAA of the outcome of third party audits and provide them with a copy of the report within seven days of receipt. This clause would apply, for example to the SQM Delivery Partnership carrying out an SQM audit.

---

3 www.gov.uk/government/news/civilcrime-news-providers-no-longer-need-to-buy-legal-aid-manual.

- **Clause 10**: Sets out standards of work you must meet, including Peer Review. All work must be performed with reasonable care and skill. You must achieve at least Threshold Competence (3) at Peer Review in order to hold a contract. If you fail a peer review, have to be reassessed and are unsuccessful, the LAA may re-charge the cost to you.

  You must authorise the LAA to carry out status enquiries in relation to your personnel, if required.

- **Clause 11**: Requires you to meet key performance indicators (KPIs). If you fail to do so, the LAA will first meet with you to agree an action plan to improve performance (see chapter 17 for more information about KPIs). The LAA says they may use KPI performance as entry or selection criteria for future contracts. However, the LSC never did so, due to the difficulty in treating previous contractors and new applicants fairly in the tender process.

- **Clause 12**: Relates to contract documents and precedence.

- **Clause 13**: The LAA may amend the contract to take account of legislation or the justice system. Minor or technical amendments may be made to individual organisations' contracts. If the LAA wants to make material changes, it has to terminate the contract and issue a new one.

- **Clause 14**: This clause creates a single account for all work done by the organisation which is treated globally. Claims made by you are treated as credits to your account, and any payments made by the LAA as debits. You may be required to reimburse the LAA's reasonable audit costs if you have mis-claimed costs under the Contract.

- **Clause 15**: Sets out confidentiality arrangements.

- **Clause 16**: Data protection requirements.

- **Clause 17**: Freedom of Information Act obligations. The LAA may release information about your organisation either following consultation with you, or not, in certain circumstances.

- **Clause 18**: Warranties that the information provided by you and the LAA is true and accurate.

- **Clause 19**: Indemnity and giving notices.

- **Clause 20**: Giving notices under the contract.

- **Clause 21**: You must notify the LAA as soon as reasonably practicable of any anticipated material constitutional change (within 14 days as a minimum) and any other change that might impact on your ability to do contract work.

- **Clause 22**: Novations. The LAA may, and usually will, novate the contract if a practice merges with another, as long as it would not have to split a contract (note that the civil and crime contracts are considered to be separate so the LAA will allow these to be separated if the civil and crime departments of a firm split up). There is a policy paper on the Legal Aid website which provides more information: www.gov.uk/government/uploads/system/uploads/attachment_data/file/332931/legal-aid-novations-policy.pdf
- **Clause 24**: Contract sanctions may include; refusal to pay for specified contract work, suspension of payments, or taking on any new matters or cases, exclusion of individuals from being supervisors or performing contract work, suspending or removing your rota allocation (if any) of from holding yourself out as a provider and termination. If you breach the contract, the LAA may serve a contract notice under clause 24.2, requiring you not to repeat the breach. If you do so, you risk contract termination.
- **Clause 25**: You may terminate the contract at any time on three months' notice (subject to clause 13, which gives you rights to propose amendments). The LAA can terminate the contract at any time on six months' notice.
- **Clause 26**: Unless the LAA terminates the contract due to your breach, they will authorise you to continue work on existing cases (usually for up to two years).
- **Clause 27**: Reconsidering decisions and reviews of decisions. There is an informal procedure and a formal procedure. Formal reviews may be carried out by the LAA's Chief Executive or the Contract Review Body.

18.21   The 2010 and 2015 Standard Civil and Own Client Crime Standard Terms contain very similar provisions.

Duty Provider Standard Terms 2015

18.22   There are some onerous provisions in the Duty Provider Standard Terms which are significantly different from other legal aid contracts. Firms need to ensure that they are aware of them and put additional procedures into place to minimise risk as far as possible. We highlight those differences below:

- **Clause 3**: requires a written agreement with any delivery partner and what must be in that agreement, including allowing the LAA access to premises/staff for audits. It sets out the number of delivery partners that can be used (up to three) and the percentages of work that must be done by the Lead Contractor in a 12-month period (at least 30 per cent in rural areas and 45 per cent in urban areas). If operating with a Delivery Partner, it is the Lead Contractor that carries the risk of non-compliance by the Delivery Partner for any breaches of the contract or failure to meet service standards. Note also that the client's retainer sits with the Lead Contractor, which raises issues concerning confidentiality and other professional conduct matters, such as complaints handling.

- **Clause 25**: the provider does not have an absolute right to serve notice of termination on the LAA (subject to notice). The provider can only apply to the LAA to terminate the contract where volumes are 25 per cent less than anticipated volumes and then there is a six-month notice period rather than three as in most legal aid contracts.

Civil and Crime Specifications

18.23　These contain the detailed rules that apply to the way in which cases are carried out on a day-to-day basis. We cover them in the relevant chapter, see: Taking on civil and family cases (chapter 3), Conducting a civil/family case (chapter 5), Conducting a family private law case (chapter 6), Conducting a family public law case (chapter 7), Conducting an immigration case (chapter 9), Conducitng a mental health case (chapter 10), Conducting a housing case (chapter 11), Conducting a criminal case (chapter 12) and Quality standards and performance monitoring (chapter 19).

18.24　Note that prior to 2013, civil payment rates were set out in an annex to the Contract Specification. This was removed, and payment rates are only to be found in the Civil (or Criminal) Legal Aid (Remuneration) Regulations 2013 as amended.

Applying for Civil or Family Contracts

18.25　In civil and family, the LAA allocates funds to geographical areas using a formula which attempts to estimate the number of potential legal aid clients who might experience legal problems. This is called 'indicative spend'.

18.26　The LAA uses the formula as a starting point when considering where to direct available funding.

18.27　You should note that although bidding opportunities are expressed in terms of the numbers of matter starts available, where you provide services under a schedule, it will also authorise you to undertake an unlimited number of certificated cases (licensed work).

18.28   If you are an existing supplier wanting to add a category, open a new office, or add a substantial number of new matter starts to your existing allocation, or whether you are an organisation wishing to contract with the LAA for the first time, you should contact the LAA regional office that covers your area and make enquiries of the regional contracts manager. He or she may be able to tell you whether the LAA plans to issue any tenders in your area. Tender opportunities are advertised on the LAA's current tenders page: www.gov.uk/legal-aid-for-providers/tenders.

18.29   We know that the LAA refines its tender process with every round of tenders it conducts, so it unlikely that the process will be the same in future; but it is worth considering the requirements of past tenders, as they give some indication of the LAA's preferences (see paras 18.31–18.36).

How long contracts last

18.30   In general, LAA contracts last for three years with a power for the LAA to extend for up to two years. The 2015 Crime contracts are to last for four years with the same provision to extend for two years.

- The **Standard Civil Contract 2010** – family mediation. It started on 15 November 2010, with a tender process for new providers/outreach locations which started on 1 February 2015. The contract will run until 31 October 2016.
- The **Standard Civil Contract 2010** – actions against the police, clinical negligence, and public law. It started on 15 November 2010, and will run until 01 November 2015.
- The **Standard Crime Contract 2010** started on 14 July 2010 and will run until 10 January 2016.
- The **Standard Civil Contract 2013** – this applies to face to face services in family, housing and debt and immigration law. The start date was 1 April 2013 and it is intended to run for a three-year term, subject to the LAA's early termination rights (see below). It can be extended for up to two years.
- The **CLA (telephone) Contract 2013** – the start date was 1 April 2013 and it is intended to run for a three-year term, subject to the LAA's early termination rights (see below). It can be extended for up to two years.

- The **Standard Civil Contract (welfare benefits) 2013** started on 1 October 2013 and covers London, the South-east, the Midlands and the East. It is intended to run for a three-year term, subject to the LAA's early termination rights (see below). It can be extended for up to two years.
- The **Standard Civil Contract (welfare benefits) 2014** started on 1 August 2014 and covers the North, South-west and Wales. It is intended to run for a three-year term, subject to the LAA's early termination rights (see below). It can be extended for up to two years.
- The **Standard Civil Contract 2014** – this applies to face to face services in mental health and community care. The start date was 1 August 2014 and it is intended to run for a three-year term, subject to the LAA's early termination rights (see below). It can be extended for up to two years.
- The **Standard Civil Contract 2015** – this applies to face to face services in actions against the police etc, clinical negligence and public law. The start date is 1 November 2015 and it is intended to run for a three-year term, subject to the LAA's early termination rights (see below). It can be extended for up to two years.
- The **Standard Crime Contract 2010** started on 14 July 2010 and covers criminal investigations, proceedings, appeal/reviews, associated work, and prison law. It applies until 10 January 2016.
- The **Own Client Crime Contract 2015** – will apply from 11 January 2016 and covers criminal investigations, proceedings, appeal/reviews, associated work, and prison law for 'own clients' anywhere in England and Wales. It is intended to run for a four-year term, subject to the LAA's early termination rights (see below). It can be extended for up to one year.
- The **Duty Provider Crime Contract 2015** will apply from 11 January 2016 and covers criminal investigations, proceedings, appeal/reviews, associated work, and prison law for all those who are authorised to do Duty work in specified police stations and magistrates' courts. It is intended to run for a four-year term, subject to the LAA's early termination rights (see below). It can be extended for up to one year.

Tenders

18.31   The LAA uses an online tendering process through on online portal, https://legalaid.bravosolution.co.uk/web/login.shtml, hosted by a commercial company, Bravo Solution.

18.32   Bidders usually have to complete a pre-qualification questionnaire (PQQ) covering basic information about the organisation and its history of compliance with legal and regulatory requirements.

18.33   Bidders have to satisfy the LAA that they meet essential criteria and there is usually a competitive element to tenders including selection criteria based on previous experience of delivering legal services. However, where the LAA perceives there may be a lack of supply, there may be a simple registration process instead. Some tenders (for example the CLA telephone service) may include price competition.

18.34   Face to face contracts for legal work starting in 2013 were guaranteed to those submitting technically correct bids and meeting minimum requirements. Larger numbers of matter starts were allocated on a pro rata basis to those meeting defined requirements.

Applying for Crime Contracts

18.35   The tender of Crime contracts to start in 2016 was highly controversial and subject to two significant legal challenges (see chapter 21 for more information). The process for applying for an Own Client Contract was relatively straightforward and based on meeting essential criteria. Only those awarded Own Client Contracts were eligible to bid for Duty Contracts. The process for applying for Duty Provider contracts was extremely complex and included writing responses to three shortlisting questions and 17 award questions, relating to the way the organisation would deliver services in a procurement area. The answers were limited to 4000 characters each. The process was designed so that bidders would have only nine weeks to interpret the complex invitation to tender document, formulate and submit their bids. Due to legal action, the closing date was postponed and closed on 5 May 2015.

18.36   At the time of writing, the results of the Duty tender were expected to be announced in September 2015.

The Public Defender Service

18.37 As well as contracting with private practice to deliver criminal defence work, the LAA also employs a small number of salaried lawyers in the Public Defender Service (PDS). This service was set up to benchmark the cost and quality of services provided by private practice and was never intended to be a nationwide scheme. At the time of writing, there are four PDS offices: Cheltenham, Darlington, Pontypridd and Swansea. They are guaranteed Duty Provider contracts from 2016.

Crime – very high cost case accreditation

18.38 The LAA's Complex Crime Unit (CCU) manages membership of the very high cost case (VHCC) scheme. Only firms that are accredited under this scheme can represent clients in VHCC cases – any case where the trial is expected to last for more than 60 days.

18.39　From 14 July 2010, organisations and self-employed advocates wishing to work on cases classified as VHCCs have had to obtain VHCC accreditation. There is information about the VHCC arrangements and how to apply at www.gov.uk/high-cost-cases-crime.

Community Legal Advice services

18.40 The Community Legal Service was a concept embodied in the Access to Justice Act 1999. In some areas, the LSC contracted with a single provider to deliver a face-to-face legal advice and representation service concentrating on welfare benefits, debt, employment, housing, education and community care (sometimes referred to as social welfare law (SWL) categories), sometimes with family law services. These were known as Community Legal Advice Centres (CLACs) in urban areas, and in rural areas Community Legal Advice Networks (CLANs). LASPO proved fatal to these developments and in April 2012, the LSC announced that it would be ending those contracts at the end of March 2013.

Other kinds of contract with the LAA

18.41   The LAA has contracts with organisations for other kinds of service, for example:

- immigration/asylum advice and representation for people in detention;
- telephone advice, representation and casework for members of the public as part of the Civil Legal Advice telephone service in housing and debt, education (special educational needs), discrimination and family categories. This comprises an operator service which takes initial calls and a specialist adviser service which provides advice, casework and representation;
- telephone advice to people in police stations (Criminal Defence Service Direct).

18.42   Opportunities are publicised on the LAA's tenders page: www.gov.uk/legal-aid-for-providers/tenders

CHAPTER 19

Quality standards and performance monitoring

continued

Introduction

19.1   This chapter deals with quality standards and performance monitoring under contracts with the Legal Aid Agency (LAA), from a management perspective. We will cover the Standard Civil Contract 2013 as this covers the main family, immigration and asylum and housing and debt contracts and we also cover the 2010 and 2015 Crime contracts. There are also others, see chapter 18.

19.2   Whatever kind of contract you have with the LAA, there is no substitute for reading it! The worst-case scenario is that you overlook something fundamental, for example your supervisor may not meet the supervisor standards, the LAA discovers this and your contract is terminated, because there is nothing you can do to remedy the historic breach.

Practice management and quality of advice standards

19.3   The LAA has set quality standards for practice management, known as the Specialist Quality Mark (SQM), which applies to professional legal services, with additional requirements for telephone services. The LAA also accepts the Law Society's Lexcel standard in place of the SQM. The Mediation Quality Mark applies to family mediation. An organisation must be accredited to one of the acceptable standards in order to hold a contract.

19.4   The Quality Assurance Scheme for Advocates (QASA) is to be introduced for all advocates in criminal courts (see chapter 17) but at the time of writing the timetable had been suspended.

19.5   The LAA worked with the Institute of Advanced Legal Studies to create a peer review scheme that assesses the quality of legal advice. See www.gov.uk/legal-aid-agency-audits. If selected for peer review, organisations with face to face contracts must reach at least Threshold Competence in order to demonstrate that they meet contractual requirements.

19.6   At the time of writing, the current version of the SQM is V 2.1 dated December 2014. It can be downloaded from the LAA's web pages at www.gov.uk/legal-aid-agency-quality-standards.

Specialist Quality Mark

19.7   Organisations wanting a contract with the LAA must hold the SQM (or Lexcel – see below) by the contract start date.

19.8   The LAA has appointed the SQM Delivery Partnership to deliver auditing services for the SQM. It is a consortium of three established bodies and has significant audit experience as it conducts assessment processes for both Lexcel and Investors in People amongst other quality standards. For information about assessment, including cost, see the SQM Delivery Partnership's website: www.sqm.uk.com

Desktop audit

19.9   This is the first stage of assessment. The documentation submitted will be reviewed against the requirements of the Quality Mark. If the documentation is incomplete or so deficient that it is clear the organisation cannot meet the standard, the application will be refused. The documentation will be returned within 28 days with comments so that the organisation knows the issues it needs to address.

19.10   If the organisation passes the desktop audit, and its application for a contract is also successful (see chapter 18 for more information), it will be awarded a provisional quality mark and a contract.

Pre-Quality Mark audit

19.11   Before the QM is confirmed, an on-site audit will be carried out, usually four to six months after the desk top audit, to make sure that the QM requirements are in effective operation.

Opening meeting

19.12   The audit will start with an opening meeting at which the auditor will explain its scope and purpose. It is useful to have a copy of the Self-Assessment Audit Checklist (SAAC) to hand as the auditor is likely to check his or her understanding of procedures and check any queries.

Discussions with the auditor

19.13   If it appears that an auditor is requiring procedures to operate in a certain way, which does not coincide with the organisation's interpretation of QM requirements, (and particularly if it appears that implementing such a system could cause difficulty), it is advisable to ask him or her to refer you to the requirement in the standard. It may be that the organisation has not understood the requirement. On the other hand, as auditors are human too, they can make mistakes. Many QM requirements are so detailed that there is a limited number of ways in which they can be met. Auditors can become so used to seeing something being implemented in a certain way that they fail to recognise that an unusual system may still comply. Some auditors conduct assessments against both Lexcel and the SQM. It is not unknown for them to assess against eg a Lexcel requirement which is not in the SQM by mistake. If you both consider the system against the actual wording of the requirement, and any mandatory definition, you are most likely to reach a consensus.

SQM audit procedure and outcomes

19.14 The result will be one of:

- pass;
- pass with acceptable corrective action – usually relating to general quality concerns in non-critical management areas – this is the most common result; or
- fail (recommendation not to award or to terminate the QM) – this usually relates to critical quality concerns which cannot be addressed.

There is a representation process which can be invoked if the organisation considers that the audit was not correctly carried out, a critical quality concern should have been disregarded, or any other reasonable grounds.

Quality Mark requirements

19.15 First, the standard itself is set out. It is split into 'Requirements', which are mandatory, and 'Definitions'. The definitions are only mandatory where the word 'must' is used. See following page for a compliance aide-memoire, to assist you in maintaining compliance with SQM and contract requirements.

SQM
A: Access to service
Business plan – in detail for one year and outline for two further years. Non-discrimination in the provision of services. Six-monthly review of plan. Providing information about service provision.
B: Seamless service
Signposting – as a minimum providing the Civil Legal Advice call centre details. Note that under the Standard Contract Specification, para 2.49, in those categories of law delivered exclusively through the telephone gateway from April 2013, you must signpost clients or potential clients to the helpline unless that Client or potential Client is an Exempted Person as described in the Procedure Regulations. The exclusive categories are Debt (post LASPO, where the client's owner-occupied home is at risk and involuntary bankruptcy), Education (post LASPO, special educational needs cases) and Discrimination (eg consumer and employment cases). Exemptions to the mandatory single gateway include where the client is a child or in detention or has previously been assessed by CLA as requiring advice face-to-face, In emergency situations the client is not exempt but where representation is required the gateway should immediately refer the client to face to face advice. Telephone advice is available for in-scope matters in Housing and Family, but it is not the mandatory route for clients to access legal aid in these categories. Referral – records kept when a client is referred elsewhere on an existing matter.
C: Running the organisation
Staff structure. Key roles and decision-making structure. Financial control. Demonstrate independence.

D: People management

Job descriptions, responsibilities and objectives.

Equality and diversity.

Open recruitment process.

Induction procedure.

Annual performance review and feedback.

Training plans, training and records.

Named Supervisors – *meeting very detailed technical requirements (see note below for more information)*.

Supervisory skills and conditions for supervision.

Limits of individual competence.

Legal qualifications or 12 hours' casework per week.

E: Running the service

File management – *file lists, conflict of interest, locating files and tracing documents, key dates, solicitor undertakings, monitoring files for inactivity, identifying all matters for one client, logical and orderly files.*

File reviews for all conducting cases – *including legal and procedural issues – by Supervisor with corrective action taken where required (see note below for more information).*

File review records monitored annually.

F: Meeting clients' needs

Procedures for recording and confirming information and advice at the outset, during and at the end of the case.

Code of Conduct chapter one requirements; case plans in complex cases; costs and cost/benefit advice; considering legal aid entitlement.

Confidentiality and privacy.

Use of approved suppliers *(eg counsel, experts, interpreters) – selected on the basis of objective assessment, evaluation, consultation with the client, instructions in prescribed form.*

G: Commitment to quality

Complaints procedure.

Quality management – *responsibility for, review of all quality procedures annually, Quality Manual.*

Client satisfaction feedback.

Lexcel

19.16   The requirements of Lexcel are more demanding than the SQM and more closely aligned with the SRA Code of Conduct. Accrediting to Lexcel makes sense for firms which do non-contentious work or undertake work with a higher risk profile than legal aid. However, firms that have a low risk profile, for example those specialising in criminal defence work only, may find that the simpler SQM standard suits them best.

Supervisors – technical legal competence

19.17   Supervisors must demonstrate that they have experience in their category of 1,050 casework hours over the preceding three years if full-time, or five years if part-time (supervisors who have been on maternity leave or long-term sick in the last three years can demonstrate the five-year requirement even if they work full-time).

19.18   In some categories, supervisors must be members of a specialist panel, eg family, mental health; in immigration, supervisors must be accredited to that level under the IAAS, as well as providing evidence of 350 hours' case involvement over the preceding 12 months. Evidence of that experience can be direct casework (which may be easier as that will be time-recorded in any event), or it can include up to 115 hours' supervision, file review, training and research for publication.

19.19   The Supervisor Self-Declaration Forms have caused some confusion. Practitioners should remember that in Case Involvement table (table 4) in many versions boxes (b), (c), (d) and (e) are optional, not mandatory, as long as the individual can show 350 hours' direct personal casework in box (4)(a).

19.20   In categories where there is no panel, supervisors must demonstrate that they have closely defined experience of case types. As for panel members, this must be maintained by at least 350 hours' experience in that category annually.

Supervisor standards in the 2013 Standard Civil Contract

19.21   The rules are to be found in the Standard Civil Contract 2013 Specification paras 2.10–2.27. Under the Contract you must (unless Category Specific Rules specify otherwise – which they do not for family, housing/debt or immigration) employ at least one full-time equivalent supervisor in that category. This means you need at least one full time equivalent in those categories (and you may need more if there are more than four people to supervise or multiple office arrangements mean that is the only practical way to ensure cover).

19.22   For this purpose 'full time equivalent' means the equivalent of one individual working five days a week and seven hours on each day (excluding breaks).

19.23   The contract goes on to say that a supervisor must at all times during their working hours (except as required for the proper performance of their role, (such as attending court and/or clients)) work from one of or any combination of your offices. Note this is not exactly the same as requiring them to be in the office at all times during working hours and does allow a degree of flexibility.

19.24   In addition, supervisors must be a sole principal, an employee or a director of or partner in or member of your organisation if your practice is a company, partnership (other than an LLP) or an LLP. Consultants are therefore not permitted to be supervisors.

19.25   The LAA will only authorise external supervisors at its discretion and for temporary periods, for example if your supervisor becomes unwell and is unable to discharge their duties for six weeks.

Supervisor standards in the 2015 Crime Contracts

19.26   The requirements in both the Own Client and Duty Contracts are very similar to the 2013 Civil Contracts above. There are some particular issues relating to Crime Contracts, which are set out below.

19.27   The 1:4 supervisor to caseworker ratio applies,[1] with the exception of prison law where the ratio under the 2015 contract is 1:6.[2]

19.28   Under the Duty Provider contract, you cannot employ a supervisor who also works for another organisation.[3]

19.29   Under the 2010 contract, there are five crime supervisor forms, offering three 'routes' to qualification as a supervisor of mainstream crime work, (duty solicitor route, duty solicitor equivalent route, 350 hours a year crime casework route) and separate routes to qualify to supervise appeals and review work and prison law.

---

1 Standard Crime Own Client Contract Specification para 2.21; Standard Crime Duty Provider Contract Specification para 2.16.
2 Standard Crime Own Client Contract Specification para 2.22.
3 Standard Crime Duty Provider Contract Specification para 2.16.

19.30   This changes with the new contracts starting in 2016. Under both the Own and Duty contracts,[4] the supervisor must hold Criminal Litigation Accreditation Scheme qualification, and have undertaken six police station attendances in the past 12 months and have:

- three years' unqualified practising certificates;
- a minimum of 20 magistrates' court representations and advocacy under a representation order in the past 12 months; or
- a minimum of ten magistrates' court representations and advocacy and five Crown Court representations and advocacy in the past 12 months.

There will continue to be separate supervisor standards for those specialising in appeals and reviews work and prison law. The requirements in relation to practising certificates do not apply to prison law supervisors.

Supervisors – file reviews

19.31   File reviews under the SQM must cover legal and procedural points (Lexcel allows for file reviews limited to procedural points but that would be risky from the point of view of peer review under the contract). This can cause problems when considering who should review the supervisor's files. If there is another experienced practitioner in the same area of law, they can review each other's files. Where there is not, perhaps because there is no one else who practises in that specialism, the supervisor will have to review his or her own files (as objectively as possible!) for legal issues and someone else will review it for procedural points. The LAA does not expect an organisation to incur the expense of an external supervisor in these circumstances.

---

4 Standard Crime Duty Provider Contract Specification para 2.13; Standard Crime Own Client Contract Specification para 2.14.

Key supervision issues from recent audits

- Have file reviews been carried out by the named supervisor (or delegated to a deputy with a training and development plan to meet full supervisor status)?

- Do the management/organisation structure and individual job descriptions agree? *It's amazing how disorganised you can look to an outsider if they don't!*

- If the supervisor has to demonstrate compliance through the portfolio route (as opposed to panel membership), can they do so over the last 12 months? *Consider the numbers of hours required and the range of cases.*

- Were independent file reviews undertaken by an appropriate person? *If you are developing a member of staff as a deputy supervisor and delegating some file reviews to them, make sure this is all properly documented.*

- Are the independent file review records completely up to date – *if there are gaps, eg someone was on maternity leave or on the holiday of a lifetime, are the reasons for them clear?*

- *If you have not been able to do file reviews for a period due to pressures such as sickness absence or additional work demands, catch up later and put a note onto your central record explaining why some file reviews were done late*

- Is corrective action required recorded on the file review forms, with appropriate dates?

- Do they also show what action was taken and by when?

- Did file reviews identify any non-compliances with SQM or contract requirements? If the supervisor is lenient, the LAA cannot be confident that the organisation meets its requirements.

Peer review

19.32   Peer review is the measure that the LAA uses to assess quality of advice. It has been developed over many years under the auspices of the Institute of Advanced Legal Studies (IALS). Peer reviewers have carried out thousands of assessments since 2000 and refined the process over the years. There is information about the process at www.gov.uk/legal-aid-agency-audits.

19.33   There are five possible scores: excellence (1), competence plus (2), threshold competence (3), below competence (4) and failure in performance (5). The LAA has defined the level of skill required under the Contract as at least threshold competence. At below competence level, the provider will be given six months to improve, if they do not achieve at least threshold competence at their next assessment, their contract will be terminated. An organisation assessed at failure in performance will have its contract terminated quickly, because of the risk to clients.

19.34   The LSC disseminated good practice guides. These got good feed-back from practitioners who generally found them helpful. Unfor-tunately, they did not get updated and did not transfer to the LAA website. The LAA has undertaken to commission updated guides from the IALS but at the time of writing, these had not yet been pub-lished. The old guides still give an indication of what peer reviewers are looking for and can be downloaded from the Legal Aid Handbook resources page http://legalaidhandbook.com/laspo-resources/.

The peer review process

19.35   All peer reviewers are experienced practitioners, trained by the IALS to carry out peer review using their framework. A sample of their own files has to be assessed at competence plus or above. Peer reviewers are consistency-checked against each other and receive regular train-ing. There are various reasons why a review might be carried out, eg routine bench-marking, or concern about quality raised by a contract manager; but the reviewer is not told what it is. This ensures that they can approach all peer reviews with an open mind.

19.36   Twenty files are requested, of which at least 15 are assessed. They are selected to cover all the different types of work carried out by the organisation within a category of law and are cases closed during the preceding 12 months. Peer reviewers carry out the assessment at an LAA regional office. They do not meet the staff of the organisation being reviewed, which never finds out the identity of its particular reviewer, although they are sent a list of all the reviewers and asked to identify any possible conflict of interest. It usually takes one to two days to do an assessment and write a report.

19.37   The reviewers evaluate issues that relate to quality of advice and service. They do not look at how long was spent on the file and they do not carry out a transaction criteria[5] audit. They apply the 'pick up test', which is the basic question – if I, as another fee-earner, picked

5   Transaction criteria will be remembered by many legal aid practitioners from the early days of 'franchising'. They enabled the Legal Aid Board, and later the LSC, to assess the extent to which a lawyer had obtained appropriate information and followed steps associated with best practice. They did not

up this file, could I understand what had been done and why, and what remained to be done?

19.38　　They assess individual files and then consider the sample as a whole and form a conclusion about its overall quality. In many cases this involves a balancing act as some files may be good, others less so. Organisations scoring competence plus tend to have a higher level of consistency. For example, if there is a change of caseworker part way through the case the peer reviewer would look at the whole case, and in order to score competence plus or excellence, both caseworkers would need to achieve that level.

19.39　　They also apply the 'friend and family test', which is simply 'would I refer a friend or family member to this organisation?' If the answer is 'no', the sample will be assessed below threshold competence or worse.

19.40　　Peer reviewers use checklists of criteria, which they score individually; but the overall score is not simply an average of the scores on individual files. Peer reviewers take account of any trends and patterns identified, including evidence of supervision. Having assessed the 15 files, the reviewer compiles a report identifying; positive findings, major areas of concern (if any), areas for development, suggested areas for improvement and any other comments.

19.41　　Reports are checked by IALS to ensure that the score reflects the comments the reviewer has made about the files. So, for example they would pick up a contradiction if the sample scored competence plus but the reviewer had identified major areas of concern, and ask the reviewer to look at the report again. IALS does not double-check the assessment. The provider should receive the final report within 28 days.

Tips for passing peer review

19.42　The peer reviewers emphasise that good practice helps to improve peer review scores, for example:

- file review and supervision support;
- ensuring workload is appropriate;
- training;
- providing appropriate advice on legal and procedural issues on every file;

allow any assessment to be made of the quality of legal advice. They were superseded by peer review.

- confirming the client's initial instructions and your advice in writing.

Standard letters and documentation

19.43   Peer reviewers accept that standard letters have their place; but that it is important to take an individual approach to them. This means ensuring that standard letters should not be 'catch-alls' which try to cover all eventualities; but should be specific to a client's circumstances. So, for example, a letter setting out the different possession proceedings in relation to both owner-occupiers and tenants would not impress a peer reviewer, who would expect the client to be given only the information that applied to his or her case.

19.44   As in all kinds of file-based assessment, it is vital that the file is complete. Some organisations send information leaflets to clients; but do not put a copy of standard information on the file, in order to save paper and printing costs. Peer reviewers advise that if that is the way you work, it is important to include copies of all standard information leaflets with the file sample.

Peer review representations

19.45   Representations can only be made if the assessment is category 4 or 5. The LAA's rationale is that since a category 3 is acceptable for a contract, there is no point in allowing representations when only the organisation's professional pride is at stake.

19.46   Possible grounds are that: you dispute the overall peer review rating, the sample does not appear to be sufficiently representative, any other reasonable grounds.

19.47   Representations must be made on the appropriate form and reach the LAA within 28 days following receipt of the report and the file sample. The representations will be considered by the original peer reviewer and a senior panel member. They may uphold the original rating, revise the original rating, request a new review, or not reach agreement. Where the latter occurs an external expert who is not a peer reviewer will be asked to help the peer reviewers reach a consensus. At the time of writing, 17 per cent of representations resulted in an improved assessment score. Note that, if an appeal is unsuccessful, you may have to pay the costs of assessment under the Standard Civil Contracts 2013 and 2014, and both Own and Duty Provider Standard Crime Contracts 2015, clause 10.8.

LAA monitoring

19.48   The LAA is increasingly monitoring firms remotely, using the data firms supply, for example when applying for legal aid or submitting claims for costs. The LAA calls this 'management Information' (MI). You can access some of your MI at www.gov.uk/legal-aid-management-information-online. You can access financial statements; but at the time of writing it was not possible for organisations to access all MI data to monitor the Contract Key Performance Indicators (KPIs) – see below for more information. Therefore, it is a good idea to ask your LAA contract manager to send you this data on a quarterly basis. They can do this and it is regarded as good practice by the LAA senior managers for them to help you in this way.

Key performance indicators

19.49   Both the civil and crime versions of the Standard Contracts have mandatory key performance indicators (KPIs).

19.50   Somebody should be monitoring key performance indicators, usually a Head of Department or Partner. Some can be monitored at individual file level, others will require the collection of data by department/work type. Contract managers monitor KPI reports, which are flagged as 'red', 'amber' or 'green'. Failing to meet KPIs will not in itself result in sanctions being taken against you or contract notices being raised. However, your contract manager may contact you to ask you to explain the reasons that your organisation is 'out of profile'. If it is an issue which the contract manager thinks should be corrected, then you will be asked to formulate an action plan for doing so. Being 'out of profile' may also trigger an on-site or other type of audit.

19.51   Both the civil and crime versions of the Standard Contract have key performance indicators (KPIs).

19.52   The LAA monitors KPIs on a three-month rolling basis rather than on individual files, with minimum numbers where volumes are low.

Standard Civil Contract 2013: Key performance indicators[6]

KPI 1 – Controlled work (non-fixed fee) – assessment reduction 10 per cent max

19.53   When your 'escape cases' are assessed (these are the cases where the costs on a time and item basis are 3 x the fixed fee), the costs claimed must not be reduced by more than 10 per cent. This includes disbursements but not VAT.

KPI 2 – Licensed work – assessment reduction 10 per cent max

19.54   This sets the same target in relation to licensed work cases that are claimed on a time and item basis.

KPI 3 – Fixed fee margin – 20 per cent max

19.55   The LAA is concerned that some organisations will select clients with straightforward cases that do not require much work, in order to retain a high surplus under each fixed fee case. This KPI can only be met if the total cost of cases under fixed fees when calculated on a time and item basis is at least 80 per cent of the appropriate fixed fees.

19.56   This KPI applies to controlled work cases, and Family Private and Public Law Representation Scheme cases that are paid by way of fixed fees.

KPI 4 – Rejection rates for licensed work – 5 per cent max in the schedule period

19.57   Rejections are when applications or claims are refused because of technical errors in form completion, or lack of enclosures etc. This applies to applications for legal aid (known as applications for determinations that an individual qualifies for legal aid in the post LASPO scheme), and claims for payment.

KPI 5 – Refusal rates for licensed work – 15 per cent max in the schedule period

19.58   This applies to applications for legal aid which are refused because the LAA considers that the practitioner has failed to show that they meet the applicable merits test.

---

6   Standard Civil Contract 2013 Specification paras 2.50–2.66.

KPI 6 – Immigration CLR positive outcome – 40% minimum

19.59   This KPI is taken as an indicator of quality and applies to Immigration CLR work only.

Service Standards – Civil and Family

19.60   Service standards are to be found in the applicable contract specification.

19.61   The general rules under the 2013 Contract are set out in the Standard Civil Contract 2013 Specification paras 2.1–2.66.

19.62   **Use of agents and third parties.** You may use agents, counsel and third parties where it is in your client's best interests. The specification allows independent consultants to carry out work under the contract as long as the supervision conditions are met. However, it is important to note that you cannot use an agent to meet the service standards. So, for example, you cannot use an agent to meet the Supervisor standards.

19.63   **Supervisor standards.** See above for Supervisor standards under the 2013 Contract and below for subsequent contracts.

19.64   **Minimum numbers of matter starts.** Although the specification allows minimum numbers to be specified, usually they are not. See below for exceptions.

19.65   **Presence in the procurement area.** You must comply with the presence requirements set out in your schedule, that is, your office must comply with the requirements for a permanent or part time presence[7]. You may be allowed to deliver outreach services. If so, these must be noted on your schedule.

19.66   **Referral and signposting arrangements.** You must have referral and signposting arrangements in place. For those categories of law delivered exclusively through the telephone gateway from April 2013, you must signpost clients or potential clients to the helpline unless that Client or potential Client is an Exempted Person as described in the procedure regulations.

19.67   The exclusive categories are debt (post-LASPO, where the client's owner-occupied home is at risk and involuntary bankruptcy), education (post-LASPO, special educational needs cases) and discrimination (eg consumer and employment cases).

19.68   Exemptions to the mandatory single gateway include where the client is a child or in detention or has previously been assessed by CLA as requiring advice face-to-face for this case.

---

7   Standard Civil Contract 2013 Specification paras 2.33–2.36.

19.69   Telephone advice is also available in those cases remaining in-scope, in housing and family, but is not the mandatory route for clients to access legal aid in those categories.

Additional service and monitoring requirements

19.70   There are additional service standards for family, actions against the police and public law, immigration and mental health, see below. Organisations with contracts to deliver housing possession court duty schemes also need additional monitoring systems, also shown below.

Family

19.71   There are appointment service standards in the Family category. When you are contacted by a client for whom you intend to provide services, (and have sufficient matter starts) you must offer a first appointment to the client within 48 hours of the initial contact in Emergency Cases, or within ten working days of the initial contact in all other cases.[8]

Actions against the police etc and clinical negligence

19.72   KPI 6: The Standard Contract 2013 KPI6 was replaced with a requirement to obtain a substantive benefit outcome in 30 per cent of cases funded under legal representation.[9]

19.73   KPI7: In cases that proceed beyond initial investigation, substantive benefit outcomes must be 50 per cent in sctions against the police etc and 60 per cent in clinical negligence.

Immigration and asylum

19.74   The Immigration Specification paras 8.15–8.22) sets down requirements for caseworkers and supervisors to be accredited under the Immigration and Asylum Accreditation Scheme. It also limits the type of work that can be done by reference to the level of accreditation. For example, only level 2 caseworkers can conduct CLR cases or use devolved powers to grant CLR.

19.75   In this category you must use 90% of your Asylum matter starts to clients who are physically located in the designated Immigration/Asylum Procurement Area.

---

8 Standard Contract Specification 2013 para 7.165.
9 Standard Contract Specification 2015 para 2.63.

Community care

19.76 The Standard Civil Contract 2014 applies.

19.77 You must also employ a 0.5 FTE Authorised Litigator who can demonstrate experience of undertaking Community Care cases.

Mental health

19.78 The Standard Civil Contract 2014 applies.

19.79 There are particular presence requirements, which are set out in paragraphs 7.4–7.5 of the 2014 Mental Health Specification. The requirements you have to meet will be recorded in your Contract schedule.

19.80 You must employ an Authorised Litigator.

19.81 In addition to the overall requirement to employ a FTE Supervisor per four caseworkers in a procurement area, you must employ a supervisor in each procurement area where you have a schedule for at least 17.5 hours a week.

19.82 All advocates before the MHT (except self-employed counsel) must be members of the Law Society Mental Health Accreditation Scheme.[10]

19.83 In this category 70 per cent of clients must be physically located in the Procurement Area in which you have been granted matter starts. 30 per cent of your matter starts may be used for clients who are not physically located in the Procurement Area in which you have been granted matter starts.

Housing possession court duty schemes

19.84 If you provide a client with advice at court and, within six months of doing so, subsequently open a new housing matter start in relation to the same case then you cannot claim any payment for providing the service at court. The costs of providing the service will be included in the housing matter start fixed fee.[11]

19.85 You need a monitoring system to monitor these cases and make adjustments where necessary.

---

10 Standard Civil Contract Specification 2014 para 7.6.
11 Standard Civil Contract Specification 2013 para 10.24.

Key performance indicators – Standard Crime Contract 2010

19.86   Under the Crime Specification 2010, para 2.50, failure to achieve a key performance indicator may result in the application of a sanction under clause 11 of the Standard Contract 2010. A repeated breach may result in contract termination.

Crime KPIs		
1	Assessment reduction on claims for magistrates' courts non-standard fees and police station advice and assistance exceptional cases.	Maximum of 15% reduction on assessment on all your claims for these fees in any three-month period during the contract term.
2	Acceptance of calls from Defence Solicitor Call Centre (DSCC) for police station telephone advice and police station attendance when you are allocated supplier on rota duty solicitor scheme.	Minimum of 90% of calls made to you by the DSCC during each of the quarter periods accepted and dealt with appropriately.

Service standards – Standard Crime Contract 2010

19.87   Section 2 of the Crime Specification 2010 contains the service standards for criminal defence work.

19.88   **Supervisors**: You must have at least one person who meets the LAA's standard for supervisors and they must carry out their duties in accordance with the contract – which contains the familiar Specialist Quality Mark standards for supervision and file review.

19.89   In the crime category there is no specified ratio of supervisors to designated fee earners or caseworkers, with the exception of Prison law, where you must have at least one full-time equivalent Supervisor for every six full-time equivalent caseworkers (Standard Crime Contract Specification para 2.25).

19.90   You must designate the staff who work under the Crime Contract and the work they can do. Designating staff means naming the people who do work under the Criminal Contract, ensuring they meet the standards required by the contract, Specialist Quality Mark and Duty Solicitor Arrangements and keeping records as shown below.

19.91 Fee earners should be 'designated', unless they do less than three hours' contract work a month. Those who regularly undertake fee earning criminal work under the contract: crime supervisors, FILEX supervisors, duty solicitors, accredited and probationary representatives, must be designated.

19.92 Under the previous Unified Contract, where an individual undertook work for more than one practice, one could be identified as a 'lead' practice and would be responsible for keeping records and carrying out independent file review and other procedures. Practices that make regular use of freelance agents will need to implement much more rigorous supervision procedures than previously to ensure that all required procedures are carried out.

19.93 Clause 3.3(ii) of the Standard Contract allows you to employ agents and subcontractors as long as your 'supervision of them is, in all respects, equal to your supervision of your employed solicitors and legal advisers'.

19.94 Paragraph 2.14 of the Specification states: 'Each Supervisor must conduct file reviews for each Designated Fee Earner or Case-worker they supervise.'

19.95 The Contract Specification sets out percentages of Crime Contract work which must be performed by designated fee earners:

- Advocacy in the magistrates' court: 50 per cent must be done by designated staff.
- Police station advice and assistance: 80 per cent must be done by designated staff.

19.96 **Location**: You may only perform contract work from the office(s) specified in your schedule. Offices must be physically accessible for clients from Monday to Friday, and you must have arrangements in place to ensure that during opening hours, clients are able to speak to someone by telephone to arrange appointments and to contact you about emergency matters. If you move your office out of your original postcode area, you must ask the LAA's permission. Even if the LAA consents they may make it a condition that your duty solicitors may not undertake work on additional duty schemes which are accessible only by virtue of your new office address.

19.97 **Referral and signposting arrangements**: You must have appropriate arrangements in operation to refer clients or potential clients to another provider if you do not provide the services that the client requires or for some other reason are unable to take on their case.

19.98 If you are in Wales, you must comply with the Welsh Language Act 1993.

Key performance indicators – Standard Own Client and Duty Provider Crime Contracts 2015

19.99   Under the Own Client Crime Specification 2015 para 2.42 (para 2.33 in the Duty Provider Contract Specification), failure to achieve a key performance indicator is not an automatic breach of contract. The KPIs in both versions of the contract are the same:

KPIs 2015 Duty and Own Client Contracts	
KPI Number	**The Key Performance Indicators that you must meet in performing Contract Work in any three month rolling period**
1	To avoid a reduction of more than 15% of your costs on Assessment on any of your claims for: Police station advice and assistance (escape fee cases); free standing advice and assistance claims; advocacy assistance claims; Magistrates' court non-standard fees; Prison law escape fee cases; Prison law non-standard fees. If your costs are reduced by more than 15% on Assessment in any 3-month rolling period, then you have not met KPI 1.
2	To accept and deal appropriately with a minimum of 90% of communications (howsoever received) from the DSCC for police station advice and assistance.
3	To ensure that 95% or more of your cases conclude before any change of provider under the contract.

Service standards – Standard Own Client Crime Contract 2015

19.100   Section 2 of the Crime Specification 2015 contains the service standards for own client criminal defence work.

19.101   **Supervisors**: See above for supervisor requirements.

19.102   You must designate the staff who work under the Crime Contract and the work they can do. Designating staff means naming the people who do work under the Criminal Contract, ensuring they meet the standards required by the contract and applicable quality standard.

19.103 Fee earners should be 'designated', unless they do less than three hours' contract work a month. Those who regularly undertake fee earning criminal work under the contract: crime supervisors, FILEX supervisors, duty solicitors, accredited and probationary representatives, must be designated.

19.104 Crime contract work which must be performed by designated fee earners:

- Advocacy in the magistrates' court: 75 per cent (by value of work) must be done by designated staff
- Police station advice and assistance: 75 per cent (by value of work) must be done by designated staff.

19.105 **Location**: You must have at least one office. Offices must have suitable private interview facilities, separate waiting area, secure storage of client files, satisfy any professional requirements of your regulator and be registered as appropriate; have infrastructure including: landline telephone; Internet access including secure email; fax; post or DX. Clients must be able to arrange appointments during business hours.

19.106 **Referral and signposting arrangements**: You must have appropriate arrangements in operation to refer clients or potential clients to another provider if you do not provide the services that the client requires or for some other reason are unable to take on their case.

Service standards – Standard Duty Provider Crime Contract 2015

19.107 Section 2 of the Crime Specification 2015 contains the service standards for duty scheme criminal defence work.

19.108 **Supervisors**: See above for supervisor requirements.

19.109 You must designate the staff who work under the Crime Contract and the work they can do. Designating staff means naming the people who do work under the Criminal Contract, ensuring they meet the standards required by the contract and applicable quality standard, and by keeping records as shown below.

19.110 Fee earners should be 'designated', unless they do less than three hours' contract work a month. Those who regularly undertake fee earning criminal work under the contract: crime supervisors, FILEX supervisors, duty solicitors, accredited and probationary representatives, must be designated.

19.111 **Location**: The location of offices which you are required to maintain will be set out in your schedule. Offices must have suitable private interview facilities, separate waiting area, secure storage of client files, satisfy any professional requirements of your regulator and be registered as appropriate; have infrastructure including: landline telephone; Internet access including secure email; fax; post or DX. Clients must be able to arrange appointments during business hours.

19.112 **Referral and signposting arrangements**: You must have appropriate arrangements in operation to refer clients or potential clients to another provider if you do not provide the services that the client requires or for some other reason are unable to take on their case.

Duty Scheme Rules – Standard Duty Provider Crime Contract 2015

19.113 These are contained in Section 6 of the Crime Specification 2015. You are only allowed to do duty work in those procurement areas set out in your schedule. The obligation to perform duty work rests with the firm, not individual lawyers. You will be allocated an equal share of duty slots along with all other firms in the procurement area.

19.114 You have to ensure that Duty Lawyers are competent. They must undertake least two hours CPD annually on issues relevant to the law, practice and procedure in the police station or magistrates' courts; and continue to undertake Contract Work generally as evidenced by conducting at least 24 police station attendances and 12 magistrates' court attendances (Duty Lawyer or Own Provider) in each 12-month rolling period, including at least one police station attendance each month and one magistrates' court attendance every four months.[12]

19.115 You have to comply with rotas produced by the LAA.[13]

19.116 You must ensure that clients know they have the right to instruct their own solicitor and you must not act for a client who has their own solicitor unless the own solicitor does not attend, the court is sitting on a non-business day or it is unclear whether the client has their own solicitor.[14]

19.117 See also chapter 18 for the requirements imposed under the Standard Duty Provider Contract standard terms for obligations regarding any delivery partners.

---

12 Standard Duty Provider Crime Contract 2015 Specification para 6.9.
13 Standard Duty Provider Crime Contract 2015 Specification para 6.12.
14 Standard Duty Provider Crime Contract 2015 Specification paras 6.26–6.32.

CHAPTER 20

Financial and contract management

Introduction

20.1   This chapter deals with issues that affect an organisation's financial and contractual position: reconciliation, payments on account, key performance indicators (KPIs), contract compliance audits, contract manager visits and audits.

20.2   Much legal aid work, with the exception of civil certificates and Criminal Crown Court cases, is paid by way of a monthly payment under either the Civil or the Crime Contract.

20.3   Each contract has a schedule, which sets out what the LAA will pay you each month if you have opted for the standard monthly payment option (see below). At the end of each month, you submit bills for concluded cases via the LAA's online claim portal.

Payment for Civil controlled work and Crime Lower

20.4   There are two options for payment of this work. You can opt for variable monthly payments (VMP) reflecting each month's claim, plus the value of any escape fee cases credited to you by the LAA during the month, (sometimes referred to as 'pay as you go') or you can be paid Standard Monthly Payments (SMP).

20.5   The advantage of 'pay as you go' is that reconciliation of claims against payments should be fairly straightforward.

20.6   If you opt for an SMP, it will be the amount the LAA expects to pay you over the lifetime of the schedule, divided by that number of months. The advantage is that you get a regular amount, which can help with budgeting; but since it is rare to hit contract targets exactly, it can involve you in complex reconciliation calculations. If you opt for an SMP, you will also have to keep your eye on the reconciliation protocol (see below).

SMP or pay as you go, which is best?

20.7   The LAA allows you to choose your payment method; but this means reconciling the contract to give the new arrangement a fresh start. If you have a strong cash position, or the LAA owes you money, you may want to opt for 'pay as you go'. However, if you have been paid more money than you have claimed and do not wish to make repayments at once, then you may prefer to stick with the SMP (subject to the reconciliation protocol below). If you are owed money by the LAA, assuming that this figure is less than £20,000, a single ad hoc payment will be made to you. If you owe money to the LAA, then you can choose to make a single payment or spread the payments over a six month period.

20.8 If you have a Crime contract and have taken advantage of the one month's 'pull forward' option, that cannot be combined with 'pay as you go'. There is more information about this on the Legal Aid Agency website at www.gov.uk/government/uploads/system/uploads/attachment_data/file/318538/LAA-variable-monthly-payments-guidance.pdf.

Reconciliation of contracts

20.9 You should always keep your own figures for the value of your monthly submissions and monitor them against your payments. You can obtain more information and check the LAA's figures at www.gov.uk/legal-aid-management-information-online. The LAA will do the same, and periodically will seek to adjust the payments to ensure that your contract remains on course. As a result of the adjustment, your payments may go up or down. The purpose is to ensure that at the end of the contract, claims equal payments, or at least that the difference between them is within an agreed band. This process is known as reconciliation, and where parity has been achieved the contract has been successfully reconciled. Where it hasn't, arrangements will need to be made to resolve the outstanding balance, either by payment of a lump sum or recovering the balance during the schedule. The LAA is usually reluctant to allow recovery over more than one schedule or six months; but it can be done.

The reconciliation protocol

20.10 The reconciliation protocol sets out the approach the LAA will take which can also be downloaded at www.gov.uk/government/uploads/system/uploads/attachment_data/file/340267/LAA-monthly-payments-protocol.pdf (or see appendix I). The key is that the target is always reconciliation to 100 per cent (though the reconciliation protocol confirms that crime providers can choose instead to have a one-month 'pull-forward' – ie to reconcile to 92.5 per cent instead of 100 per cent) – that is, for claims to equal payments over the course of the schedule. It is recognised that in practice it will often work out that 100 per cent is not exactly achieved. Therefore the LAA will look at the position twice a year – April and September – and determine whether the contract is within the acceptable margin of 90 to 110 per cent (calculated over the shorter of the life of the contract or the last 12 months). Where it is, no action will be taken. Where the contract is outside the acceptable margin, the monthly payment will be revised with a view to paying off any balance within six months.

20.11　　It is important to remember that each month you claim less than your standard monthly payment (SMP) then the closer to the 90 per cent trigger point you will be. You need to try to avoid any cumulative decline in performance that takes you below 90 per cent. Once you go below the trigger point, the reduction happens automatically and the LAA would not warn you about this in advance. The new payment would remain in place for three months to monitor that it would achieve the desired effect. You would have to ensure that claims stayed at or around the level of the previous SMP, otherwise it could trigger a further reduction at the three-month review stage.

Case study

My firm has Criminal and Civil Contracts. The Civil Contract is currently paid at £10,000 per month. After 12 months, we have claimed £102,000. The Criminal Contract is paid at £5,000 per month and after 12 months we have claimed £64,000. Are we in band? Are the LAA likely to change our payments?

Civil: Total claims = £102,000 over the life of the contract. Payments are £120,000, so the balance on the account is £18,000 owed to the LAA. This is a margin of 82 per cent, so outside the acceptable band (ie below 90 per cent). The payment will be amended. The target is 100 per cent. Average monthly claim is £8,500 (£102,000/12) and you owe the LAA £18,000, which must be repaid over the next six months. The new payment will be £8,500 – (£18,000/6) = £5,500 per month.

Crime: Total claims = £64,000, and payments are £60,000. 10 per cent of claims = £6,400, so the acceptable band is £60,000 ± £6,400 – between £53,600 and £66,400. Therefore you are within band and the LAA will not automatically amend your contract payment. However, you are entitled to ask the LAA to amend your payments at any time and may want to ask for an increase. The LAA do not have to agree, but if you can demonstrate that you are likely to continue to claim more than you are paid, they should do so.

Payments on account

20.12 You are entitled to be paid your costs on civil certificates at the end of the case following assessment by the LAA or court – see chapter 13 for details. In recognition of the fact that such cases often last a considerable time and costs can be substantial, there is provision for you to claim payments on account during the life of the case.

20.13 The Standard Civil Contract 2013 entitles you to claim a payment on account of profit costs at any time, provided that a) you may not apply for the first until three months have elapsed since the certificate was issued, and b) you may not apply more than twice in any 12-month period. Also, cumulatively, you are not entitled to be paid more than 75 per cent of your profit costs to date[1], (or standard fee in applicable Family cases[2]) You can make a payment on account for disbursements incurred, or about to be incurred, at any time.[3]

Case study

It is 1 May 2015. I have two certificate files. On the first, the certificate was issued on 1 February 2015 and I have spent £1,000. On the second, the certificate was issued on 1 April 2014. I have spent £5,000 in total, and I received a payment on account of £2,000 in January. Am I entitled to any payments on account? If so, how much?

The first certificate was issued exactly three months ago, so you are entitled to a payment on account. The second was issued more than three months ago and you have only made one application in the 12 months leading up to today, so you are entitled to a payment on account.

You should complete a CIVPOA1, one line for each certificate. You should report your total profit costs to date for each claim, and you will be paid £750 on the first case and £1,750 on the second (75 per cent of £5,000, less the £2,000 already paid).

You could opt to make a POA application online using an eform: www.gov.uk/legal-aid-eforms.

If you are using CCMS, payments on account have to be submitted using CCMS.

---

1 Standard Civil Contract 2013 Specification para 6.22.
2 Standard Civil Contract 2013 Specification para 7.25.
3 Standard Civil Contract 2013 Specification para 6.21.

Payments on account are paid into your office account (Specification para 6.26).

20.14　Payments on account are re-payable at the end of the case. When each case concludes and the bill is assessed, the LAA will pay the value of the bill and then recoup the payments on account, so that the net effect is that you are paid only the outstanding balance. Where you receive costs from the other side in part or in full, you should notify the LAA even where you are making no claim for legal aid costs so that payments on account can be recouped.

Payment on account limits

20.15　Paragraph 6.24 of the Specification entitles the LAA to impose a maximum payment on account limit. This would be set in each individual contract schedule, and could vary from category of law to category of law, and indeed from firm to firm.

20.16　The limit is calculated by comparing the value of debits (payments to you) as against credits (claims received) on your account with the LAA. The maximum amount by which debits are allowed to exceed credits is the maximum payment on account limit, and once the limit is reached the LAA would refuse to make any further payments on account and would require repayment of the excess.

20.17　However, although this clause is in the contract, no schedules currently specify a limit and the LSC undertook not to introduce one without further consultation when the Unified Contract was introduced in 2007. The power in the 2013 contract is discretionary, and the LAA have, at the time of writing, given no indication of whether or in what circumstances they intend to introduce the limit.

Key performance indicators

20.18　The LAA monitors organisations remotely, using the data they supply as a matter of course when applying for funding or claiming at the end of the case. You need to be able to monitor your own performance against these.

20.19　The Standard Contracts include key performance indicators (KPIs). See chapter 19 for more information about KPIs.

Service Standards

20.20   The Standard Contracts include service standards. You need to comply with them. See chapter 19 for more information about service standards.

Costs audits

20.21   Historically, cost auditing of controlled work has always been a bone of contention between the LSC/LAA and practitioners. Practitioners tend to feel that LSC/LAA staff do not understand the work that has been done and the LSC/LAA tends to feel that practitioners are not sufficiently stringent in applying the Contract requirements. The LAA has published a list of 14 different types of audit and validation process.[4]

20.22   The LAA's approach is that if, from the management information evidence that they have, it appears that you are complying with contractual requirements, it is likely that you will only have one contract manager visit a year and will not be audited further. The LAA distinguishes between a contract manager visit, which it does not count as a formal audit, and formal audits, carried out by members of the Operational Assurance team. The distinction is lost on many practitioners, who often emerge from whichever process the LAA has used having to repay money. The way to avoid this is by robust supervision and monitoring, especially before final claims for payment are submitted. To ensure all your claims are made correctly, the LAA's Costs Guidance is helpful and can be found here www.gov.uk/funding-and-costs-assessment-for-civil-and-crime-matters.

20.23   The LAA's audits are undertaken to provide the Ministry of Justice assurance that the legal aid fund has been spent correctly and to eliminate the cause of irregularities and errors identified in the past by the National Audit Office, which has led to the LSC's annual accounts being qualified. The LAA needs to achieve an overall level of 'materiality of error' of less than one per cent in order to meet NAO targets.

20.24   This means that in the small samples taken by contract managers when they come to visit, you are aiming for a 0% error rate. This is not easy!

---

4 See www.gov.uk/legal-aid-agency-audits.

20.25   The main problem areas are in controlled work (Legal Help, Controlled Legal Representation and Family Help Lower) cases:

- assessing the eligibility of clients incorrectly or retaining insufficient evidence on file; and
- incorrect claims for payment for:
  - private law family cases; and
  - immigration and asylum cases

So, these tend to be the main focus of visits/audits in civil and family categories (see below for crime).

20.26   If you disagree with an LAA decision about costs, see costs appeals, para 20.45 below.

Evidence of means

20.27   The contract manager will select at least five Legal Help Forms. If even one of them fails, (due to no or invalid evidence of means) a further sample will be selected. This is then audited by the organisation itself and two files are checked by the contract manager. If three or more of the aggregated sample fail, the organisation may be invited to agree an extrapolation rate across all similar work, or may be asked to self-assess all the files which could possibly exhibit the same failing.

Family level 1 and 2 fees

20.28   The contract manager will be checking that level 2 fees have been claimed correctly, see below.

Private Family Law – conditions for level 2

20.29   Up to and including 08 May 2011, paragraph 10.55 of the Family Contract Specification required two meetings with the client in order to justify a level 2 fee.

20.30   Note also that following certification of PoP CLA 54 – definition of 'meeting' was broadened from 20 December 2010 to include phone calls.

20.31   The LSC removed the requirement for a second meeting from 9 May 2011 and instead practitioners had to show that 'substantive negotiations' had taken place. This remains the position under the 2013 Standard Contract.

Standard Contract 2013 Specification

7.60 You may only make a determination that a Client qualifies for Family Help (Lower) where all relevant criteria in the Merits Regulations, Financial Regulations and Procedure Regulations are satisfied including the criteria in Paragraph 35 of the Merits Regulations. In addition, the fee for Family Help (Lower) may only be claimed for those Family Disputes:

(a) which involve more than simply taking instructions from and advising the Client, and providing any follow up written or telephone advice; and

(b) where you are involved in substantive negotiations with a third party (either by conducting the negotiations yourself or by advice and assistance in support of mediation); and

(c) where the dispute, if unresolved, would be likely to lead to family proceedings; and

(d) which do not primarily concern processing a divorce, nullity, judicial separation or dissolution of a civil partnership; and

(e) which do not primarily concern advice relating to child support.

Crime

20.32 In crime, contract managers will check:

- evidence of means on CRM1 and 2 cases;
- incorrect claiming of court duty work:
  - claiming under a subsequent representation order as well as court duty for the same case;
  - claiming under a representation order when the case concluded on the same day as a court duty session;
  - incorrect claiming of travel for court duty work;
- 'duplicate' claims where more than one police station case fee has been claimed, where the contract manager considers that there was a 'series of offences' and only one fee was payable.

Contract notices

20.33 Contract managers may, and usually will, issue a contract notice, even though the organisation does not accept their interpretation of whether a file has met the relevant contract rule and whether any review or appeal process has been invoked. This appears to us to be poor practice; but is usual.

20.34 A contract notice requires a significant improvement in performance in relation to the relevant issue within six months, when the contract manager will come back to see whether improvements have been achieved. Clause 24 of the Standard Contract (all versions, both civil and crime) allows the LAA to suspend or even terminate contracts for 'persistent breaches',that is three breaches of the same term in a 24-month period (or six different breaches). It is very rare indeed for the LAA to invoke this clause; but it has been known and undoubtedly gives practitioners cause for concern.

20.35   The contract manager will also recoup money against any over-payments or ineligible payments.

Appeals

20.36   If you disagree with your contract manager see Contract Compliance Appeals below.

20.37   You cannot actually appeal against a contract notice as such. It is not an appealable decision under clause 27 of the Standard Contract Terms. What you can do is appeal against any wrong decision which has led to a contract notice, and therefore undermine the basis on which it was issued.

20.38   If you accept that you made an error, and so there was a breach of the contract; but it was minor, say on one file, you should write to your contract manager stating why you consider a contract notice to be disproportionate in the circumstances. It probably will not make any difference in the short term; but may be useful in the long term if the LAA wishes to suspend or terminate your contract under the 'totting up' provisions in clause 24.

Contract compliance audits

20.39   If they have concerns, the LAA may choose to carry out a contract compliance audit (CCA). A minimum of 30 and maximum of 50 files will be assessed, depending on the level of claims you have made across the 12-month sample period. The LAA employs a formula used by the National Audit Office to select samples to test the accuracy of assessments.

20.40   CCAs are carried out off-site on the LAA's premises. They check compliance with the civil/crime contracts, guidance, the criminal bills assessment manual, and civil costs assessment guidance. The LAA assesses whether there is appropriate evidence of eligibility, work done and disbursements on the file, costs incurred are reasonable and the bill is in line with the appropriate guidance.

Contract compliance audit outcomes

20.41   Files are either nil assessed, because the file should not have been funded at all (eg the client was not financially eligible or the matter was out of scope) or reduced by a percentage because a higher fee was claimed than was appropriate (eg a Family level 2 fee was claimed when the LAA says it should have been level 1).

20.42   Firms used to be given a categorisation, depending on the outcome of a CAA. The LSC stopped doing that and the LAA simply applies reductions in fees and takes action as follows:

Final % value assessed down	Action and sanctions	Old rating name
0.00%–10.00%	Recoup or credit value of incorrectly claimed files within audit sample.	Category 1
10.01%–20.00%	Extrapolation of % reduction. Re-audit to be scheduled. Contract notice/s.	Category 2
20.01% or more	Extrapolation of % reduction. Re-audit to be scheduled. Contract notice/s (Further action, including possible termination, to be taken on an individual basis if result of re-audit not improved).	Category 3

Extrapolation

20.43   Extrapolation is the reason that CCAs are dreaded by practitioners as an audit of a relatively small sample can result in significant sums having to be repaid. The Standard Contract allows the LAA to apply the findings of a controlled work costs audit back to the date when the file sample was requested for the previous CCA, or 12 months prior to the date the sample was requested in the current CCA, whichever is the most recent. For example, suppose the file sample of 20 files was requested on 01 July 2015 and the eventual reduction was 25 per cent. If the value of claims 1 July 2015–30 June 2014 = £146,000, the recoupment would be 25 per cent of £146,000, ie £36,500.

Contract compliance audit – appeal process

20.44   The appeal process is the same as other types of costs appeal, see below.

Costs appeals

20.45   The first stage of the appeal process (see eg the Standard Contract 2013 Specification para 6.67 et seq; the Standard Contract Specification para 7.19 et seq. The substantive provisions in relation to the initial stages are the same in the different contracts, only the paragraph numbers differ) is an internal review by another member of the LAA's audit team. You must set out the reasons for the appeal in writing within 28 days and send the file(s) back with the appeal. If you need an extension of time, you must have a 'good reason' and request the extension within 21 days. It is likely to be granted; but only up to a further 14 days. If the initial stage is not successful, you move to independent costs assessment. Independent costs assessors (ICAs) are solicitors or barristers who are members of the LAA's Review Panel; but are contracted on a sessional basis and are not LAA employees.

20.46   ICA appeals are generally considered on the papers only, although in exceptional circumstances either party can apply to the assessor for an oral hearing, although these are rarely granted. The assessor reviews the assessment and may confirm, increase or decrease the amount assessed. In contracts issued after 2013, the process ends here. Any further challenge would need to be brought by way of judicial review.

Points of principle

20.47   In contracts issued up to and including the Standard Civil Contract 2013, there is a further appeal after the ICA's decision. At any point not later than 21 days after receipt of the final decision, you (or the LAA) can seek clarification on the costs rules. You do this by applying for a certificate of a point of principle of general importance (PoP). It is important to note that your PoP must deal with an issue which is generally applicable, you cannot appeal on the basis that the ICA has simply made a mistake, for example. Applications can be made to the LAA or direct to an assessor if one has been appointed. The application must set out the exact wording of the PoP sought. However, these are rarely certified. There is more information at www.gov. uk/legal-aid-points-of-principle-of-general-importance-pop.

20.48   The LAA will decide whether the matter should progress to the Costs Appeals Committee. Applications for PoPs are considered on the papers only. You will be sent the LAA's and/or the Costs Appeals Committee's decision.

Legal aid policy

Big fall in legal aid expenditure

21.1   Practitioners have to keep an eye on policy changes in legal aid. These have come thick and fast over the last couple of years. This chapter gives an update on the main developments since the last edition of this handbook was published.

21.2   Driven by the coalition government's austerity measures, the Legal Aid Sentencing and Punishment of Offenders Act 2012 (LASPO) introduced cuts to the scope of civil legal aid which radically altered the scheme from 1 April 2013. In response, practitioners have had to adapt, accepting that they can no longer serve many people who were previously eligible for help. This process has been difficult, resulting as it has in a loss of income and redundancies for many legal aid providers.

21.3   Overall expenditure on legal aid has fallen dramatically in the last five years, as figure 1 opposite illustrates. Most of these reductions in spending have come from civil legal aid (see paras 21.40–21.48 below), but expenditure on criminal legal aid has also gone down because of fee cuts and falling crime rates.[1] Spending on cases is now under £1.6 billion, a fall of around £500 million over five years. The budget for administration, despite an overall reduction in expenditure of approximately 24 per cent, has stayed at over £100 million.

21.4   LAG clashed with officials at the Ministry of Justice (MoJ) over our estimate in July 2014 that the Legal Aid Agency (LAA) was underspending its budget by over £100 million. The MoJ argued that our figures were incorrect and could be explained by differences in accounting.[2] While the amount might be in dispute, it seems irrefutable that there is a considerable underspend in the legal aid budget which is in addition to the planned cuts.

21.5   In November 2013 Sadiq Khan, then shadow Justice Secretary, highlighted the fact that the MoJ had underspent the legal aid budget by £56.4m in 2012/13 – £28.9m in criminal legal aid and £27.5m in civil legal aid. The ministry did not challenge this figure, but blamed the reduction in spending on criminal legal aid on reduced demand, among other reasons. The civil fund underspend was accounted for by 'changes in provider behaviour and the introduction of remuneration cuts'.[3]

---

1   There is evidence to suggest that the crime figures are lower than they should be due to the use of warnings by the police and the interviewing of suspects on a 'voluntary' basis: *Transforming Legal Aid: Next Steps*, February 2014, Otterburn Legal Consulting pp34 and 35.

2   www.legalactiongroupnews.org.uk/moj-deny-underspend/.

3   www.theguardian.com/law/2013/nov/26/legal-aid-cuts-underspend.

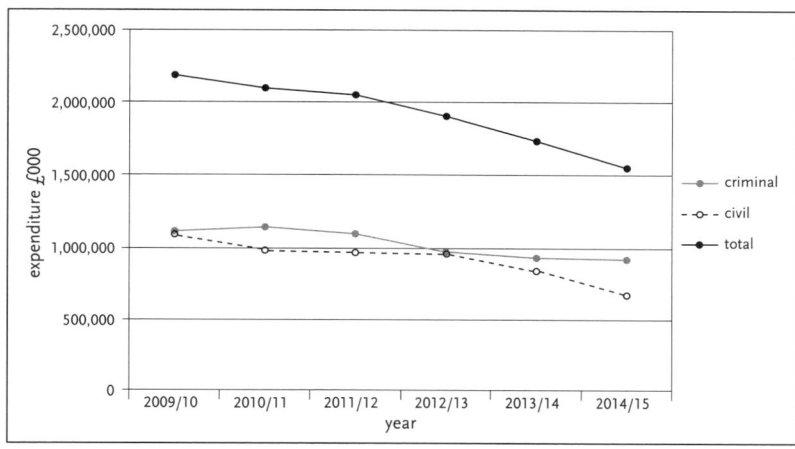

Figure 1: Reduction in spending on legal aid[4]

21.6   According to the National Audit Office, in a report published in November 2014, the MoJ had exceeded its spending reductions for civil legal aid by £32m owing to the LAA funding fewer cases than it had anticipated.[5] LAG believes that fee cuts and other changes to the scheme have combined with a public perception that civil legal aid especially is no longer available. This has had a chilling effect on the demand for services.

21.7   It might have been hoped that, after LASPO came into force, the government would opt for a period of steady state for the legal aid scheme, but in April 2013, only days after providers began their new civil legal aid contracts, a consultation was announced on further drastic changes to legal aid.[6] In contrast to LASPO, this time the government had criminal legal aid as its main target, as well as further changes to civil legal aid.

Criminal legal aid

Competitive tendering proposals

21.8   *Transforming legal aid: delivering a more credible and efficient system,*[7] set out the main policies which were to be pursued in Chris Grayling's

---

4   Figures from LSC and LAA annual reports and accounts.
5   *Implementing reforms to civil legal aid* NAO, November 2014, p6.
6   *Transforming legal aid: delivering a more credible and efficient system* MoJ, 9 April 2013.
7   MoJ, 9 April 2013.

tenure at the MoJ. Chris Grayling secured a footnote in history by being the first non-lawyer to hold the position of Lord Chancellor in a thousand years. Ironically, this non-lawyer managed at times in his term of office to accomplish the difficult task of uniting all lawyers, albeit against the policies he promulgated.

21.9 Chris Grayling's predecessor as Lord Chancellor, Ken Clarke, had delayed attempts to introduce competitive tendering in criminal legal aid,[8] but Chris Grayling decided to force the pace of change. The consultation paper outlined a competitive tendering system for contracts for duty work in police stations and magistrates' courts, as well as non-advocacy (litigation) work in the Crown Court. Under the proposals the number of providers would be cut from 1,600 to 400.[9]

21.10 In his foreword to the document, the Lord Chancellor stated: 'we are proposing a model of competitive tendering, where solicitors firms must compete to offer the best price they can for work in their local area'. Under the proposed model, firms would compete for contracts in 42 procurement areas, with between four and 38 contracts allowed in each. London would be split into three procurement areas and four of the smaller existing areas would be merged into two.[10]

21.11 Crown Court advocacy and Very High Cost Cases were excluded from the competitive tendering proposal. The government argued that, because 75 per cent of the barristers who undertook advocacy work in the Crown Court were self-employed, they could not tender for the full range of criminal legal aid work on offer.[11] The consultation paper also suggested that a tender process for Crown Court work would effectively introduce a 'one case one fee' system in which solicitors would control the budget, which could threaten the viability of the independent Bar.[12]

21.12 At the time LAG thought that the government was being disingenuous in its reasoning behind excluding higher courts advocacy from competitive tendering. We argued that it was done to try and buy off opposition from the higher end of the Bar 'which because of its size and specialist skills in complex cases is much better placed to organise a boycott or strike in Crown Court and higher court cases'. In contrast LAG suggested that the more junior members of the Bar would potentially be squeezed out from magistrates' court work

8 Steve Hynes, *Austerity Justice* LAG, 2012, p114.
9 *Transforming legal aid* paras 4.58–4.66.
10 *Transforming legal aid* para 4.66.
11 *Transforming legal aid* para 4.35.
12 *Transforming legal aid* para 4.36.

by firms of solicitors employing in-house advocates 'leading to the gradual withering of the new talent which is essential for the long-term health of the criminal Bar'.[13]

Split among solicitors

21.13   At the Law Society, a decision was taken to try and reach a compromise with the government. Des Hudson, then CEO, felt that a line of outright opposition was not going to sway the government. His view seems to have been informed by the failure of the campaign against the LASPO Bill. The Society spent hundreds of thousands of pounds on the 'Sound Off For Justice' campaign, but the bill became law with few concessions being made by ministers.

21.14   In the summer of 2013 high level talks were going on behind the scenes between the MoJ and the Law Society. Patricia Greer, Head of Corporate Affairs at the Society, played a key role in these discussions. She had previous experience at the heart of government because she had spent four years as deputy director of the Prime Minister's Strategy Unit.

21.15   According to Law Society insiders, Patricia Greer agreed to the package of changes around duty tenders without consultation with the Society's internal committees, which represent practitioners. The key issue in what was agreed was the government's decision to back down on competitive tendering and to introduce a system of two-tier contracts. The senior leadership at the Law Society believed that these were major concessions by the government.

21.16   Under the two-tier system, criminal legal aid firms were allowed to apply for own client contracts, but would have to tender for duty contracts for police and magistrates' court work. We are currently awaiting the results of the duty tender round. Own and duty contracts for successful bidders are due to start in January 2016.

21.17   There was an immediate backlash against the agreement which the Law Society had reached with the government. While the shelving of competitive tendering was welcome, firms did not want to lose out on duty work because this is important to provide new clients. Surviving on own client work alone is just not viable for most of them.

21.18   Opposition to the agreement coalesced around a motion of no confidence against Des Hudson and the then President of the Law Society, Nicholas Fluck. This was proposed by Liverpool solicitor James Parry, who collected over 100 signatures from solicitors in support.

---

13 Criminal price competition', editorial *Legal Action*, May 2013.

21.19   The profession was split on the issue. In contrast to James Parry's supporters, the Big Firms Group (BFG) of criminal defence firms backed the Hudson/Greer deal. The BFG consists of around 40 firms each with a turnover from legal aid of over £1.5m. They believed that a radical reduction in the number of criminal defence firms was needed. In an article on the *Times* website in November 2013 the smaller firms were accused by Anthony Edwards, senior partner at TV Edwards, of being 'headstrong with their heads in the sand' over the government's intention to make cuts. Edwards said he believed that the 'market should consolidate down to 200 firms', and that the government should be told that to make cuts 'they must consolidate the market'.[14]

21.20   The associations representing many criminal legal aid practitioners were opposed to the deal. The Criminal Law Solicitors Association and the London Criminal Courts Solicitors Association took an officially neutral stance, but many of their members supported the vote of no confidence. This took place in December 2013 at a special general meeting of the Law Society. In a close vote, the leadership lost by 228 to 213, but decided to tough it out rather than resign. Both sides had the option of forcing a full vote of all solicitors in a postal ballot, but did not take this up.

Grayling Day

21.21   Following two consultations which, according to the MoJ, elicited 18,000 responses, the vast majority of which were overwhelming hostile, Chris Grayling announced what he described as a 'final decision on a modified model of competitive tendering for criminal legal aid contracts' on 27 February 2014.[15] Carol Storer, director of the Legal Aid Practitioners Group, warned that the government's plans to spread 525 duty contracts across 97 procurement areas would have a 'devastating impact on the numbers of firms and access to justice'.[16]

21.22   Just over a week after the government's announcement, solicitors and barristers took to the streets in protest at the government's plans. A co-ordinated day of action, which was dubbed 'Grayling Day', took place on 7 March 2014. Criminal lawyers refused to work and joined protests across the country.

14 See www.legalactiongroupnews.org.uk/big-firms-break-cover/.

15 HL Hansard, 27 February 2014, col WS 115.

16 www.legalactiongroupnews.org.uk/criminal-legal-aid-disaster/.

21.23   At a rally in London, Nigel Lithman, leader of the Criminal Bar Association, said that these were exceptional times which had forced lawyers 'to take to the streets and to close the courts'.[17] In the weeks leading to the protests of Grayling Day, senior barristers refused to take on Very High Cost Cases (VHCCs) because of a 30 per cent fee cut imposed by the government.[18] At the rally Nigel Lithman confirmed that the Bar would step up their action by refusing to take returns (cases in which the original barrister instructed is no longer able to represent in the case).

21.24   In response to the threat of a boycott of VHCCs by the Bar, the government had established a specialist advocacy unit employing salaried advocates,[19] but the refusal to take returns had an almost immediate impact, forcing the government into doing a deal with the criminal Bar. In the week after the Grayling Day demonstrations, the government agreed to call off the planned 6 per cent cut in advocacy fees in the Crown Court, which was to be introduced later in the year, and to review the VHCC fees. At the time, Nigel Lithman claimed that barristers had got 89 per cent of what they wanted.

21.25   Nigel Lithman's deal was a rather hypocritical move, given his previous opposition to the agreement the Law Society had struck with the government. At a highly charged meeting of criminal legal aid lawyers organised by the Criminal Law Solicitors Association and the London Criminal Courts Solicitors Association, which took place in October 2013, Nigel Lithman had been scathingly critical of Des Hudson, who also spoke at the meeting. The Criminal Bar Association leader said he had been 'stunned, shocked and disappointed by the Law Society's U-turn' and that the agreement 'maybe is acceptable to the executive of the Law Society, but I doubt your members agree'.[20]

Solicitors fight on

21.26   While many individual barristers still oppose the changes, the Criminal Bar Association agreement with the government fractured the

---

17   www.legalactiongroupnews.org.uk/grayling-day/.

18   A high profile example of a case affected by the VHCC boycott was a fraud case in which Alex Cameron QC (the prime minister's brother) acted pro bono. See '£5m fraud case collapses after David Cameron's brother attacks legal aid cuts', *Telegraph* 1 May 2014.

19   According to the LAA's *Annual Report and Accounts 2014/15*, the unit currently employs 24 advocates, including seven QCs.

20   www.legalactiongroupnews.org.uk/commotion-in-camden/.

unity between the Bar and solicitors. According to sources at the Law Society, just before the agreement was made public Chris Grayling rang Nick Fluck, then president of the Society, to say that he had been forced to cave in to the barristers' demands. Chris Grayling was able to offer the sweetener of £9m in interim payments a year early, but for solicitors there was no avoiding the fact that the Bar had a stronger negotiating hand than theirs.

21.27   Protests against the government's changes to criminal legal aid continued with another round of demonstrations in early April 2014. The Justice Alliance, a campaign group with a wide base of members including charities as well as individual lawyers and firms, has proved to be an effective organisation, staging events including a comedy show, a relay march from Runnymede to mark the anniversary of Magna Carta in February 2015 and a short film featuring celebrities endorsing the message 'I am for justice: are you?'

21.28   Changes at the Law Society helped solicitors in re-establishing some unity against the government's proposals. Des Hudson announced his retirement in March 2014, Patricia Greer also left her post and a new president, Andrew Caplen, took office in July 2014. This sense of common purpose among criminal legal aid practitioners was also facilitated by the opening of a new front in opposition to Chris Grayling's plans.

Judicial reviews launched

21.29   Early in 2014, two judicial review challenges were brought, one by the Criminal Law Solicitors Association and the London Criminal Courts Solicitors Association and the other by the Law Society. The cases were joined in the same proceedings and centred on the government's failure to consider properly the findings of two reports commissioned by the MoJ to provide an assessment of the likely impact of the proposals on the criminal legal aid market.

21.30   The KPMG report,[21] provided a financial analysis of the viability of the market. The Otterburn report,[22] which was jointly commissioned by the Law Society and the MoJ, looked at the financial position of firms and the likely impact of the changes in detail. The Otterburn report, published in February 2014 at the same time as the government's 'final decision' on criminal legal aid tenders, described the

---

21 *Procurement of Criminal Legal Aid Services: Financial Modelling,* March 2014, KPMG.

22 *Transforming Legal Aid: Next Steps,* February 2014, Otterburn Legal Consulting.

finances of the 1,500 criminal legal aid firms as 'fragile' and said that many were unlikely to withstand the 8.75 per cent cut which was due to hit them in March 2014.

21.31   In September 2014 the government was forced into conceding a short reconsultation on the two reports after losing in a judicial review.[23] Solicitors scored another significant victory when they were granted interim relief, meaning that the tender process had to be suspended pending the result of the full hearing of a further judicial review on the government's decision to go ahead with the tenders. However, at the full hearing in January 2015, they lost the case and Chris Grayling decided to go ahead with the tender round.[24]

Strike action

21.32   In a parliamentary statement published in June 2015 the government announced that it will continue with the tenders for police and magistrates' court duty work and that a further 8.75 per cent fee cut would go ahead from 1 July.[25] Responding to the statement, Bill Waddington, chair of the Criminal Law Solicitors Association, said that they were 'beside themselves with grief' because the government had 'not listened to the arguments of the last two to three years at all'. While the government has agreed to undertake a review of the impact of the fee cut and tenders a year after their implementation, Bill Waddington believes that this 'will not be so much a review but a body count'.[26]

21.33   The judicial reviews on the duty tenders had delayed the tender process so that it straddled the general election in May 2015. The Labour party had promised to scrap the duty tenders and reconsider the planned further fee cut if they were to form the government, but the Conservative victory meant it was perhaps inevitable that the government would press ahead with the tenders.

21.34   From 1 July 2015 many criminal legal aid solicitors and barristers started to boycott new cases. On 15 July the Criminal Bar Association voted by a margin of 10 per cent to support the boycott. They hoped

23 R *(London Criminal Courts Solicitors Association and Criminal Law Solicitors Association) v The Lord Chancellor* [2014] EWHC 3020 (Admin).

24 R *(London Criminal Courts Solicitors Association, Criminal Law Solicitors Association and Nelson Guest and Partners) v The Lord Chancellor* [2015] EWHC 295 (Admin).

25 HC Written Statement (HCWS22) by Parliamentary Under-Secretary of State for Courts and Legal Aid (Shailesh Vara) on 10 June 2015.

26 '"Body count" warning over further fee cut' July/August *Legal Action* 5.

to force the government to re-think its policies. As the use of this tactic by the criminal Bar has shown, this is the most effective means of winning concessions from the government.

21.35   Some solicitors have been reluctant to take action and risk their firm being in breach of contract with the LAA. At the time of writing (July 2015) it is unclear how widespread the boycott is – strike action in all but name. The biggest obstacle to solidarity breaking out among firms is that many of them are competing for duty tenders.

21.36   According the LAA, a total of 1,099 bids for tenders were received from just over 500 firms. They were currently only short of bids in three out of 85 procurement areas. Some firms with decisions pending on contracts to start in January 2016 might not want to jeopardise these by taking strike action. However, many are now contemplating a future without duty work and so they have nothing to lose. The boycott might at least force a six-month delay in the fee cut.

21.37   All practitioners accept that there has been a drop in the numbers of cases in police stations and magistrates' courts, though arguments continue about the reasons for this. LAG believes that the policy makers at the MoJ have accepted the BFG's position that firms need increased volumes to make duty work pay. It is therefore inconsistent, we think, to introduce the fee cut six months before the new contracts.

Follow the money

21.38   The Criminal Bar Association's victory over fees should be seen only as a short-term one. In the last few years many solicitors have responded to falling margins in criminal work by providing more advocacy services in-house, often using employed solicitor advocates with higher courts rights of audience. This is a trend which is likely to continue as firms follow the money which can be made from providing advocacy services directly or by finding means to retain a larger portion of the fees currently paid to the Bar.

21.39   The government's headlong pursuit of a strategy of consolidation in the criminal defence market mirrors what is happening in other markets, as companies look to produce savings of scale through take-overs and mergers. There are risks to this approach. In a service dependent on professionally qualified staff, costs can be reduced by only a finite amount before quality suffers. LAG is unconvinced that larger firms necessarily lead to cost savings. We also believe that a much reduced number of suppliers in the market will threaten competition.

Civil legal aid

Thousands excluded from civil legal aid

21.40 From April 2013 the major changes to scope in civil legal aid introduced by LASPO has reduced the number of firms and other providers undertaking legal aid work. The scope changes have also excluded many thousands of people from help with civil legal problems. The main cuts have been to discontinue legal aid for most private law family matters, along with all welfare benefits cases (apart from a few hundred Upper Tribunal cases) and reductions in what is covered by the scheme for housing, immigration and debt.

21.41 Before 2012/13 the Legal Service Commission (LSC) reported on the total acts of assistance in the civil legal aid scheme which had commenced in the previous year. The overall figure included new Legal Help, Controlled Legal Representation, housing duty scheme and telephone helpline cases. The figures were given a prominent position in the LSC's annual report and accounts. Post LASPO, the LAA does not mention these figures in its annual report and accounts.

21.42 Before the implementation of the LASPO scope changes, the LSC reported that it had funded a total of 925,200 acts,[27] but this dropped by nearly half to 441,500 in 2013/14.[28] Figure 2 overleaf traces the decline in the number of new acts of assistance over the last parliament against the final full year of the previous government. It shows a total reduction of just under one million (1,431,200 in 2009/10[29] to 441,500 in 2013/14). LAG believes that these figures illustrate that under the last government there was a decisive shift away from providing early advice for members of the public with civil legal problems.

21.43 If the telephone and duty rota acts are excluded from the count, the decline in numbers is still dramatic. Figure 3 overleaf shows the reduction in the total number of new civil legal help and representation cases from 2009/10 to 2014/15. The increased demand for civil legal advice and an adjustment to the means test had led to a peak of 933,815 cases in 2009/10.

27 See *LSC Annual Report and Accounts 2012/13* p15.
28 See tables in *Legal Aid Statistics in England and Wales 2013/14*, MoJ, 24 June 2014, pp48 and 52.
29 *LSC Annual Report and Accounts 2009/10*, p5.

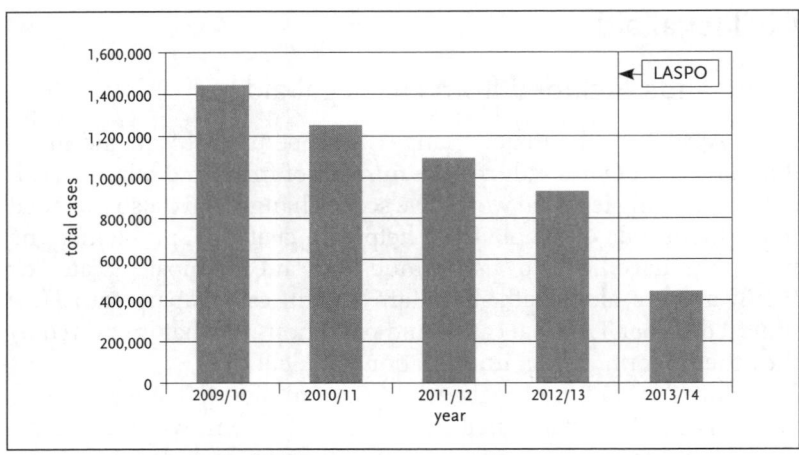

Figure 2: Decline in total number of acts of assistance[30]

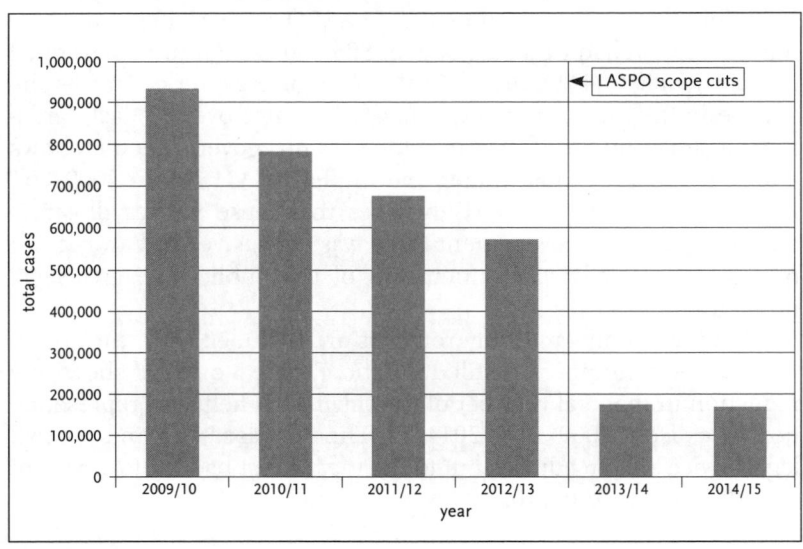

Figure 3: Decline in new civil legal aid cases[31]

30 Figures from LSC and LAA Annual report and accounts.
31 These statistics are drawn from *Legal Aid Statistics main tables*, MoJ, 25 June 2015, table 5.1.

21.44 Again figure 3 shows that prior to the scope changes there had been a steady decline in the number of cases under the coalition government which took office in May 2010. This pre-LASPO reduction was caused by a number of factors including cuts in fees, adjustments to the means test and stricter administrative controls on the granting of legal aid. In 2014/15 785,377 fewer cases were commenced compared with 2009/10 (the last full year of the Labour government).

21.45 Claims for payment of legal aid submitted to the LAA are always greater than the number of new cases.[32] Controlled Legal Representation cases particularly can take a number of years to complete. This means that after the scope changes of April 2013 there is still a tail of work in progress, moving towards completion, which was granted legal aid under the old rules.

21.46 In 2012/13, the year before the scope changes, 601,514 claims were made. The following year this dropped to 318,306 and in 2014/15 it was 196,164. Work in progress has cushioned to some extent the impact of the scope changes in legal aid on providers who undertake Controlled Legal Representation cases, but for firms which mainly carried out Legal Help work the impact of the changes was almost immediate.

21.47 The number of civil legal aid providers has fallen from around 3,500 in April 2013 to under 3,000 in April 2015. Not-for-profit (NfP) agencies were particularly affected by the LASPO cut to Legal Help work and had shrunk by around half to 231 by April 2015.[33]

21.48 Over the last two years eleven law centres have been forced to close. These have included two in Manchester, Trafford and Wythenshawe; Greenwich in London, and Cross Street Law Centre in Kent. Barnet Law Service in North London was another casualty. David Rommer, the supervising solicitor there, told LAG in February 2014 that they were closing for good as a 'direct consequence' of LASPO. According to him, the cuts to legal aid for employment, immigration, housing, benefits and debt cases 'knocked out our main source of income'. The law centre had employed six caseworkers, including three solicitors.[34]

---

32 See *Legal Aid Statistics main tables: January to March 2015*, MoJ, 25 June 2015, table 5.2.

33 See *Legal Aid Statistics main tables: January to March 2015*, MoJ, 25 June 2015, table 9.1.

34 'Law Centre closures', 12 February 2014, LAG News Blog.

Judicial review challenges

21.49   There have been a number of judicial reviews of government policy in civil legal aid over the last two years. A case backed by the charity Rights of Women on the domestic violence gateway regulations has so far been unsuccessful, but is subject to appeal.[35] However, the government has been fighting a losing battle over the exceptional case funding (ECF) regulations.

21.50   The number of successful applications for ECF has been much lower than anticipated. The low take-up of cases has been commented on by the House of Commons Justice and Public Accounts Committees. The LAA planned for between 5,000 and 7,000 applications,[36] but in 2014/15 out of a total of 1,172 applications received only 214 were ultimately granted.[37]

21.51   Revised guidance on ECF cases was published by the LAA in June 2015 in response to a successful judicial review.[38] A further judicial review of the regulations, brought by the Official Solicitor on behalf of a severely disabled person, was decided against the government as this book was going to press. According to the court, the exceptional case provisions are 'not providing the safety net promised by Ministers'.[39] LAG expects that further adjustments will have to be made to the guidance to comply with the High Court's judgment.

21.52   Perhaps the most politically embarrassing court defeat for Chris Grayling was the successful judicial review of the residence test regulations. The regulations, which are intended to block foreign nationals from claiming legal aid, were struck down by the High Court the week after parliament had approved them in the face of warnings from the opposition and legal experts that they were illegal. The court held that there was no lawful basis for the implementation of the test:

> ... it is not possible to justify such discrimination in an area where all are equally subject to the law, resident or not, and equally entitled to its protection, resident or not.[40]

35 *R (Rights of Women) v The Lord Chancellor and Secretary of State for Justice* [2015] EWHC 35 (Admin).

36 *Implementing reforms to civil legal aid*, NAO, 20 November 2014, p7, para 15.

37 *Legal Aid in England and Wales: statistics bulletin: January to March 2015*, MoJ, 25 June 2015, p38, figure 30.

38 *R (Gudanaviciene and Others) v Director of Legal Aid Casework and Others* [2014] EWCA Civ 1622.

39 *IS (by the Official Solicitor as Litigation Friend) v The Director of Legal Casework and The Lord Chancellor* [2015] EWHC 1965 (Admin) para 107.

40 *R (Public Law Project) v Secretary of State for Justice* [2014] EWHC 2365 (Admin) para 84.

21.53   Lord Chancellor Michael Gove made a speech in June 2015 on the importance of the rule of law and the need to reform the 'creaking, outdated' and 'dysfunctional' justice system.[41] This was his first major speech in his new post and marked a distinct change in tone from his predecessor, who seemed to have little appreciation or understanding of the unique role of the Lord Chancellor.

21.54   The residence test, arguably, was more about political symbolism than saving cash. Very few cases would be caught by the test if it was introduced. LAG believes that Michael Gove should drop the appeal against the court's decision, thus adding some positive action to his rhetoric about the importance of the rule of law.

Strain on the courts system

21.55   Private law family cases were the subject of the largest cut under LASPO. In the year after the implementation of the Act, there was a 60 per cent drop in the number of family cases. The number of civil representation cases in private law Children Act cases alone went down by over 30,000.[42]

21.56   Despite the government committing more funds to mediation (the only silver lining in the cloud of LASPO cuts), the number of family mediations fell from 13,609 in 2012/13 to 8,400 in the following year.[43] With a change in the rules to allow for the initial mediation to be paid for if one of the parties qualifies for legal aid, the number of mediations is now increasing.

21.57   For a while it looked as if an alternative legal aid might be developed by the courts. The President of the Family Division, Sir James Munby, suggested in *Q v Q*[44] that, in some circumstances, the court should order payment of costs including representation to ensure a fair trial. However, in *K and H (Children)*, Lord Dyson MR in the Court of Appeal concluded that a court did not have the power to require the government to bear the costs of representation other than through the provisions of LASPO.[45]

21.58   Munby P's decision in *Q v Q* can be seen as symptomatic of the widespread concern which is felt by the senior judiciary and other informed opinion about the increase in litigants in person (LiPs)

---

41   www.gov.uk/government/speeches/what-does-a-one-nation-justice-policy-look-like.

42   *Legal Aid Statistics in England and Wales 2013/14* p20.

43   *Legal Aid Statistics in England and Wales 2013/14* p21.

44   [2014] EWFC 31.

45   [2015] EWCA Civ 543.

before the courts, caused by the removal of many family cases from legal aid.[46] In response to this, in October 2014 the government came up with £1.4m in extra funding for pro bono and other support for LiPs. While this is of course welcome, LAG believes that, because of the LASPO cuts, it is inevitable that there will continue to be an increase in LiPs, especially in family cases, and that this will place an increasing strain on the courts system.

Widening access to justice

21.59   A new government and new ministers often lead to an outbreak of optimism among interest groups that things might improve. Michael Gove has encouraged this view by saying that he has 'no plans to cut legal aid further'.[47] He seems to be pursuing a strategy of sounding at least more conciliatory towards lawyers and especially the Bar. This may well be because he is, as outlined in his speech in June 2015, committed to a radical shake-up of the justice system and he will need the co-operation of the legal profession to achieve this. LAG is concerned that all the signs are that his focus will be on the courts and tribunals system rather than access to justice in any wider sense.

21.60   As outlined above, nearly 800,000 cases have been lost from the civil legal aid scheme in the last five years. This figure is closer to one million if telephone and duty rota cases are included. Some of the people affected will be in the courts system as LiPs, but many more are effectively excluded from enforcing their rights. They are joined by the thousands who never manage to resolve their legal problems. Hazel Genn, in her ground-breaking research *Paths to Justice*, found that many people with legal problems never managed to tackle them. For example, 65 per cent of tenants with problems relating to landlords had not been able to resolve them at the time that they were interviewed for the Genn research.[48]

21.61   Taking what Michael Gove has said at face value, but assuming that there will be no general restoration of scope, there is still much that the government could do to widen access to justice. Its first priority should be to comply with the High Court's recent judgment on ECF (see para 21.51) and to redraft the guidance, followed by a revi-

46 www.newlawjournal.co.uk/nlj/content/litigants-person-facing-miscarriages-justice.
47 '"Do more unpaid work", Gove tells lawyers', *The Times* 24 June 2015.
48 Hazel Genn, *Paths to Justice*, Hart, 1999, p163.

sion of the domestic violence gateway regulations. LAG also argues that advice on benefits should be brought back into scope for housing cases, because there is a strong argument in support of this, in that early intervention can prevent the expense of repossession actions.

21.62   Figure 1, above at para 21.6, show that spending on legal aid has reduced by around a quarter since 2009/10. However, the cuts so far have fallen disproportionately on civil legal aid and particularly on Legal Help. The reduction in acts of assistance for civil legal aid (see figure 2), shows that the number of people helped by the scheme has fallen by around 70 per cent. The scheme now has far less emphasis on early advice and assistance in civil cases.

21.63   In social welfare law, LAG believes that the government should implement the recommendations of the Low Commission report which was published in January 2014.[49] A main plank of the commission's recommendations is the creation of a fund to support social welfare law services to deliver the early advice and intervention which have been lost from civil legal aid. The Low Commission has also published a joint report with the Advice Services Alliance, which makes a compelling case for investing in social welfare law services as part of a holistic approach to health care.[50]

21.64   Over the last few years, government policy has had a devastating impact on legal aid and access to justice. LAG hopes that Michael Gove will stick to his promise not to pursue further cuts and that the policy makers in general will adopt a more positive attitude to what is, after all, a vital part of the fabric of our justice system.

---

49 www.lowcommission.org.uk/dyn/1389221772932/Low-Commission-Report-FINAL-VERSION.pdf.

50 *The Role of Advice Services in Health Outcomes*, Low Commission/ASA, June 2015.

APPENDICES

New applications checklist – civil

If you are using CCMS, the software should ensure that it is only possible to submit an application when it is correctly completed. Unfortunately, that can be a lengthy process. This checklist is designed for paper applications.

- Have you used the correct version of the form?
- Have all the forms been signed and dated by the client and the legal representative?
- Are the signatures original and less than two months old?
- Have you submitted the relevant means form?
  - CIV Means 1 (clients not in receipt of passporting benefits);
  - CIV Means 2 (clients on passporting benefits).
- Has the applicant (and partner if appropriate) completed all sections of the means form and signed/dated it?
- Have you submitted the relevant evidence – eg bank statements for each account, wage skips, evidence of childcare costs? Please use the checklist in form CIV Means 1 or 2
- If using Form L17 is it fully completed and signed/dated by the employer?
- If the client or their partner is self-employed, submit a CIV Means 1 form together with:
  - CIV Means 1A if sole trader;
  - CIV Means 1B if in partnership;
  - CIV Means 1C if a company director
  - CIV MEANS1 and CIV MEANS1 P if a prisoner.
- CIV APP1 – the section relating to conditional fee agreements asks you to confirm whether a case is unsuitable for a CFA. If you believe it is unsuitable, you should answer 'yes' and give full reasons.

New applications checklist – crime

This checklist is designed for paper applications. For more information see the Criminal Legal Aid Manual at www.gov.uk/government/publications/criminal-legal-aid-manual.

You may wish to use the online version of the form CRM14. It gets good feedback from practitioners regarding ease of use. See www.gov.uk/legal-aid-eforms.

- Have the forms been signed and dated by the client and the legal representative?
- Are the signatures original?
- Have you included the client's National Insurance number?
- Have you addressed the interests of justice test on the CRM14?
- Has the applicant (and partner if appropriate) completed all sections of the CRM15 form and signed/dated it?
- Have you included evidence of means?
- Has the client provided evidence of the benefits they are receiving?
- Have you included any supporting documents? Not always necessary, but if for example you are relying on the client's previous convictions to tip the balance into a potential loss of liberty case, it is useful to include the PNC print-out.

Legal Aid, Sentencing and Punishment of Offenders Act 2012[1]

SCHEDULE 1: CIVIL LEGAL SERVICES

Section 9

PART 1: SERVICES

Care, supervision and protection of children

1 (1) Civil legal services provided in relation to–
- (a) orders under section 25 of the Children Act 1989 ('the 1989 Act') (secure accommodation);
- (b) orders under Part 4 of the 1989 Act (care and supervision);
- (c) orders under Part 5 of the 1989 Act (protection of children);
- (d) approval by a court under paragraph 19 of Schedule 2 to the 1989 Act (arrangements to assist children to live abroad);
- (e) parenting orders under section 8 of the Crime and Disorder Act 1998 ('the 1998 Act');
- (f) child safety orders under section 11 of the 1998 Act;
- (g) orders for contact under section 26 of the Adoption and Children Act 2002 ('the 2002 Act');
- (h) applications for leave of the court to remove a child from a person's custody under section 36 of the 2002 Act;
- (i) placement orders, recovery orders or adoption orders under Chapter 3 of Part 1 of the 2002 Act (see sections 21, 41 and 46 of that Act);
- (j) orders under section 84 of the 2002 Act (parental responsibility prior to adoption abroad).

(2) Civil legal services provided in relation to an order under an enactment made–
- (a) as an alternative to an order mentioned in sub-paragraph (1), or
- (b) in proceedings heard together with proceedings relating to such an order.

Exclusions

(3) Sub-paragraphs (1) and (2) are subject to the exclusions in Parts 2 and 3 of this Schedule.

Definitions

(4) In this paragraph 'children' means persons under the age of 18.

---

1 © Crown copyright. Reproduced, as amended, up to date to 1 August 2015.

Special educational needs

2 (1) Civil legal services provided in relation to–

(a) matters arising under Part 4 of the Education Act 1996 or Part 3 of the Children and Families Act 2014 (special educational needs);

(b) assessments relating to learning difficulties under section 140 of the Learning and Skills Act 2000.

Exclusions

(2) Sub-paragraph (1) is subject to the exclusions in Parts 2 and 3 of this Schedule.

Abuse of child or vulnerable adult

3 (1) Civil legal services provided in relation to abuse of an individual that took place at a time when the individual was a child or vulnerable adult, but only where–

(a) the services are provided to the individual, or

(b) the individual has died and the services are provided–

(i) to the individual's personal representative, or

(ii) for the purposes of a claim under the Fatal Accidents Act 1976 for the benefit of the individual's dependants.

General exclusions

(2) Sub-paragraph (1) is subject to–

(a) the exclusions in Part 2 of this Schedule, with the exception of paragraphs 1, 2, 3, 8 and 12 of that Part, and

(b) the exclusion in Part 3 of this Schedule.

Specific exclusions

(3) The services described in sub-paragraph (1) do not include services provided in relation to clinical negligence.

(4) The services described in sub-paragraph (1) do not include services provided in relation to a matter arising under a family enactment.

Definitions

(5) In this paragraph–

'abuse' means physical or mental abuse, including–

(a) sexual abuse, and

(b) abuse in the form of violence, neglect, maltreatment and exploitation;

'child' means a person under the age of 18;

'clinical negligence' means breach of a duty of care or trespass to the person committed in the course of the provision of clinical or medical services (including dental or nursing services);

'family enactment' has the meaning given in paragraph 12;

'personal representative', in relation to an individual who has died, means–

(a) a person responsible for administering the individual's estate under the law of England and Wales, Scotland or Northern Ireland, or

(b) a person who, under the law of another country or territory, has functions equivalent to those of administering the individual's estate;

'vulnerable adult' means a person aged 18 or over whose ability to protect himself or herself from abuse is significantly impaired through physical or mental disability or illness, through old age or otherwise.

Working with children and vulnerable adults

4 (1) Civil legal services provided in relation to–

    (a) the inclusion of a person in a barred list or the removal of a person from a barred list;

    (b) a disqualification order under section 28, 29 or 29A of the Criminal Justice and Court Services Act 2000 (disqualification from working with children);

    (c) a direction under section 142 of the Education Act 2002 (prohibition from teaching etc).

Exclusions

(2) Sub-paragraph (1) is subject to the exclusions in Parts 2 and 3 of this Schedule.

Definitions

(3) In this paragraph 'barred list' means a list maintained under–

    (a) section 2 of the Safeguarding Vulnerable Groups Act 2006 (persons barred from regulated activities relating to children or vulnerable adults);

    (b) section 81 of the Care Standards Act 2000;

    (c) section 1 of the Protection of Children Act 1999.

Mental health and mental capacity

5 (1) Civil legal services provided in relation to matters arising under–

    (a) the Mental Health Act 1983;

    (b) paragraph 5(2) of the Schedule to the Repatriation of Prisoners Act 1984;

    (c) the Mental Capacity Act 2005.

General exclusions

(2) Sub-paragraph (1) is subject to the exclusions in Parts 2 and 3 of this Schedule.

Specific exclusion

(3) The services described in sub-paragraph (1) do not include services provided in relation to–

    (a) the creation of lasting powers of attorney under the Mental Capacity Act 2005, or

    (b) the making of advance decisions under that Act.

(4) Sub-paragraph (3) does not exclude services provided in relation to determinations and declarations by a court under the Mental Capacity Act 2005 as to the validity, meaning, effect or applicability of–

    (a) a lasting power of attorney that has been created, or

    (b) an advance decision that has been made.

Community care

6 (1) Civil legal services provided in relation to community care services.

Exclusions

(2) Sub-paragraph (1) is subject to the exclusions in Parts 2 and 3 of this Schedule.

Definitions

(3) In this paragraph–

'community care services' means services which a relevant person may provide or arrange to be provided under–

    (a) Part 3 of the National Assistance Act 1948 ('the 1948 Act') (local authority support for children and families);

    (b) section 47 of the 1948 Act (removal to suitable premises of persons in need of care and attention);

    (c) section 48 of the 1948 Act (temporary protection for property of persons admitted to hospital);

    (d) section 45 of the Health Services and Public Health Act 1968 (arrangements for promoting welfare of old people);

    (e) section 117 of the Mental Health Act 1983 (after-care);

    (f) section 17 of the Children Act 1989 ('the 1989 Act') (provision of services for children in need);

    (g) section 20 of the 1989 Act (provision of accommodation for children);

    (h) sections 22A, 22B, 22C and 23 of the 1989 Act (accommodation and maintenance for children in care and looked after children);

    (i) sections 23B and 23C of the 1989 Act (local authority functions in respect of relevant children);

    (j) sections 24, 24A and 24B of the 1989 Act (provision of services for persons qualifying for advice and assistance);

    (k) section 2 of the Carers and Disabled Children Act 2000 (services for carers);

    (l) [Repealed.]

    (m) section 192 of, and Schedule 15 to, the National Health Service (Wales) Act 2006 (functions of local social service authorities);

    (n) Part 1 of the Care Act 2014 (local authority's functions of meeting an adult's needs for care and support);

'relevant person' means–

    (a) a district council;

    (b) a county council;

    (c) a county borough council;

    (d) a London borough council;

    (e) the Common Council of the City of London;

    (f) a Primary Care Trust established under section 18 of the National Health Service Act 2006;

    (g) a Local Health Board established under section 11 of the National Health Service (Wales) Act 2006;

    (h) any other person prescribed for the purposes of this paragraph.

Facilities for disabled persons

7 (1) Civil legal services provided in relation to grants under Part 1 of the Housing Grants, Construction and Regeneration Act 1996 for the provision of facilities for disabled persons.

Exclusions

(2) Sub-paragraph (1) is subject to the exclusions in Parts 2 and 3 of this Schedule.

Definitions

(3) In this paragraph 'disabled person' has the meaning given in section 100 of the Housing Grants, Construction and Regeneration Act 1996.

Appeals relating to welfare benefits

8 (1) Civil legal services provided in relation to an appeal on a point of law to the Upper Tribunal, the Court of Appeal or the Supreme Court relating to a benefit, allowance, payment, credit or pension under–
   (a) a social security enactment,
   (b) the Vaccine Damage Payments Act 1979, or
   (c) Part 4 of the Child Maintenance and Other Payments Act 2008.

Exclusions

(2) Sub-paragraph (1) is subject to–
   (a) the exclusions in Part 2 of this Schedule, with the exception of paragraphs 1 and 15 of that Part, and
   (b) the exclusion in Part 3 of this Schedule.

Definitions

(3) In this paragraph 'social security enactment' means–
   (a) the Social Security Contributions and Benefits Act 1992,
   (b) the Jobseekers Act 1995,
   (c) the State Pension Credit Act 2002,
   (d) the Tax Credits Act 2002,
   (e) the Welfare Reform Act 2007,
   (f) the Welfare Reform Act 2012, or
   (g) any other enactment relating to social security.

Inherent jurisdiction of High Court in relation to children and vulnerable adults

9 (1) Civil legal services provided in relation to the inherent jurisdiction of the High Court in relation to children and vulnerable adults.

Exclusions

(2) Sub-paragraph (1) is subject to the exclusions in Parts 2 and 3 of this Schedule.

Definitions

(3) In this paragraph–
   'adults' means persons aged 18 or over;
   'children' means persons under the age of 18.

Unlawful removal of children

10 (1) Civil legal services provided to an individual in relation to the following orders and requirements where the individual is seeking to prevent the unlawful removal of a related child from the United Kingdom or to secure the return of a related child who has been unlawfully removed from the United Kingdom–
   (a) a prohibited steps order or specific issue order (as defined in section 8(1) of the Children Act 1989);
   (b) an order under section 33 of the Family Law Act 1986 for disclosure of the child's whereabouts;

(c) an order under section 34 of that Act for the child's return;

(d) a requirement under section 37 of that Act to surrender a passport issued to, or containing particulars of, the child.

(2) Civil legal services provided to an individual in relation to the following orders and applications where the individual is seeking to secure the return of a related child who has been unlawfully removed to a place in the United Kingdom–

(a) a prohibited steps order or specific issue order (as defined in section 8(1) of the Children Act 1989);

(b) an application under section 27 of the Family Law Act 1986 for registration of an order relating to the child;

(c) an order under section 33 of that Act for disclosure of the child's whereabouts;

(d) an order under section 34 of that Act for the child's return.

Exclusions

(3) Sub-paragraphs (1) and (2) are subject to the exclusions in Parts 2 and 3 of this Schedule.

Definitions

(4) For the purposes of this paragraph, a child is related to an individual if the individual is the child's parent or has parental responsibility for the child.

(5) In this paragraph 'child' means a person under the age of 18.

Family homes and domestic violence

11 (1) Civil legal services provided in relation to home rights, occupation orders and non-molestation orders under Part 4 of the Family Law Act 1996.

(2) Civil legal services provided in relation to the following in circumstances arising out of a family relationship–

(a) an injunction following assault, battery or false imprisonment;

(b) the inherent jurisdiction of the High Court to protect an adult.

Exclusions

(3) Sub-paragraphs (1) and (2) are subject to–

(a) the exclusions in Part 2 of this Schedule, with the exception of paragraphs 3 and 11 of that Part, and

(b) the exclusion in Part 3 of this Schedule.

Definitions

(4) For the purposes of this paragraph–

(a) there is a family relationship between two people if they are associated with each other, and

(b) 'associated' has the same meaning as in Part 4 of the Family Law Act 1996 (see section 62 of that Act).

(5) For the purposes of this paragraph, the Lord Chancellor may by regulations make provision about when circumstances arise out of a family relationship.

Victims of domestic violence and family matters

12 (1) Civil legal services provided to an adult ('A') in relation to a matter arising out of a family relationship between A and another individual ('B') where–

(a) there has been, or is a risk of, domestic violence between A and B, and

(b) A was, or is at risk of being, the victim of that domestic violence.

General exclusions

(2) Sub-paragraph (1) is subject to the exclusions in Part 2 of this Schedule, with the exception of paragraph 11 of that Part.

(3) But the exclusions described in sub-paragraph (2) are subject to the exception in sub-paragraph (4).

(4) The services described in sub-paragraph (1) include services provided in relation to conveyancing, but only where–
   (a) the services in relation to conveyancing are provided in the course of giving effect to a court order made in proceedings, and
   (b) services described in that sub-paragraph (other than services in relation to conveyancing) are being or have been provided in relation to those proceedings under arrangements made for the purposes of this Part of this Act.

(5) Sub-paragraph (1) is subject to the exclusion in Part 3 of this Schedule.

Specific exclusion

(6) The services described in sub-paragraph (1) do not include services provided in relation to a claim in tort in respect of the domestic violence.

Definitions

(7) For the purposes of this paragraph–
   (a) there is a family relationship between two people if they are associated with each other, and
   (b) 'associated' has the same meaning as in Part 4 of the Family Law Act 1996 (see section 62 of that Act).

(8) For the purposes of this paragraph–
   (a) matters arising out of a family relationship include matters arising under a family enactment, and
   (b) (subject to paragraph (a)) the Lord Chancellor may by regulations make provision about when matters arise out of a family relationship.

(9) In this paragraph–
   'adult' means a person aged 18 or over;
   'domestic violence' means any incident, or pattern of incidents of controlling, coercive or threatening behaviour, violence or abuse (whether psychological, physical, sexual, financial or emotional) between individuals who are associated with each other;
   'family enactment' means–
      (a) section 17 of the Married Women's Property Act 1882 (questions between husband and wife as to property);
      (b) the Maintenance Orders (Facilities for Enforcement) Act 1920;
      (c) the Maintenance Orders Act 1950;
      (d) the Maintenance Orders Act 1958;
      (e) the Maintenance Orders (Reciprocal Enforcement) Act 1972;
      (f) Schedule 1 to the Domicile and Matrimonial Proceedings Act 1973 (staying of matrimonial proceedings) and corresponding provision in relation to civil partnerships made by rules of court under section 223 of the Civil Partnership Act 2004;
      (g) the Matrimonial Causes Act 1973;
      (h) the Inheritance (Provision for Family Dependants) Act 1975;
      (i) the Domestic Proceedings and Magistrates' Courts Act 1978;

(j)   Part 3 of the Matrimonial and Family Proceedings Act 1984 (financial relief after overseas divorce etc);

(k)   Parts 1 and 3 of the Family Law Act 1986 (child custody and declarations of status);

(l)   Parts 1 and 2 of the Children Act 1989 (orders with respect to children in family proceedings);

(m)   section 53 of, and Schedule 7 to, the Family Law Act 1996 (transfer of tenancies on divorce etc or separation of cohabitants);

(n)   Chapters 2 and 3 of Part 2 of the Civil Partnership Act 2004 (dissolution, nullity and other proceedings and property and financial arrangements);

(o)   section 54 of the Human Fertilisation and Embryology Act 2008 (applications for parental orders);

(p)   section 51A of the Adoption and Children Act 2002 (post-adoption contact orders).

Protection of children and family matters

13 (1) Civil legal services provided to an adult ('A') in relation to the following orders and procedures where the child who is or would be the subject of the order is at risk of abuse from an individual other than A–

(a)   orders under section 4(2A) of the Children Act 1989 ('the 1989 Act') (removal of father's parental responsibility);

(b)   orders under section 6(7) of the 1989 Act (termination of appointment of guardian);

(c)   orders mentioned in section 8(1) of the 1989 Act (child arrangements and other orders);

(d)   special guardianship orders under Part 2 of the 1989 Act;

(e)   orders under section 33 of the Family Law Act 1986 ('the 1986 Act') (disclosure of child's whereabouts);

(f)   orders under section 34 of the 1986 Act (return of child);

(g)   orders under section 51A of the Adoption and Children Act 2002 (post-adoption contact).

Exclusions

(2) Sub-paragraph (1) is subject to the exclusions in Parts 2 and 3 of this Schedule.

Definitions

(3) In this paragraph–

'abuse' means physical or mental abuse, including–

(a)   sexual abuse, and

(b)   abuse in the form of violence, neglect, maltreatment and exploitation;

'adult' means a person aged 18 or over;

'child' means a person under the age of 18.

Mediation in family disputes

14 (1) Mediation provided in relation to family disputes.

(2) Civil legal services provided in connection with the mediation of family disputes.

Exclusions

(3) Sub-paragraphs (1) and (2) are subject to the exclusions in Part 2 of this Schedule, with the exception of paragraph 11 of that Part.

(4) But the exclusions described in sub-paragraph (3) are subject to the exception in sub-paragraph (5).

(5) The services described in sub-paragraph (2) include services provided in relation to conveyancing, but only where–

    (a) the services in relation to conveyancing are provided in the course of giving effect to arrangements for the resolution of a family dispute, and

    (b) services described in that sub-paragraph or sub-paragraph (1) (other than services in relation to conveyancing) are being or have been provided in relation to the dispute under arrangements made for the purposes of this Part of this Act.

(6) Sub-paragraphs (1) and (2) are subject to the exclusion in Part 3 of this Schedule.

Definitions

(7) For the purposes of this paragraph–

    (a) a dispute is a family dispute if it is a dispute between individuals about a matter arising out of a family relationship between the individuals,

    (b) there is a family relationship between two individuals if they are associated with each other, and

    (c) 'associated' has the same meaning as in Part 4 of the Family Law Act 1996 (see section 62 of that Act).

(8) For the purposes of this paragraph–

    (a) matters arising out of a family relationship include matters arising under a family enactment, and

    (b) (subject to paragraph (a)) the Lord Chancellor may by regulations make provision about when matters arise out of a family relationship.

(9) In this paragraph–

'child' means a person under the age of 18;

'family enactment' has the meaning given in paragraph 12.

Children who are parties to family proceedings

15 (1) Civil legal services provided to a child in relation to family proceedings–

    (a) where the child is, or proposes to be, the applicant or respondent;

    (b) where the child is made a party to the proceedings by a court under rule 16.2 of the Family Procedure Rules;

    (c) where the child is a party to the proceedings and is conducting, or proposes to conduct, the proceedings without a children's guardian or litigation friend in accordance with rule 16.6 of the Family Procedure Rules.

Exclusions

(2) Sub-paragraph (1) is subject to the exclusions in Parts 2 and 3 of this Schedule.

Definitions

(3) For the purposes of this paragraph–

    (a) proceedings are family proceedings if they relate to a matter arising out of a family relationship,

(b) there is a family relationship between two individuals if they are associated with each other, and

(c) 'associated' has the same meaning as in Part 4 of the Family Law Act 1996 (see section 62 of that Act).

(4) For the purposes of this paragraph–

(a) matters arising out of a family relationship include matters arising under a family enactment, and

(b) (subject to paragraph (a)) the Lord Chancellor may by regulations make provision about when matters arise out of a family relationship.

(5) In this paragraph–

'child' means a person under the age of 18;

'family enactment' has the meaning given in paragraph 12.

Female genital mutilation protection orders

15A(1) Civil legal services provided in relation to female genital mutilation protection orders under paragraph 1 of Schedule 2 to the Female Genital Mutilation Act 2003.

Exclusions

(2) Sub-paragraph (1) is subject to the exclusions in Parts 2 and 3 of this Schedule.

Forced marriage

16 (1) Civil legal services provided in relation to forced marriage protection orders under Part 4A of the Family Law Act 1996.

Exclusions

(2) Sub-paragraph (1) is subject to the exclusions in Parts 2 and 3 of this Schedule.

EU and international agreements concerning children

17 (1) Civil legal services provided in relation to–

(a) an application made to the Lord Chancellor under the 1980 European Convention on Child Custody for the recognition or enforcement in England and Wales of a decision relating to the custody of a child;

(b) an application made to the Lord Chancellor under the 1980 Hague Convention in respect of a child who is, or is believed to be, in England and Wales;

(c) the recognition or enforcement of a judgment in England and Wales in accordance with Article 21, 28, 41, 42 or 48 of the 2003 Brussels Regulation.

Exclusions

(2) Sub-paragraph (1) is subject to the exclusions in Parts 2 and 3 of this Schedule.

Definitions

(3) In this paragraph–

'the 1980 European Convention on Child Custody' means the European Convention on Recognition and Enforcement of Decisions concerning Custody of Children and on the Restoration of Custody of Children which was signed in Luxembourg on 20 May 1980;

'the 1980 Hague Convention' means the Convention on the Civil Aspects of International Child Abduction which was signed at The Hague on 25 October 1980;

'the 2003 Brussels Regulation' means Council Regulation (EC) No 2001/2003 of 27 November 2003 concerning jurisdiction and the recognition and enforcement of judgments in matrimonial matters and the matters of parental responsibility.

(4) For the purposes of this paragraph, an application is made to the Lord Chancellor if it is addressed to the Lord Chancellor or transmitted to the Lord Chancellor in accordance with section 3 or 14 of the Child Abduction and Custody Act 1985.

EU and international agreements concerning maintenance

18 (1) Civil legal services provided in relation to an application under the following for the recognition or enforcement in England and Wales of a maintenance order–

(a) the 1968 Brussels Convention;
(b) the 1973 Hague Convention;
(c) the 1989 Lugano Convention;
(d) the 2000 Brussels Regulation;
(e) the 2007 Lugano Convention.

(2) Civil legal services provided in relation to an application under Article 56 of the EU Maintenance Regulation (applications relating to maintenance decisions).

(3) Civil legal services provided to an individual in relation to proceedings in England and Wales relating to the recognition, enforceability or enforcement of a maintenance decision in circumstances in which the individual falls within Article 47(2) or (3) of the EU Maintenance Regulation (parties who benefited from free legal aid etc in Member State of origin).

(3A) Civil legal services provided in relation to an application under Article 10 of the 2007 Hague Convention (applications relating to maintenance decisions).

(3B) Civil legal services provided to an individual in relation to proceedings in England and Wales relating to the recognition or enforcement of a maintenance decision in circumstances in which–

(a) Article 17(b) of the 2007 Hague Convention (free legal assistance for persons who benefited from such assistance in State of origin) applies to the proceedings by virtue of Article 37(2) of that Convention (direct request to competent authority of Contracting State), and
(b) the individual falls within Article 17(b) as so applied.

Exclusions

(4) Sub-paragraphs (1) to (3B) are subject to–

(a) the exclusions in Part 2 of this Schedule, with the exception of paragraph 11 of that Part, and
(b) the exclusion in Part 3 of this Schedule.

Definitions

(5) In this paragraph–

'the 1968 Brussels Convention' means the Convention on jurisdiction and the enforcement of judgments in civil and commercial matters (including the Protocol annexed to that Convention) signed at Brussels on 27 September 1968;

'the 1973 Hague Convention' means the Convention on the recognition and enforcement of decisions relating to maintenance obligations concluded at The Hague on 2 October 1973;

'the 1989 Lugano Convention' means the Convention on jurisdiction and the enforcement of judgments in civil and commercial matters (including the Protocols annexed to that Convention) opened for signature at Lugano on 16 September 1988 and signed by the United Kingdom on 18 September 1989;

'the 2000 Brussels Regulation' means Council Regulation (EC) No 44/2001 of 22 December 2000 on jurisdiction and the recognition and enforcement of judgments in civil and commercial matters;

'the 2007 Hague Convention' means the Convention on the international recovery of child support and other forms of family maintenance concluded at The Hague on 23 November 2007;

'the 2007 Lugano Convention' means the Convention on jurisdiction and enforcement of judgments in civil and commercial matters, between the European Community and the Republic of Iceland, the Kingdom of Norway, the Swiss Confederation and the Kingdom of Denmark signed on behalf of the European Community on 30 October 2007;

'the EU Maintenance Regulation' means Council Regulation (EC) No 4/2009 of 18 December 2008 on jurisdiction, applicable law, recognition and enforcement of decisions and co-operation in matters relating to maintenance obligations;

'maintenance order', in relation to a convention or regulation listed in this paragraph, means a maintenance judgment within the meaning of that convention or regulation.

Judicial review

19 (1) Civil legal services provided in relation to judicial review of an enactment, decision, act or omission.

General exclusions

(2) Sub-paragraph (1) is subject to–

   (a) the exclusions in Part 2 of this Schedule, with the exception of paragraphs 1, 2, 3, 4, 5, 6, 8, 12, 15, 16 and 18 of that Part, and

   (b) the exclusion in Part 3 of this Schedule.

Specific exclusion: benefit to individual

(3) The services described in sub-paragraph (1) do not include services provided to an individual in relation to judicial review that does not have the potential to produce a benefit for the individual, a member of the individual's family or the environment.

(4) Sub-paragraph (3) does not exclude services provided in relation to a judicial review where the judicial review ceases to have the potential to produce such a benefit after civil legal services have been provided in relation to the judicial review under arrangements made for the purposes of this Part of this Act.

Specific exclusions: immigration cases

(5) The services described in sub-paragraph (1) do not include services provided

in relation to judicial review in respect of an issue relating to immigration where–

(a) the same issue, or substantially the same issue, was the subject of a previous judicial review or an appeal to a court or tribunal,

(b) on the determination of the previous judicial review or appeal (or, if there was more than one, the latest one), the court, tribunal or other person hearing the case found against the applicant or appellant on that issue, and

(c) the services in relation to the new judicial review are provided before the end of the period of 1 year beginning with the day of that determination.

(6) The services described in sub-paragraph (1) do not include services provided in relation to judicial review of removal directions in respect of an individual where the directions were given not more than 1 year after the latest of the following–

(a) the making of the decision (or, if there was more than one, the latest decision) to remove the individual from the United Kingdom by way of removal directions;

(b) the refusal of leave to appeal against that decision;

(c) the determination or withdrawal of an appeal against that decision.

(7) Sub-paragraphs (5) and (6) do not exclude services provided to an individual in relation to–

(a) judicial review of a negative decision in relation to an asylum application (within the meaning of the EU Procedures Directive) where there is no right of appeal to the First-tier Tribunal against the decision;

(b) judicial review of certification under section 94 or 96 of the Nationality, Immigration and Asylum Act 2002 (certificate preventing or restricting appeal of immigration decision).

(8) Sub-paragraphs (5) and (6) do not exclude services provided in relation to judicial review of removal directions in respect of an individual where prescribed conditions relating to either or both of the following are met–

(a) the period between the individual being given notice of the removal directions and the proposed time for his or her removal;

(b) the reasons for proposing that period.

Definitions

(9) For the purposes of this paragraph an individual is a member of another individual's family if–

(a) they are relatives (whether of the full blood or half blood or by marriage or civil partnership),

(b) they are cohabitants (as defined in Part 4 of the Family Law Act 1996), or

(c) one has parental responsibility for the other.

(10) In this paragraph–

'EU Procedures Directive' means Council Directive 2005/85/EC of 1 December 2005 on minimum standards on procedures in Member States for granting and withdrawing refugee status;

'an issue relating to immigration' includes an issue relating to rights described in paragraph 30 of this Part of this Schedule;

'judicial review' means–

(a) the procedure on an application for judicial review (see section 31 of the Senior Courts Act 1981), but not including the procedure after the application is treated under rules of court as if it were not such an application, and

(b) any procedure in which a court, tribunal or other person mentioned in Part 3 of this Schedule is required by an enactment to make a decision applying the principles that are applied by the court on an application for judicial review;

'removal directions' means directions under–

(a) paragraphs 8 to 10A of Schedule 2 to the Immigration Act 1971 (removal of persons refused leave to enter and illegal entrants);

(b) paragraphs 12 to 14 of Schedule 2 to that Act (removal of seamen and aircrew);

(c) paragraph 1 of Schedule 3 to that Act (removal of persons liable to deportation);

(d) section 10 of the Immigration and Asylum Act 1999 (removal of certain persons unlawfully in the United Kingdom);

(e) [Repealed.]

Habeas corpus

20 (1) Civil legal services provided in relation to a writ of habeas corpus ad subjiciendum.

Exclusions

(2) Sub-paragraph (1) is subject to the exclusions in Parts 2 and 3 of this Schedule.

Abuse of position or powers by public authority

21 (1) Civil legal services provided in relation to abuse by a public authority of its position or powers.

General exclusions

(2) Sub-paragraph (1) is subject to–

(a) the exclusions in Part 2 of this Schedule, with the exception of paragraphs 1, 2, 3, 4, 5, 6, 8 and 12 of that Part, and

(b) the exclusion in Part 3 of this Schedule.

Specific exclusion

(3) The services described in sub-paragraph (1) do not include services provided in relation to clinical negligence.

Definitions

(4) For the purposes of this paragraph, an act or omission by a public authority does not constitute an abuse of its position or powers unless the act or omission–

(a) is deliberate or dishonest, and

(b) results in harm to a person or property that was reasonably foreseeable.

(5) In this paragraph–

'clinical negligence' means breach of a duty of care or trespass to the person committed in the course of the provision of clinical or medical services (including dental or nursing services);

'public authority' has the same meaning as in section 6 of the Human Rights Act 1998.

Breach of Convention rights by public authority

22 (1) Civil legal services provided in relation to–
  (a) a claim in tort, or
  (b) a claim for damages (other than a claim in tort),
  in respect of an act or omission by a public authority that involves a significant breach of Convention rights by the authority.

General exclusions
  (2) Sub-paragraph (1) is subject to–
  (a) the exclusions in Part 2 of this Schedule, with the exception of paragraphs 1, 2, 3, 4, 5, 6, 8 and 12 of that Part, and
  (b) the exclusion in Part 3 of this Schedule.

Specific exclusion
  (3) The services described in sub-paragraph (1) do not include services provided in relation to clinical negligence.

Definitions
  (4) In this paragraph–
  'clinical negligence' means breach of a duty of care or trespass to the person committed in the course of the provision of clinical or medical services (including dental or nursing services);
  'Convention rights' has the same meaning as in the Human Rights Act 1998;
  'public authority' has the same meaning as in section 6 of that Act.

Clinical negligence and severely disabled infants

23 (1) Civil legal services provided in relation to a claim for damages in respect of clinical negligence which caused a neurological injury to an individual ('V') as a result of which V is severely disabled, but only where the first and second conditions are met.
  (2) The first condition is that the clinical negligence occurred–
  (a) while V was in his or her mother's womb, or
  (b) during or after V's birth but before the end of the following period–
    (i) if V was born before the beginning of the 37th week of pregnancy, the period of 8 weeks beginning with the first day of what would have been that week;
    (ii) if V was born during or after the 37th week of pregnancy, the period of 8 weeks beginning with the day of V's birth.
  (3) The second condition is that–
  (a) the services are provided to V, or
  (b) V has died and the services are provided to V's personal representative.

General exclusions
  (4) Sub-paragraph (1) is subject to–
  (a) the exclusions in Part 2 of this Schedule, with the exception of paragraphs 1, 2, 3 and 8 of that Part, and
  (b) the exclusion in Part 3 of this Schedule.

Definitions
  (5) In this paragraph–
  'birth' means the moment when an individual first has a life separate from

his or her mother and references to an individual being born are to be interpreted accordingly;

'clinical negligence' means breach of a duty of care or trespass to the person committed in the course of the provision of clinical or medical services (including dental or nursing services);

'disabled' means physically or mentally disabled;

'personal representative', in relation to an individual who has died, means–

- (a) a person responsible for administering the individual's estate under the law of England and Wales, Scotland or Northern Ireland, or
- (b) a person who, under the law of another country or territory, has functions equivalent to those of administering the individual's estate.

Special Immigration Appeals Commission

24 (1) Civil legal services provided in relation to proceedings before the Special Immigration Appeals Commission.

Exclusions

(2) Sub-paragraph (1) is subject to the exclusions in Parts 2 and 3 of this Schedule.

Immigration: detention

25 (1) Civil legal services provided in relation to–

- (a) detention under the authority of an immigration officer;
- (b) detention under Schedule 3 to the Immigration Act 1971;
- (c) detention under section 62 of the Nationality, Immigration and Asylum Act 2002;
- (d) detention under section 36 of the UK Borders Act 2007.

Exclusions

(2) Sub-paragraph (1) is subject to the exclusions in Parts 2 and 3 of this Schedule.

Immigration: temporary admission

26 (1) Civil legal services provided in relation to temporary admission to the United Kingdom under–

- (a) paragraph 21 of Schedule 2 to the Immigration Act 1971;
- (b) section 62 of the Nationality, Immigration and Asylum Act 2002.

Exclusions

(2) Sub-paragraph (1) is subject to the exclusions in Parts 2 and 3 of this Schedule.

Immigration: residence etc restrictions

27 (1) Civil legal services provided in relation to restrictions imposed under–

- (a) paragraph 2(5) or 4 of Schedule 3 to the Immigration Act 1971 (residence etc restrictions pending deportation);
- (b) section 71 of the Nationality, Immigration and Asylum Act 2002 (residence etc restrictions on asylum-seekers).

Exclusions

(2) Sub-paragraph (1) is subject to the exclusions in Parts 2 and 3 of this Schedule.

Immigration: victims of domestic violence and indefinite leave to remain

28 (1) Civil legal services provided to an individual ('V') in relation to an application by V for indefinite leave to remain in the United Kingdom on the grounds that–

(a) V was given leave to enter or remain in the United Kingdom for a limited period as the partner of another individual present and settled in the United Kingdom, and

(b) V's relationship with the other individual broke down permanently because V was the victim of domestic violence.

General exclusions

(2) Sub-paragraph (1) is subject to the exclusions in Parts 2 and 3 of this Schedule.

Specific exclusion

(3) The services described in sub-paragraph (1) do not include attendance at an interview conducted on behalf of the Secretary of State with a view to reaching a decision on an application.

Definitions

(4) For the purposes of this paragraph, one individual is a partner of another if–

(a) they are married to each other,

(b) they are civil partners of each other, or

(c) they are cohabitants.

(5) In this paragraph–

'cohabitant' has the same meaning as in Part 4 of the Family Law Act 1996 (see section 62 of that Act);

'domestic violence' means any incident, or pattern of incidents, of controlling, coercive or threatening behaviour, violence or abuse (whether psychological, physical, sexual, financial or emotional) between individuals who are associated with each other (within the meaning of section 62 of the Family Law Act 1996);

'indefinite leave to remain in the United Kingdom' means leave to remain in the United Kingdom under the Immigration Act 1971 which is not limited as to duration;

'present and settled in the United Kingdom' has the same meaning as in the rules made under section 3(2) of the Immigration Act 1971.

Immigration: victims of domestic violence and residence cards

29 (1) Civil legal services provided to an individual ('V') in relation to a residence card application where V–

(a) has ceased to be a family member of a qualified person on the termination of the marriage or civil partnership of the qualified person,

(b) is a family member who has retained the right of residence by virtue of satisfying the conditions in regulation 10(5) of the Immigration (European Economic Area) Regulations 2006 (SI 2006/1003) ('the 2006 Regulations'), and

(c) has satisfied the condition in regulation 10(5)(d)(iv) of the 2006 Regulations on the ground that V or a family member of V was the victim of domestic violence while the marriage or civil partnership of the qualified person was subsisting.

General exclusions

(2) Sub-paragraph (1) is subject to the exclusions in Parts 2 and 3 of this Schedule.

Specific exclusion

(3) The services described in sub-paragraph (1) do not include attendance at an interview conducted on behalf of the Secretary of State with a view to reaching a decision on an application.

Definitions

(4) In this paragraph–

'domestic violence' means any incident, or pattern of incidents, of controlling, coercive or threatening behaviour, violence or abuse (whether psychological, physical, sexual, financial or emotional) between individuals who are associated with each other (within the meaning of section 62 of the Family Law Act 1996);

'family member' has the same meaning as in the 2006 Regulations (see regulations 7 and 9);

'family member who has retained the right of residence' has the same meaning as in the 2006 Regulations (see regulation 10);

'qualified person' has the same meaning as in the 2006 Regulations (see regulation 6);

'residence card application' means–

(a) an application for a residence card under regulation 17 of the 2006 Regulations, or

(b) an application for a permanent residence card under regulation 18(2) of the 2006 Regulations.

Immigration: rights to enter and remain

30 (1) Civil legal services provided in relation to rights to enter, and to remain in, the United Kingdom arising from–

(a) the Refugee Convention;

(b) Article 2 or 3 of the Human Rights Convention;

(c) the Temporary Protection Directive;

(d) the Qualification Directive.

General exclusions

(2) Sub-paragraph (1) is subject to the exclusions in Parts 2 and 3 of this Schedule.

Specific exclusion

(3) The services described in sub-paragraph (1) do not include attendance at an interview conducted on behalf of the Secretary of State with a view to reaching a decision on a claim in respect of the rights mentioned in that sub-paragraph, except where regulations provide otherwise.

Definitions

(4) In this paragraph–

'the Human Rights Convention' means the Convention for the Protection of Human Rights and Fundamental Freedoms, agreed by the Council of Europe at Rome on 4 November 1950 as it has effect for the time being in relation to the United Kingdom;

'the Qualification Directive' means Council Directive 2004/83/EC of 29 April 2004 on minimum standards for the qualification and status of third country nationals or stateless persons as refugees or as persons who otherwise need international protection and the content of the protection granted;

'the Refugee Convention' means the Convention relating to the Status of Refugees done at Geneva on 28 July 1951 and the Protocol to the Convention;

'the Temporary Protection Directive' means Council Directive 2001/55/EC of 20 July 2001 on minimum standards for giving temporary protection in the event of a mass influx of displaced persons and on measures promoting a balance of efforts between Member States in receiving such persons and bearing the consequences thereof.

Immigration: accommodation for asylum-seekers etc

31 (1) Civil legal services provided in relation to the Secretary of State's powers to provide, or arrange for the provision of, accommodation under–

(a) section 4 or 95 of the Immigration and Asylum Act 1999 (accommodation for persons temporarily admitted and asylum-seekers);

(b) section 17 of the Nationality, Immigration and Asylum Act 2002 (support for destitute asylum-seekers).

Exclusions

(2) Sub-paragraph (1) is subject to the exclusions in Parts 2 and 3 of this Schedule.

Victims of trafficking in human beings

32 (1) Civil legal services provided to an individual in relation to an application by the individual for leave to enter, or to remain in, the United Kingdom where–

(a) there has been a conclusive determination that the individual is a victim of trafficking in human beings, or

(b) there are reasonable grounds to believe that the individual is such a victim and there has not been a conclusive determination that the individual is not such a victim.

(2) Civil legal services provided in relation to a claim under employment law arising in connection with the exploitation of an individual who is a victim of trafficking in human beings, but only where–

(a) the services are provided to the individual, or

(b) the individual has died and the services are provided to the individual's personal representative.

(3) Civil legal services provided in relation to a claim for damages arising in connection with the trafficking or exploitation of an individual who is a victim of trafficking in human beings, but only where–

(a) the services are provided to the individual, or

(b) the individual has died and the services are provided to the individual's personal representative.

Exclusions
(4) Sub-paragraph (1) is subject to the exclusions in Parts 2 and 3 of this Schedule.
(5) Sub-paragraphs (2) and (3) are subject to–
    (a) the exclusions in Part 2 of this Schedule, with the exception of paragraphs 1, 2, 3, 4, 5, 6 and 8 of that Part, and
    (b) the exclusion in Part 3 of this Schedule.

Definitions
(6) For the purposes of sub-paragraph (1)(b) there are reasonable grounds to believe that an individual is a victim of trafficking in human beings if a competent authority has determined for the purposes of Article 10 of the Trafficking Convention (identification of victims) that there are such grounds.
(7) For the purposes of sub-paragraph (1) there is a conclusive determination that an individual is or is not a victim of trafficking in human beings when, on completion of the identification process required by Article 10 of the Trafficking Convention, a competent authority concludes that the individual is or is not such a victim.
(8) In this paragraph–
    'competent authority' means a person who is a competent authority of the United Kingdom for the purposes of the Trafficking Convention;
    'employment' means employment under a contract of employment or a contract personally to do work and references to 'employers' and 'employees' are to be interpreted accordingly;
    'employment law' means an enactment or rule of law relating to employment, including in particular an enactment or rule of law conferring powers or imposing duties on employers, conferring rights on employees or otherwise regulating the relations between employers and employees;
    'exploitation' means a form of exploitation described in section 4(4) of the Asylum and Immigration (Treatment of Claimants, etc) Act 2004 (trafficking people for exploitation); section 3 of the Modern Slavery Act 2015 (meaning of exploitation for purposes of human trafficking offence in section 2 of that Act);
    'personal representative', in relation to an individual who has died, means–
    (a) a person responsible for administering the individual's estate under the law of England and Wales, Scotland or Northern Ireland, or
    (b) a person who, under the law of another country or territory, has functions equivalent to those of administering the individual's estate;
    'the Trafficking Convention' means the Council of Europe Convention on Action against Trafficking in Human Beings (done at Warsaw on 16 May 2005);
    'trafficking in human beings' has the same meaning as in the Trafficking Convention.

Victims of slavery, servitude or forced or compulsory labour
32A(1) Civil legal services provided to an individual in relation to an application by the individual for leave to enter, or to remain in, the United Kingdom where–
    (a) there has been a conclusive determination that the individual is a victim of slavery, servitude or forced or compulsory labour, or

(b) there are reasonable grounds to believe that the individual is such a victim and there has not been a conclusive determination that the individual is not such a victim.

(2) Civil legal services provided in relation to a claim under employment law arising in connection with the conduct by virtue of which an individual who is a victim of slavery, servitude or forced or compulsory labour is such a victim, but only where–

(a) the services are provided to the individual, or

(b) the individual has died and the services are provided to the individual's personal representative.

(3) Civil legal services provided in relation to a claim for damages arising in connection with the conduct by virtue of which an individual who is a victim of slavery, servitude or forced or compulsory labour is such a victim, but only where–

(a) the services are provided to the individual, or

(b) the individual has died and the services are provided to the individual's personal representative.

Exclusions

(4) Sub-paragraph (1) is subject to the exclusions in Parts 2 and 3 of this Schedule.

(5) Sub-paragraphs (2) and (3) are subject to–

(a) the exclusions in Part 2 of this Schedule, with the exception of paragraphs 1, 2, 3, 4, 5, 6 and 8 of that Part, and

(b) the exclusion in Part 3 of this Schedule.

Definitions

(6) For the purposes of sub-paragraph (1)(b) there are reasonable grounds to believe that an individual is a victim of slavery, servitude or forced or compulsory labour if a competent authority has determined that there are such grounds.

(7) For the purposes of sub-paragraph (1) there is a conclusive determination that an individual is or is not a victim of slavery, servitude or forced or compulsory labour when a competent authority concludes that the individual is or is not such a victim.

(8) For the purposes of this paragraph 'slavery', 'servitude' and 'forced or compulsory labour' have the same meaning as they have for the purposes of article 4 of the Human Rights Convention.

(9) The 'Human Rights Convention' means the Convention for the Protection of Human Rights and Fundamental Freedoms, agreed by the Council of Europe at Rome on 4 November 1950, as it has effect for the time being in relation to the United Kingdom.

(10) The definitions of 'competent authority', 'employment', 'employment law' and 'personal representative' in paragraph 32(8) also apply for the purposes of this paragraph.

Loss of home

33 (1) Civil legal services provided to an individual in relation to–

(a) court orders for sale or possession of the individual's home, or

(b) the eviction from the individual's home of the individual or others.

(2) Civil legal services provided to an individual in relation to a bankruptcy order against the individual under Part 9 of the Insolvency Act 1986 where–

(a) the individual's estate includes the individual's home, and

(b) the petition for the bankruptcy order is or was presented by a person other than the individual,

including services provided in relation to a statutory demand under that Part of that Act.

General exclusions

(3) Sub-paragraphs (1) and (2) are subject to the exclusions in Part 2 of this Schedule, with the exception of paragraph 14 of that Part.

(4) But the exclusions described in sub-paragraph (3) are subject to the exceptions in sub-paragraphs (5) and (6).

(5) The services described in sub-paragraph (1) include services provided in relation to proceedings on an application under the Trusts of Land and Appointment of Trustees Act 1996 to which section 335A of the Insolvency Act 1986 applies (application by trustee of bankrupt's estate).

(6) The services described in sub-paragraph (1) include services described in any of paragraphs 3 to 6 or 8 of Part 2 of this Schedule to the extent that they are–

(a) services provided to an individual in relation to a counterclaim in proceedings for a court order for sale or possession of the individual's home, or

(b) services provided to an individual in relation to the unlawful eviction from the individual's home of the individual or others.

(7) Sub-paragraphs (1) and (2) are subject to the exclusion in Part 3 of this Schedule.

Specific exclusion

(8) The services described in sub-paragraph (1) do not include services provided in relation to–

(a) proceedings under the Matrimonial Causes Act 1973;

(b) proceedings under Chapters 2 and 3 of Part 2 of the Civil Partnership Act 2004 (dissolution, nullity and other proceedings and property and financial arrangements).

Definitions

(9) In this paragraph 'home', in relation to an individual, means the house, caravan, houseboat or other vehicle or structure that is the individual's only or main residence, subject to sub-paragraph (10).

(10) References in this paragraph to an individual's home do not include a vehicle or structure occupied by the individual if–

(a) there are no grounds on which it can be argued that the individual is occupying the vehicle or structure otherwise than as a trespasser, and

(b) there are no grounds on which it can be argued that the individual's occupation of the vehicle or structure began otherwise than as a trespasser.

(11) In sub-paragraphs (9) and (10), the references to a caravan, houseboat or other vehicle include the land on which it is located or to which it is moored.

(12) For the purposes of sub-paragraph (10) individuals occupying, or beginning occupation, of a vehicle or structure as a trespasser include individuals who do so by virtue of–

(a) title derived from a trespasser, or

(b) a licence or consent given by a trespasser or a person deriving title from a trespasser;

(13) For the purposes of sub-paragraph (10) an individual who is occupying a vehicle or structure as a trespasser does not cease to be a trespasser by virtue of being allowed time to leave the vehicle or structure.

Homelessness

34 (1) Civil legal services provided to an individual who is homeless, or threatened with homelessness, in relation to the provision of accommodation and assistance for the individual under–

(a) Part 6 of the Housing Act 1996 (allocation of housing accommodation);

(b) Part 7 of that Act (homelessness).

(c) Part 2 of the Housing (Wales) Act 2014 (homelessness).[2]

Exclusions

(2) Sub-paragraph (1) is subject to the exclusions in Parts 2 and 3 of this Schedule.

Definitions

(3) In this paragraph 'homeless' and 'threatened with homelessness' have the same meaning as in section 175 of the Housing Act 1996.

Risk to health or safety in rented home

35 (1) Civil legal services provided to an individual in relation to the removal or reduction of a serious risk of harm to the health or safety of the individual or a relevant member of the individual's family where–

(a) the risk arises from a deficiency in the individual's home,

(b) the individual's home is rented or leased from another person, and

(c) the services are provided with a view to securing that the other person makes arrangements to remove or reduce the risk.

Exclusions

(2) Sub-paragraph (1) is subject to–

(a) the exclusions in Part 2 of this Schedule, with the exception of paragraphs 6 and 8 of that Part, and

(b) the exclusion in Part 3 of this Schedule.

Definitions

(3) For the purposes of this paragraph–

(a) a child is a relevant member of an individual's family if the individual is the child's parent or has parental responsibility for the child;

(b) an adult ('A') is a relevant member of an individual's family if–

(i) they are relatives (whether of the full blood or half blood or by marriage or civil partnership) or cohabitants, and

(ii) the individual's home is also A's home.

(4) In this paragraph–

'adult' means a person aged 18 or over;

'building' includes part of a building;

'child' means a person under the age of 18;

2   Not yet in force.

'cohabitant' has the same meaning as in Part 4 of the Family Law Act 1996 (see section 62(1) of that Act);

'deficiency' means any deficiency, whether arising as a result of the construction of a building, an absence of maintenance or repair, or otherwise;

'harm' includes temporary harm;

'health' includes mental health;

'home', in relation to an individual, means the house, caravan, houseboat or other vehicle or structure that is the individual's only or main residence, together with any garden or ground usually occupied with it.

Anti-social behaviour

36 (1) Civil legal services provided to an individual in relation to an application for, or proceedings in respect of, an injunction against the individual under section 1 of the Anti-social Behaviour, Crime and Policing Act 2014.

Exclusions

(2) Sub-paragraph (1) is subject to the exclusions in Parts 2 and 3 of this Schedule.

Protection from harassment

37 (1) Civil legal services provided in relation to–

(a) an injunction under section 3 or 3A of the Protection from Harassment Act 1997;

(b) the variation or discharge of a restraining order under section 5 or 5A of that Act.

Exclusions

(2) Sub-paragraph (1) is subject to the exclusions in Parts 2 and 3 of this Schedule.

Gang-related violence and drug-dealing activity

38 (1) Civil legal services provided in relation to injunctions under Part 4 of the Policing and Crime Act 2009 (injunctions to prevent gang-related violence and drug-dealing activity).

Exclusions

(2) Sub-paragraph (1) is subject to the exclusions in Parts 2 and 3 of this Schedule.

Sexual offences

39 (1) Civil legal services provided in relation to a sexual offence, but only where–

(a) the services are provided to the victim of the offence, or

(b) the victim of the offence has died and the services are provided to the victim's personal representative.

Exclusions

(2) Sub-paragraph (1) is subject to–

(a) the exclusions in Part 2 of this Schedule, with the exception of paragraphs 1, 2, 3, 8 and 12 of that Part, and

(b) the exclusion in Part 3 of this Schedule.

Definitions

(3) In this paragraph–

'personal representative', in relation to an individual who has died, means–
- (a) a person responsible for administering the individual's estate under the law of England and Wales, Scotland or Northern Ireland, or
- (b) a person who, under the law of another country or territory, has functions equivalent to those of administering the individual's estate;

'sexual offence' means–
- (a) an offence under a provision of the Sexual Offences Act 2003 ('the 2003 Act'), and
- (b) an offence under section 1 of the Protection of Children Act 1978 ('the 1978 Act') (indecent photographs of children).

(4) The references in sub-paragraph (1) to a sexual offence include–
- (a) incitement to commit a sexual offence,
- (b) an offence committed by a person under Part 2 of the Serious Crime Act 2007 (encouraging or assisting crime) in relation to which a sexual offence is the offence which the person intended or believed would be committed,
- (c) conspiracy to commit a sexual offence, and
- (d) an attempt to commit a sexual offence.

(5) In this paragraph references to a sexual offence include conduct which would be an offence under a provision of the 2003 Act or section 1 of the 1978 Act but for the fact that it took place before that provision or section came into force.

(6) Conduct falls within the definition of a sexual offence for the purposes of this paragraph whether or not there have been criminal proceedings in relation to the conduct and whatever the outcome of any such proceedings.

Proceeds of crime

40 (1) Civil legal services provided in relation to–
- (a) restraint orders under section 41 of the Proceeds of Crime Act 2002 ('the 2002 Act') including orders under section 41(7) of that Act (orders for ensuring that restraint order is effective);
- (b) orders under section 47M of the 2002 Act (detention of property);
- (c) directions under section 54(3) of the 2002 Act (distribution of funds in the hands of a receiver);
- (d) directions under section 62 of the 2002 Act (action to be taken by receiver);
- (e) orders under section 67A of the 2002 Act (realising property), including directions under section 67D of that Act (distribution of proceeds of realisation);
- (f) orders under section 72 or 73 of the 2002 Act (compensation);
- (g) applications under section 351 of the 2002 Act (discharge or variation of a production order or order to grant entry);
- (h) applications under section 362 of the 2002 Act (discharge or variation of disclosure order);
- (i) applications under section 369 of the 2002 Act (discharge or variation of customer information order);
- (j) applications under section 375 of the 2002 Act (discharge or variation of account monitoring orders).

General exclusions

(2) Sub-paragraph (1) is subject to–

   (a) the exclusions in Part 2 of this Schedule, with the exception of paragraph 14 of that Part, and

   (b) the exclusion in Part 3 of this Schedule.

Specific exclusions

(3) Where a confiscation order has been made under Part 2 of the 2002 Act against a defendant, the services described in sub-paragraph (1) do not include services provided to the defendant in relation to–

   (a) directions under section 54(3) of that Act (distribution of funds in the hands of a receiver), or

   (b) directions under section 67D of that Act (distribution of proceeds of realisation),

that relate to property recovered pursuant to the order.

(4) Where a confiscation order has been made under Part 2 of the 2002 Act against a defendant and varied under section 29 of that Act, the services described in sub-paragraph (1) do not include services provided in relation to an application by the defendant under section 73 of that Act (compensation).

Inquests

41 (1) Civil legal services provided to an individual in relation to an inquest under the Coroners Act 1988 into the death of a member of the individual's family.

Exclusions

(2) Sub-paragraph (1) is subject to–

   (a) the exclusions in Part 2 of this Schedule, with the exception of paragraph 1 of that Part, and

   (b) the exclusion in Part 3 of this Schedule.

Definitions

(3) For the purposes of this paragraph an individual is a member of another individual's family if–

   (a) they are relatives (whether of the full blood or half blood or by marriage or civil partnership),

   (b) they are cohabitants (as defined in Part 4 of the Family Law Act 1996), or

   (c) one has parental responsibility for the other.

Environmental pollution

42 (1) Civil legal services provided in relation to injunctions in respect of nuisance arising from prescribed types of pollution of the environment.

Exclusions

(2) Sub-paragraph (1) is subject to the exclusions in Parts 2 and 3 of this Schedule.

Equality

43 (1) Civil legal services provided in relation to contravention of the Equality Act 2010 or a previous discrimination enactment.

Exclusions

(2) Sub-paragraph (1) is subject to–

(a) the exclusions in Part 2 of this Schedule, with the exception of paragraph 15 of that Part, and

(b) the exclusion in Part 3 of this Schedule.

Definitions

(3) In this paragraph 'previous discrimination enactment' means–

(a) the Equal Pay Act 1970;

(b) the Sex Discrimination Act 1975;

(c) the Race Relations Act 1976;

(d) the Disability Discrimination Act 1995;

(e) the Employment Equality (Religion or Belief) Regulations 2003 (SI 2003/1660);

(f) the Employment Equality (Sexual Orientation) Regulations 2003 (SI 2003/1661);

(g) the Equality Act 2006;

(h) the Employment Equality (Age) Regulations 2006 (SI 2006/1031);

(i) the Equality Act (Sexual Orientation) Regulations 2007 (SI 2007/1263).

(4) The reference in sub-paragraph (1) to contravention of the Equality Act 2010 or a previous discrimination enactment includes–

(a) breach of a term modified by, or included by virtue of, a provision that is an equality clause or equality rule for the purposes of the Equal Pay Act 1970 or the Equality Act 2010, and

(b) breach of a provision that is a non-discrimination rule for the purposes of the Equality Act 2010.

Cross-border disputes

44 (1) Civil legal services provided in relation to proceedings in circumstances in which the services are required to be provided under Council Directive 2002/8/EC of 27 January 2003 to improve access to justice in cross-border disputes by establishing minimum common rules relating to legal aid for such disputes.

No exclusions

(2) Sub-paragraph (1) is not subject to the exclusions in Parts 2 and 3 of this Schedule.

Terrorism prevention and investigation measures etc

45 (1) Civil legal services provided to an individual in relation to a TPIM notice relating to the individual.

(2) Civil legal services provided to an individual in relation to control order proceedings relating to the individual.

Exclusions

(3) Sub-paragraphs (1) and (2) are subject to the exclusions in Parts 2 and 3 of this Schedule.

(4) In this paragraph–

'control order proceedings' means proceedings described in paragraph 3(1)(a) to (e) of Schedule 8 to the Terrorism Prevention and Investigation Measures Act 2011 ('the 2011 Act');

'TPIM notice' means a notice under section 2(1) of the 2011 Act.

Extension of time for retention of travel documents

45A(1) Civil legal services provided in relation to proceedings under paragraph 8 of Schedule 1 to the Counter-Terrorism and Security Act 2015.

Exclusions

(2) Sub-paragraph (1) is subject to the exclusions in Parts 2 and 3 of this Schedule.

Connected matters

46 (1) Prescribed civil legal services provided, in prescribed circumstances, in connection with the provision of services described in a preceding paragraph of this Part of this Schedule.

Exclusions

(2) Sub-paragraph (1) is subject to—
   (a) the exclusions in Parts 2 and 3 of this Schedule, except to the extent that regulations under this paragraph provide otherwise, and
   (b) any other prescribed exclusions.

PART 2: EXCLUDED SERVICES

The services described in Part 1 of this Schedule do not include the services listed in this Part of this Schedule, except to the extent that Part 1 of this Schedule provides otherwise.

1   Civil legal services provided in relation to personal injury or death.
2   Civil legal services provided in relation to a claim in tort in respect of negligence.
3   Civil legal services provided in relation to a claim in tort in respect of assault, battery or false imprisonment.
4   Civil legal services provided in relation to a claim in tort in respect of trespass to goods.
5   Civil legal services provided in relation to a claim in tort in respect of trespass to land.
6   Civil legal services provided in relation to damage to property.
7   Civil legal services provided in relation to defamation or malicious falsehood.
8   Civil legal services provided in relation to a claim in tort in respect of breach of statutory duty.
9   Civil legal services provided in relation to conveyancing.
10   Civil legal services provided in relation to the making of wills.
11   Civil legal services provided in relation to matters of trust law.
12 (1) Civil legal services provided in relation to a claim for damages in respect of a breach of Convention rights by a public authority to the extent that the claim is made in reliance on section 7 of the Human Rights Act 1998.
    (2) In this paragraph—
       'Convention rights' has the same meaning as in the Human Rights Act 1998;
       'public authority' has the same meaning as in section 6 of that Act.
13   Civil legal services provided in relation to matters of company or partnership law.

14   Civil legal services provided to an individual in relation to matters arising out of or in connection with–
  (a) a proposal by that individual to establish a business,
  (b) the carrying on of a business by that individual (whether or not the business is being carried on at the time the services are provided), or
  (c) the termination or transfer of a business that was being carried on by that individual.

15 (1) Civil legal services provided in relation to a benefit, allowance, payment, credit or pension under–
  (a) a social security enactment,
  (b) the Vaccine Damage Payments Act 1979, or
  (c) Part 4 of the Child Maintenance and Other Payments Act 2008.
  (2) In this paragraph 'social security enactment' means–
  (a) the Social Security Contributions and Benefits Act 1992,
  (b) the Jobseekers Act 1995,
  (c) the State Pension Credit Act 2002,
  (d) the Tax Credits Act 2002,
  (e) the Welfare Reform Act 2007,
  (f) the Welfare Reform Act 2012, or
  (g) any other enactment relating to social security.

16   Civil legal services provided in relation to compensation under the Criminal Injuries Compensation Scheme.

17   Civil legal services provided in relation to changing an individual's name.

18 (1) Civil legal services provided in relation to judicial review of an enactment, decision, act or omission.
  (2) In this paragraph 'judicial review' means–
  (a) the procedure on an application for judicial review (see section 31 of the Senior Courts Act 1981), but not including the procedure after the application is treated under rules of court as if it were not such an application, and
  (b) any procedure in which a court, tribunal or other person mentioned in Part 3 of this Schedule is required by an enactment to make a decision applying the principles that are applied by the court on an application for judicial review.

PART 3: ADVOCACY: EXCLUSION AND EXCEPTIONS

The services described in Part 1 of this Schedule do not include advocacy, except as follows–
  (a) those services include the types of advocacy listed in this Part of this Schedule, except to the extent that Part 1 of this Schedule provides otherwise;
  (b) those services include other types of advocacy to the extent that Part 1 of this Schedule so provides.

Exceptions: courts

1   Advocacy in proceedings in the Supreme Court.
2   Advocacy in proceedings in the Court of Appeal.
3   Advocacy in proceedings in the High Court.
4   Advocacy in proceedings in the Court of Protection to the extent that they concern–

(a) a person's right to life,

(b) a person's liberty or physical safety,

(c) a person's medical treatment (within the meaning of the Mental Health Act 1983),

(d) a person's capacity to marry, to enter into a civil partnership or to enter into sexual relations, or

(e) a person's right to family life.

5   Advocacy in proceedings in a county court.

5A   Advocacy in proceedings in the family court.

6   Advocacy in the following proceedings in the Crown Court–

(a) proceedings for the variation or discharge of an order under section 5 or 5A of the Protection from Harassment Act 1997,

(aa) proceedings on an appeal under section 10(1)(b) of the Crime and Disorder Act 1998 against the making of a parenting order where an injunction is granted under section 1 of the Anti-social Behaviour, Crime and Policing Act 2014,

(b) proceedings under the Proceeds of Crime Act 2002 in relation to matters listed in paragraph 40 of Part 1 of this Schedule'

(c) proceedings on an appeal under section 46B of the Policing and Crime Act 2009,

(d) proceedings on an appeal under section 15 of the Anti-social Behaviour, Crime and Policing Act 2014, and

(e) proceedings for the variation or discharge of an order under paragraph 1 of Schedule 2 to the Female Genital Mutilation Act 2003.

7   Advocacy in a magistrates' court that falls within the description of civil legal services in any of the following provisions of Part 1 of this Schedule–

(a) paragraph 1(1)(e),

(b) paragraph 1(2) so far as relating to paragraph (1)(1)(e), and

(c) paragraphs 11(2), 12, 13(1)(e), 15][, 17 (1)(a) and (b), 36 and 38.

8   Advocacy in the following proceedings in a magistrates' court–

(a) proceedings under section 47 of the National Assistance Act 1948,

(b) proceedings in relation to–

(i) bail under Schedule 2 to the Immigration Act 1971, or

(ii) arrest under Schedule 2 or 3 to that Act,

(c) proceedings for the variation or discharge of an order under section 5 or 5A of the Protection from Harassment Act 1997, and

(d) proceedings under the Proceeds of Crime Act 2002 in relation to matters listed in paragraph 40 of Part 1 of this Schedule, and

(e) proceedings for the variation or discharge of an order under paragraph 1 of Schedule 2 to the Female Genital Mutilation Act 2003.

Exceptions: tribunals

9   Advocacy in proceedings in the First-tier Tribunal under–

(a) the Mental Health Act 1983, or

(b) paragraph 5(2) of the Schedule to the Repatriation of Prisoners Act 1984.

10   Advocacy in proceedings in the Mental Health Review Tribunal for Wales.

11   Advocacy in proceedings in the First-tier Tribunal under–

(a) Schedule 2 to the Immigration Act 1971, or

(b) Part 5 of the Nationality, Immigration and Asylum Act 2002.

12   Advocacy in proceedings in the First-tier Tribunal under–

(a) section 40A of the British Nationality Act 1981, or

(b) regulation 26 of the Immigration (European Economic Area) Regulations 2006 (SI 2006/1003),

but only to the extent that the proceedings concern contravention of the Equality Act 2010.

13   Advocacy in the First-tier Tribunal that falls within the description of civil legal services in paragraph 28, 29, 32(1) or 32A(1) of Part 1 of this Schedule.

14   Advocacy in proceedings in the First-tier Tribunal under–

(a) section 4 or 4A of the Protection of Children Act 1999 (appeals and applications relating to list of barred from regulated activities with children or vulnerable adults),

(b) section 86 or 87 of the Care Standards Act 2000 (appeals and applications relating to list of persons unsuitable to work with vulnerable adults),

(c) section 32 of the Criminal Justice and Court Services Act 2000 (applications relating to disqualification orders), or

(d) section 144 of the Education Act 2002 (appeals and reviews relating to direction prohibiting person from teaching etc).

15   Advocacy in proceedings in the Upper Tribunal arising out of proceedings within any of paragraphs 9 to 14 of this Part of this Schedule.

16   Advocacy in proceedings in the Upper Tribunal under section 4 of the Safeguarding Vulnerable Groups Act 2006.

17   Advocacy in proceedings in the Upper Tribunal under section 11 of the Tribunals, Courts and Enforcement Act 2007 (appeals on a point of law) from decisions made by the First-tier Tribunal or the Special Educational Needs Tribunal for Wales in proceedings under–

(a) Part 4 of the Education Act 1996 (special educational needs),

(b) the Equality Act 2010, or

(c) Part 3 of the Children and Families Act 2014 (children and young people in England with special education needs or disabilities).

18   Advocacy in proceedings which are brought before the Upper Tribunal (wholly or primarily) to exercise its judicial review jurisdiction under section 15 of the Tribunals, Courts and Enforcement Act 2007.

19   Advocacy where judicial review applications are transferred to the Upper Tribunal from the High Court under section 31A of the Senior Courts Act 1981.

20   Advocacy in proceedings in the Employment Appeal Tribunal, but only to the extent that the proceedings concern contravention of the Equality Act 2010.

Other exceptions

21   Advocacy in proceedings in the Special Immigration Appeals Commission.

22   Advocacy in proceedings in the Proscribed Organisations Appeal Commission.

22A   Advocacy in proceedings before a District Judge (Magistrates' Courts) under paragraph 8 of Schedule 1 to the Counter-Terrorism and Security Act 2015.

23   Advocacy in legal proceedings before any person to whom a case is referred (in whole or in part) in any proceedings within any other paragraph of this Part of this Schedule.

24   Advocacy in bail proceedings before any court which are related to proceedings within any other paragraph of this Part of this Schedule.
25   Advocacy in proceedings before any person for the enforcement of a decision in proceedings within any other paragraph of this Part of this Schedule.

PART 4: INTERPRETATION

1   For the purposes of this Part of this Act, civil legal services are described in Part 1 of this Schedule if they are described in one of the paragraphs of that Part (other than in an exclusion), even if they are (expressly or impliedly) excluded from another paragraph of that Part.
2   References in this Schedule to an Act or instrument, or a provision of an Act or instrument–
(a) are references to the Act, instrument or provision as amended from time to time, and
(b) include the Act, instrument or provision as applied by another Act or instrument (with or without modifications).
3   References in this Schedule to services provided in relation to an act, omission or other matter of a particular description (however expressed) include services provided in relation to an act, omission or other matter alleged to be of that description.
4   References in this Schedule to services provided in relation to proceedings, orders and other matters include services provided when such proceedings, orders and matters are contemplated.
5 (1) Where a paragraph of Part 1 or 2 of this Schedule describes services that consist of or include services provided in relation to proceedings, the description is to be treated as including, in particular–
(a) services provided in relation to related bail proceedings,
(b) services provided in relation to preliminary or incidental proceedings,
(c) services provided in relation to a related appeal or reference to a court, tribunal or other person, and
(d) services provided in relation to the enforcement of decisions in the proceedings.
(2) Where a paragraph of Part 3 of this Schedule describes advocacy provided in relation to particular proceedings in or before a court, tribunal or other person, the description is to be treated as including services provided in relation to preliminary or incidental proceedings in or before the same court, tribunal or other person.
(3) Regulations may make provision specifying whether proceedings are or are not to be regarded as preliminary or incidental for the purposes of this paragraph.
6   For the purposes of this Schedule, regulations may make provision about–
(a) when services are provided in relation to a matter;
(b) when matters arise under a particular enactment;
(c) when proceedings are proceedings under a particular enactment;
(d) when proceedings are related to other proceedings.
7   In this Schedule 'enactment' includes–
(a) an enactment contained in subordinate legislation (within the meaning of the Interpretation Act 1978), and
(b) an enactment contained in, or in an instrument made under, an Act or Measure of the National Assembly for Wales.

Category definitions 2010[1]

Introduction

1. These are the Category Definitions 2010 as referred to in the 2010 Standard Civil Contract and 2010 Standard Crime Contract. Definitions of terms set out in those Contracts also apply to these Category Definitions.
2. In these Category Definitions:
   a. References to 'Legal Help' include Help at Court;
   b. References to 'proceedings in a Category' cover the provision of Legal Representation (including Controlled Legal Representation) in that Category.
3. Services within the Crime Category are automatically excluded from all Civil Categories, except for any overlap between Categories specified in this document.

Legal Aid, Sentencing and Punishment of Offenders Act 2012

4. The Legal Aid, Sentencing and Punishment of Offenders Act 2012 (hereafter referred to as 'the Act' in this document) sets out the matters for which civil and criminal legal services may be provided.
5. In some cases advice and assistance may only be provided to certain clients e.g. Clinical Negligence cases. In addition, there may be some instances where legal services may only be provided as a result of an application for exceptional funding (the parameters of which are described below). The Category Definitions show into which Category cases will fall but providers will need to satisfy themselves before undertaking work for any individual client that it is within the scope of the Act or that an application for exceptional funding has been approved.
6. Descriptions in this document of matters within scope of Part 1 of Schedule 1 to the Act are not exhaustive and should be read subject to the full provisions in Part 1 of Schedule 1 to the Act. For example, services described in Part 1 of Schedule 1 to the Act may be subject to exclusions in Parts 2 and 3 of Schedule 1 to the Act.

Crime

7. Representation in all proceedings defined as criminal proceedings under section 14 of the Legal Aid, Sentencing Punishment of Offenders Act 2012 and regulations made under that section.

---

1 Available at www.gov.uk/government/uploads/system/uploads/attachment_data/file/406159/2010-category-definitions-2015-anti-social-behaviour-amendments.pdf. Updated 1 April 2013.

8. All criminal Advice and Assistance as defined in section 13 and 15 of the Legal Aid, Sentencing Punishment of Offenders Act 2012 and regulations made under those sections.
9. All appeals in relation to criminal proceedings including applications for case stated arising out of criminal proceedings.
10. The Crime Category also includes Advice and Assistance and Representation in the following areas (as defined in the 2010 Standard Crime Contract):
    (a) Prison Law;
    (b) Associated Civil Work.
11. The undertaking of civil proceedings is excluded from the Crime Category unless falling within the definitions given above. Proceedings brought under the Environmental Protection Act 1990 for a statutory nuisance where the client is the complainant are excluded from the Crime Category as are proceedings under the Animal Welfare Act 2006 for the destruction of animals.

Overlaps between Categories

12. The Categories are drafted to ensure that the majority of cases clearly fall within one Category or another. However, there will be some cases which genuinely fall within more than one Category in which case you can choose in which Category to carry the case out. An example of this is in Mental Capacity Act cases that can fall within the Mental Health Category, but may fall equally within Community Care.
13. Another example of this is discrimination cases, which may be dealt with either within the Discrimination Category itself, or, where the underlying matter arises from an individual category such as Actions Against the Police etc, within that category.
14. Some cases will arise as the result of a number of different underlying issues, which may either be in scope or the subject of an exceptional funding application, and in those instances classification to a Category will depend upon the overall substance or predominant issue of the case when taken as a whole.

Exceptional Funding

15. Civil legal services that do not fall within the scope of Part 1 of Schedule 1 to the Act will fall to be funded under section 10 if the Director makes either: (i) an exceptional case determination (under section 10(2)(a) of the Act), or (ii) a wider public interest determination (under section 10(4)(b) of the Act).
16. Matters that are funded by virtue of a determination of the Director under section 10 of the Act will fall within the Category to which the primary problem or issue relates or, in the case of matters that are wholly unrelated to in-scope categories within the Miscellaneous Category.

Inquests

17. Legal Help in relation to an inquest under the Coroners Act 1988 into the death of a member of the client's family (paragraph 41 of Part 1 of Schedule 1 to the Act) will fall into the Category which relates to the underlying subject matter of the inquest. For example, Legal Help for an inquest where the client died in prison will be funded in the Actions Against the Police etc Category. Where an inquest does not fall within one of the Categories, it will be included in the Miscellaneous Category.
18. Where any relevant grant of exceptional funding is made (in accordance

with section 10 of the Act) for advocacy at an inquest, this will fall into the Category which relates to the underlying subject matter of the inquest, and where the inquest does not fall within any given Category, it will be included in the Miscellaneous Category.

Judicial Review and Public Law

19. Public law challenges to the acts, omissions or decision of public bodies (including under the Human Rights Act 1998), in particular challenges by way of judicial review (as described in paragraph 19 of Part 1 of Schedule 1 to the Act) and habeas corpus (as described in paragraph 20 of Part 1 of Schedule 1 to the Act) are covered by the Category in which the principal matter or proceedings appear or by the Category which relates to the underlying substance of the case (as referenced by the widest Category Definition incorporating excluded work). They are also covered by the Public Law Category.

20. If arising in respect of matters or proceedings within the Crime Category, these cases will also fall within the Crime Category.

21. Note that the fact that a Defendant is a Public Authority does not bring a case within the Public Law Category. For a case to constitute a public law challenge it must be determined according to judicial review principles (limited to paragraph 19 Part 1 of Schedule 1 to the Act). Claims for damages against Public Authorities, other than Human Rights Act claims, do not usually fall within Public Law but may come within Actions Against the Police etc. Claims under the Human Rights Act may well come within both Public Law and Actions Against the Police etc.

Minor Civil/Criminal Overlaps

22. Work falling within the Crime Category is generally excluded from any other Category, but there is one minor exception under the 2010 Standard Civil Contracts: Associated Civil Work as defined in the 2010 Standard Crime Contract, which includes judicial review proceedings or proceedings for habeas corpus, provided those proceedings arise from a Matter or Case within the Crime Category, and proceedings under the Proceeds of Crime Act 2002.

23. The exception in paragraph 22 can be carried out under the 2010 Standard Civil Contract as well as by criminal practitioners under the 2010 Standard Crime Contract.

Clinical Negligence Category

24. Legal Help and all proceedings in relation to a claim for damages in respect of clinical negligence which caused a neurological injury to an infant as a result of which they are now severely disabled (paragraph 23(1) of Part 1 of Schedule 1 to the Act), where the client is the infant. The clinical negligence must have occurred while the infant was in his or her mother's womb, or during or after their birth but before the end of the period specified in paragraph 23(2)(b) of Part 1 of Schedule 1 to the Act.

25. To the extent that any relevant grant of exceptional funding is made (in accordance with section 10 of the Act) this Category also includes Legal Help and all proceedings in relation to a claim for damages or a complaint to a relevant professional body in respect of an alleged breach of duty of care or trespass to the person committed in the course of the provision of clinical or medical

services (including dental or nursing services); or a claim for damages in respect of alleged professional negligence in the conduct of such a claim.

Mental Health Category

26. Legal Help and proceedings under paragraph 5 of Part 1 of Schedule 1 to the Act.
27. To the extent that any relevant grant of exceptional funding is made (in accordance with section 10 of the Act), this category also includes advocacy for matters arising under the Mental Capacity Act 2005 which are not listed in paragraph 4 of Part 3 of Schedule 1.

Community Care Category

28. Legal Help and related proceedings concerning the provision of community care services, as defined in paragraph 6 of Part 1 of Schedule 1 to the Act, and the provision of facilities for disabled persons, as set out in paragraph 7 of Part 1 of Schedule 1 to the Act. This includes legal services provided in relation to community care assessments, service provision decisions, and issues around the delivery of services, but excludes any matter falling within the Welfare Benefits Category or Clinical Negligence Category and proceedings before the First-Tier Tribunal (Mental Health).
29. Legal Help on issues arising under the Mental Capacity Act 2005, and advocacy in proceedings to extent set out at paragraph 4 of Part 3 of Schedule 1 to the Act, regarding a person's capacity, their best interests (welfare and/or medical treatment) and deprivation of liberty issues.
30. To the extent that any relevant grant of exceptional funding is made (in accordance with section 10 of the Act), this category also includes advocacy for matters arising under the Mental Capacity Act 2005 which are not listed at paragraph 4 of Part 3 of Schedule 1.

Action Against the Police Etc Category

31. Legal Help and proceedings in cases under the following paragraphs of Schedule 1 to the Act:
    (a) paragraph 3 (abuse of a child or a vulnerable adult)
    (b) paragraph 21 (abuse of position or power by a public authority)
    (c) paragraph 22 (significant breach of convention rights)
    (d) paragraph 39 (sexual offences)
    to the extent that the defendant is a public authority with the power to prosecute, detain, or imprison or the case is a claim for personal injury based on allegations of deliberate abuse of a person whilst in the care of a public authority or other institution.
32. Subject to the above, claims for damages for clinical negligence (including claims funded via exceptional funding) are included only if the clinical negligence forms part of a claim which includes another cause of action against a body or person with power to detain or imprison.
33. To the extent that any relevant grant of exceptional funding is made (in accordance with section 10 of the Act) this Category also includes Legal Help and all proceedings concerning any claim against a public authority with the power to prosecute, detain or imprison. To the extent that any relevant grant of exceptional funding is made (in accordance with section 10 of the Act) this Category also includes Legal Help and all proceedings concerning:

a. Applications to the Home Office under s. 133 of the Criminal Justice Act 1988 or the ex gratia scheme for compensation for wrongful conviction.
b. Claims under the Criminal Injuries Compensation Scheme, including any applications to the First-Tier Tribunal arising out of a matter falling within the category.
c. Claims for damages in respect of alleged professional negligence in the conduct of a matter included in the category.

Public Law Category

34. Legal Help and related proceedings concerning:
    a. the human rights of the client or a dependant of the client other than matters which fall within the definition of another Category;
    b. public law challenges to the acts, omissions or decisions of public bodies, including challenges by way of judicial review or habeas corpus.
35. To the extent that any relevant grant of exceptional funding is made (in accordance with section 10 of the Act) this Category also includes Legal Help and all proceedings concerning data protection and freedom of information issues.

Miscellaneous Work

36. The following matters or proceedings (including Legal Help in relation to those matters and related appeals) are likely to fall outside all Civil Categories:

Working with children and vulnerable adults

Legal Help and all proceedings in relation to:
(a) The inclusion of a person in a barred list or the removal of a person from a barred list (paragraph 4(1)(a) of Part 1 of Schedule 1 to the Act);
(b) A disqualification order under section 28, 29, or 29A of the Criminal Justice and Court Services Act 2000 (disqualification from working with children) (paragraph 4(1)(b) of Part 1 of Schedule 1 to the Act);
(c) A direction under section 142 of the Education Act 2002 (prohibition from teaching etc) (paragraph 4(1)(c) of Part 1 of Schedule 1 to the Act).

Protection from Harassment

Legal Help and all proceedings in relation to:
(a) An injunction under section 3 or 3A of the Protection from Harassment Act 1997 (paragraph 37(1)(a) of Part 1 of Schedule 1 to the Act);
(b) The variation or discharge of a restraining order under section 5 or 5A of that Act (paragraph 37(1)(b) of Part 1 of Schedule 1 to the Act),
(other than where they arise within the context of a Category).

Proceeds of Crime

Legal Help and proceedings in relation to:
(a) Restraint orders under section 41 of the Proceeds of Crime Act 2002 (POCA) including orders under section 41(7) of POCA (orders for ensuring that restraint order is effective) (paragraph 40(1)(a) of Part 1 of Schedule 1 to the Act);
(b) Orders under section 47M of POCA (detention of property) (paragraph 40(1)(b) of Part 1 of Schedule 1 to the Act);
(c) Directions under section 54(3) of POCA (distribution of funds in the hands of a receiver) (paragraph 40(1)(c) of Part 1 of Schedule 1 to the Act);

(d) Directions under section 62 of POCA (action to be taken by receiver) (paragraph 40(1)(d) of Part 1 of Schedule 1 to the Act);

(e) Orders under section 67A of POCA (realising property), including directions under section 67D of POCA (distribution of proceeds of realisation) (paragraph 40(1)(e) of Part 1 of Schedule 1 to the Act);

(f) Orders under section 72 or 73 of POCA (compensation) (paragraph 40(1)(f) of Part 1 of Schedule 1 to the Act);

(g) Applications under section 351 of POCA (discharge or variation of a production order or order to grant entry) (paragraph 40(1)(g) of Part 1 of Schedule 1 to the Act);

(h) Applications under section 362 of POCA (discharge or variation of disclosure order) (paragraph 40(1)(h) of Part 1 of Schedule 1 to the Act);

(i) Applications under section 369 of POCA (discharge or variation of customer information order) (paragraph 40(1)(i) of Part 1 of Schedule 1 to the Act);

(j) Applications under section 375 of POCA (discharge or variation of account monitoring orders) (paragraph 40(1)(j) of Part 1 of Schedule 1 to the Act).

Note that where a confiscation order has been made against a defendant under Part 2 of POCA, civil legal services provided to the defendant in relation to directions under section 54(3) or section 67D of POCA that relate to property recovered pursuant to the order (paragraph 40(3) of Part 1 of Schedule 1 to the Act) are not within scope of Part 1 of Schedule 1 to the Act.

Note that where a confiscation order has been made under Part 2 of POCA against a defendant and varied under section 29 of POCA, civil legal services provided in relation to an application by the defendant under section 73 of POCA are not within scope of Part 1 of Schedule 1 to the Act.

Environmental Pollution

Legal Help and all proceedings in relation to injunctions in respect of nuisance arising from pollution of the environment (paragraph 42(1) of Part 1 of Schedule 1 to the Act).

Sexual offences

Legal help and all proceedings in relation to a sexual offence where the client is the victim of the offence, including incitement to commit a sexual offence, encouraging or assisting a sexual offence which the person intended or believed would be committed, conspiracy to commit a sexual offence, and an attempt to commit a sexual offence (paragraph 39(1) and (4) of Part 1 of Schedule 1 to the Act). This will include conduct which would be a sexual offence under the Sexual Offences Act 2003 or under section 1 of the Protection of Children Act 1978 but for the fact the conduct occurred before those provisions were in force (paragraph 39(5) of Part 1 of Schedule 1 to the Act).

Victims of trafficking in human beings

Legal Help and all proceedings in connection with:

(a) a claim for damages arising in connection with the trafficking or exploitation of an individual who is a victim of human trafficking (paragraph 32(3) of Part 1 of Schedule 1 to the Act); and

(b) claims under employment law arising in connection with the exploitation of an individual who is a victim of human trafficking (paragraph 32(2) of Part 1 of Schedule 1 to the Act).

Injunction to prevent gang-related violence
Legal Help and all proceedings in relation to injunctions to prevent gang-related violence under Part 4 of the Policing and Crime Act 2009 (paragraph 38(1) of Part 1 of Schedule 1 to the Act).

Abuse of child or vulnerable adult
Legal Help and all proceedings in relation to abuse of an individual that took place at a time when the individual was a child or vulnerable adult (paragraph 3(1) of Part 1 of Schedule 1 to the Act), excluding any matter that falls within the Actions Against the Police etc. or any other Category

Anti-social behaviour injunctions
Legal Help and proceedings in relation to an injunction in respect of alleged anti-social behaviour arising under Part 1 of the Anti-social Behaviour, Crime and Policing Act 2014 and related parenting orders (para-graph 36(1) of Part 1 of Schedule 1 and paragraph 1(1)(e) of Part 1 of Schedule 1).

APPENDIX E

Category definitions 2013[1]

Introduction

1. These are the Category Definitions 2013 as referred to in the 2013 Standard Civil Contract. Definitions of terms set out in those Contracts also apply to these Category Definitions.
2. In these Category Definitions:
    i) References to 'Legal Help' include Help at Court and in the Family Category only, Family Help (Lower) and Help with Family Mediation.
    ii) References to 'proceedings in a Category' cover the provision of Legal Representation (including Controlled Legal Representation) in that Category and, in the Family Category only, Family Help (Higher).
3. Services within the Crime Category are automatically excluded from all Civil Categories, except for any overlap between Categories specified in this document.

Legal Aid, Sentencing and Punishment of Offenders Act 2012

4. The Legal Aid, Sentencing and Punishment of Offenders Act 2012 (hereafter referred to as 'the Act' in this document) sets out the matters for which civil legal services may be provided. In some cases advice and assistance may only be provided to certain clients eg in private law children cases where the client must show evidence of having suffered domestic violence. In addition, there may be some instances where legal services may only be provided as a result of an application for exceptional funding (the parameters of which are described below). The category definitions show into which category cases will fall but providers will need to satisfy themselves before undertaking work for any individual client that it is within the scope of the Act or that an application for exceptional funding has been approved.
5. Descriptions in this document of matters within scope of Part 1 of Schedule 1 to the Act are not exhaustive and should be read subject to the full provisions in Part 1 of Schedule 1 to the Act. For example, services described in Part 1 of Schedule 1 to the Act may be subject to exclusions in Parts 2 and 3 of Schedule 1 to the Act.

Overlaps between Categories

6. The Categories are drafted to ensure that the majority of cases clearly fall within one Category or another. For example, mortgage arrears possession

---

1   Available at www.gov.uk/government/uploads/system/uploads/attachment_data/file/441385/category-defenitions-2013.pdf. Updated July 2015.

cases fall within the debt category and are excluded from the housing category. However, there will be some cases which genuinely fall within more than one Category in which case you can choose in which Category to carry the case out.

7. An example of this is in discrimination cases, which may be dealt with either within the discrimination category itself or, where the underlying matter arises from an individual category such as education, within that category.

8. Some cases will arise as the result of a number of different underlying issues, which may either be in scope or the subject of an exceptional funding application, and in those instances classification to a Category will depend upon the overall substance or predominant issue of the case when taken as a whole.

Exceptional Funding

9. Civil legal services that do not fall within the scope of Part 1 of Schedule 1 to the Act will fall to be funded under section 10 if the Director makes either: (i) an exceptional case determination (under section 10(2)(a) of the Act), or (ii) a wider public interest determination (under section 10(4)(b) of the Act).

10. Matters that are funded by virtue of a determination of the Director under section 10 of the Act will fall within the category to which the primary problem or issue relates or, in the case of matters that are wholly unrelated to in-scope categories within the Miscellaneous category.

Inquests

11. Legal Help in relation to an inquest under the Coroners Act 1988 into the death of a member of the client's family (paragraph 41 of Part 1 of Schedule 1 to the Act) will fall into the Category which relates to the underlying subject matter of the inquest. For example, Legal Help for an inquest where the client died in prison will be funded in the Actions Against the Police etc Category. Where an inquest does not fall within one of the Categories, it will be carried out as Miscellaneous Work.

12. Where any relevant grant of exceptional funding is made (in accordance with section 10 of the Act) for advocacy at an inquest, this will fall into the Category which relates to the underlying subject matter of the inquest, and where the inquest does not fall within any given Category, it will be included be carried out as Miscellaneous Work.

Judicial Review and Public Law

13. Public law challenges to the acts, omissions or decision of public bodies (including under the Human Rights Act 1998), in particular challenges by way of judicial review (as described in paragraph 19 of Part 1 of Schedule 1 to the Act)) and habeas corpus (as described in paragraph 20 of Part 1 of Schedule 1 to the Act) are covered by the category in which the principal matter or proceedings appear or by the category which relates to the underlying substance of the case (as referenced by the widest category definition incorporating excluded work). They are also covered by the Public Law Category.

14. If arising in respect of matters or proceedings within the Crime Category, these cases will also fall within the Crime Category.

15. Note that the fact that a Defendant is a Public Authority does not bring a case within the Public Law Category. For a case to constitute a public law

challenge it must be determined according to judicial review principles (limited to paragraph 19 Part 1 of Schedule 1 to the Act). Claims for damages against Public Authorities, other than Human Rights Act claims, do not usually fall within Public Law but may come within Actions Against the Police etc. Claims under the Human Rights Act may well come within both Public Law and Actions Against the Police etc.

Minor Civil/Criminal Overlaps
16. Work falling within the Crime Category is generally excluded from any other category, but there are some minor exceptions:
    (a) Enforcement proceedings in the magistrates court arising out of the breach of an order of that court made in family proceedings where there is a risk of imprisonment also fall within the Family Category;
    (b) Civil proceedings in the magistrates' court arising out of the breach of a financial order of that court where there is a risk of imprisonment also fall within the Debt Category;
    (c) Associated CLS Work as defined in the 2010 Standard Crime Contract including civil proceedings under the Proceeds of Crime Act 2002;
    (d) Proceedings against a child for a Sexual Harm Prevention Order and any associated Parenting Order, and for a Parenting Order made on the conviction of a child where the parent cannot be reasonably represented by the child's solicitor also fall within the Family Category.
17. These exceptions can be carried out under the 2013 Standard Civil Contract as well as by criminal practitioners under the 2010 Standard Crime Contract.

CATEGORY DEFINITIONS
Debt
18. Legal Help and all proceedings in relation to:
    (a) Court orders for sale of an individual's home (under paragraph 33(1)(a) of Part 1 of Schedule 1 to the Act);
    (b) Court orders for possession of an individual's home arising out of failure to make payment due under a mortgage (under paragraph 33(1)(a) of Part 1 of Schedule 1 to the Act). Possession of the home arising out of any other matter fall within the housing category and cannot be undertaken in this category.
    (c) A bankruptcy order against the individual under Part 9 of the Insolvency Act 1986 where the estate includes the individual's home and where the petition for bankruptcy was not presented by the client, including in relation to a statutory demand under Part 9 of that Act (paragraph 33(2) of Part 1 to Schedule 1 to the Act).
19. To the extent that any relevant grant of exceptional funding is made (in accordance with section 10 of the Act), this category includes Legal Help and all proceedings:
    (a) For the payment of monies due or the enforcement of orders in such proceedings (excluding any matter which falls within the housing category); and
    (b) Arising out of personal insolvency, including bankruptcy, administration, Debt Relief representation or IVA proceedings, but excluding representation in proceedings against parties in default of a fine or other

order in criminal proceedings in the magistrates' court who are at risk of imprisonment.

Discrimination

20. Legal Help and proceedings in relation to:
   (a) Contravention of the Equality Act 2010 (under paragraph 43(1) of Part 1 of Schedule 1 to the Act);
   (b) Contravention of a previous discrimination enactment (as defined in paragraph 43(3) of Part 1 of Schedule 1 to the Act), namely;
      i)   The Equal Pay Act 1970;
      ii) The Sex Discrimination Act 1976;
      iii) The Race Relations Act 1976;
      iv) The Disability Discrimination Act 1995;
      v)   The Employment Equality (Religion or Belief) Regulations 2003 (SI No 1660);
      vi) The Employment Equality (Sexual Orientation) Regulations 2003 (SI No 1661);
      vii) The Equality Act 2006;
      viii) The Employment Equality (Age) Regulations 2006 (SI No 1031);
      ix) The Equality Act (Sexual Orientation) Regulations 2007 (SI No 1263).
21. For the avoidance of doubt, the following matters/proceedings are included in the category:
   (a) Legal Help for a claim in the Employment Tribunal in so far as it relates to a contravention of the Equality Act 2010 or a previous discrimination enactment;
   (b) Legal Help and Representation on an appeal to the Employment Appeal Tribunal, and onward appeals to the higher courts in so far as it relates to contravention of the Equality Act 2010 or a previous discrimination enactment.

Education (Special Educational Needs)

22. Legal Help and all proceedings in relation to:
   (a) matters arising under Part 4 of the Education Act 1996 (Special Educational Needs) (under paragraph 2(1)(a) of Part 1 of Schedule 1 to the Act);
   (b) assessments relating to learning difficulties under sections 139A and 140 of the Learning and Skills Act 2000 (under paragraph 2(1)(b) of Part 1 of Schedule 1 to the Act); and
   (c) any other matter within the scope of Part 1 of Schedule 1 to the Act where the primary problem or issue relates to the provision of, or failure to provide, education or funding for education.
23. For the avoidance of doubt, the following are included in the category:
   (a) Legal Help and all proceedings in relation to a contravention of Part 6 of the Equality Act 2010 (Education); and
   (b) Legal Help and all proceedings in relation to a contravention of a previous discrimination enactment as far as the matter concerns the provision or funding of education.
24. Proceedings in relation to judicial review of an enactment, decision, act or omission as far as this concerns the provision or funding of education. To the extent that exceptional funding is granted (in accordance with section 10 of the Act) this category includes Legal Help and proceedings in relation to

any matter where the primary problem or issue relates to the provision of or failure to provide education or funding for education.

Family

25. Legal Help on matters and proceedings which arise out of family relationships as prescribed in Part 1 of Schedule 1 to the Act and in Regulations under the Act including proceedings in which the welfare of children is determined.

26. Included with the family category are Legal Help and all proceedings under the following legislation:
    (a) Orders under section 25 of the Children Act 1989 ('the 1989 Act') (secure accommodation);
    (b) Orders under Parts 4 and Part 5 of the 1989 Act (care and supervision and the protection of children);
    (c) Approval by a court under paragraph 19 of Schedule 2 to the 1989 Act (arrangements to assist children to live abroad);
    (d) Proceedings under sections 8 and 11 of the Crime and Disorder Act 1998 for a Child Safety Order or for a Parenting Order made in proceedings for a Child Safety Order or a Parenting Order made on the conviction of a child;
    (e) Applications under the Adoption and Children Act 2002;
    (f) Orders under Part 4 of the Family Law Act 1996;
    (g) Forced marriage protection orders under Part 4A of the Family Law Act 1996;
    (h) Proceedings under ss 3, 3A or 5 of the Protection from Harassment Act 1997 arising out of a family relationship;
    (i) Proceedings under the Child Abduction and Custody Act 1985;
    (j) The inherent jurisdiction of the High Court in relation to children;
    (k) Proceedings under Part 1 of the Maintenance Orders (Reciprocal Enforcement) Act 1972 relating to a maintenance order made outside the United Kingdom;
    (l) Proceedings under the 2003 Brussels Regulation (No 2001/2003);
    (m) Proceedings under the EU Maintenance Regulation (No 4/2009);
    (n) Proceedings relating to the Convention on the International Recovery of Child Support and other forms of Family Maintenance concluded at The Hague on 23 November 2007;
    (o) Female genital mutilation protection orders under the Female Genital Mutilation Act 2003.

27. In addition, the proceedings below are also included in the family category. These proceedings are only within the scope of Part 1 of Schedule 1 of the Act where the client meets certain criteria eg the client is a child, a victim of domestic violence, or where the proceedings involve the unlawful removal of children or the protection of children. However, the matters also fall generally within the family category for the purposes of applications for exceptional funding (made in accordance with section 10 of the Act). These are:
    (a) Parts 1 and 2 of the Children Act 1989;
    (b) Proceedings under the Family Law Act 1986;
    (c) The Matrimonial Causes Act 1973;
    (d) The Inheritance (Provision for Family and Dependants) Act 1975;
    (e) Section 17 of the Married Women's Property Act 1882;

(f) Proceedings under section 14 of the Trust of Land and Appointment of Trustees Act 1996 which arise out of a family relationship;

(g) Section 53 and Schedule 7 to the Family Law Act 1996;

(h) Maintenance Orders (Facilities for Enforcement) Act 1920;

(i) Proceedings under the Maintenance Orders Act 1950 and 1958;

(j) Domestic Proceedings and Magistrates' Courts Act 1978;

(k) Part 3 of the Matrimonial and Family Proceedings Act 1984;

(l) Chapters 2 and 3 of Part 2 of the Civil Partnership Act 2004;

(m) Schedule 1 to the Domicile and Matrimonial Proceedings Act 1973 and corresponding provision in relation to civil partnerships.

(n) Applications for a parental order under the Human Fertilisation and Embryology Act 2008.

(See paragraphs 1, 9, 10, 11, and 14 to 18 of Part 1 of Schedule 1 to the Act).

Housing

28. Legal Help and proceedings in relation to:

(a) Possession of an individual's home (other than mortgage possession) (paragraph 33(1)(a) of Part 1 of Schedule 1 to the Act). Possession arising from mortgage arrears and court orders for sale of the home fall within the debt category and cannot be undertaken in this category.

(b) Eviction from an individual's home of the individual or others, including unlawful eviction and planning eviction matters (paragraph 33(1)(b) of Part 1 of Schedule 1);

(c) The provision of accommodation and assistance under Parts 6 and 7 of the Housing Act 1996 for an individual who is homeless or threatened with homelessness (paragraph 34 of Part 1 of Schedule 1 to the Act). References to Part 7 of the Housing Act 1996 (or to provisions within Part 7 of the Housing Act 1996) include reference to Part 2 of the Housing (Wales) Act 2014 (or equivalent provisions within Part 2 of the Housing (Wales) Act 2014);

(d) The provision of accommodation by way of community care services as specified in paragraph 6 of Part 1 of Schedule 1 to the Act, in relation to an individual who is homeless or threatened with homelessness;

(e) Housing disrepair matters described in paragraph 35 of Part 1 of Schedule 1 to the Act, namely removing or reducing a serious risk of harm to the health or safety of the individual or relevant family member where the risk arises from a deficiency in the individual's rented or leased home and the legal services are provided with a view to securing that the landlord makes arrangements to remove or reduce the risk. This includes Legal Help for applications under section 82 of the Environmental Protection Act 1990 for a statutory nuisance, where the application falls within the terms of paragraph 35 of Part 1 of Schedule 1.

(f) Applications to vary or discharge an injunction under section 153A of the Housing Act 1996;

(g) Injunctions under the Protection from Harassment Act 1997 arising from matters within paragraphs 1 and 2 of this section (paragraph 37 of Part 1 of Schedule 1 to the Act); and

(h) The powers of the Secretary of State to provide or arrange to provide accommodation under section 4 or 95 of the Immigration and Asylum

Act 1999 (accommodation for persons temporarily admitted and asylum seekers) and section 17 of the Nationality, Immigration and Asylum Act 2002 (support for destitute asylum seekers) (paragraph 31 of Part of Schedule 1 to the Act).

29. To the extent that any relevant grant of exceptional funding is made (in accordance with section 10 of the Act) this category also includes any matters which concern the possession, status, terms of occupation, repair, improvement, eviction from, quiet enjoyment of, or payment of rent or other charges for premises (including vehicles and sites they occupy) which are occupied as a residence, including the rights of leaseholders under the terms of their lease or under any statutory provision (including enfranchisement). Cases including allocation, transfers and the provision of sites for occupation are also included.

Immigration and Asylum

30. Legal Help on matters and all proceedings in relation to:
    (a) Immigration-related detention powers referred to in paragraph 25(1) of Part 1 of Schedule 1 to the Act;
    (b) Temporary admission to the UK under provisions referred to in paragraph 26(1) of Part 1 of Schedule 1 to the Act;
    (c) Restrictions imposed on an individual under the provisions referred to in paragraph 27(1) of Part 1 of Schedule 1 to the Act;
    (d) An application for indefinite leave by a victim of domestic violence as described in paragraph 28 of Part 1 of Schedule 1 to the Act;
    (e) A residence card application by a victim of domestic violence as described in paragraph 29 of Part 1 of Schedule 1 to the Act;
    (f) Rights to enter and to remain in the United Kingdom under the provisions referred to in paragraph 30(1) of Part 1 of Schedule 1 to the Act;
    (g) An application by a victim of human trafficking for leave to enter or remain in the United Kingdom (paragraph 32(1) of Part 1 of Schedule 1 to the Act);
    (h) A Terrorism Prevention and Investigation Measure notice as described in paragraph 45 of Part 1 of Schedule 1 to the Act.
    For the avoidance of doubt it should be noted that services in relation to an application for judicial review are subject to paragraph 19 of Part 1 of Schedule 1 to the Act

31. Legal help and all proceedings before the Special Immigration Appeals Commission as described in paragraph 24 of Part 1 of Schedule 1 to the Act.

32. To the extent that any relevant grant of exceptional funding is made (in accordance with section 10 of the Act) this category includes Legal Help and all proceedings in relation to any matter where the primary problem or issue is an immigration or asylum matter.

Welfare Benefits 2013 (the Welfare Benefits Category of Law does not apply to the 2013 Standard Civil Contract)

33. Legal Help in relation to appeals on a point of law in the Upper Tribunal, Court of Appeal and Supreme Court for all welfare benefits (including housing benefit, war pensions, state pensions and other similar benefits under a social security enactment, the Vaccine Damage Payments Act 1979 or Part 4 of the Child Maintenance and Other Payments Act 2008).

34. Legal Help in relation to appeal on a point of law relating to a council tax reduction scheme from the Valuation Tribunal England and the Valuation Tribunal Wales to the High Court, Court of Appeal and Supreme Court.[2]
35. Legal representation for appeals to the Court of Appeal and the Supreme Court on a point of law in relation to all welfare benefits (including housing benefit, war pensions, state pensions and other similar benefits under a social security enactment, the Vaccine Damage Payments Act 1979 and Part 4 of the Child Maintenance and Other Payments Act 2008) and appeals on a point of law relating to a [council tax reduction scheme] to the Court of Appeal and Supreme Court.[3]
36. To the extent that any grant of exceptional funding is made this category includes:
    (a) Legal Help in relation to all welfare benefits (including [council tax reduction scheme appeals], housing benefit, war pensions, state pensions and vaccine damage payments or similar payments), and in relation to proceedings before any welfare benefit review or appeal body;
    (b) any subsequent or related proceedings before a court.

Miscellaneous work

37. The following matters or proceedings (including Legal Help in relation to those matters and related appeals) are likely to fall outside all Civil Categories:

Working with children and vulnerable adults
Legal Help and all proceedings in relation to
(a) The inclusion of a person in a barred list or the removal of a person from a barred list (paragraph 4(1)(a) of Part 1 of Schedule 1 to the Act);
(b) A disqualification order under section 28, 29, or 29A of the Criminal Justice and Court Services Act 2000 (disqualification from working with children) (paragraph 4(1)(b) of Part 1 of Schedule 1 to the Act);
(c) A direction under section 142 of the Education Act 2002 (prohibition from teaching etc) (paragraph 4(1)(c) of Part 1 of Schedule 1 to the Act).

Protection from Harassment
Legal Help and all proceedings in relation to:
(a) An injunction under section 3 or 3A of the Protection from Harassment Act 1997 (paragraph 37(1)(a) of Part 1 of Schedule 1 to the Act);
(b) The variation or discharge of a restraining order under section 5 or 5A of that Act (paragraph 37(1)(b) of Part 1 of Schedule 1 to the Act),
(other than where they arise within the context of a Category).

Proceeds of Crime
Legal Help and proceedings in relation to:
(a) Restraint orders under section 41 of the Proceeds of Crime Act 2002 (POCA) including orders under section 41(7) of POCA (orders for

---

2   This is contained in the Legal Aid, Sentencing and Punishment of Offenders Act 2012 (Amendment of Schedule 1) Order 2013 which is subject to Parliamentary approval.
3   This is contained in the Legal Aid, Sentencing and Punishment of Offenders Act 2012 (Amendment of Schedule 1) Order 2013 which is subject to Parliamentary approval.

ensuring that restraint order is effective) (paragraph 40(1)(a) of Part 1 of Schedule 1 to the Act);

(b) Orders under section 47M of POCA (detention of property) (paragraph 40(1)(b) of Part 1 of Schedule 1 to the Act);

(c) Directions under section 54(3) of POCA (distribution of funds in the hands of a receiver) (paragraph 40(1)(c) of Part 1 of Schedule 1 to the Act);

(d) Directions under section 62 of POCA (action to be taken by receiver) (paragraph 40(1)(d) of Part 1 of Schedule 1 to the Act);

(e) Orders under section 67A of POCA (realising property), including directions under section 67D of POCA (distribution of proceeds of realisation) (paragraph 40(1)(e) of Part 1 of Schedule 1 to the Act);

(f) Orders under section 72 or 73 of POCA (compensation) (paragraph 40(1)(f) of Part 1 of Schedule 1 to the Act);

(g) Applications under section 351 of POCA (discharge or variation of a production order or order to grant entry) (paragraph 40(1)(g) of Part 1 of Schedule 1 to the Act);

(h) Applications under section 362 of POCA (discharge or variation of disclosure order) (paragraph 40(1)(h) of Part 1 of Schedule 1 to the Act);

(i) Applications under section 369 of POCA (discharge or variation of customer information order) (paragraph 40(1)(i) of Part 1 of Schedule 1 to the Act);

(j) Applications under section 375 of POCA (discharge or variation of account monitoring orders) (paragraph 40(1)(j) of Part 1 of Schedule 1 to the Act).

Note that where a confiscation order has been made against a defendant under Part 2 of POCA, civil legal services provided to the defendant in relation to directions under section 54(3) or section 67D of POCA that relate to property recovered pursuant to the order (paragraph 40(3) of Part 1 of Schedule 1 to the Act) are not within scope of Part 1 of Schedule 1 to the Act.

Note that where a confiscation order has been made under Part 2 of POCA against a defendant and varied under section 29 of POCA, civil legal services provided in relation to an application by the defendant under section 73 of POCA are not within scope of Part 1 of Schedule 1 to the Act.

Environmental Pollution
Legal Help and all proceedings in relation to injunctions in respect of nuisance arising from pollution of the environment (paragraph 42(1) of Part 1 of Schedule 1 to the Act).

Sexual offences
Legal help and all proceedings in relation to a sexual offence where the client is the victim of the offence, including incitement to commit a sexual offence, encouraging or assisting a sexual offence which the person intended or believed would be committed, conspiracy to commit a sexual offence, and an attempt to commit a sexual offence (paragraph 39(1) and (4) of Part 1 of Schedule 1 to the Act). This will include conduct which would be a sexual offence under the Sexual Offences Act 2003 or under section 1 of the Protection of Children Act 1978 but for the fact the conduct occurred before those provisions were in force (paragraph 39(5) of Part 1 of Schedule 1 to the Act).

Victims of trafficking in human beings

Legal Help and all proceedings in connection with:

(a) a claim for damages arising in connection with the trafficking or exploit-ation of an individual who is a victim of human trafficking (paragraph 32(3) of Part 1 of Schedule 1 to the Act); and

(b) claims under employment law arising in connection with the exploitation of an individual who is a victim of human trafficking (paragraph 32(2) of Part 1 of Schedule 1 to the Act).

Injunction to prevent gang-related violence

Legal Help and all proceedings in relation to injunctions to prevent gang-related violence under Part 4 of the Policing and Crime Act 2009 (paragraph 38(1) of Part 1 of Schedule 1 to the Act).

Abuse of child or vulnerable adult

Legal Help and all proceedings in relation to abuse of an individual that took place at a time when the individual was a child or vulnerable adult (paragraph 3(1) of Part 1 of Schedule 1 to the Act), excluding any matter that falls within the Actions Against the Police etc. or any other Category.

Anti-social behaviour injunctions

Legal Help and proceedings in relation to an injunction in respect of alleged anti-social behaviour arising under Part 1 of the Anti-social Behaviour, Crime and Policing Act 2014 and related parenting orders (paragraph 36(1) of Part 1 of Schedule 1 and paragraph 1(1)(e) of Part 1 of Schedule 1).

Category definitions 2014[1]

Introduction

1. These are the Category Definitions 2014 as referred to in the 2014 Standard Civil Contract. Definitions of terms set out in those Contracts also apply to these Category Definitions.

2. In these Category Definitions:
   i) References to 'Legal Help' include Help at Court and in the Family Category only, Family Help (Lower) and Help with Family Mediation.
   ii) References to 'proceedings in a Category' cover the provision of Legal Representation (including Controlled Legal Representation) in that Category and, in the Family Category only, Family Help (Higher).

3. Services within the Crime Category are automatically excluded from all Civil Categories, except for any overlap between Categories specified in this document.

Legal Aid, Sentencing and Punishment of Offenders Act 2012

4. The Legal Aid, Sentencing and Punishment of Offenders Act 2012 (hereafter referred to as "the Act" in this document) sets out the matters for which civil legal services may be provided. In some cases advice and assistance may only be provided to certain clients eg in private law children cases where the client must show evidence of having suffered domestic violence. In addition, there may be some instances where legal services may only be provided as a result of an application for exceptional funding (the parameters of which are described below). The Category Definitions show into which Category cases will fall but providers will need to satisfy themselves before undertaking work for any individual client that it is within the scope of the Act or that an application for exceptional funding has been approved.

5. Descriptions in this document of matters within scope of Part 1 of Schedule 1 to the Act are not exhaustive and should be read subject to the full provisions in Part 1 of Schedule 1 to the Act. For example, services described in Part 1 of Schedule 1 to the Act may be subject to exclusions in Parts 2 and 3 of Schedule 1 to the Act.

Overlaps between Categories

6. The Categories are drafted to ensure that the majority of cases clearly fall

---

1 Available at www.gov.uk/government/uploads/system/attachment_data/file/406173/2014-category-definitions-2015-anti-social-behaviour-act-amendments.pdf. February 2014.

within one Category or another. For example, mortgage arrears possession cases fall within the debt category and are excluded from the housing category. However, there will be some cases which genuinely fall within more than one Category in which case you can choose in which Category to carry the case out.

7. An example of this is in discrimination cases, which may be dealt with either within the discrimination category itself or, where the underlying matter arises from an individual category such as education, within that category.

8. Some cases will arise as the result of a number of different underlying issues, which may either be in scope or the subject of an exceptional funding application, and in those instances classification to a Category will depend upon the overall substance or predominant issue of the case when taken as a whole.

Exceptional Funding

9. Civil legal services that do not fall within the scope of Part 1 of Schedule 1 to the Act will fall to be funded under section 10 if the Director makes either: (i) an exceptional case determination (under section 10(2)(a) of the Act), or (ii) a wider public interest determination (under section 10(4)(b) of the Act).

10. Matters that are funded by virtue of a determination of the Director under section 10 of the Act will fall within the Category to which the primary problem or issue relates or, in the case of matters that are wholly unrelated to in-scope categories within Miscellaneous Work.

Inquests

11. Legal Help in relation to an inquest under the Coroners Act 1988 into the death of a member of the client's family (paragraph 41 of Part 1 of Schedule 1 to the Act) will fall into the Category which relates to the underlying subject matter of the inquest. For example, Legal Help for an inquest where the client died in prison will be funded in the Actions Against the Police etc Category. Where an inquest does not fall within one of the Categories, it will be carried out as Miscellaneous Work.

12. Where any relevant grant of exceptional funding is made (in accordance with section 10 of the Act) for advocacy at an inquest, this will fall into the Category which relates to the underlying subject matter of the inquest, and where the inquest does not fall within any given Category, it will be included be carried out as Miscellaneous Work.

Judicial Review and Public Law

13. Public law challenges to the acts, omissions or decision of public bodies (including under the Human Rights Act 1998), in particular challenges by way of judicial review (as described in paragraph 19 of Part 1 of Schedule 1 to the Act) and habeas corpus (as described in paragraph 20 of Part 1 of Schedule 1 to the Act) are covered by the Category in which the principal matter or proceedings appear or by the Category which relates to the underlying substance of the case (as referenced by the widest Category Definition incorporating excluded work). They are also covered by the Public Law Category.

14. If arising in respect of matters or proceedings within the Crime Category, these cases will also fall within the Crime Category.

15. Note that the fact that a Defendant is a Public Authority does not bring a case within the Public Law Category. For a case to constitute a public law

challenge it must be determined according to judicial review principles (limited to paragraph 19 Part 1 of Schedule 1 to the Act). Claims for damages against Public Authorities, other than Human Rights Act claims, do not usually fall within Public Law but may come within Actions Against the Police etc. Claims under the Human Rights Act may well come within both Public Law and Actions Against the Police etc.

Minor Civil/Criminal Overlaps

16. Work falling within the Crime Category is generally excluded from any other category, but there are some minor exceptions:
    (a) Enforcement proceedings in the magistrates court arising out of the breach of an order of that court made in family proceedings where there is a risk of imprisonment also fall within the Family Category;
    (b) Civil proceedings in the magistrates' court arising out of the breach of a financial order of that court where there is a risk of imprisonment also fall within the Debt Category;
    (c) Associated CLS Work as defined in the 2010 Standard Crime Contract" including civil proceedings under the Proceeds of Crime Act 2002;
    (d) Proceedings against a child for an Anti-Social Behaviour Order or Sex Offender Order and any associated Parenting Order, and for a Parenting Order made on the conviction of a child where the parent cannot be reasonably represented by the child's solicitor also fall within the Family Category;
    (e) Proceedings for an Anti-Social Behaviour Order sought by a local authority against a tenant or a person living with him or her, or by way of an appeal against such an order to the Crown Court, also fall within the Housing Category.
17. These exceptions can be carried out under the 2013 Standard Civil Contract as well as by criminal practitioners under the 2010 Standard Crime Contract.

CATEGORY DEFINITIONS
Community Care

18. Legal Help and related proceedings concerning the provision of community care services, as defined in paragraph 6 of Part 1 of Schedule 1 to the Act, the provision of facilities for disabled persons as set out in Paragraph 7 of Part 1 of Schedule 1 to the Act and the inherent jurisdiction of the high court in relation to vulnerable adults, as set out in paragraph 9 of Part 1 of Schedule 1 to the Act. This includes legal services provided in relation to community care assessments, service provision decisions, and issues around the delivery of services, but excludes any matter falling within the Welfare Benefits Category or Clinical Negligence Category and proceedings before the First-Tier Tribunal (Mental Health).
19. Legal Help on issues arising under the Mental Capacity Act 2005 and advocacy in proceedings to extent set out at paragraph 4 of Part 3 of Schedule 1 to the Act, regarding a person's capacity, their best interests (welfare and/or medical treatment) and deprivation of liberty issues.
20. To the extent that any relevant grant of exceptional funding is made (in accordance with section 10 of the Act), this category also includes advocacy for matters arising under the Mental Capacity Act 2005 which are not listed at

paragraph 4 of Part 3 of Schedule1 and the public law obligations of other health authorities.

Mental Health Category

21. Legal Help and proceedings under paragraph 5 of Part 1 of Schedule 1 to the Act.
22. The inherent jurisdiction of the High Court in relation to vulnerable adults, as set out Paragraph 9 of Part 1 of Schedule 1 to the Act.
23. To the extent that any relevant grant of exceptional funding is made (in accordance with section 10 of the Act), this category also includes advocacy for matters arising under the Mental Capacity Act 2005 which are not listed in paragraph 4 of Part 3 of Schedule 1.

Miscellaneous Work

24. The following matters or proceedings (including Legal Help in relation to those matters and related appeals) are likely to fall outside all Civil Categories:

Working with children and vulnerable adults

Legal Help and all proceedings in relation to:

(a) The inclusion of a person in a barred list or the removal of a person from a barred list (paragraph 4(1)(a) of Part 1 of Schedule 1 to the Act);
(b) A disqualification order under section 28, 29, or 29A of the Criminal Justice and Court Services Act 2000 (disqualification from working with children) (paragraph 4(1)(b) of Part 1 of Schedule 1 to the Act);
(c) A direction under section 142 of the Education Act 2002 (prohibition from teaching etc) (paragraph 4(1)(c) of Part 1 of Schedule 1 to the Act).

Protection from Harassment

Legal Help and all proceedings in relation to:

(a) An injunction under section 3 or 3A of the Protection from Harassment Act 1997 (paragraph 37(1)(a) of Part 1 of Schedule 1 to the Act);
(b) The variation or discharge of a restraining order under section 5 or 5A of that Act (paragraph 37(1)(b) of Part 1 of Schedule 1 to the Act),
(other than where they arise within the context of a Category).

Proceeds of Crime

Legal Help and proceedings in relation to:

(a) Restraint orders under section 41 of the Proceeds of Crime Act 2002 (POCA) including orders under section 41(7) of POCA (orders for ensuring that restraint order is effective) (paragraph 40(1)(a) of Part 1 of Schedule 1 to the Act);
(b) Orders under section 47M of POCA (detention of property) (paragraph 40(1)(b) of Part 1 of Schedule 1 to the Act);
(c) Directions under section 54(3) of POCA (distribution of funds in the hands of a receiver) (paragraph 40(1)(c) of Part 1 of Schedule 1 to the Act);
(d) Directions under section 62 of POCA (action to be taken by receiver) (paragraph 40(1)(d) of Part 1 of Schedule 1 to the Act);
(e) Orders under section 67A of POCA (realising property), including direc-

tions under section 67D of POCA (distribution of proceeds of realisation) (paragraph 40(1)(e) of Part 1 of Schedule 1 to the Act);

(f) Orders under section 72 or 73 of POCA (compensation) (paragraph 40(1)(f) of Part 1 of Schedule 1 to the Act);

(g) Applications under section 351 of POCA (discharge or variation of a production order or order to grant entry) (paragraph 40(1)(g) of Part 1 of Schedule 1 to the Act);

(h) Applications under section 362 of POCA (discharge or variation of disclosure order) (paragraph 40(1)(h) of Part 1 of Schedule 1 to the Act);

(i) Applications under section 369 of POCA (discharge or variation of customer information order) (paragraph 40(1)(i) of Part 1 of Schedule 1 to the Act);

(j) Applications under section 375 of POCA (discharge or variation of account monitoring orders) (paragraph 40(1)(j) of Part 1 of Schedule 1 to the Act).

Note that where a confiscation order has been made against a defendant under Part 2 of POCA, civil legal services provided to the defendant in relation to directions under section 54(3) or section 67D of POCA that relate to property recovered pursuant to the order (paragraph 40(3) of Part 1 of Schedule 1 to the Act) are not within scope of Part 1 of Schedule 1 to the Act.

Note that where a confiscation order has been made under Part 2 of POCA against a defendant and varied under section 29 of POCA, civil legal services provided in relation to an application by the defendant under section 73 of POCA are not within scope of Part 1 of Schedule 1 to the Act.

Environmental Pollution
Legal Help and all proceedings in relation to injunctions in respect of nuisance arising from pollution of the environment (paragraph 42(1) of Part 1 of Schedule 1 to the Act).

Sexual offences
Legal help and all proceedings in relation to a sexual offence where the client is the victim of the offence, including incitement to commit a sexual offence, encouraging or assisting a sexual offence which the person intended or believed would be committed, conspiracy to commit a sexual offence, and an attempt to commit a sexual offence (paragraph 39(1) and (4) of Part 1 of Schedule 1 to the Act). This will include conduct which would be a sexual offence under the Sexual Offences Act 2003 or under section 1 of the Protection of Children Act 1978 but for the fact the conduct occurred before those provisions were in force (paragraph 39(5) of Part 1 of Schedule 1 to the Act).

Victims of trafficking in human beings
Legal Help and all proceedings in connection with:

(a) a claim for damages arising in connection with the trafficking or exploitation of an individual who is a victim of human trafficking (paragraph 32(3) of Part 1 of Schedule 1 to the Act); and

(b) claims under employment law arising in connection with the exploitation of an individual who is a victim of human trafficking (paragraph 32(2) of Part 1 of Schedule 1 to the Act).

Injunction to prevent gang-related violence

Legal Help and all proceedings in relation to injunctions to prevent gang-related violence under Part 4 of the Policing and Crime Act 2009 (paragraph 38(1) of Part 1 of Schedule 1 to the Act).

Abuse of child or vulnerable adult

Legal Help and all proceedings in relation to abuse of an individual that took place at a time when the individual was a child or vulnerable adult (paragraph 3(1) of Part 1 of Schedule 1 to the Act), excluding any matter that falls within the Actions Against the Police etc. or any other Category.

Anti-social behaviour injunctions

Legal Help and proceedings in relation to an injunction in respect of alleged anti-social behaviour arising under Part 1 of the Anti-social Behaviour, Crime and Policing Act 2014 and related parenting orders (paragraph 36(1) of Part 1 of Schedule 1 and paragraph 1(1)(e) of Part 1 of Schedule 1).

Category definitions 2015[1]

Introduction

1. These are the Category Definitions 2015 as referred to in the 2015 Standard Civil Contract. Definitions of terms set out in those Contracts also apply to these Category Definitions.
2. In these Category Definitions:
   a. References to 'Legal Help' include Help at Court;
   b. References to 'proceedings in a Category' cover the provision of Legal Representation (including Controlled Legal Representation) in that Category.
3. Services within the Crime Category are automatically excluded from all Civil Categories, except for any overlap between Categories specified in this document.

Legal Aid, Sentencing and Punishment of Offenders Act 2012

4. The Legal Aid, Sentencing and Punishment of Offenders Act 2012 (hereafter referred to as 'the Act' in this document) sets out the matters for which civil and criminal legal services may be provided.
5. In some cases advice and assistance may only be provided to certain clients e.g. Clinical Negligence cases. In addition, there may be some instances where legal services may only be provided as a result of an application for exceptional funding (the parameters of which are described below). The Category Definitions show into which Category cases will fall but providers will need to satisfy themselves before undertaking work for any individual client that it is within the scope of the Act or that an application for exceptional funding has been approved.
6. Descriptions in this document of matters within scope of Part 1 of Schedule 1 to the Act are not exhaustive and should be read subject to the full provisions in Part 1 of Schedule 1 to the Act. For example, services described in Part 1 of Schedule 1 to the Act may be subject to exclusions in Parts 2 and 3 of Schedule 1 to the Act.

Overlaps between Categories

7. The Categories are drafted to ensure that the majority of cases clearly fall within one Category or another. However, there will be some cases which genuinely fall within more than one Category in which case you can choose

---

1 The 2015 category definitions are in draft form, available at: www.gov.uk/government/publications/standard-civil-contract-2015. July 2015.

in which Category to carry the case out. An example of this is in Mental Capacity Act cases that can fall within the Mental Health Category, but may fall equally within Community Care.

8. Another example of this is discrimination cases, which may be dealt with either within the Discrimination Category itself, or, where the underlying matter arises from an individual category such as Actions Against the Police etc, within that category.

9. Some cases will arise as the result of a number of different underlying issues, which may either be in scope or the subject of an exceptional funding application, and in those instances classification to a Category will depend upon the overall substance or predominant issue of the case when taken as a whole.

Exceptional Funding

10. Civil legal services that do not fall within the scope of Part 1 of Schedule 1 to the Act will fall to be funded under section 10 if the Director makes either: (i) an exceptional case determination (under section 10(2)(a) of the Act), or (ii) a wider public interest determination (under section 10(4)(b) of the Act).

11. Matters that are funded by virtue of a determination of the Director under section 10 of the Act will fall within the Category to which the primary problem or issue relates or, in the case of matters that are wholly unrelated to in-scope categories within the Miscellaneous Category.

Inquests

12. Legal Help in relation to an inquest under the Coroners Act 1988 into the death of a member of the client's family (paragraph 41 of Part 1 of Schedule 1 to the Act) will fall into the Category which relates to the underlying subject matter of the inquest. For example, Legal Help for an inquest where the client died in prison will be funded in the Actions Against the Police etc Category. Where an inquest does not fall within one of the Categories, it will be included in the Miscellaneous Category.

13. Where any relevant grant of exceptional funding is made (in accordance with section 10 of the Act) for advocacy at an inquest, this will fall into the Category which relates to the underlying subject matter of the inquest, and where the inquest does not fall within any given Category, it will be included in the Miscellaneous Category.

Judicial Review and Public Law

14. Public law challenges to the acts, omissions or decision of public bodies (including under the Human Rights Act 1998), in particular challenges by way of judicial review (as described in paragraph 19 of Part 1 of Schedule 1 to the Act) and habeas corpus (as described in paragraph 20 of Part 1 of Schedule 1 to the Act) are covered by the Category in which the principal matter or proceedings appear or by the Category which relates to the underlying substance of the case (as referenced by the widest Category Definition incorporating excluded work). They are also covered by the Public Law Category.

15. If arising in respect of matters or proceedings within the Crime Category, these cases will also fall within the Crime Category.

16. Note that the fact that a Defendant is a Public Authority does not bring a case within the Public Law Category. For a case to constitute a public law challenge it must be determined according to judicial review principles (limited

to paragraph 19 Part 1 of Schedule 1 to the Act). Claims for damages against Public Authorities, other than Human Rights Act claims, do not usually fall within Public Law but may come within Actions Against the Police etc. Claims under the Human Rights Act may well come within both Public Law and Actions Against the Police etc.

Minor Civil/Criminal Overlaps

17. Work falling within the Crime Category is generally excluded from any other Category, but there is one minor exception under the 2015 Standard Civil Contract: Associated Civil Work as defined in the 2015 Standard Crime Contract, which includes judicial review proceedings or proceedings for habeas corpus, provided those proceedings arise from a Matter or Case within the Crime Category, and proceedings under the Proceeds of Crime Act 2002.
18. The exception in paragraph 22 can be carried out under the 2015 Standard Civil Contract as well as by criminal practitioners under the 2015 Standard Crime Contract.

Clinical Negligence Category

19. Legal Help and all proceedings in relation to a claim for damages in respect of clinical negligence which caused a neurological injury to an infant as a result of which they are now severely disabled (paragraph 23(1) of Part 1 of Schedule 1 to the Act), where the client is the infant. The clinical negligence must have occurred while the infant was in his or her mother's womb, or during or after their birth but before the end of the period specified in paragraph 23(2)(b) of Part 1 of Schedule 1 to the Act.
20. To the extent that any relevant grant of exceptional funding is made (in accordance with section 10 of the Act) this Category also includes Legal Help and all proceedings in relation to a claim for damages or a complaint to a relevant professional body in respect of an alleged breach of duty of care or trespass to the person committed in the course of the provision of clinical or medical services (including dental or nursing services); or a claim for damages in respect of alleged professional negligence in the conduct of such a claim.

Action Against the Police Etc Category

21. Legal Help and proceedings in cases under the following paragraphs of Schedule 1 to the Act:
    (a) paragraph 3 (abuse of a child or a vulnerable adult)
    (b) paragraph 21 (abuse of position or power by a public authority)
    (c) paragraph 22 (significant breach of convention rights)
    (d) paragraph 39 (sexual offences)
    to the extent that the defendant is a public authority with the power to prosecute, detain, or imprison or the case is a claim for personal injury based on allegations of deliberate abuse of a person whilst in the care of a public authority or other institution.
22. Subject to the above, claims for damages for clinical negligence (including claims funded via exceptional funding) are included only if the clinical negligence forms part of a claim which includes another cause of action against a body or person with power to detain or imprison.
23. To the extent that any relevant grant of exceptional funding is made (in accordance with section 10 of the Act) this Category also includes Legal Help

and all proceedings concerning any claim against a public authority with the power to prosecute, detain or imprison. To the extent that any relevant grant of exceptional funding is made (in accordance with section 10 of the Act) this Category also includes Legal Help and all proceedings concerning:

a. Applications to the Home Office under s. 133 of the Criminal Justice Act 1988 or the ex gratia scheme for compensation for wrongful conviction.

b. Claims under the Criminal Injuries Compensation Scheme, including any applications to the First-Tier Tribunal arising out of a matter falling within the category.

c. Claims for damages in respect of alleged professional negligence in the conduct of a matter included in the category.

Public Law Category

24. Legal Help and related proceedings concerning:

a. the human rights of the client or a dependant of the client other than matters which fall within the definition of another Category;

b. public law challenges to the acts, omissions or decisions of public bodies, including challenges by way of judicial review or habeas corpus.

25. To the extent that any relevant grant of exceptional funding is made (in accordance with section 10 of the Act) this Category also includes Legal Help and all proceedings concerning data protection and freedom of information issues.

Miscellaneous Work

26. The following matters or proceedings (including Legal Help in relation to those matters and related appeals) are likely to fall outside all Civil Categories:

Working with children and vulnerable adults

Legal Help and all proceedings in relation to:

(a) The inclusion of a person in a barred list or the removal of a person from a barred list (paragraph 4(1)(a) of Part 1 of Schedule 1 to the Act);

(b) A disqualification order under section 28, 29, or 29A of the Criminal Justice and Court Services Act 2000 (disqualification from working with children) (paragraph 4(1)(b) of Part 1 of Schedule 1 to the Act);

(c) A direction under section 142 of the Education Act 2002 (prohibition from teaching etc) (paragraph 4(1)(c) of Part 1 of Schedule 1 to the Act).

Protection from Harassment

Legal Help and all proceedings in relation to:

(a) An injunction under section 3 or 3A of the Protection from Harassment Act 1997 (paragraph 37(1)(a) of Part 1 of Schedule 1 to the Act);

(b) The variation or discharge of a restraining order under section 5 or 5A of that Act (paragraph 37(1)(b) of Part 1 of Schedule 1 to the Act),

(other than where they arise within the context of a Category).

Proceeds of Crime

Legal Help and proceedings in relation to:

(a) Restraint orders under section 41 of the Proceeds of Crime Act 2002 (POCA) including orders under section 41(7) of POCA (orders for ensuring that restraint order is effective) (paragraph 40(1)(a) of Part 1 of Schedule 1 to the Act);

(b) Orders under section 47M of POCA (detention of property) (paragraph 40(1)(b) of Part 1 of Schedule 1 to the Act);

(c) Directions under section 54(3) of POCA (distribution of funds in the hands of a receiver) (paragraph 40(1)(c) of Part 1 of Schedule 1 to the Act);

(d) Directions under section 62 of POCA (action to be taken by receiver) (paragraph 40(1)(d) of Part 1 of Schedule 1 to the Act);

(e) Orders under section 67A of POCA (realising property), including directions under section 67D of POCA (distribution of proceeds of realisation) (paragraph 40(1)(e) of Part 1 of Schedule 1 to the Act);

(f) Orders under section 72 or 73 of POCA (compensation) (paragraph 40(1)(f) of Part 1 of Schedule 1 to the Act);

(g) Applications under section 351 of POCA (discharge or variation of a production order or order to grant entry) (paragraph 40(1)(g) of Part 1 of Schedule 1 to the Act);

(h) Applications under section 362 of POCA (discharge or variation of disclosure order) (paragraph 40(1)(h) of Part 1 of Schedule 1 to the Act);

(i) Applications under section 369 of POCA (discharge or variation of customer information order) (paragraph 40(1)(i) of Part 1 of Schedule 1 to the Act);

(j) Applications under section 375 of POCA (discharge or variation of account monitoring orders) (paragraph 40(1)(j) of Part 1 of Schedule 1 to the Act).

Note that where a confiscation order has been made against a defendant under Part 2 of POCA, civil legal services provided to the defendant in relation to directions under section 54(3) or section 67D of POCA that relate to property recovered pursuant to the order (paragraph 40(3) of Part 1 of Schedule 1 to the Act) are not within scope of Part 1 of Schedule 1 to the Act.

Note that where a confiscation order has been made under Part 2 of POCA against a defendant and varied under section 29 of POCA, civil legal services provided in relation to an application by the defendant under section 73 of POCA are not within scope of Part 1 of Schedule 1 to the Act.

Environmental Pollution
Legal Help and all proceedings in relation to injunctions in respect of nuisance arising from pollution of the environment (paragraph 42(1) of Part 1 of Schedule 1 to the Act).

Sexual offences
Legal help and all proceedings in relation to a sexual offence where the client is the victim of the offence, including incitement to commit a sexual offence, encouraging or assisting a sexual offence which the person intended or believed would be committed, conspiracy to commit a sexual offence, and an attempt to commit a sexual offence (paragraph 39(1) and (4) of Part 1 of Schedule 1 to the Act). This will include conduct which would be a sexual offence under the Sexual Offences Act 2003 or under section 1 of the Protection of Children Act 1978 but for the fact the conduct occurred before those provisions were in force (paragraph 39(5) of Part 1 of Schedule 1 to the Act).

Victims of trafficking in human beings

Legal Help and all proceedings in connection with:

(a) a claim for damages arising in connection with the trafficking or exploitation of an individual who is a victim of human trafficking (paragraph 32(3) of Part 1 of Schedule 1 to the Act); and

(b) claims under employment law arising in connection with the exploitation of an individual who is a victim of human trafficking (paragraph 32(2) of Part 1 of Schedule 1 to the Act).

Injunction to prevent gang-related violence

Legal Help and all proceedings in relation to injunctions to prevent gang-related violence under Part 4 of the Policing and Crime Act 2009 (paragraph 38(1) of Part 1 of Schedule 1 to the Act).

Abuse of child or vulnerable adult

Legal Help and all proceedings in relation to abuse of an individual that took place at a time when the individual was a child or vulnerable adult (paragraph 3(1) of Part 1 of Schedule 1 to the Act), excluding any matter that falls within the Actions Against the Police etc. or any other Category.

Anti-social behaviour injunctions

Legal Help and proceedings in relation to an injunction in respect of alleged anti-social behaviour arising under Part 1 of the Anti-social Behaviour, Crime and Policing Act 2014 and related parenting orders (paragraph 36(1) of Part 1 of Schedule 1 and paragraph 1(1)(e) of Part 1 of Schedule 1).

Civil costs: what you can claim for

A quick reference guide

This is a summary of the LAA's Costs Assessment Guidance applicable to the 2013 and 2014 contracts, in respect of the most common queries raised by caseworkers. Paragraph numbers are from the Guidance, which can be found on the website at www.gov.uk/funding-and-costs-assessment-for-civil-and-crime-matters.

Admin work

Opening and setting up files, maintaining time costing records and other time spent in complying with the requirements of the Unified Contract are not chargeable (para 2.1). Letters confirming appointments etc with no legal content are administrative (para 2.19).

Advocacy

Normally (and where claimable), this is time on your feet before a court or tribunal; but note that in the Family Advocacy Scheme advocacy also includes travel to court, waiting time and attendance at advocates' meetings. The Costs Assessment Guidance states that where you do your own advocacy, it is reasonable to claim for preparing a brief to yourself (para 2.39).

Agents

They stand in your shoes and their costs are part of your profit costs. You cannot claim their fees as a disbursement.

Attendance

This is the conventional legal costing term for interviewing someone face-to-face, or speaking to them on the telephone. The presumption is that work will be done as quickly as possible, which can seem strange to some people in the not-for-profit sector who have been trained to let the client take their time.

All claims for attendance must be justified in an attendance note. The longer the time claimed, the more detail is expected.

You may be able to justify more than one caseworker being present; but this would be exceptional, for example, in a complex case, where different aspects of it have been split between different people (para 2.36). In a complex case you may be able to justify the time of two caseworkers in the same category of law where you would be able to justify claiming legal research (see Legal research for more details). You may be able to justify the time of two caseworkers in different categories of law if a difficult or unusual point arises and it would be reasonable. Supervision is overhead and is not chargeable (para 2.37).

Bundles

Fee earners should identify the documents for the master bundle and draft the index to the bundle. Making up or copying of additional bundles is not chargeable. Where the bundles are above average size it is reasonable for fee earners to check that copies have been properly collated and reproduced (para 2.17). See also chapter 16 for bundle payments under the Family Advocacy Scheme.

Congestion charge

This is claimable where incurred exclusively in relation to the case but not where your journey to work would have meant you incurred the charge anyway (para 3.20).

Consideration of documents

See Perusal.

Disbursements

Must be reasonably incurred and reasonable in amount (para 3.1). Sign language interpreters' costs can be claimed but must be accounted for separately as they are excluded from the statutory charge (para 3.6). See also chapter 13 for information about guideline rates and amounts for experts' fees.

Distant clients

No extra costs can be claimed that arise because you are in a location that is distant from your client, where it would be reasonable for the client to instruct someone closer (para 2.46) (see also Travel time).

Drafting documents

As a guideline, 6–12 minutes' preparation time would be expected per page of a straightforward document, but more complex documents will take longer (para 2.16). It is reasonable to re-examine the core documents to consider their effect on the case. However, the degree to which this will be justified depends entirely on the complexity of the issues (para 2.9).

Emails

See Letters.

Faxes

These are treated as letters; but you cannot claim for sending a copy by post as well as the fax. See Letters for more detail.

Form completion

Generally not claimable; but there are exceptions (paras 2.58–2.63):
- CW1 where the client is eligible;
- CLR in Immigration cases;
- application forms for certificates (30 minutes is standard but may be exceeded where justifiable);
- applications for amendments to certificates;
- POA claims;

- applications to increase financial limitations on certificates;
- Claim 1 and Claim 2 (12–18 minutes);
- Claim 4 (12 minutes).

Completion of forms on behalf of clients is only claimable where legal assistance is justified, eg sections of the Disability Living Allowance form.

Legal research

Not claimable unless on a novel, developing or unusual point of law or the impact of new legislation to the particular case (para 2.5). However, it may still be reasonable for time for checking on the application of established law or procedural rules to individual circumstances to be claimed, provided the reasons are recorded (para 2.6).

Letters in

You cannot claim for reading routine letters received in any Legal Help matters (para 2.23). You can only charge for reading routine letters received in Family proceedings (para 2.23). You can charge for reading non-routine letters received.

Letters out

These are either 'routine' and claimed at the item rate, because they are stand-ard letters or take up to six minutes to write, or they are preparation rate letters, because they take longer to write than six minutes (para 2.18).

You cannot charge for administrative letters, eg confirming an appointment, with no legal content. You cannot charge for multiple letters sent to the same client or party on the same day, unless there is a good reason that justifies it. You cannot charge for a letter correcting your own mistake (para 2.19).

Office overheads

The following are office overheads and not claimable: costs of postage, stationery, faxes, scanning, typing and the actual cost of telephone calls and most photocopying, but see below for exceptional costs (para 2.1). Supervision is an overhead (para 2.37).

Overnight expenses

These can only be claimed in exceptional circumstances, where it would be unreasonable to travel the distance there and back and carry out whatever was required in one day (para 3.18).

Perusal

This is also known as consideration of documents. An initial brief perusal of all the documents to identify which documents are relevant is reasonable. Later detailed consideration of documents may also be reasonable (para 2.8). As a very rough guide it takes approximately two minutes per A4 page to read the most simple document. Time taken will depend on the quality and layout of the document, eg whether handwritten or typed, single- or double-spaced, large or small font, etc. More complex documents may take a longer (para 2.12).

Photocopying

Photocopying in-house is generally an overhead expense, but if there are 'unusual circumstances', or documents are unusually numerous (as a rule of thumb, 500 pages), you may claim the lowest commercial photocopying rate as a disbursement, even when carried out in-house (para 3.38).

Preparation
Includes drafting of documents, consideration of documents and evidence provided by the client or other parties, and general consideration of strategy, evidence needed and evidence to be put forward and whether to make or accept offers to settle a case, and 'thinking time' (para 2.7).

Reviewing files
You are expected to be familiar with your own files, so you would need to justify any claim for reading a file, eg prior to seeing a client when you had not dealt with the file for some time (para 2.39). You cannot charge for reviewing a file when it is reallocated from one caseworker to another, unless this is due to unforeseeable circumstances, eg the client needs to give urgent instructions and the first caseworker is not available (para 2.41).

Telephone calls
These are either 'routine' and claimed at the item rate, because they take up to six minutes, or they are attendance rate calls, because they take longer than six minutes (para 2.26). You can claim for an unsuccessful call; but if you make repeated calls to the same number, you would have to justify it. You can claim a routine call for leaving a message on an answering machine. If you are put 'on hold', after the first six minutes on the call, you can charge the waiting time at the waiting rate (para 2.27). However, bear in mind that it may be more efficient to write a letter.

Texts
These are treated as telephone calls. See Telephone calls for more detail.

Transferring files between fee earners
See Reviewing files.

Travel time
The general rule is that if the round trip travel time is five hours or more, it is usually more reasonable to instruct an agent than to go yourself. However, in some circumstances it may be reasonable to go (para 2.44):
(a) court applications, other than those that are straightforward;
(b) conference with counsel;
(c) interviewing a witness where the fee earner will wish to test the witnesses credibility for him or herself;
(d) because of the specialised nature of the case, the fee earner's close personal understanding of the matter or the nature of the client,
(e) where there is a lack of suitably qualified agents in the area concerned. The reason for making the journey must be recorded on the file.

Travel time to clients
Usually, the client should come to you; but if the client is housebound, in hospital or detention, it may be reasonable for you to travel to the client (para 2.47).

Travelling expenses (caseworkers')

Caseworkers' travelling expenses can be claimed where the journey was necessary and the most appropriate form of transport used (para 3.11). The LAA considers that public transport should normally be used; but time saved will be considered as well as travel fares or mileage. Taxis may be justified, eg when transporting heavy bundles. Local travelling expenses to court cannot be claimed (eg within a ten-mile radius) unless public transport is known to be poor. Documentary evidence must support claims over £10 (except mileage) (para 3.17).

Travelling expenses (clients')

You can pay clients' expenses to attend court and claim them back from the LAA as a disbursement (documentary evidence is required as for caseworkers). Prior authority can be sought for a clients' travelling expenses to an expert where the client cannot afford them and a report is essential for the proper conduct of proceedings (para 3.26).

Waiting

You should not normally arrive at court more than 30 minutes before a hearing. If you have to, perhaps due to transport timetables, you should record the reason on file (para 2.53). You cannot claim waiting time during the lunchtime adjournment.

Waiting on the telephone

If you are out 'on hold', after the first six minutes on the call, you can charge the waiting time at the waiting rate (para 2.27).

Criminal costs: what you can claim for

A quick reference guide

This is a summary of the LAA's Costs Assessment Guidance for criminal defence work, in respect of the most common queries raised by caseworkers. Paragraph numbers are from the Criminal Bills Assessment Manual, April 2013 edition.

Admin work

Opening and setting up files, taxes, postage, stationery, typing, faxing, and telephone bills are not chargeable (para 3.1.1). Letters confirming appointments etc with no legal content are administrative (para 3.8.17).

Advocacy

Normally (and where claimable), this is time on your feet before a court, including time while the bench (or jury) has retired (para 6.8.38), as long as the solicitor has not been released from the court.

Agents

They stand in your shoes and their costs are part of your profit costs. You cannot claim their fees as a disbursement (para 3.6.3).

Attendance

All claims for attendance must be justified in an attendance note. The longer the time claimed, the more detail is expected. Time spent dictating an attendance note may be allowed as long as it is reasonable (or typing it up if the fee-earner is self servicing) (3.3.3)

You may be able to justify more than one caseworker being present; but this would be exceptional, for example, in a complex case, where different aspects of it have been split between different people (para 3.5.5).

Congestion charge

This is claimable where incurred exclusively in relation to the case but not where your journey to work would have meant you incurred the charge anyway (para 3.9.30).

Consideration of documents

See Perusal.

Disbursements

Must be reasonably incurred and reasonable in amount (para 4.1.1). See section 4 CBAM for disbursements generally.

Distant clients

No extra costs can be claimed that arise because you are in a location that is distant from your client, where it would be reasonable for the client to instruct someone closer (para 3.9.7) (see also Travel time).

Drafting documents

As a guideline, 6–12 minutes' preparation time would be expected per page of a straightforward document, but more complex documents will take longer (para 3.8.8).

Emails

See Letters.

Faxes

These are treated as letters; but you cannot claim for sending a copy by post as well as the fax. See Letters for more detail.

Legal research

Not claimable unless on a novel, developing or unusual point of law or the impact of new legislation to the particular case (para 3.4.1). However, it may still be reasonable for time for checking on the application of established law or procedural rules to individual circumstances to be claimed, provided the reasons are recorded case (para 3.4.1).

Letters in

You cannot claim for reading routine letters received (para 3.8.10). You can charge for non-routine items at the preparation rate (para 3.8.8). Letters sent will not automatically allowed. It has to be reasonable to send them (para 3.8.2).

Letters out

These are either 'routine' and claimed at the item rate, because they are standard letters or are the equivalent of the item rate (para 3.8.1), or they are preparation rate letters, because they take longer than six minutes, although confusingly the guidance suggests that timed letters should take more than 12 minutes (para 3.8.8).

You cannot charge for administrative letters, eg confirming an appointment, with no legal content. You cannot charge for multiple letters sent on the same day, unless there is a good reason that justifies it. You cannot charge for a letter correcting your own mistake (para 3.8.3).

Office overheads

The following are office overheads and not claimable: costs of postage, stationery, faxes, scanning, typing and the actual cost of telephone calls and most photocopying, but see below for exceptional costs (para 3.1). Supervision is an overhead.

Overnight expenses

These can only be claimed in exceptional circumstances, where it would be unreasonable to travel the distance there and back and carry out whatever was required in one day (para 3.9.28).

Perusal

This is also known as consideration of documents. An initial brief perusal of all the documents to identify which documents are relevant is reasonable. Later detailed consideration of documents may also be reasonable. As a very rough guide it takes approximately two minutes per A4 page to read the most simple document. Time taken will depend on the quality and layout of the document eg whether handwritten or typed, single- or double-spaced, large or small font etc. More complex documents may take a longer (para 3.3.10).

Photocopying

Photocopying in-house is generally an overhead expense but if there 'unusual circumstances' or documents are unusually numerous (as a rule of thumb 500 pages), you may claim the lowest commercial photocopying rate as a disbursement, even when carried out in-house (para 7.14.1).

Preparation

Includes drafting of documents, consideration of documents and evidence provided by the client or other parties, and general consideration of strategy, evidence needed and evidence to be put forward and 'thinking time'.

Reviewing files

You are expected to be familiar with your own files, so you would need to justify any claim for reading a file, eg prior to seeing a client when you had not dealt with the file for some time (para 6.9.1).

Telephone calls

These are either 'routine' and claimed at the item rate, because they take up to six minutes, or they are attendance rate calls, because they take longer than the item charge (again, as for letters CBAM says more than 12 minutes) (para 3.8.12). You cannot claim for an unsuccessful call, ie where it is not answered and no message is left. You can claim a routine call for leaving a message on an answering machine (para 3.8.19).

Texts

These are treated as telephone calls. See Telephone calls for more detail.

Transferring files between fee earners

See Reviewing files.

Travel time

Travel and waiting may only be claimed in respect of standard fees and non-standard fees. No travel or waiting may be claimed in respect of revised standard fees or revised non-standard fees (para 3.6.5). A useful rule of thumb is that if the round trip travel time is more than two hours, it would not be reasonable and you should instruct a local agent or the client should instruct someone more local to them. In some circumstances you may be able to justify greater travelling times (para 3.9.7), eg

a) There is no other more local contractor available.

b) The client's problem is so specialised that, in the solicitor's reasonable view, there is no more local contractor with the expertise to deal with the case.

c) The solicitor has significant previous knowledge of the case or dealings with the client in relation to the issues raised by the case so as to justify renewed involvement even though the client is at a distance.

d) The local court or the remand centre where the client is located is more than one hour's travelling time away.

The reason for making the journey must be recorded on the file.

Travel cost is not included in the calculation to determine whether a case is an Escape Fee Case. However, once a case has become eligible for payment at hourly rates, payment for travel time is claimable (para 12.12.3).

Travel time to clients

Usually, the client should come to you; but if the client is housebound, in hospital or detention, it may be reasonable for you to travel to the client (para 3.9.13).

Travelling expenses (caseworkers)

Caseworkers' travelling expenses can be claimed where the journey was necessary and the most appropriate form of transport used (see para 3.9 generally). The LAA takes as a starting point that public transport should normally be used; but time saved will be considered as well as travel fares or mileage. Travel expenses will not normally accepted if the Court is within walking distance, although issues such as the need to transport bulky files or sensitivity of documentation may be taken into consideration. Taxis may be justified, eg for an out-of-hours attendance at a police station. Documentary evidence must support claims, eg ticket or print out from the internet (except mileage) over £20.00 (para 3.9.21).

Travelling expenses (clients)

You can pay clients' expenses to attend court and claim them back from the LAA as a disbursement using eform CRM4 submitted electronically (documentary evidence is required as for caseworkers) (para 7.3.3). Prior authority can be sought for a clients' travelling expenses to an expert where the client cannot afford them and a report is essential for the proper conduct of proceedings (7.3.2).

Waiting

If at court, you cannot claim waiting time during the lunchtime adjournment (para 3.9.24).

Standard monthly payment reconciliation process[1]

1 Introduction

The Legal Aid Agency (LAA) offers providers a choice as to how they are paid for Civil (Legal Help) and Crime (Lower) work. Providers can be paid a Standard Monthly Payment (SMP) or can opt for a Variable Monthly Payment (VMP).

2 Standard Monthly Payments

The Standard Monthly Payment reconciliation process implements the Protocol set out in the Deed of Settlement as agreed between the Ministry of Justice and the Law Society in 2008. The information in this section provides a guide on how the LAA applies the process.

The aim is to reconcile accounts (claims versus payments) to a 100% balanced position.[2] The contract position percentage is calculated using the following formula:

$$\frac{\text{Claims in last 12 months}}{\text{Total payments aligned to last claim} - (\text{Total Claims} - \text{Claims in last 12 months})} \times 100\%$$

Where an account is within the 90%–110% band no action will be taken to change the SMP. Where an account is below 90% (meaning payments exceed claims by a variance of more than 10%) we will take action to adjust the SMP with the aim of recovering the balance over a period of 6 months to return the contract position to 100%. Likewise where an account is in excess of 110% we will adjust the payment upwards with the aim of bringing the account back to 100% in 6 months.

The new SMP is calculated by taking the average claim value over the preceding 6 months and adding or subtracting 1/6th of the current balance (whether overpaid or underpaid at the time of the review).

Although this initial action is intended to return the account to 100% balanced, it may not have the desired effect due to fluctuations in claims. Prior to the setting of the 6th payment following the initial review, if the account is still outside of the 90%-110% band further action will be taken to clear the

---

1 Contract Payments (Legal Help and Crime Lower Work) March 2014. Available at: www.gov.uk/government/uploads/system/uploads/attachment_data/file/340267/LAA-monthly-payments-protocol.pdf.

2 Criminal legal aid providers who have requested a pull forward of 7.5% (of previous 12 months claims) will have a balance target of 92.5% instead of 100% (of previous 12 months claims) for the purposes of setting future payment levels.

remaining balance over a 3-month period. This is achieved by setting the SMP to the 6 month average claim figure with a series of 3 credits or debits (depending on whether the account is underpaid or overpaid).

If at any time the contract position is less than 50% or in excess of 150% action will be taken to clear the balance over a 3-month period (as above).

Any proposed change to your SMP will be communicated one month in advance of the date of the first SMP at the revised amount.

Every account will be reconciled in accordance with this process, but there may be exceptional circumstances where it is appropriate to vary the action required to reconcile an account. Any exceptions are subject to agreement on a case by case basis with the Operational Assurance Reconciliation team. Examples of such exceptions may include (please note this is not an exhaustive list):

• Novations
• Mergers/Acquisitions
• Significant balance discrepancies
• Significant increase in number of Duty Solicitors

New accounts will be paid for the value of work claimed for the first six months and then providers have the option of requesting an SMP or remaining on a Variable Monthly Payment (further details below).

When a Legal Aid provider's contract ends, and is not replaced, the right to an SMP also ends.

3 Variable Monthly Payments

If you elect to receive a Variable Monthly Payment (VMP) this is calculated using the amount of the latest monthly submission plus or minus any changes to claims since the previous payment, for example, claim amendments and escape fee case assessments.

All other aspects of the contract payments process including the payment dates and submissions deadlines will remain the same.

The intention of VMP is to make a balancing payment each month so there may be a period of transition required in order to achieve a zero account balance.

On transition if an account is underpaid the balance will be cleared in a single payment and VMPs will commence from the following month.

If an account is overpaid on transition the balance will generally be recovered over a period of six months by reducing the variable payments by 1/6th of the balance. Providers have the opportunity to discharge the balance by making a single payment or by requesting payments are stopped until the account moves into a position of credit, or by a combination of these options. Providers should contact the Operational Assurance Reconciliation team to discuss transitional arrangements.

When a Legal Aid provider's contract ends, and is not replaced, the right to a VMP also ends.

Contact Details

By email: reconciliation@legalaid.gsi.gov.uk

By telephone: 0191 428 3738

By DX: Operational Assurance Reconciliation Team, Legal Aid Agency, DX 742350, Jarrow 2

By Post: Operational Assurance Reconciliation Team, Legal Aid Agency, South Tyneside Office, Berkley Way, Viking Business Park, Jarrow, NE31 1SF

Index